◆世紀之交：觀念動向與

第二屆中瑞漢學國際學術

淡江大學中國文學

臺灣

序

孟子曰：「東海有聖人焉，此心同此理同；西海有聖人焉，此心同此理同。」在以往，我們是由書本上去體會此中之意義，如今，我們在中瑞漢學國際學術會議裡，卻是以眞實生命去體悟其中之深意。

無論是瑞典人還是中國人，只要是人，都有共通的人性與理想，在此基礎上，我們才能有合作與討論的可能。當然，「心同理同」自是一義，然而此心此理卻可以有種種不同之表現背景與表現方式，由是而有中國與歐洲、台灣與瑞典的差異。也正是在此差異上，對話與交談便成爲彼此開放、相互學習的重要憑藉，也是彼此成長的必經歷程。除了心同理同之外，此時的人類還共同面對一重要課題，此即全球化與廿一世紀的人類展望。在第一屆的中瑞漢學會議中，我們已就全球化問題做了初步的討論。全球化趨勢是一已然的事實，我們要注意的是，這樣的發展應該遵循怎麼樣的規範，才能帶給人類較爲積極而正面的影響。即就眼前的事實而言，當歐美先進國家將有毒的廢棄電腦大量輸往中國大陸之時，我們便發現全球化並非在一開放而公平的條件下進行，除非我們完全放棄人類的理想、責任與尊嚴，否則我們不得不對全球化提出較爲具體的規範，以使全球化發展成爲人類共進大同的開端，而不致落入另類殖民的危機。

全球化是以往人類未曾眞正面對的經驗，然而今天出現了，此時，我們根據以往經驗所構成之知識，能否有效地掌握此嶄新之現象，此即爲當前人類的重大挑戰。例如前文提及全球化的規範問題，如今便有「普世倫理」（globle ethics）的提出；而生命科學、基因工程之發展，也逼出「生命倫理」（bioethics）的問題。這說明在新世紀的來臨下，我們將面對許多與以往經驗完全斷裂而異質的現象，這些現象有待我們以新觀點、新方法加以回應。這也正是本次會議的基本關懷所在了。其實，中瑞漢學會議的召開，本身也正是全球化的結果之一啊！我們對此問題之反省，其實也正是對自身意義之反省。當然，我相信此次會議在全球化的意義上必然是正面的，我們是通過具體的討論與交談，使全球化不只是一種事實的趨勢，而且也帶有強烈的價値色彩。我們不是隨波逐流地在全球化的浪潮下翻新，我們更要以理想性爲大趨勢找尋更爲合理的方向。

此次會議由於羅多弼教授感冒未能來台赴會，是大會唯一的遺憾，但我們隨即在台北市政府文化局主辦，而由淡江大學中文系承辦的朱子學國際會議中，再邀請羅教授出席，總算彌補了這一小缺憾。舉辦會議的行政程序及問題頗爲繁重，此要多謝瑞典的陳邁平教授，充當二系的重要連絡橋樑。同時，當時的中文系主任周彥文教授對此會議的全力支持，方使會議順利進行。此外，黃麗卿老師、吳春枝助教、黃慧鳳助教、吳麗雯助教的行政辛勞，更是功不可沒，在此要鄭重致謝。當然，全體與會的學者及各指導贊助單位，都是此次會議的主角，也都是令人感佩的學術同道。我想，「君子以文會友，以友輔仁」，正是此次會議的寫眞，而「苟日新，日日新，又日新」，將是我們持續中歐漢學整合的努力原則，尚祈學界師友多予指導與支持。

高柏園 序於淡江大學中文系 2002.3.7

第二屆中瑞國際學術研討會議程

本屆主題：世紀之交--觀念動向與文化變遷

舉辦地點：淡江大學覺生國際會議廳

	日期	1999/11/18(星期四)		
場次	時間 (Time)	主　席 (Chair)	主　講 (Speaker)	論　文　題　目(TOPIC)
	8:30 | 9:00	報　到		
	9:00 | 9:20	開幕典禮Opening Ceremony		
第一場	9:20 | 9:50	周彥文	袁保新	主題演講：中國哲學與廿一世紀人類命運的展望
🍸	9:50 | 10:10	茶敘(Tea and Coffee)		
第二場	10:10 | 12:10	韓耀隆	高柏園	廿一世紀的人文學
		陳大道	黃基明	The Renewal of Nations: World-wide Waves and Domestic Dynamics
		熊　彪	馬良文	The legacy of Sun - Wukung:on being (post)modern without Modernity in China
	12:10 | 14:00	午餐 (Lunch and rest)		
第三場	14:10 | 15:20	張維邦	魏萼	中國資本論：富有中國特色的新《資本論》

		馬　丁	柯塞北	The Japanese, the Opium Wars and the Unequal Treaties 1839-95
Ɏ	15:20 ｜ 15:40	茶敘(Tea and Coffee)		
第四場	15:40 ｜ 17:00	龔鵬程	蓋瑪雅	Conceptual Challenges Facing the Student of Popular Literature in Mainland China and Taiwan
		陳瑞秀	潘錫堂	台灣與大陸對於兩岸關係定位之認知比較： 「特殊國與國關係論」的意涵、反應與影響
	18:00 ｜	會後餐敘		
	日期	1999/11/19(星期五)		
	時間(Time)	主席(Chair)	主講(Speaker)	論文題目(TOPIC)
	8:50 ｜ 9:10	報到		
第五場	9:10 ｜ 10:20	黃基明	陳大道	從《玉臺新詠》到《全唐詩看舞者之形象轉變
		王仁鈞	宋永珠	韓中詩學比較研究： 李朝李德懋與清朝王士禛詩學關係
Ɏ	10:20 ｜ 10:40	茶敘(Tea and Coffee)		

第六場	10:40 | 12:10	蓋瑪雅	陳邁平	「鐵屋」中的個人—大陸當代文學中「自我」的品格
		李本京	盧國屏	台灣地區語言政策的跨世紀省思
	12:10 | 14:00	午餐（Lunch and rest）		
第七場	14:00 | 15:40	周彥文	羅多弼	Cultural Traditions and the Quest for Modernity in China: A Multi-Dimensional Problematique
		柯塞北	熊　彪	The 'Native' Researcher Revisited Some Reflections on Personal and Structural Components of Otherness
		高柏園	黃麗卿	由《聊齋誌異》觀「唯情意識」
T	15:40 | 16:00	茶敘(Tea and Coffee)		
第八場	16:00 | 17:10	范銘如	馬銘浩	東坡「以詩為詞」在文學史上的意涵
		陳邁平	馬　丁	Treasures of Another kind: The Celebration and Condemnation of Metaphor, Lie and Illusion in Classical Chinese Poetics
	17:10 | 17:20	周彥文	閉幕式(Close Ceremony)	
	17:20 |	會後餐敘(圓山The Grand Hotel)		

世紀之交：觀念動向與文化變遷——第二屆中瑞漢學國際學術會議論文集

目　錄

序-- I

第二屆中瑞國際學術研討會議程-- V

中國哲學與廿一世紀人類命運的展望 ------------------------ 袁保新　1

廿一世紀的人文學-- 高柏園　9

The Renewal of Nations:World-wide Waves and
Domestic Dynamics -- 黃基明　25

The legacy of Sun Wukung : on being (post) modern without
Modernity in China-- 馬良文　51

中國資本論——富有中國特色的新《資本論》 ----------- 魏　萼　73

The Japanese, the Opium Wars and
the Unequal Treaties 1839-95 ---------------------------- 柯塞北　95

Conceptual Challenges Facing the Student of Popular Literature
in Mainland China and Taiwan ---------------------------- 蓋瑪雅　127

臺灣與大陸對於兩岸關係定位之認知比較——「特殊國與國關係論」的意涵、反應與影響 ---------------- 潘錫堂 147

The Change in the Depiction of Dancers from the *Yu-t'ai hsin- yung* to the *Ch'uan T'ang-shih* ---------------------------------- 陳大道 175

韓中詩學比較研究——李朝李德懋與清朝王士禎詩學關係 -- 宋永珠 203

「鐵屋」中的個人——中國大陸當代文學中「自我」的品格 -- 陳邁平 229

臺灣地區語言政策的跨世紀省思---------------------------- 盧國屏 257

Cultural Traditions and the Quest for Modernity in China：A Multi-Dimensional Problematique -------------------- 羅多弼 287

The 'Native' Researcher Revisited Some reflections on personal and structural components of Otherness----------------- 熊　彪 295

由《聊齋誌異》觀「唯情意識」---------------------------- 黃麗卿 323

東坡「以詩爲詞」在文學史上的意涵 ------------------- 馬銘浩 335

Treasures of Another Kind: The Celebration and Condemnation of Metaphor, Lie and Illusion in Classical Chinese Poetics--- 馬　丁 355

中國哲學與廿一世紀人類命運的展望

袁保新*

摘　要

一、前　言

二、廿世紀人類文明的成就及其潛在危機

1.上不在天：超越價值世界的隱沒

2.下不在地：自然山水的物質化

3.外不在人：人間世界蛻變爲殺戮戰場

4.內不在己：自我認同的迷惘

三、道與存有（Being, Sein）

1.存有在西方哲學思考中，主要擔負的是存有物可理解性的說明；存有的探索亦即世界可理解性秩序的建立。

2.道在中國哲學思考中，主要擔負的是存在界（天、

＊　淡江大學中文系教授

地、人、我）共生、長生、生生的最終保證；對道的探尋亦即試圖掌握天、地、人、我共生互動的規範性原理。

四、結　論

關鍵詞　存有　危機　物質化　自我認同

在人類歷史上，沒有那一個時代比今天更富足，也沒有那一個時代比今天更貧乏。對於未來人類文化的前景，現代人一方面覺得充滿了希望光明，另一方面又感到黯淡沮喪。

科技所推動的理性化歷程，既深刻又廣泛，不僅展現在理論與技術的不斷翻新，就是社會、政治、經濟、藝術方面，二十世紀也都在經歷一場嶄新的變化。

環顧當前這個由科技所結晶的現代文明，雖然它將人類從傳統的迷思中釋放出來，並且賜予現代人從所未有的富庶，但是在無情地瓦解傳統世界觀之後，俗眾文化的氾濫，也使得當代心靈陷入空前的意義危機中。

面對這個世紀的寵兒——科技，我們實在不知道它究竟是對人類的一項祝福，還是咀咒。

不快樂的現代人

二十世紀最傑出的科學心靈愛因斯坦，就曾經感嘆過：

為什麼成果若是輝煌的應用科學，它減少了我們的工作，讓我們的生活較前容易，但卻沒有給我們帶來多少快樂呢？

是的！爲什麼我們不快樂呢？科技難道不是我們人類經歷過幾個世紀的奮鬥才創造出來的輝煌成果？它不曾經是無數高貴的心靈用生命、智慧來灌溉的一片園地？爲什麼它碩大飽滿的果實不能解除現代心靈的焦渴？是什麼原因使得我們成爲不快樂的現代人？而我們又應該如何才能找回失去的快樂？

這一連串的質疑，顯然只有在科技之外，乞靈於將人類所有經驗予以整體透視的哲學智慧，才能找到令人滿意的解答。

危機時代中的哲學

在二十世紀風起雲湧的哲學思潮中，也許存在主義是最能忠於這個時代感受的哲學。

存在主義的興起，可以從許多角度來分析，簡單說來，主要是源於哲學家意識到科技文明對傳統世界觀的衝激，已然使得現代人在存在意義的攝受上，陷入四不掛搭，無家可歸的命運中。

在此，所謂「四不掛搭」，藉唐君毅先生的觀念，也就是指當代西方人「上不在天，下不在地，外不在人，內不在己」的存在危機而言。其具體涵義，又可以還原到西方近代文化史上，作以下的說明。

上不在天：這是指十九世紀以來，基督宗教的俗世化，尼采宣布上帝死亡，在諸神隱退的情況下，西方人頓失神聖超越世界的嚮往與庇護。

下不在地：文藝復興以來，數學物理學的順利發展，使科技理性一枝獨秀，自然世界淪爲科技理性認知與征服的對象，不再呈現可供人類心靈「修、遊、藏、息」的情趣。

外不在人：產業革命之後，工商企業的發達，都市文明的崛起，徹底改變了西方社會的結構，傳統的人際關係轉化爲組織分工的角色互動，相照相溫的人間情感完全由冰冷的權利義務關係所取代。

內不在己：繼天、地、人的失落，在俗眾文化的氾濫流行中，人類原本寧靜自足的心靈，也拱手讓給爭奇鬥妍的意識形態，淪爲紛擾不安的戰場。

換言之，存在主義之所以重視人之具體存在，並且對當代文明展開嚴厲的批判，正是因爲他們敏銳地察覺到現代人的不快樂，根本是一個「存在意義」的問題，一個因爲科技理性獨大所造成的世界觀危機。

因此，就存在主義而言，當代哲學的首要課題不是什麼別的，主要就是回到滋生一切意義理解的根源——「存有」（Being），重建天、地、人、我之間的溝通管道，使西方文明再次得到活水源頭的滋潤。

存在主義的洞見與盲點

遺憾的是，存在主義在當代哲學史上並未結成正果。在它最興盛的時候，它被誤解爲一切頹廢思想的淵藪，在它代表性哲學家相繼辭世之後，它又迅速的遭人遺忘。

雖然繼存在主義而起的各種歐洲思潮，無論是詮釋學、法蘭克福學派、結構主義，均多少繼承了批判科學主義的精神傳統，但是在文化危機意識以及根源性的反省方面，無疑地，存在主義仍是當代世界最深刻的一支哲學思潮。

問題是：究竟是什原因使存在主義迅速的沒落？答案可能非常複雜，一方面固然是因爲當代科技文明乃是西方世界幾百年來所結胎生出的龐然大物，有其自身的結構與堅韌的生命力，另一方面可能是存在主義哲學家各自爲政，在後繼乏人的情況下，根本無法形成強而有力的傳統。

但最重要的是，存在主義哲學作爲一種文化治療學，雖然能夠從一切意義滋生的根源——「存有」——來揭露科技的本質與侷限性，可是在背負西方傳統哲學的包袱下（或者對照於中國傳統哲學的特質來看），它潛存著有兩項基本的困難：

存有與價值的二分

存在主義對科技文明所帶來的存在危機，的確能夠從存有學的層面予以根源性的解析，但是在昧於文化問題也就是價值問題的情況下，我們發現存在主義始終不能針對現代人價值的顚倒與誤置，徹底地展開對近代文明以來工具理性獨大的批判，並進而重建價值理性的合法性。

換言之，存在主義對「存有」情有獨鍾的思考方式，由於不能正視存在界就是人類在天、地、人、我之間尋求價值實現的行動之場，從而打通存有之源與價值之源的隔障，因此儘管他們對存有的思辨是如何的精微，但仍然不能觸及現代心靈的迷惘，指出脫困的方向與途徑。

理論與實踐的二分

存在主義對於現代人在科技文明中飽受意義失落的威脅，誠有其深度的體會與分析，但是對於如何建立眞實自我此一關乎實踐修養的課題，卻因爲避諱價值問題，不僅無法提出中肯的建議，連帶著對於社會實踐也無法提供正確的方向。這一點，只要對照中國哲學，無論是孔、孟，還是老、莊，就不得不承認是存在主義的一項嚴重的缺失。

我們查閱存在主義的歷史，海德格一度加入納粹，沙特曾經醉心於共產主義，而六〇年代的學生運動與嬉皮風潮也都與存在主義脫不了關係，僅從這一段不甚佳的紀錄來看，我們就可以確認：莊子「有眞人而後有眞知」的卓見，也許是所有將理論、實踐二分，或者只重社會實踐而不重主體人格修養的哲學，都應該善加體會的智者之言。

未來哲學的期待

中國兩千多年前的莊子，曾經寓意深長的說過一個故事：有一天，惠施對莊子說：「魏王送給我一種大葫蘆的種子，種植收成之後，居然有五石那麼大的容量，用來盛水嘛，它不夠堅硬，不能承受。剖開來作瓢吧，又虛大的沒有水缸可以容納它。這個葫蘆誠然是件大物了，但是對我卻絲毫沒有用處，因此我把它打碎了。」莊子一聽，就回答道：「你這個人眞是不善於運用大物啊！……你爲什麼不把它當作腰舟，浮游在江湖之上呢？居然還在發愁沒有大水缸來容納它，看來你的心早已被茅草杜塞住了，一點也不通達！」從這段故事讓我們聯想到，二十世紀科技文明可能就是這麼一個令人又愛又憎、「瓠落無所容」的大物罷！它既然曾經得到無數傑出心靈的灌溉，必定有它的可貴之處，但是如果使用者的心靈杜塞不通，那麼這個龐然大物就可能不是一項禮物，而變成了一個可怕的惡夢。

事實上，二十世紀科技文明所造成的存在危機，與其歸咎於科技，倒不如歸咎於現代人在接受科技理性獨尊之後，自己將心靈禁錮在遼闊的價值世界之外，最後落得坐擁大物，卻苦於不得自由的惡果。

當代存在主義的興起，代表著當代哲學心靈對於這項困境的覺醒，雖然它的奮鬥並沒有成功，但無論如何，只要現代人的心靈保持這種對文化的不安悱惻之情，我們相信當代科技文明的詛咒，終將在未來哲學的導引下，轉化爲甜美的祝福。

廿一世紀的人文學

高柏園*

摘　要

本文主要目標，在對比著自然科學，說明人文學所面臨的挑戰與困境，以及其可能的回應之道。人文學目前所充斥的考古化、煩瑣化、泡沫化的特質，正是阻礙人文學的主要原因，而其連續性、詮釋性與非量化性則是更深層的主要原因。因此，我們必須在非連續性的形式上加以努力，以徹底解放人文學，進而以「新經驗主義」的方法與態度，重新建構廿一世紀人文學，並對自然科學之發展目的、方向及價值問題，提出人文學的主張與意見。

關鍵詞　人文學　自然科學　連續性　詮釋　量化　新經驗主義

*　淡江大學中文系教授

Human Science in 21th Century

Kao Pa-Yuan

Abstract

The main purpose in this paper is to compared with the natural science to describe the challenges and straits the humanity science in face of as well as the rebuttal and refutation. The main reasons to impede humanity science today are the characteristic of archaize, complicate and bubblize of human science. And the series, interpretation and non-quantification are the further reasons. Therefore, we have to do our best on the formation of non-series in order to liberate humanity science through and through and reconstruct the human science in 21th century by the way of 'neo-experiencism'（新經驗主義）as well as form some opinions from humanity science towards to the purpose, the way and the problem of value of the natural science.

Keywords: humanity science, natural science, interpretation, quantification, neo-experiencism

一、問題的提出

廿一世紀即將來到，人類即將迎接有史以來的第二個千禧年。然而，廿一世紀的來臨固然令人興奮，但是也同時帶來許多的問題與疑慮。例如，電腦在面對Ｙ２Ｋ問題時，便充滿著許多不可知的變數與可能，在今日幾乎完全依賴電腦的時代，這樣的衝擊不可謂不大。又例如，人類在廿世紀末對生命科學與基因工程學的重大突破，使人類在某一意義上窺見了上帝創造的奧祕。這樣的發展一方面誠然是一種努力的成果與進步，但是相對而來的生態問題及倫理問題，也足以使人類坐立難安。

人是社會的動物，當自然科學大量改變人類環境及自身的同時，當然也會引發一些人文的問題，對以上問題的回應也就有自然科學與人文學的二個面向。一方面我們要繼續自然科學之研究，另一方面我們也要回應其所帶來的人文學問題。易言之，單單由科學所引發之人文問題就已然十分可觀了，然而，我們也不能忽視人文學本身所遭遇的問題。

無論這個世界是由資本主義或社會主義的意識型態所主導，其共同的特質之一，便是對自然科學之尊重與利用。科學無國界，科學亦無意識型態之區別與對立，因此，眞正改變人類及其環境的最實質動力，便是自然科學。正是因爲自然科學在現實經驗的掌握及控制上是如此成功，因而也使自然科學在自覺或不自覺中，成爲一切學問之典範，進而使人文學亦呈現出強烈之自然科學化的現象。這樣的現象其價値與得失，是本文首要處理的問題。其次，人文學雖然在典範上，甚至方法上取法於自然科學，但是在研究對象上仍然十分封閉與被動。例如有爲數頗多的人文學研究，仍是以過去的對象爲研究範圍，形成考古化的趨勢。另外也有不少人則完全追逐自然科學的成果，進行第二序的詮釋，人文學在此似乎成了自然科學的婢女了。因此，人文學自身之定位、研究典範、研究對象等問題，便成爲本文所要處理的第二個問題。由於人文學範圍極大，加上筆者個人研究範圍之限制，爲求論題較爲集中，是以將主題偏重在中國人文學，以討論其在廿一世紀的可能處境及回應之道。

二、典範的混淆與研究的困境

關於人文學典範的混淆，我們可以從現有的現象中開始反省。首先，所有的人文學學術論文之形成，基本上仍是以自然科學學術論文爲典範的。例如引文、註釋之形式，便是其中之一例。其次，在人文學學域中也開始進行大量的量化評量。例如某學者在某等級的學術期刊中發表一篇論文則得多少點數，由是來衡量學者的研究成就。暫且不論此種做法的優劣得失，我們只要經由如下的檢證，便可發現其中的困結：我們試著將眞正影響人文學界的經典著作找出來，便可發現以上二種要求，無法充分說明這些經典著作的合理地位。例如，牟宗三先生的《心體與性體》一書共有三巨冊，其中只有引用古代文獻，根本沒有引用近代的二手研究成果；而且，書中沒有今日所要求的註釋；至於其中內容也未必在所謂的學術期刊上發表過。然而，《心體與性體》卻是當代研究宋明理學不可不讀的經典作品。另就時間性關係而言，則以上之經典作品在諸如牟先生般的大師之後，似乎亦成爲絕響。新一代的學者大多著力在短篇的論文寫作上，罕見有大部頭的巨作出現。例如時下的學術著作大多是以論文集的形式出現，此便是一例。不但論文本身已趨向輕薄短小，連研究主題亦是如此。在牟先生之後，中國人文學似乎已然不見百科全書式的學術作品，例如，我們根本找不到一本有關宋明理學的研究著作，可以在研究主題之全面性、內容之創造性及理論系統的建構上，能與《心體與性體》一書相匹敵。現在我們要問的是，這些現象到底隱含了什麼意義？

（一）連續性與非連續性

在自然科學與人文學之間，其間典範意義差異之一，便是自然科學乃是非連續性的，而人文學則是連續性的。易言之，自然科學基本上的實證性與經驗性，使得以往理論系統與今日理論系統之間，有著較明顯的非連續性與斷裂性，這樣的特點明顯反映在以下的事實。例如，一門電腦課程，根本不必先討論電腦史，一門生物學課程，也不會將重點放在生物學史上。反之，乃是將重點，放在最新的經驗結果及理論系統。換言之，就自然科學而言，以往理論系統與今日發展出之理論系統間，乃是有著非連續性與斷裂性關係之存在。吾人不必了解以往的理論系統，這並不會造成對今日理論系統在理解上的困擾。反之，文學史、哲學史、史學史，卻是人文學永遠的必要，由是顯示出人文學的連續性。如果以上的分析是可以成立的話，那麼，在自然科學中理解的內容與意義便顯然與人文學不同。例如，自然科學所引用的資料基本上有實證性與時效性，而以最新的資料爲首要訴求，也因此，資料來源的時間與地點，也就必須十分的清楚。但是，在人文學上是否需要以如此的方式做詮釋呢？

（二）詮釋性與發現性

人文學之所以會是連續性的，與其學問的詮釋性有關。易言之，人文學當然會發現新的現象與事實，但是，它卻不是以發現為重點，而是以對此發現對象加以詮釋其意義與價值為重點。當然，我們也可以很形上學地說，詮釋出對象的新意義，也就是發現了新的對象，但是這樣的發現與自然科學之發現仍有很大的差異。人是歷史的動物，人的詮釋根據仍須由歷史文化提供，是以人文學的詮釋必然會涉及與其詮釋根據相關之歷史文化的理解，由是而展開其連續性的特質。另一方面，自然科學則是以發現新現象為主要用心，任何的詮釋都必須納入新的現象加以實證，因而新經驗的產生便意味著新理論的產生，由此發現性自然導出其新舊理論間的非連續性。

（三）非量化與量化

連續性的詮釋既是重在意義與價值之闡發，因此，其特質顯然是非量化、非實證的。易言之，至少量化及實證都無法做為人文學詮釋優劣之標準。另一方面，自然科學根本就是通過經驗的實證與量化為基礎，展開其理論系統的建立，此中，數學正是其中的根本基礎所在。而不同理論之優劣，亦可經由實證及量化的方式加以判別。由於實證與量化是可以通過客觀操作程序而加以掌握的，因此，自然科學也就較人文學具有更高的客觀性與可檢證性（verifiability）。同時，自然科學的實證性與量化性，亦使自然科學擁有較高的非累積性與不可逆性。所謂非累積性，是說自然科學知識的累積性是斷裂的，舊的理論可能完全被新的理論所取代。愈新的理論代表愈高的經驗支持，也代表更加地可靠，舊的資料在自然科學的領域裏，往往根本是明日之黃花，毫無價值可言，此即其不可逆性。相對於人文學來說，則新的詮釋未必比舊的詮釋更有價值，因而有著較高的累積性與可逆性。

現在，我們再回到前文所論及的註釋問題。自然科學對註釋的嚴格要求，正是因爲自然科學中高度的非連續性、發現性、量化與非累積性的特色上。如果我們不能掌握最新的研究成果，則註定是落後與重複無意義的工作罷了。此外，自然科學的客觀性與實證性，亦可支持其間之優劣判準的成立，進而評比研究者的客觀成果。問題是，這樣的方式用在人文學上是否適用，便值得懷疑了。

首先，由於人文學是連續性的，因此，有許多的意見與看法，可能都是一般的或非創造性的，在研究時是否要一一註明，則似乎是無必要的。也因此，我們發現許多人文學的論文，如果去掉註釋，似乎也不會比較不健全。尤有進者，當我們把其中的引文或註釋去除，一篇論文眞正屬於作者個人的意見可能少得可憐。易言之，以自然科學的論著形式作爲要求，不但未必能提昇人文學的素質，反而可能成爲人文學貧乏化、煩瑣化的藉口，進而造成創造力的喪失。試想，當人文學學者必須窮盡一切以往的研究成果，又要著力於所謂最新的研究成果，不但可能只是製造出一些無關痛癢的泡沫，也可能造成創造力無從發揮的困境。

其次，由於人文學的連續性特質，也使得人文學研究在強調以自然科學模式展開時，造成考古化、貧乏化、煩瑣化與泡沫化的後果。例如一個要研究老子思想的人文學者，在依照人文學連續性的特質要求下，便不得不對老子的相關研究進行全面性的掌握。而在時間的長期累積，加上現代資訊的爆炸事實而言，這樣的努力註定不可能成功，即便成功，也只是在資料中更製造出一些資料罷了，其結果就註定是考古化、煩瑣化、貧乏化與泡沫化。易言之，資訊爆炸的結果，使得人文學連續性的特質，產生了無限後退的困境，而考古化、煩瑣化、貧乏化與泡沫化都只是此中的現象罷了。由於無限後退，也使得人文學落入一種考古式的詮釋循環中，我們似乎遠離了原初的對象，而迷失在既有的詮釋系統中。其結果，便是創造性的喪失與深入感的缺乏，這正是人文學大量落後在自然科學之原因之一，也造成人文學對時代回應的無力感與距離感。此中，最明顯的例子之一，便是人文學界每年大量的博士碩士論文的出現以及種種學術會議的召開，到底是研究成果的展現與累積，還是已往成果的泡沫化結果，便十分值得討論。而且，這些研究成果又與我們的生命與現存的社會有多少意義的關聯呢？這些研究成果對你我而言，其意義究竟何在呢？

或許，我們可以較為樂觀地認為：人文學雖然是連續性的，但是其中研究成果仍然是會產生自然淘汰的現象。例如，許多論文便完全無法進入核心，而慘遭淘汰的命運。因此，人文學論述的自然淘汰，應可使人文學傳統之負擔不致過重。這樣的說法誠然是有理由的，但是卻仍不足以解決以上所論之困境。首先，人文學研究成果的產生速度較其淘汰速率為高，因而仍然大量地累積研究成果等待克服。其次，自然淘汰到底能否淘汰所謂較無價值之論著，依然是可懷疑的。再其次，人文學既無如自然科學般地實證性與量化性，因此如何找到「有價值或無價值」之標準，依然不易客觀地建立。由此看來，訴諸人文學的自然淘汰，並不足以面對資訊時代下人文學的困境。

必須說明的是，筆者並不認為人文學論文採用註釋是錯誤的，反之，適當的使用乃是合理而有價值的。然而，對註釋等形式的過分強調，只是對自然科學與人文學特質及其典範之混淆。它不但不能增加人文學的研究價值，反而會使人文學落入考古化、煩瑣化及泡沫化的惡果。

三、人文學根本意義之反省

當我們說自然科學與人文學之特質是不同的，似乎也就預設了對人文學特質之肯定。問題是：人文學的特質究竟是什麼呢？

首先，我們不得不承認，這是一個難解的問題，因為人文學仍是一個發展中的存在，既沒完成，又如何規定其本質呢？因此我們只能以描述式定義的方法加以回答：在人文學既有的發展而言，人文學仍是以意義的詮釋為主要的關懷，尤其是對以往之詮釋進行再詮釋的工作，佔了其中極大的部份。筆者在前文已指出，為了避免人文學的考古化、煩瑣化及泡沫化，這類的再詮釋似乎可以做適度的調整與控制，而將更多的力量放在現有問題甚至未來可能問題的研究上。一如自然科學，人文學在不同的時代有其不同的問題與關懷，歷史上偉大的自然科學或人文學領袖，無一不是因為他們充分回應其時代問題使然，而不是由於他們對以往的偉大提出更偉大的詮釋，即使提出詮釋，也是在其相應之關懷下所提出的，而不是純然的考古式興趣與意義。果如此，則人文學正應該重新體認如是的反省，進而開創出廿一世紀的人文學新風貌。況且，人類的文明自工業革命以來，已然不是一種漸進式、程度上的改進，而是以一種突進式、異質性的變化進行發展。托佛勒（Alvin Toffler）所提出的「第三波」（The Third Wave）就十分明確地說明了這點。因此，我們實在無法堅持人文學在面對廿一世紀之際，仍然能一成不變地因循以往的研究方法、態度及內容。中國先秦時代的哲學家韓非在〈五蠹篇〉便指出：「世異則事異，事異則備變。」時至今日，人文學沒有新的反省實在是令人驚訝的。

或許有人會認爲，人文學之所以會對以往的論著進行再詮釋，乃是因爲人文學並不重在結論的提出與獲致，而是以自我的自覺爲主要的目的，因而自覺的過程才是重點，至於自覺所信賴之對象並不重要。從另外的角度而言，自然科學的學者其提出種種的理論，其實也都是人對世界的一種理解的方式罷了，這和人文學者對世界的理解一樣，都會有強烈的主觀成份。就此而言，一個哲學家以論證說明世界，文學家以文學描寫世界，電腦學家以程式說明世界，都是一種主觀的理解與說明罷了，其不同，也僅在於使用之工具及切入角度之差異而已！果如此，則人文學的結論並不重要，因而書架上的博、碩士論文雖然有考古化、煩瑣化及泡沫化的傾向，然而只要它們能達成自我自覺的目的，也就有其價值了。

其實，這樣的反省不但頗具說服力，而且在某種意義下，也是十分深刻的洞見。無疑地，人類的知識與反省是無法脫離生命經驗而展開的，人的經驗在時間中展開，而時間又尚未結束，因而我們的經驗及因此而開出之知識，便亦在發展中而未完成。果如此，則人類對知識之追求與反省，亦正是人自我成長、發展的一種形式罷了。結論的正確與否雖然是我們所關切的，但卻也不必是我們能保證的或唯一關切的目的。

在此意義下，筆者要提出二點反省：

首先，我承認知識，無論是人文的或自然的，最後都僅只是人類理解過程的形式表現罷了，存在的意義仍然是永恆的奧祕。然而，我們卻不能因此過分誇張人文學與自然科學的相似性。反之，我們更應該深入探討此中之差異性。例如，人文學爲什麼不能提出如自然科學般地實用知識呢？爲什麼發展不出較客觀的知識形態呢？

其次，如果知識或學問對吾人的意義，只是個人生命反省的歷程罷了，那麼藉由何種管道並不是決定性的因素，因而考古化亦不必是大病。易言之，我們也能由對過去之反省而獲得自我反省的可能。然而，我們也不能過分強調此義，因爲人的自覺過程畢竟要依賴一對象而展開，我們爲什麼不選擇我們最親切、最熟悉的經驗內容，而要以考古的方式想像已過去的一切呢？再者，人文學的創始者又要如何展開其考古式的反省呢？他不正是對其現實生命進行最眞實、最深切的反省嗎？筆者以爲，人文學的確含有自我自覺的要求，因而過程的意義十分重要，但是它卻不應該被誇張爲人文學唯一的內容與要求。人的自覺與反省並非憑空展開，而是相應於經驗內容展開，因而經驗內容的選取固然不必排斥以往的經驗，但是也沒有理由只限定在以往的經驗。尤有進者，人的自覺亦不只是爲自覺而自覺，人的自覺乃是爲進一步安頓自我生命內容的一種過程與方法。因此，自覺過程所賴以支持的內容，便應選擇與吾人生命更爲親切相關者爲優先。因爲唯有自覺過程與賴以支持的經驗內容是與吾人之生命直接相關者，才會引發吾人的興趣，滿足吾人實踐的要求，甚至滿足某種實用的目的。例如，與其以古代社會為研究主題，就不如以當代甚至未來的社會為主題，更能直接與吾人之生活習習相關，並能提供實踐及實用的幫助。否則，人文學在強調考古式的研究態度下，將使人文學陷入與社會及自我生命極為疏離的境地，此不但將使人文學喪失了實踐的活力，而且也無法得到社會的認同與對社會的發言權。

四、廿一世紀的人文學

廿一世紀人文學的確呈現出十分特殊的風貌，而與以往的人文學有重大的差異。例如，影音媒體的大量普遍化，使得人的思維方式亦從以往的抽象式思考，逐步轉為具象式思考，此對於以往考古的內容，一方面將使著人們興趣缺缺，而另一方面亦顯得格格不入。例如，在中國文學領域中，我們只能在學院，而且大都只是在學院的中文系裡，面對古典詩詞的存在。一般人早就進入白話文學的世界中，從而使古典文學成為極小眾文學，完全不在一般的文化媒體中出現。同樣的情形也在中國哲學中發現，對古典哲學的閱讀能力、理解能力及學習興趣，都只是少數學生的專長，已然退出大眾的舞台，而成為小眾的事業，當然也就無法直接影響大眾所處的社會與時代了。

面對以上的情況，我們應如何面對廿一世紀人文學呢？筆者願提供以下幾點看法：

（一）非連續性的形式：

一如前論，人文學的連續性特質乃是一種既存的事實與傳統，時至今日亦未有重大的改變。當然，這種連續性的特質對人文學而言亦有奇特有之意義，此即提供吾人對自身之存在以及由此存在性而開發出之理解態度與要求，有一全面之反省與繼承。人是歷史的動物，也是社會的動物，無論是歷史或社會都有其連續性的一面，因而我們對人文學的連續性反省，也正是回應做爲人文學基礎的歷史及社會特質之反省。只是有關的連續性反省固然是有意義的，但是也同時形成一種莫大的負擔，進而導致人文學發展的遲滯，甚至有考古化、煩瑣化及泡沫化的危機。

現在，我們可以問的問題是：如果在廿一世紀所展現的人類文化與社會，乃是與其從前的人類文化、社會是完全異質而斷裂的話，我們是否可以因此取消人文學中連續性的特質。例如，資訊化的高度發展、知識的爆炸、生物學的長足進步，凡此皆使廿一世紀的人類，與其前的人類有著完全不同的存在情境與環境。在此意義下，以往的人文學與今日的人文學之間還有多少連續性與同質性是頗値得討論的。或許我們仍然可以說，人類即使到了廿一世紀，人類對美的追求、對善的肯定以及對眞的嚮往，仍然與昔日無別，是以其間依然有連續性與同質性。這樣的說法誠然有理由成立，但是，這樣的肯定似乎只是形式上的肯定，我們大可接受如是形式化的連續性，而完全排除內容上的連續性，進而可以合理地宣稱以往人文學的過時與死亡，從而拋棄千百年來的枷鎖，而使人文學獲得空前的解放，而將心力完全投注在現有問題的處理與回應上，此甚至可能獲致如自然科學般地成功。這是第一步。

第二步，則不是對以往人文學的排除，而是如何面對當代已有以及將有的研究成果。易言之，我們雖然以文化與社會之斷裂性，使廿一世紀人文學免於傳統之束縛，但是，即使廿一世紀人文學自身亦因為資訊的爆炸，形成無法完全掌握的困境，因此，我們也需要找出新的方法與標準，以便能在當前幾乎無限多的人文研究成果中，避免無限後退的困境。易言之，也就是要找出一種評量、過濾資訊的方式。至於在此不能訴諸自然淘汰的理由，其一是自然淘汰未必是合理的淘汰；其二是自然淘汰也未必能滿足、克服資訊爆炸的困境。至於在自然淘汰之外，還有什麼具體的回應方式，筆者亦仍未能在此提供較完善的主張，只有留待日後的努力了。

（二）新經驗主義：

相對於非連續性的形式，人文學在廿一世紀亦將展開一種「新經驗主義」。由於廿一世紀是與其從前之文化與社會有如此高的異質性，因而吾人在廿一世紀所面對的經驗亦是一全新的經驗，而人文學也正是要以這類新經驗為關懷對象，遠離以往人文學考古化的陷阱。就此新經驗主義而言，由於人類資訊的發達，全球化趨勢日趨形成，因而人文學在此趨勢下將有其共同的關懷，此為其同質性。另一方面，人類不同的歷史文化並不會因全球化的趨勢而立即消失，反之，它也可能形成不同區域的特殊經驗，此為其異質性。而就新經驗主義的異質性而言，我們必須回到各個區域之特殊經驗，也就是所謂「本土化」的內容，由是而形成屬於不同區域的特有人文學內容與風貌。

（三）人文學與自然科學之互動

以往的人文學在受到連續性所產生之巨大傳統的壓力下，在詮釋已有之理論便已力不從心，遑論去發現新的經驗與理論。因此，眼前的事實便是人文學總是尾隨自然科學之後而做詮釋性的第二序工作。現在，如果人文學的非連續性特質能形成，新經驗主義能建立，則人文學便有充分的心力去關懷現在、展望未來，從而對自然科學提出新的要求與評價，進而使得自然科學不再只是訴諸自然的演化，而使人類能逐漸主導自然科學發展的方向與目標。例如某些知識或技術應否開發？由誰開發？其成果是否可壟斷牟利？凡此，皆可在人文學日趨成熟之時，加以合理的回應。

五、結　論

實踐性是知識發展的重要動力之一，缺乏了實踐性，自然使人失去興趣而不願深入，此在人文學尤其明顯。本文主要反省人文學所以落後於自然科學的可能原因，並試圖找出廿一世紀人文學拋棄侷限，勇於開創的理由與方法。筆者在此乃是貫徹文中所提出之新經驗主義原則，也就是對自身切實遭遇的疑難與困惑，提出說明與反省。當然，也正因爲是由自身經驗出發，因而不免有以偏概全之弊，同時在理解、詮釋及解決方法上也未必周延，凡此，尚祈學者方家不吝賜正。

The Renewal of Nations:World-wide Waves and Domestic Dynamics*

Ooi Kee Beng**

Now that we seek to save the human race from its miseries, to bring about the happiness and advantages of complete peace-and-equality, to seek the universal benefits of One World, we must begin with the destruction of state boundaries and the abolishment of nationalism (or perhaps better, the idea of the state).

Kang Youwei 康有爲 (*Datong shu* 大同書)

Introduction: Describing the Modern Project as Nation Renewal

The history of the modern age, especially in the Far East, is very

* 國家改新化：全球波浪與國內動力

** 黃基明，瑞典斯德歌爾摩大學中文系博士生暨兼任講師

much the story of the renewal of political entities. How much of old discourses and institutions is to be jettisoned is of course the key question. The pressing project of renewal is largely a response to those new dynamic forms of political and economic organisation developed by North Atlantic nations that have exerted more pressure than traditional political structures can withstand. More than merely evolving new forms of political and social co-operation and coercion, this process requires the formation of new identities and new loyalties. Nations, ancient and modern, new and otherwise, have to undergo unending rejuvenation.

This article presents terms that together amount to a perspective on this ubiquitous project of nation renewal. The term "Nation Renewal" is introduced to capture the variations of radical political changes during at least the Twentieth Century. Being of the opinion that many important *human* aspects of modern political life are not given due attention and are subsequently not captured by conventional terms, I attempt to present conceptual dimensions that simultaneously describe the international scene as well as the domestic scene. To the extent I find useful, I adopt Chinese terms as alternatives. The history of Chinese political science is a long and exciting one and the absence of concepts from it in international usage is unfortunate.

After playing around with the terms "Modernisation" and "Nation-state Building", to describe this process, I finally settled for Nation Renewal instead, since any study of the subject would principally cover the restructuring of political entities.

It should also be mentioned that "Nation-state Building", however, was found preferable to "Modernisation" for a number of reasons. Differentiating between "nation" and "state" does provide some space for conceiving of the state at once as the expression of the cultural nation and also the moulder of future national identities, and as something separate from the nation. Furthermore, while capturing the essentials of the political and cultural changes of our times, it does not leave us with social-darwinistic implications the way the second term obviously does. It avoids the discussion of whether a political project and event is an expression of modernisation or the dying spasms of traditionalism and conventionalism. The tendency of the term "modernisation" to create controversy before an analysis has even started is avoided if all contemporary wide-ranging political and cultural events are instead placed within a ubiquitous nation-state building context. Thus, the Iran of Khomeini, the Libya of Gaddafi, the twists and turns of modern German political history, the creating and destroying of Japanese political structures, the racialist democracy of Malaysia or the corporate capitalism of Scandinavia, the big brother foreign policies of the USA, Korean state patronism or the *laissez faire* system of Hong Kong, all become expressions of unprecedented nation-state building, and not variations of a struggle between revolutionary and reactionary, progressive and conservative, or in other words, acceptable or not acceptable forces *per se.* We need not therefore label the Beijing student revolt of 1989 as progressive or the *Falungong* demonstrations of 1999 as reactionary. Both are occurrences within a larger process.

Despite these advantages, however, the terms nation, state and nation-state are admittedly controversial. Since what is important is the describing of endless changes experienced on a social level on the one hand, and of the pragmatic application of ideologies and masterplans for staving off cultural anachronism or political irrelevance on the other, I find the term "**Nation Renewal**" preferable, firstly because it is new and unstained, secondly because it connotes unended endeavour. Nation renewal is never over and done with.

"Modernising", in most, if not all cases, is deemed an inevitability and not a choice, and the conflicts involved in the renewal of a nation on the geographical and cultural grounds of old ones are part and parcel of this project. Where the language-defined nation and the sovereign state coincide, the way they seem to have done relatively well in Sweden, cultural differences have so far not been very pertinent. When one state takes root where different cultures congregate, the situation is much more volatile, as the case was in the USSR and Yugoslavia, and as it is in Russia, India, and to a lesser extent, China.

In modern international politics, where world views and broad national interests easily come into conflict, cultural, and even civilizational differences have always been highly relevant. Samuel Huntington's recent depiction of present and impending civilizational tension, interestingly enough, describes a reality that "Third World" populations have been conscious about for at least 150 years.

At the present moment, we have the interesting example of one of the first modern nations, Great Britain, going through not only a transformation of political and social institutions, but also an attempt at the renewal of national identification, not only among the Welsh and the Scottish, but also among the English themselves, and among the sizable migrant population. The hybrid model formed from First and Third Wave ideologies is undergoing profound change (see below for explanation of these terms).

Components of the Sufficient Discursive Commonality (常道構件圖)

THEORETICAL PRE-CONDITIONS (理論先決條件)：

INTERNAL DYNAMICS (國內社會動力)

• Structuring level of social dynamics (社會動力的構思層次)

Ideologies, blueprints, masterplans, education, symbol-building, rituals, etc.

• Spontaneous level of social dynamics (社會動力的自發層次)

Ethnic differences, recent migration effects, economic life, artistic forms, rituals, etc.

• Li-Fa dichotomy of social cohesion (社會內聚性的禮法範圍)

Social control and socialisation through reliance on conventionalism and law.

EXTERNAL DYNAMICS (國際關係動力)

History of relations to neighbours and the first modern nations, present power constellations in the vicinity, role in previous Waves of nation-renewal and effects of earlier national projects.

• **Li-Fa dichotomy of international relations** (國際關係的禮法範圍)

Mutual recognition and respect, co-existence or conflict, superior or inferior roles.

PRACTICAL SOLUTION (實際答案)：

SUFFICIENT DISCURSIVE COMMONALITY (CHANGDAO 常道)

Generating the national rationale (*daoli* 道理) and morality (*daode* 道理)

Interwoven ideas about the Renewing Nation (國家改新化) and the World Order (國際組織) propagandized through mass medial discursive conservatism, obligatory schooling, language reforms, etc.

Standardisations (標準化) deemed conducive to domestic strength and wealth (強富)

Intense interplay (強列的相互影響)

Nei Dao (內道) ⟷ **Wai ~Dao** (外道)

Nei Dao (內道)	**Wai ~Dao** (外道)
Balance between structuring and spontaneous levels and stance between Li and Fa generate forms of domestic co-operation or conflict, wealth or poverty, stability or chaos, and high or low compatibility with democracy	1.Isolationism/ Globalism 2. Regionalism Acceptance or rejection Co-operation or conflict Independence and Influence as driving forces

The Two Levels of Social Dynamics

The rush of changes in any given area and at any given time is not always comprehensible to the nation renewer. His attitude lies between the ideological and the pragmatic. The cultures and peoples he is to smelt into a stable citizenry, even as he plans, are in change, being influenced greatly in ways not always predictable. And so even as he works, necessarily on a more abstract level, the concrete lower level of society changes according to its own loose logic.

That is one factor of nation renewal that should be captured in an analysis of the subject. This I try to do by introducing the Two Levels of Social Dynamic—the **Structuring Level** (社會動力的構思層次) and the **Spontaneous Level** (社會動力的自發層次).

The Structuring Level subsumes central policies and analyses, ideological ambitions and politics in general. Here, although very often in an *ad hoc* manner, masterplans are drawn, powers balanced, symbols created and identities weaved, all with much consideration being paid, on the one hand, to the traditions and conventions of the region, and the more spontaneous changes these are going through, and on the other, to the reality of political powers and discourses influential in the nation's immediate vicinity and also further afield. This level deals with concept creation, through concrete symbols and lingual abstractions, and through the physical linking and defining of national territory, citizenship and jurisdiction. Identification here is largely a rather consciously orchestrated affair. (Note that the adjective "Structuring" and not "Structural" is used. This is to suggest the inventive and not the discovering element in thought).

The Spontaneous Level denotes society's more unstructured solutions and expedient forms of relationships. Concretely, this can mean changes in migration, technological influence, educational levels, living standards, the spread of ideas and attitudes, etc. Identification here would be of a more individualistic nature, less standardized by wider political considerations. Influences and responses here happen with little state control. For example, the Falungong demonstrations in China in the Summer of 1999, was a culmination of changes at a lower social level that had taken place without state planning, and was therefore considered subversive.

Sufficient Discursive Commonality: Changdao 常道*, daoli* 道理 *and daode* 道理

The term **Renewing Nation** is adopted in place of terms like New Nation, Nation-state or merely Nation, to stress the point that nations are never completed entities and that a people's national identity is always in need of reformation or reconfirmation. Only in realising this identity to a sufficient level can the project, for the moment, be considered successful and conducive to a nation's independence (duli獨立) and influence (*shili*實力), wealth, power and stability (*fuguo*富國, *qiangbing*強兵, *wending*穩定). This involves depicting a world and a nation bound on some commendable venture within which this image has currency. This is the Nation Renewal Project (*guojia gaixinhua* 國家改新化). A masterplan in application will in most cases be modified beyond recognition by time and circumstances, and will generate not only successes and failures, but most importantly, also a discourse on co-operation and conflict. The rationale and morality formed will function in a rather self-fulfilling manner. This construction I call the **Sufficient Discursive Commonality**. A functional national identity relies on the attainment and upkeep of the common use of a network of concepts. At some point, this commonality reaches critical mass as it were, and becomes sufficient and effective. A sufficiently functional citizenry thus comes into being.

I find it useful here to import a Chinese term and call this discursive commonality the ***Changdao*,** the Constant Discourse, using it totally in a relativistic sense. There are a few reasons for this choice. Firstly, the term's connotations of 'speech' and 'prescriptiveness' are extremely useful to what I wish to suggest here. Secondly, continuity is essential to it. Thirdly, it generates easily the further claim I make that the ***daoli*** (道理 rationale) and the ***daode*** (道德 morality) of the project command relevance only within it. Fourthly, it serves well as a general term for the different combinations of ***Li*** (禮 conventionalism) and ***Fa*** (法 jurisdiction) which go into making a political structure viable.

As mentioned earlier, for this *changdao* to function, a symbiotic relationship between an internal and an external discourse (***neidao*** 内道 and ***waidao*** 外道) must be effected. A depiction of significant others is needed to describe the self. The attainment and the continual rejuvenation of this requires both an educational and mass medial propaganda apparatus. The measures thus taken to generate this *changdao* are tantamount to the specific nation renewal project.

Language reforms, together with ethnic mapping, are surprisingly common in the early history of a Renewing Nation. Such Structuring Level changes try to work out what is necessary to integrate and what is safe to eradicate of the variety of inherited phenomena. We also see that resistance to the *changdao* that is being generated, when not violent, generally involves the defence of old symbols and rituals, lingual or otherwise, that are threatened. The *changdao,* successfully propagandized, serves as the lasting discourse, "the element in which arguments have their life" which must pretend to be *eternal.*

The Li-Fa dichotomy (禮法範圍)

Another dimension of the generation of *changdao* is as old as Confucius and Lao Zi. I mean of course the dichotomy of *Li* and *Fa.* I consider this to be the theoretical base for social cohesion. Individuals become functioning social units through these two elements. *Fa* is the method of jurisdiction, where laws are formulated and passed by due process, and the punishment for breaking them is also comprehensively written down and, at least theoretically, predictable. *Li* is the method of conventionalism, a wide term that covers all the different aspects of socialisation from simple social habits to social (excepting judicial) controls and sanctions.

Many conflicts common to contemporary intercontinental politics can be understood within the Fa-Li dimension in terms of differing solutions in social organisation.

The long-standing discussion about Rule of Man against Rule of Law, Asian values (which generally are expressive of a state of prolonged loss of cultural initiative) against Western values (ethnocentric modernity), governmental paternalism against democracy, social stability against human rights-all these can, I believe, be fruitfully seen as scales of conflict created when different Fa-Li balances function as unquestionable *changdao* in intercontinental dialogue. What makes these conflicts so difficult to dissolve is this fact: *To work effectively, the changdao, strives to be amnesiac about the compromises that went into forming it!*

The generation of the *changdao,* always a hybrid of the old and the modern (Meiji Japan's *hehun yangcai* 和魂洋才, the Tongzhi restoration's *zhongti xiyong* 中體西用) is in fact the essence of the eagerness for standardisation exhibited by any would-be nation renewer from the time of the legalists and Qin Shihuang Di (秦始皇帝) to the era of Mao Zedong (毛澤東).

The *Neidao,* being a balancing of Li and Fa forms of socialisation and social control, essentially propagandises a top-down framework where being represented (or even the acceptance of being unrepresented within a democracy), on the one hand, or being centrally controlled, on the other, sometimes do not differ much in practice in terms of individual influence in politics. However, even when the political arena is exclusive and authoritarian, the economic arena might not be.

Paradoxically, Deng's reforms, or the examples of the Four Dragons, allow much Spontaneous Level freedom, an act made possible by the patronage of a tightly controlled Structring Level. Social mobility in such an exercise appears extremely high. A sensitive rein on unleashed spontaneous change is the thin and loose tightrope to be walked in such a case.

Extra-national bodies like financial institutions, international or global organisations, mass medial conglomerates and international companies and political, economic and military constructions whose relevance is undeniable to the nation are important elements in the calculus of the nation renewer today. Together with the influence of strong nations on international affairs, these constitute the perceived World Order. The Renewing Nation must also be studied through the expressions of its understanding of its own relation to it.

The Three Forms of International Relations: The Waidao外道

Depicting other nations and powers in a comprehensive way is part and parcel of the generation of a *changdao.* Once a World Order is described, it is very much a matter of strategy how the description of the domestic order, the *neidao,* is to relate to it. A functioning stability that will generate wealth and influence, and in specific cases, attain other pressing goals like the preservation or regaining of cultural pride or greatness, is what nation renewal blueprints amount to.

This is necessary if a functional idea of nationhood and citizenship is to evolve within national borders. Regional political considerations-the relationship between the National Self and National Others in the vicinity—are therefore an indispensably illuminating factor in nation renewal, both in how they form domestic discourse and in insights they give into the more informal labours involved in the generation of a national image.

This identification process is effected on a discursive level and its concepts possess a basically prescriptive function. The descriptive or scientific function is of secondary importance. *Asian Values* is such a term. There is of course a strong case to be made that clear or sudden threats to a nation's *changdao* more than to its wealth and independence, will give cause to limit spontaneous change.

A highly significant aspect of the amnesiac *changdao* is that an old *changdao* once created to handle earlier, but now defunct, circumstances tends to linger and cause contradictions until such a time that calls for *reformasi* are made. Often, radical events at the Spontaneous Level exert pressure upon the Structuring Level to resolve the tension. A *changdao* once created for confrontation, for example, Maoism, American cold-war ideology or Khomeinism, does, for a time at least, continue to dictate conditions and to re-stage the same play, with new actors in old familiar roles.

At this point, the case of China serves as an illuminative example.

Her old World Order finally fell apart after the fall of the Manchurian dynasty. This demise was, despite the division into mutually antagonistic regions typical of periods of dynastic disaster, quite unlike the disappearance of earlier dynasties. No longer could another family set itself up as the founder of a new dynasty. The republican idea had grown too strong, a fact evidenced by the fatal lack of support for the attempt by Yuan Shikai to become emperor in 1915. Yuan's failure, despite having strong executive powers as president and a history of skilful political manoeuvring within the old system, heralded the end of that very system, though not the coming of any specific new one.

Why was there such weak support for the founding of yet another glorious dynasty? The inflow of new ideas of political organisation and analysis was of course a major factor, but this was mainly a change brewing within the ranks of certain intellectuals. Without subtracting from the importance of this, one could suggest that, more importantly, it was aggressive powers with radically different *changdao* which had forced the doors of China and then implanted themselves at strategic points across the fallen empire, making it impossible for the national consciousness to harbour continued faith in the old *changdao*.

The *external conditions* for the existence of a "universal empire" simply no longer obtained! This in no way suggests that the old discourse and the habits of thought inculcated by it would no longer continue to exert significant influence. Inarguably, the truth is to the contrary.

By the turn of the century, a new World Order threatened to engulf all in its way who did not play the Game of Nations. And so a new China had to be born and the old buried. The decades between the fall of Yuan in 1916 and the victory of Mao in 1949 was a time when factions and ideologies not only strove to impose new institutions on the Empire, it was more comprehensively an era when men propagandized, by peaceful and other means, their conclusions about this unstoppable new World Order: how it was superior to the dynastic system, and, more importantly, which new system could take its place. What structure could strengthen and enrich the nation and influence to China's advantage the further development of the World Order?

This preoccupation with the World Order, this *waidao* aspect in renewing the nation, is common to practically all nations in the East at least, and has basically three lines of development:

1. Isolationism（孤立主義）By this, I mean the kind of *changdao* that closes a nation's borders to all spontaneous influences from without and consequently inhibits physical, social and political mobility among its citizenry.

This alternative has been practised now and again by certain Far Eastern nations, including Maoist China. Myanmar and North Korea are other examples that come immediately to mind. Oriental Communism, often seen in the West as part and parcel of Global Communism and an active participant in the Cold War, was very often no more than such an isolationist solution fenced in by the deceptive Red Flag of Global Communism. Non-participation in the World Order and the protection of domestic change from foreign influence, proven in all cases to be no more than a temporary solution, has not been acceptable to global powers.

The forms of adjustment at the Structuring Level common to a nation isolating itself would reflect the reasons for that ambition. Antipathy towards foreign influence and intolerance towards domestic dissidents would provide the framework for political conceptualisation. Militarisation on all fronts becomes the result. Independent of whether the regime names itself rightist or leftist, religious or secular, nationalist or ethnicist, an *authoritarian defensive policy* characterises it.

Not much room is left for personalised and unstructured discourse. The politicisation of society is enforced thoroughly. Take the example of Burma, where ethnic differences have led to unending civil war, or the case of Kampuchea, where cultural suicide in the name of political correctness was mercilessly committed, or the Cultural Revolution in Maoist China, when adjustments at the Structuring Level were pushed to the extreme and any spontaneous discourse was rendered totally unadvisable.

The discursive balance in these cases can be said to have been maintained purely under the strict conditions imposed from the Structuring Level. This unrelenting coercion cannot possibly hope to maintain stability for too long.

2. **Regionalism** (地區主義) views nation renewal efforts as being irretrievably intertwined with the ambitions and the fate of neighbouring nations.

This tendency seems most common among smaller states. Countries that feel that they cannot go it alone seek co-operation with more or less sympathetic neighbours, the ideology being of strength in numbers and based on mutual aid. Regionalism may also be a way to keep stronger powers at bay to gain time and opportunity for weaker and newer nations to develop without overbearing foreign influence. The successful currency controls imposed on 1st September 1997 by Malaysia to protect the *ringgit* is an obvious case in point.

The flora of bodies of regional co-operation blooming in Southeast Asia attests to the popularity of this solution. Malaysia's foreign policy is an illuminative example: she is an active party in regional bodies from SIJORI (Singapore, Johor, Malaysia and Riau, Indonesia) Growth Triangle and IMT-GT (Indonesia, Malaysia and Thailand Growth Triangle) to the gigantic APEC (Asia Pacific Economic Co-operation which includes most East Asian nations plus Australia, New Zealand and the USA) via organs like EAGA (East ASEAN Growth Area including The Philippines, Brunei, Malaysia and Indonesia), AFTA (ASEAN Free Trade Area), ASEAN itself, and EAEC (East Asia Economic Caucus which pointedly excludes the USA), among others.

The conflict between the concepts of EAEC and APEC is a case of smaller nations whose identity, growth and security, and above all, *internal structure,* rely greatly on the benefits of regionalism, feeling extremely uneasy about being again dominated by global powers. The very structure of APEC seems globalist to its lesser members and threatens to nullify the idea of regional co-operation itself.

The sentiments of outrage at this state of affairs are echoed in the speech made by the Malaysian Prime Minister Mahathir Mohamad at the Caracas meeting of the G5 nations in November 1991:

> Yet the East Asians are not allowed even to consult each other or indeed to call themselves East Asians. The United States rejects and opposes vehemently the East Asia Economic Caucus or EAEC and demands that Japan and South Korea dissociate themselves from the formation of this consultative group. South Korea is told that it owes a debt of blood to the United States and it owes nothing to Malaysia and should therefore toe the US line. (Mahathir Mohamad. See Govin Alagasari, 1994:238. Mahathir, The Awakening, Malaysia: Uni-Strenth Sdn.Bhd.)

For a nation investing in *open regionalism* (as opposed to, for example, the closed regionalism of the former Warsaw Pact states), adjustments at the Structuring Level will be concerned with the benefits and ills of multi-ethnicity and pluralism (as opposed to the preoccupation with cultural and ideological homogeneity of the isolationistic state) and the advantages and disadvantages of free trade (as opposed to the benefits and ills of the planned economy).

Adjusted discourse at the Spontaneous Level will, in a country wed to open regionalism, supposedly dwell on consensual forms of relationships (as opposed to a moralist or legalistic form common to closed societies) and social mobility of the individual (as opposed to the benefits and ills of the stable social roles of a centrally controlled society and the statistically conceived citizenry produced within an isolationistic mode of thought).

In a renewing nation less hostile to the World Order than the isolationist nation is, new abstractions relevant to that World Order must be absorbed and transformed in such a way that they effectively facilitate the transition from the traditional to the new. This adjustment must necessarily come into some form of conflict with older habits of daily living. Though adjustments at the Spontaneous Level do take place, one cannot expect them to keep up with or follow neatly the adjustments made at the Structuring Level. An elite is born whose job is, on the one hand, to create a new and functional political discourse, and on the other, to achieve this with minimal friction with the old habits of the populace. At the same time, this feat has to be both didactic and propagandistic, building support for, and participation in, the *changdao* being born.

Regionalism seems on the whole to have succeeded better in terms of stability and steady growth. By withstanding the temptation of globalist terminology, a feat harder for larger nations like China to accomplish, and instead concentrating on concrete regional solutions, smaller states seem able to achieve a better balance between adjustments made at the Structuring Level and those made at the Spontaneous Level. Apparently, the dual dangers of xenophobia and utopism tend more to plague countries with higher ambitions.

3. **Globalism**（全球主義）A globalist ideology conceives of national aims as being inherently connected to revolutionary changes in the world as a whole and within which the renewing nation itself must play a strong contributive role.

The most comprehensive form of globalism in the 20th Century was the proposed Communist World Order. It taught that a World Order could be achieved, initially as a parallel to, and finally as a substitute for, the imperialist Western one constructed over the previous 200 years. It is doubtful if this globalism was totally sincere since history has shown that communist states usually practice isolationism instead. One can of course debate whether or not this tendency was forced on them from the outside, and whether such a development was incidental to, or inherent in, the ideology. The fact remains that this form of globalism is in practice highly reminiscent of the isolationist solution. Indeed, I venture that isolationism and globalism tend towards synonymity, given the hostile geopolitical terrain within which nations practice renewal.

The Structuring Discourse necessary to a globalist ideology puts the Renewing Nation in an enviable historical and moral role against the seemingly ineffaceable World Order. The arguments thus produced in turn help define the domestic order itself. Given the threatening atmosphere of such a discourse, one cannot expect much elbow room to be given to activities at the Spontaneous Level. Here, as in isolationism, the discursive balance is maintained by a coercive Structuring Discourse.

At this point, I would like to introduce a depiction of the modern political history of the world that I call the Five Waves of Nation Renewal.

*The Five Waves of Nation Renewal*新國化之五大波

Let us start by going back to the dawn of the Age of Modern Nations. The exact dates for the start of this are not important. What is clear is that revolution and reforms, scientific developments and ideological innovations in countries like Holland, France, England and the earlier USA provided the grounds for a phenomenal growth in economic and military strength, not to mention political stability. This was the First Wave, or the Atlantic Wave. As the highly successful expansionist politics of these first modernised nations of the Atlantic coast strengthened them beyond then thinkable levels, it became imperative for other ethnic and political groupings to imitate, to seek to limit and, in fact, to challenge that strength.

The efforts of the nations that started nation renewal at the end of the 1860's, specifically Germany, Italy and Japan, all involved a globalist *realpolitik*. By this, I do not mean that each of these nations planned to take over the world. However, quite unavoidably it seems, the foreign affairs of the nations of this Second Wave (the Fascist Wave) were played out on the global stage. The final showdown between the Atlantic Wave and the Fascist Wave of Nation Renewal is more commonly known as the Second World War. The indecisive and misnamed First World War, however, helped to create the next wave of nation renewal. The forces unleashed by the Bolshevik Revolution of 1917 were of course globalist in essence, being Marxist, and came to involve huge areas, in truth stretching from Poland to North Korea. Besides the Warsaw Pact states and China and other minor states, the so-called Third World was profoundly affected. The Cold War, which could just as well have been called the War Between the First and Third Waves, forced international discourse for a time into a single dimension, that of Left versus Right.

At the same time, as a sort of ideological compromise between Communism and Capitalism, the Fourth Wave grew forth. It was initially small but its influence was to be deep and lasting. This Social Democratic Wave occurred principally in Scandinavia and came to have profound effects on the renewal of other nations in west Europe, including the Atlantic nations themselves.

As the impetus of the communist inspiration died down, nations at the edge of American influence in East Asia elbowed for room under the umbrella of US nuclear defence. These effected in fact a new wave of successfully renewing nations straddled across the West Pacific Rim, forming the next explosion of economic expansion. This is the Pacific Wave.

This depiction of nation renewal postulates that political cultures, through experienced hostility or through other destabilising external influence, force themselves through profound social, philosophical and political changes that may even threaten the very means and criteria by which they had until then defined themselves. The chronological and geographical demarcations of these waves are what make them obvious.

Some interesting points about them, given the isolationism-regionalism-globalism forms of *waidao* laid forth earlier, are that, firstly, the first three waves can all to a large extent be termed globalist, and secondly, and this is of much higher significance, the second and the third waves are more continental and militant in nature, in contrast to the more maritime and mercantile nature of the first, fourth and fifth❶

The waves model provides us with a theoretical framework of world-wide nation renewal large enough and flexible enough to be used as a common means for periodising any nation's modern history. In

---

❶ See Bariington Moore Jr. (*Social Origins of Dictatorship and Democracy. Lord and Peasant in the Making of the Modern World* 1987 (1966), Penguin), where what are principally the three first waves are thoroughly discussed as routes to modernization. My aims are to show through the addition of a fourth and fifth that there is a clear contrast between maritime and continental cultures involved in modernization, and, through the use of the image of waves, reveal a chronological and geographical pattern in modern global history. Though Moore's book was not the source of inspiration for me, I mention it here to ease my argumentation.

studying Malaysia, for example, the effects of the waves would tentatively be as follows:

The Atlantic Wave came ashore with the creation of the Straits Settlements and of British Malaya over 150 years ago, followed by the short occupation by the Second Wave representative, Japan, in the early part of the 1940's, which was in turn followed by the Communist Insurgency of the 1950's, and finally the economic upsurge of the whole East Asia region from early in the 1980's. The influence of the Social Democratic Wave is significantly missing. This periodisation helps explain upheavals in social conditions and variations in political discourse.

To prove further my point that this framework is able to provide significant variations in periodisation for different countries, we can also take the case of China. The modern history of China can be divided into the English period from the First Opium War of 1840 up to the time of the First Sino-Japanese War of 1895, from which date the Fascist Period commences, only to end with the defeat of Japan in 1945 and the Kuomintang in 1949. The Communist Period for China would start around that final year. There is an overlap from 1980, when China, still under the Communist structure, but now under Deng Xiaoping, reforms itself economically and becomes to a large extent a major part of the Pacific Wave.

Even in China, the Scandinavian Wave seems not to have made any ripples, so to speak. It would seem that this model has not left any deep impression in the Far East, nor have the sentiments important to it been propagandized.

Are the four modernizations formulated by Deng Xiaoping a sufficient collection of factors for most nation renewers? Developing defence capabilities, propagandizing the scientific mode of thought, industrializing production and mechanising agriculture do seem to sum up much of what is the core of "*realmodernization*". The softer side of human existence, where concepts like individual freedom, self-determination, humaneness, even the search for happiness, etc., are important, is difficult to include in five-year plans. Radical political measures involve control and comprehensibility, and so one would expect the softer side to be operationalised into hard concepts that have clear indicators of change, and to subsequently lose priority. For example, the feminism of early communism in China, as elsewhere, had to be sacrificed on the altar of the crass class struggle.

The call for political reform that Chinese dissidents like Wei Jingsheng came to embody after 1980, did not express clearly enough the need for freedom in terms that suggested compromise within the nation renewal context. Even European parliamentary democracy is historically a compromise between radical calls for freedom and the established order's need for stability. It is the renewing of a nation into a stable and strong political unit able to exert itself globally that has become the modern project, despite earlier ideals. Other more humane factors are given supporting roles. It would seem that in order to give right of place to the softer side of politics, it is necessary to express it together with the hard side. The Structuring and Spontaneous Levels introduced above will hopefully contribute towards this.

Conclusion: Trends in Nation Renewing Discourse in the Last Decade of the Millennium

The end of the Cold War, or in *Reaganspeak,* the Fall of the "Evil Empire" in 1991, does indeed mark the passing away of the old Left-

Right discourse. At about the same time in Asia, just before the fall of the Berlin Wall in 1989, the Tiananmen Crackdown backfired badly on the legitimacy of the Chinese Communist Party and on the integrity of the People's Liberation Army.

Within Western societies, on the cultural level, the search for variation within the one remaining global alternative took the place of the battle of opposites. Alternativeness in Social Life becomes more relevant than Alternative Societies. Pluralism becomes the catchword when democracies experience strong centralisation tendencies justified by crass economic considerations.

In the United States, the publication of Francis Fukuyama's triumphalist *The End of History* in 1992 articulated the self-satisfaction of the victor of the 40-year-long Cold War. From now on, who can imagine anything other than the continued success of the Liberal world order?

In 1996, Samuel Huntington formulated the *Clash of Civilizations* as if it were something new, while in areas outside the Western hemisphere, this clash, though still relevant, is ancient. This suggests that this centuries-old clash is finally becoming obvious to the West, possibly through the rise of a Pacific Wave. This wave is a broad answer to what was until recently, except for the ill-fated Japanese challenge of the 1940s, a one-sided civilizational crisis. For example, a phrase like East-West dialogue could not properly be used until fairly recent times, for example, after the first ASEM (Asia-Europe Meeting) in 1996.

The First, Third and Fourth Waves seem to be smelting into one with the pending entry of Great Britain and Scandinavia, excepting Norway, into the economist melting pot that is the European Monetary Union. The coming into being of the *Euro* currency inspires similar ambitions elsewhere.

Asian aspirations expressed in wishful projects like the EAEC or the forming of a regional currency zone centred around the Japanese Yen may be viewed as expressions of new dynamics in the relationship between nations and civilizations.

Changes in methods of war and foreign intervention since the Gulf War are also part of the creation of a new world order, or more correctly, they express the hurried reorientation of nations towards one sole centre.

This is also a period of democratisation, a stage in the decolonisation of former colonies and dependencies that follows the era of insecurities that was very much a part of the newly attained nationhood of most countries since India's independence in 1947. The patriotic and patronist regimes of *Independence* that froze into the global battle between communism and non-communism are now defrosting, and new dimensions of nation renewal are coming into being.

Given the speed of economic and political development nowadays, national realities seem to play a mere supporting role in the forming of a larger international discourse.

The effective regime created by Mahathir in Malaysia since 1981 has now lost much of its authority, and worse, its integrity. A vision of change in the structure of politics is now thinkable to a broad segment of the population. An unholy alliance of opposition parties, putting their contradictions aside, has been formed (*Barisan Alternatif*), using *Reformasi* as its catchword, challengingly vowing to put the convicted Anwar Ibrahim in the Prime Minister's seat if it should against all odds win the impending election. Although this seems unlikely to happen at the moment of writing (September 1999), tension does remain between priorities on the international stage and those in domestic politics.

The racial nature of political alliances in Malaysia is no longer given. This is clearly a development away from the solutions of the

Merdeka era. After gaining independence, certain compromises had successively been made and certain freedoms taken away, all purportedly to make it possible for a strong nation to emerge. That was 40 years ago. With the self-confidence gained through economic development, the old compromises have lost much of their relevance. A draconian law like the ISA (Internal Security Act) of 1960 appears ridiculous. Internal security, despite the rioting in Kuala Lumpur in 1999, is not as serious an issue as it used to be. In fact, the rioting shows that security is no longer the issue. The demonstrations, though carried out without permission, were often peaceful. The society had become stable enough for youths to take to the streets without the demonstrations getting totally out of hand or turning inte racial riots, a real and dampening fear in the history of the nation.

The growth of the *Internet* must not be forgotten of course. It offers a totally new industry open to all nations with a sufficient level of education to get into the fray. The revolutionary strength of this lies not merely in the off reported use of it as a means of communication and for propaganda, as during the Beijing Summer of 1989, or the disturbances following Anwar Ibrahim's arrest, trial and conviction, and continuing trial, etc. It lies also in its ability to sweep away much of the old discourse, potentially including the advantage more developed nations have in total economic development and in industrial infrastructure.

And so, changes in world views are happening on many fronts. Within the West itself, the project of building and propagandising an essential West continues. In the East, continuing decolonisation leads to calls for a solid Asianness, essentially amounting to a non-Westenmess that needs not necessarily be anti-Western. In between these two, an East-West dialogue has arisen. A future clash of civilizations needs not occur.

The legacy of Sun Wukung: on being (post)modern without Modernity in China*

Vladimir V. Maliavin**

Abstract

Perhaps the most remarkable feature of Chinese traditional philosophical terms is their deeply rooted ambiguity readily observed in the absence of strictly technical vocabulary in Chinese science and philosophy which upsets so much the scholars obsessed with the precision of their language ❶ Epistemologically this ambiguity refers to the contingency of subjective and objective or symbolical and empirical aspects of human experience. The task of thinking in Chinese tradition is not to secure the intellect's hold of consciousness, the rule of the subjective ego over the totality of experience but, on the contrary, to dissolve ego's boundaries and, so to say, to universalize consciousness,

---

* 孫悟空的遺產：沒有現代的後現代主義

** 馬良文，淡江大學俄羅斯研究所教授

❶ One of the recent examples is Dr. M. Porkert's effort to create a technical vocabulary, based on Latin, for the language of Chinese medicine.

in Chinese terms – "to embody the heart of Heaven and Earth".

According to Feng Yulan the history of Chinese thought is a movement towards ever more encompassing non-duality of "heavenly" and "mundane" values in human life – a point which, no matter how true it is to the spirit of Chinese culture, leaves no room for history *per se* for the simple reason that various degrees of "non-duality" cannot be demonstrated.

The study of the meaning of emotions and related concepts in the 17th century China can provide an interesting data for speculating on the destiny of the *Weltanschauung* based on "non-duality" thinking. It was in fact the time when Chinese thought made the most decisive turn for the philosophical synthesis sanctioned by tradition. Wang Yangming's philosophy of innate and "intrinsically good" knowledge (*liang zhi*) opened new vistas for preaching the inherent goodness of emotional life in its spontaneity. Emotion in Chinese thought was understood as essentially a relation between the ego and non-ego actualized within "one body" (*yi ti*) of Tao so ot was not separated from the moral will. The radical followers of Wang Yangming pushed this line of thinking to its logical end that it is precisely strong feelings, for instance a mania for some object (*pi*) or a passionate love (*zhi qing*), that generates moral strength in man and eventually heightens the inner awareness to the point of achieving complete calmness and "supreme enlightenment". Writings on courtly love, so fashionable at the time ❷ and basically in tune, let us note, with the Taoist tradition of "bedchamber art", stress the significance of erotic desire as a way to self-

❷ I would refer specifically to the works of writers close to Li Zhi, mostly Tang Xianzu and Yuan Hungdao, as well as Feng Menglung and many minor writers like Wei Yung, Yu Huai et al.

control. However, this trend by the last decades of Ming rule led some enthusiastic writers to accepting the sexual passion (often affiliated with dreaming or ghostly state) as a gateway to salvation or even restoration of the Confucian order – a situation that amounted paradoxically to the tradition's self-affirmation through self-denial. This sort of tradition's "deadlock" precluded the passage to modernity if we understand by this term the autonomy of the subjective Self and its spontaneous desires. [3]

Now the drive of Desire (the world of dreaming, of sexuality etc.) reveals "profound and subtle" (*you, wei, miao*) roots of experience which constitute the repertoire of type-forms (*pin*) – a real heritage of Chinese traditional culture. These type-forms come most closely to Deleuze's notion of haecceity. [4] These are not substances or ideas but the hierarchies of forces, the contingencies of shadows and echoes which exist "between presence and absence", in proximity of everything and they immediately dissolve in the light of the "critical reflection". The very capacity to perceive these "semen of things" is generated by the heightening of the inner awareness through the Will's working.

I have argued elsewhere that the greatest problem of Chinese cultural theory was the passage from the micro-perceptions of inner experience to the micro-images of culture which bear only the semblance of natural forms. [5] The real meaning of the post-traditional situation in China achieved in Late Ming times was the acute awareness

---

[3] Cf. R. Girard. Deceit, Desire and Novel. Baltimore: Johns Hopkins University Press, 1988.

[4] Cf. J.Deleuze., F. Guattari. A Thousand Plateau: Capitalism and Schizophrenia Minnesota University Press, 1987.

[5] Cf. V. Maliavin. The East, the West and the Russian Idea. – Tamkang Journal of International Affairs. Vol.1, no.2., 1997.

of the illusionary nature of external images which resulted in deliberate creating of phantom-like worlds in arts and literature. The wanderings of Sun Wukung, a model schizophrenic subject who embraces the whole of the world history, serves the best example of this extreme point in the development of tradition.

The "culture of fantasies", however, proved to be only transitory. To become socially acceptable the phantasm was to be downgraded to the status of "reality". So, quite soon a realistic vision superceded the former inner quest and the Qing culture is characterized by the ever deepening gap between fantasy (reduced to nightmare) and reality (downplayed to life's trivia). Yet this change marked the fulfillment of traditional thought's potential because creation itself was conceived in China in terms of the "fall" of holistic experience into its fragment or, in other words, of spirit's

em-bodiment. This accounts for the ironic mood pervading Chinese culture of the last few centuries.

One should conclude that China's effort to modernize herself hides in itself a good deal of the "post-modern situation" as long as post-modernity means the radical critique of autonomous subject while affirming the priority of actuality.

Perhaps the most remarkable feature of Chinese traditional philosophical terms is their all-pervading ambiguity readily observed in the absence of strictly technical vocabulary in Chinese science and philosophy . This fact is a source of great nuisance to the scholars who tend to identify scientific spirit with the positivist precision of the terms they use ❻ Epistemological root of this ambiguity is the contingency of

❻ One of the recent examples is Dr. M. Porkert's effort to create a technical vocabulary, based on Latin, for the language of Chinese medicine.

subjective and objective or, better say, symbolical and empirical aspects of human experience. The task of thinking in Chinese tradition canot be reduced to securing the intellect's hold of consciousness, the rule of subjective ego over the totality of experience. On the contrary, it consists in overcoming ego's boundaries and, so to say, universalizing consciousness, or what in Chinese is expressed in somewhat mysterious terms – "embodying the heart of Heaven and Earth".

What kind of a history could such thinking have? Evidently, it resists all procedures for objectifying the spirit, accomplished dialectically or otherwise; procedures that cast the history in a form of linear development. The difficulties in dealing with this problem are well illustrated by a historical scheme suggested by one of the most influential Chinese philosophers Fung Youlan. According to Fung Youlan, [7] the history of Chinese thought is a movement towards ever more encompassing non-duality of "heavenly" and "mundane" values in human life – a point which, no matter how true it is to the spirit of Chinese culture, leaves no room for history *per se* for the simple reason that various degrees of "non-duality" cannot be determined still less demonstrated. So Fung Youlan's history of Chinese thought ends where it starts. This setback, though, reveals one important side of Chinese tradition: the latter stands as a meta-logical limit for individual systems of thought based on empirical evidence and formal reasoning. Such is the difference between the Way (*dao*) and partial Teachings (*jiao*). The former must be apprehended or rather realized through direct experience beyond words, the latter can be verbally taught and learned.

The main value of Chinese cultural tradition is neither knowledge nor even creation but embodiment of truth. The Chinese sage does not

---

[7] Cf. Fung Youlan. *A Short History of Chinese Philosophy*. NY., Macmillan, 1948.

look for ideas, substances or facts; he "empties himself", i.e. releases his subjective Self thus withdrawing to the source of his life which is the Great Void of Heaven. In a way quite similar to Heidegger's *Gelassenheit*, he opens himself to the absolute openness, a great (W)hole-ness of Being. Heidegger thought of Gelassenheit as an alternative to the nihilism of modern civilization. Many would think now of Heidegger's "turn" as one of the salient features of the so called "Postmodern condition" (to use the title of the pathbreaking book by J.-F. Lyotard). In fact "self-emptying" may be fully positive and universal event that provides an important perspective on the history of Chinese thought as well.

Recently quite a few scholars, both Chinese and foreign, have pointed at the significance of the Late Ming period in the history of Chinese thought and culture. Until now, though, the intellectual changes at that time have been described somewhat formalistically in terms mostly borrowed from the West such as the rise of novel, empirical philosophy and critical thought etc. In my opinion these changes signify even more that facts can tell for we are witnessing here a decisive turn in Chinese history, the change of the whole "epistemological paradigm" of culture which determined the course of China's development for subsequent centuries. The purpose of this presentation is to outline, by necessity in a general and tentative manner,. the inherent logic of this change.

To begin with, let us recall briefly the fundamentals of the Chinese view of subjectivity. The chief metaphor of authentic consciousness in China is that of clean mirror. The latter does not contain the reflection of reality which is accessible to sight otherwise. Thus it has no cognitive value. It is the only means to see at all; it signifies the opening of vision as such, a vision *of* vision. It reminds that whatever we see, we see *within* and as if through the multiplying glass. The mirror metaphor is a reminder of the inner and hidden depth of consciousness. I call this depth symbolical because it is for ever absent in our world-picture and precedes all existence. This "mirror of darkness" (Lao-tzu's words) belongs to the world of virtual being where things "have not yet begun to exist". This dark abyss of experience (designated by terms *xuan, ming, miao*) serves as a space of gathering (without reduction to formal unity) of all things. It is essentially a mediative and functional reality which in Chinese bears many different definitions: the Void, The Magic Tower, The Treasury of Things, The Womb of the World, the Chaos etc. The latter name highlights the fluid and concrete nature of symbolic reality: it is the elusiveness of moment culminating in the immovable Aeon, a force of becoming that never ceases to be, a change of all changes (itself unchangeable), a limit of all limits (itself limitless) and so on. This symbolic vortex of being exists, as it were, in the mode of pulsation: it is permeated with the flash of creativity but in the very moment of self-transcendence it discloses the abyss within itself. In all its metamorphoses it contains a hidden "power of things" (*shi*), a "deep impulse" (*shen ji*) that act in the direction *opposite* to the actual tendency. In every transformation things secretly return to their virtual, or "heavenly", source – the *a priori* dimension of this world which is the inverted image of its external appearance.

In terms of culture this symbolic world is represented by a variety of symbolic types (*p'in, ge*), testimonies to the inner transformations of experience. ❽ Essentially, the Chinese cultural tradition is nothing but a

---

❽ A definition of symbol, given by J.Deleuze, as "the sign in as much as it interiorizes the conditions of its own repetition" seems to be relevant here. Cf. J.Deleuze. *Difference et repetition*. P., P.U.F. 1968. P.92.

repertoire of such types – suffice is to recall the sets of normative chords in Chinese music, normative gestures in all sorts of ritual practice or in Chinese boxing, theatre and even sexual practices, artistic forms in painting, calligraphy, architecture etc. The closest analogies of Chinese *p'in* in Western philosophy are Leibniz's monads and especially the notion of haecceity suggested by J. Deleuze and F.Guattari. ❾ These symbolic types are used not for description or definition but for recalling qualities of experience. They signify not substances, ideas or even facts but the (infinitely) complex assemblages of events, hierarchies of forces, the contingencies of shadows and echoes which exist "between presence and absence", in proximity of everything, in the dark vortex of virtual reality which appears to the outsider as a "fleeting instance of stillness" (*xi*). ❿ These quasi-forms are described by means of metaphors pointing at a certain quality of situation: "the dragon soaring up to the sky", "eight immortals crossing the sea", "the snake creeping down the valley" etc. The metaphors, as P. Ricoeur showed, are literary correlates of imagination, ⓫ and the world of *p'in*-endowed objects was indeed attributed to the world of imagination. (*yi jing*).

Now the power of imagination makes us abandon ourselves, go astray. Accordingly, symbolic types of Chinese tradition signify the act of "dispersal" (*san*) which already Ts'ai Yung, the founder of Chinese

---

❾ Cf. J.Deleuze., F. Guattari. *A Thousand Plateau: Capitalism and Schizophrenia* Minnesota University Press, 1987.

❿ Cf. The words of the Taoist treatise "Kuan Yin-tzu" spoken in the manner of sacred riddle: "One instant of Tao's stillness (*xi*) can make disappear (*ming*) ten thousand things. But when the things disappear where can Tao abide in?"

⓫ Cf. P.Ricoeur, *Hermeneutic and the Human Sciences.* Cambridge University Press, 1981. P. 181.

calligraphy, called the essence of writing. ⓬ Under the light of the "critical reflection" they immediately fall apart and dissolve. The ghostly nature of symbolic types that the building of Chinese culture was composed of used to be the biggest secret of Chinese tradition carefully guarded through the centuries.

The individualized patterns of these symbolic types constituted separate schools in different realms of human practice. Learning them was the process of heightening one's sensitivity, a way of self-cultivation. Yet there is always a limit to our sensitivity. So the symbolic types come out, as it were, from the primordial Chaos, or No-Limit (*wuji*), and, having been refined to the most subtle nuances through self-perfection and cultural practices, finally merge once again with the chaotic web of differences. But this time they constitute the Chaos of another sort – sublimated by human effort, esthetically conceived secondary Chaos of the Great Limit (*t'aiji*). Thus the life of symbolic types amounts to "whirling around in the dark" (*xuan yun*), a spiral-like movement that goes on beyond the empirical time and casts its virtual "shadows" into external world. ⓭ In spatial terms this movement can be described by the figures of concentrated spheres, the double spiral and the fold. The fundamental symbols and principles of Chinese traditional art – the "world in the gourd" motif, the miniature gardens, the layout of classical Chinese gardens etc. – bear a convincing testimony to the priority of virtual space in the artistic taste of the Chinese. The necessity of school

---

⓬ Ts'ai Yung, *Jiu shi lun.*(On Nine Configurations of Force). - *Zhunghua wenhua jinghua.* Vol. 13. Beijing. 1992. P.147.

⓭ These theme received detailed treatment in numerous Taoist treatises on the "transmission of the Heart" (*xin chuan*) explained usually in terms of cosmological circular movement but refers in fact to the symbolical, or virtual, dimension of being.

in Chinese art and thought was predetermined by the deliberate , not to say hazardous, nature of symbolic types constituting the canon of the school. So Chinese school was a closed community based on disciples' confidence in their teacher. And yet, as Chinese saying goes, "Heaven is impartial to all schools".

The subject in Chinese tradition is also two-fold: it exists in the symbolic space of mutual "letting go" of Heaven and things and is constantly "forgetting himself" (*zi-wang*) or "releasing himself" (*zi-fang*) into the world. So he "follows two ways at once": he transcends himself only in order to fall down into its own shadow. Hence the unfading Chinese apology for the common sense permeated with good-tempered irony. The Chinese "man of culture" faced the task of transforming the world into infinitely complex network of symbolic types that refined his taste and sublimated his desire. Hence a great place attributed in the Chinese life ideal to the feeling of joy – a sign of self-transcendence – and the feeling of satisfaction: the sign of self-autonomy. The combination of the encompassing vision and the fragmentary nature of perception is perhaps the most distinctive feature of Chinese esthetic experience.

It was reflection on the symbolic premises of tradition that gave the greatest impetus to historical evolution of Chinese thought and culture. The stepping stone here was of course the need to clarify the nature of symbolic "non-duality" of things. Later Ming period turned out to be a decisive stage in this development. Wang Yang-ming's philosophy of innate and "intrinsically good" knowledge (*liang zhi*) as opposed to objectified knowledge made Chinese thinkers more than ever sensitive to the difference between the symbolic ("anterior to Heaven") and empirical ("posterior to Heaven") aspects of existence. For a while Wang Yangming's moderate disciples tried to preserve this distinction by identifying the "innate knowledge" with the transcendent "body of the Void" (as, for instance, in the philosophy of Wang Chi). But the very premises of symbolist thinking inevitably drew yangmingist thought towards ever closer identification of symbolic reality with . the spontaneous drives of human psyche. The radical thinkers among Wang Yang-ming's followers– I mean of course the Taichow school – would argue that every common man could be put on a par with a sage although they insisted on essentially moral and edifying nature of human emotions, so that the more passionate these emotions are the more they are moral. The literary theory inspired by Wang Yang-ming's philosophy – primary the Kung-an school of Yuan brothers – insisted on the spontaneous self-expression at the expense of stylistic adornments. For Yuan Hung-dao and writers of his circle the subject of poetry was the "mood" (*qu*) or a "soul" (*ling xing*) of the author. An innocent child who gives free rein to his emotions would be the best prototype of a poet.

This line of development reached its unexpected limit in the work of the most famous Chinese nonconformist Li Zhi. Contrary to the widespread view, Li Zhi was not an immoralist. The essence of his message was complete identification of symbolical and natural dimensions of human existences, this time conceived in Buddhist terms as the identity between "the Buddha nature" and the world of appearances. And yet achieving this goal would create an effect comparable to the mutual annihilation of matter and antimatter in physics: it would make meaningless and non-existent both symbolic and empirical values. Li Zhi's suicide in prison was the culmination of both his self-confidence and his despair.

Li Zhi won scandalous popularity for preaching the so called "wild Ch'an". The role of Buddhism is of crucial importance here. The Ch'an thought also advocated in its own way the return to the "naturalness" of the actuality. It is highly significant in this regard that in Ch'an descriptions of meditative experiences we come across not metaphors but solitary natural images, like "green willows", "blue sky". "red sun", "clean streams" etc. ⓮ These images do not presuppose any underlying pattern or rhythm of life, what is only to be expected from the advocates of absolute emptiness. The fact is that Buddhism could only imitate (and could not help imitating for lack of its own onthology of language) the forms of Chinese culture. The Ch'an "madness" was in fact the name for a kind of insight that disclosed the inner inconsistencies of symbolic types and thus threatened to ruin the cultural tradition of China. At best it could point at the pure qualities of experience that provided conditions for setting the patterns of types. Such a view is reflected in the theory that equated artistic inspiration with Ch'an. This theory gained popularity since Southern Sung dynasty when the Chinese tradition for the first time came under critical scrutiny. We can conclude that Li Zhi did not go against tradition. Rather, he carried to the logical end its epistemological premises but had neither conceptual tools nor willingness to take a step beyond traditional thinking. He stopped at undermining it. But the question persisted and a century later Yan Yuan, philosopher of a quite different brand, still tried to solve it, this time by resorting to the traditional idea of continuity between the "small" and the "big" Ego-body. ⓯

Li Zhi's failure became the source of the ever aggravating feeling

---

⓮ I refer specifically to various versions of inscriptions to "Ten pictures on taming the bull" – the most authoritative description of the stages in Ch'an spiritual practice.

⓯ Cf: Wei-Ming Tu. Yan Yuan: From Inner Experience to Lived Concreteness. – In: The Unfolding of Neo-Confucianism, NY&L., 1975, p.518.

of insecurity among later Ming Confucianists. The most sophisticated response to it came from Liu Zungchou who rebelled against the tendency "to consider knowledge acquired through senses always right" and affirmed the primacy of the moral will in man. This will represents the absolute Good and the pure transcendence of spirit revolving in the symbolic depth of the heartful Mind. As for the external world, it can perceive only dead traces of this movement. ⑯ Liu Zungchou's suicide by starvation was in its own way, as in the case of Li Zhi, as much a triumph of moral will as a victory of material world. The turn of Chinese thought towards empirical experience became inevitable.

Conservative reactions notwithstanding, in the wake of Wang Yang-ming's philosophic turn the educated elite of Chinese society faced a new intellectual situation. Since the moral will could not be separated from emotion many scholars of that time came to admit that it is precisely strong feelings, for instance a mania for some object (*pi*) or a passionate love (*zhi qing*), that generates moral strength in man and eventually heightens the inner awareness to the point of achieving complete calmness and "supreme enlightenment". ⑰ Writings on courtly love, so fashionable at the time and basically in tune, let us note, with the Taoist tradition of "bedchamber art", stress the significance of erotic desire as a way to self-control. By the last decades of Ming rule this trend led some enthusiastic writers to accepting sexual desire

---

⑯ Mou Zungsan, Cong Lu Xiangshan to Liu Jishan (From Lu Hsiang-shan to Liu Chi-shan). Taipei, Hsuesheng shuju, 1979. P.479 ff.

⑰ For more details see: Wai-Yee Li, The Collector, the Connoisseur and Late-Ming Sensibility. – T"oung Pao, Vol. 84 , 1998; VV.Maliavin. Love unto Death. Passion and Reason in Late Ming China.. – Journal of Chinese Philosophy. Vo. #3. 1999.

(often affiliated with dreaming or ghostly state) as a gateway to salvation or even restoration of the Confucian order – a situation that amounted paradoxically to the tradition's self-affirmation through self-denial This sort of tradition's "deadlock" precluded the passage to modernity if we understand by this term the autonomy of the subjective Self and its spontaneous desires. ⑱ Rather, it directed the search for the authentic Self right down to the seeds of psychic life in the symbolic realm of chaotic fusion perceived as the virtual world of fantasies, dreaming, visions etc. Yet the very feeling of estrangement generated by such experiences strengthened the inner awareness of the "genuineness" of pre-Self's existence. Self-realization was achieved just by releasing oneself into the plenitude of the Void; freedom coincided here with chance granting one's life the significance of fate.

Such were the conditions for the appearance of that great novel "Journey to the West". The hero of the novel, Sun Wukung, who was born in the beginning of time and could acquire by will any appearance could have served a classical example of schizofrenia if he did not remind to Chinese readers a dragon – the embodiment of the creative transformations of being. Sun Wukung's fantastic adventures expose the essence of tradition with its ideal of "self-emptying" as a flight into the outside, into one's own double; by revealing the phantom-like nature of symbolic types they are undoing tradition. Yet after Zhuang-tzu's book the novel for the second time in Chinese history affirms a perfect narration, the power of fiction. Sun Wukung is constantly creating masks of himself but his life follows the symbolic vortex of reality mediating between the virtual preexistence and its actual correlates. More precisely,

---

⑱ Cf. R. Girard, *Deceit, Desire and Novel*. Baltimore: Johns Hopkins University Press, 1988.

his visible image of life is the spontaneous "fall" of symbolic wholeness into the world of external forms, i.e. the plane of continuing dispersion. (in Chinese this event was designated usually by the terms *yuan* – "issuing forth" or *pu* – "tracing the genealogy"). The novel's plot represents, as it were, a projection of the empty/full "one body" of Tao on various physical bodies, a projection quite illusory in its external appearance and yet absolutely real in its inner determination. Hence a mood of good humor that fills the story and make it appeal not to the reader's erudition but to his imagination. This observation also reminds us, that the novel has a hidden dimension – a movement of transcendence, a story of "bringing to submission the licentious Heart-Mind". This more traditional theme was explored in some Taoists sects.⓳

I have argued elsewhere that the greatest problem of Chinese cultural theory was the passage from the micro-perceptions of inner experience to the macro-images of cultural public space for these macro-images represent in fact only the *semblance* , approximations of micro-perceptions under the cover of recognizable figures conceived naturalistically. These images, therefore, have neither intrinsic reality nor real continuity; they are hyper-real. ⓴ No wonder, the narrative in many Chinese novels and especially in "Journey to the West" jumps from one episode to another; like a string of aphorisms, that became so popular a genre at that time. In a word, it is ruled by pause, a pathetic silence. The images of the novel are like spontaneous crystallizations of desire that occur in the border region "between presence and absence", in

---

⓳ *Xi you ji lungmen xinchuan.* (A transmission of Heart in the Lungmen school according to "Journey to the West"). Manuscript.

⓴ Cf. V. Maliavin. The East, the West and the Russian Idea. – Tamkang Journal of International Affairs. Vol.1, no.2., 1997.

the symbolic vortex of "inter-being-ness".

The historical outcome of the post-traditional situation in China achieved in later Ming times was bringing into public space of culture the awareness of the phantom-like nature of external images – a novelty that gave the artist unconditional freedom to create and popularize imaginary worlds, to test one's own identity by the powers of imagination. This bold step was not without its price for it gave rise to the feelings of anxiety and insecurity among the intellectual elite. It was not without its contradictions either: the eccentricity of experience has now become the measure of its normative value. The remarkable ambiguity of the Chinese notion of dreaming encompassing both sleep, daydreaming and insight indicates that the "world of dreaming" served as a paradigmatic space for mediation between virtual and actual dimensions of experience. At this point creative activity for the first time in Chinese history ran into the danger of losing its ties with the foundation of tradition – the steadfastness of moral will which through the process of self-differentiation moulds symbolic types and artistic taste. Under new circumstances it would be enough to accept these fantastic images as deliberately deformed copies or reflections of objective world to let the symbolism of tradition fall into oblivion.

This is precisely what happened in history. The "culture of fantasies" proved to be too fragile and sophisticated challenge to a harsh reality of public life. Despotic government could not tolerate the eccentric freedom of the artist even if this artist claimed, like all radical late Ming scholars did, that he embodies the whole tradition. In any case, to become socially acceptable the phantasm was to be downgraded to the status of "reality". In a short while naive realism superceded the former quest for inner truth, most of the novels of dreams were suppressed under the pretext of defending morality. The type of culture that emerged under

Ch'ing dynasty was characterized by the ever deepening gap between fantasy (reduced to demonic nightmare) and reality (downplayed to life's trivia). Yet this change produced almost no open protest. The main reason, I believe, was not political oppression. As a matter of fact, this turn marked the fulfillment of traditional thought's potential because creation itself was conceived in China in terms of the "fall" of holistic experience into its fragment or, in other words, of spirit's em-bodiment. However, this time it was a kind of "mis-fall" – falling into a mis-conceived reality.

Some instructive illustrations to the cultural changes described above are provided by the history of Chinese painting. The main trend of Ming pictorial art was determined by investigation, ever more vigorous and detailed, of the symbolic types whose unlimited variety stood out as the sign of the inner continuity of the enlightened spirit. This tendency culminated in the work of Tung Qich'ang (1555-1636) who deliberately composed his landscapes as monuments to the inner work of self-transcendence. Following the fashion of the day, Tung equated the essence of painting with the Ch'an ideal. In the mouth of the late Ming scholar it meant that creation was destined to clarify the very conditions for the emergence of symbolic types. At this point the Chinese literati's theory of painting reached its limit: the hypothetical convergence of virtual and actual sustained by the moral will was exposed to critical examination to such extent that it could no longer withstand the light of reason. Already the paintings of some contemporaries and disciples of Tung Qich'ang show the signs of the former ideal's disintegration. The best example are Wu Pin's grotesque landscapes that by their very eccentricity were supposed, like the fantasies of Sun Wukung's epic, to confirm and safeguard the inner truth of the Heart. It is remarkable that Wu Pin's contemporaries, according to his biographer, believed, even contrary to established opinion about the nature of artist's work, that Wu Pin painted *actual* landscapes. ㉑ Since Tung Qich'ang and Wu Pin the Chinese lovers of painting developed a taste for "dream landscapes" – a novelty that signaled radical interiorization and, in a sense, privatization of tradition's great style. By obscuring the public message of traditional symbolism the new fashion made even more inevitable relying on empirical experience as the criteria of reality. "Dream landscapes" were doomed to be perceived eventually as actual views.

By the early Ch'ing times an amazing variety of styles sprang forth, like fresh sprouts, from the half-decomposed stump of classical tradition. In spite of great differences between them, they had in common at least one important feature: a strong awareness of the gap between imaginary and real which could be bridged now only by persuasion, even mannerisms of the individual style whether it was ironic pseudo-archaism of Ch'en Hungshou, pure expressionism of Zhu Da, the contrast between formal composition and physical grandeur in the landscapes of Kung Hsien and Hungjen or the constant search for originality in the work of Shitao. Kung Hsian once remarked that he painted "fantastic world which, under close look, turns out to be real". Indeed, the paintings of the new generation exhibit an unprecedented unity of symbolic and descriptive elements of the picture. Painting became a self-sufficient image of the world *as it is represented* – a highly ambiguous situation which, as we know already, threatened to bring about the oblivion of tradition. The spread of the woodblock printing with its stereotyped images contributed to the loss of pictorial nuances – an indispensable witness to the effort of "self-emptying". The

㉑ J.Cahill, *The Compelling Image*. NY-Tokyo. 1985. P.115.

version of landscapes rationalized in printing could only be identified with their (supposed) natural prototypes.

To be sure, the new conception of painting that emerged by the middle of the XVIIth century did not deny the message of tradition. It rendered apparent the source of traditional symbolism while liberating artistic creation from the time-worn cliches of symbolist expression. Indeed, most of the early Ch'ing geniuses of painting became the founders of separate school of painting though this time based only on the continuity of a certain painting technique. These changes made possible for the Ch'ing court to confer on the scholars' painting the academic status, in other words – to appropriate the symbolism of tradition by changing it to the statement about the actual world. It was a complete reversal of classical painting's meaning: real as illusory became illusory as real. By lumping together incompatible aesthetic values the Ch'ing dynasty destroyed the integrity of artistic tradition and reduced painting to a level of sophisticated craft. Now the door was opened to the acceptance of the naturalistic – and essentially style-less – vision of the West.

The dramatic developments in the XVIIth century Chinese painting reveal with exceptional clarity the premises of traditional thinking and their logical consequences. In particular they throw light on a very delicate problem of the "oblivion of tradition". I can venture to suggest now that the demise of traditional symbolism was not the result of some external influence (a standard materialist explanation that hardly explains anything), nor could it be ascribed, as a romantic historian would argue, to a "weakening of people's spirit". What is symbolic can be reevaluated as natural through the mediating faculties of imagination that originally helps to recognize the symbolic reality under the cover of fantastic. For a while this "culture of fantasies" is sustained by the awareness of the distance between image and experience – awareness expressed in the figures of irony and humor. However, the integrity of this cultural mode demands ever more degree of freedom in imagination and ever stronger spiritual concentration. The growing tension between virtual and actual aspects of existence finally breaks their intimate connection. In place of former integrity there emerges two parallel worlds, equally actual: actual/natural and actual/spiritual. In cultural history, it seems, the famous saying of Holderlin should be read the other way round: where salvation is, there lies the danger…

There are good reasons to believe, that the cultural transformations described above are not limited to China but point to a certain universal pattern in human history. There are obvious analogies, for instance, between Chinese art and thought of the XVIIth century and the age of Baroque in Europe as well as the crisis of icon painting in the XVIIth century Russia. In all cases we are facing the transition from the traditional culture based on symbolist thinking to the modern age.

So under the Ch'ing traditional thinking in China was left behind and yet it was not overcome. In fact, Chinese civilization was opened only to the passive reception of Western modernity, to be precise – to the degree that the technological project of the West affirmed actuality. The very fusion of symbolic and natural aspects of existence that served as a starting point of China's purported "modernization" made impossible the quest for a more realistic representation of the world that was the guiding force in the shaping of modern art and science in Europe.

> We can safely assume by now that Modernity with its oppressively transcendentalist ideologies has proved to be a transitory stage on China's way beyond modern age and

contemporary China's "modern face" is really a mask of yet unrecognized "postmodern China". If Postmodernity means the "deconstruction" of the autonomous subject and his objective knowledge while attuning culture to the virtual/symbolic dimension of experience related to the notions of self-differentiating and absolute inside, then we must admit that the "Postmodern situation" helps to recover the life attitudes and values upheld in late medieval times by Chinese philosophers, novelists and garden makers. [22] This is not the idle wish for the kind of history outlined above, though bound to remain unwritten, is being written out by the lacunae in observable history. It is the virtual being infinite rich in variations anticipating and making possible all actual qualities. In this axis of the universal vortex we are able, in the words of J. Deleuze, "to constitute a continuum with fragments of different ages" [23] In the manner of Sun Wu-kung, we can actualize the "Great Body" (*da ti*) of Tao that gathers itself by making happen the infinite number of life-worlds. This abyss of human intimacy is due to be reopened in the global community.

Does not the real meaning of the "end of history" amount to recognizing the priority of ruptures in experience and discovering a new mode of (symbolic) temporality capable of accumulating the history through contingency of things ? Will this "return of the tradition" lead to the recovery of the inner fullness of existence that makes possible the

---

[22] The first scholar to note China's affinity with the Postmodern age was, to my knowledge, D.L.Hall. Cf: D.L.Hall. *Modern China and the Postmodern West*. – In: *Culture and Modernity*. Ed. by E.Deutsch. Honolulu, 1991.

[23] J.Deleuze, *L'image-temps*. Paris: Minuit, 1985. P. 161.

free interchange, as it was once suggested in China, between the consciousness (*xin*) and unconscious (*wu-xin*), knowledge (*zhi*) and no-knowledge (*wu-zhi*), fictitious and genuine, dream and awakening? Perhaps these questions do not call for answers. Rather, they are destined to safeguard the profound existential indeterminacy and, therefore, freedom of humankind.

中國資本論
——富有中國特色的新《資本論》

魏　萼*

摘　要

亞當·史密斯（1723～1790）的《國富論》和馬歇爾（1842～1924）的《經濟原則》兩書中，同時皆強調市場機制是解決人類經濟活動的重要課題，其中包括如何生產、生產什麼及爲何生產等議題。宏觀的經地理論，涵蓋了生產、消費、交換及分布等課題，1898 年英國經濟學家馬歇爾引用了「供需決定價格」之說，來研究人類的經濟行爲，因而開啓了Neo-Classicalism學派的形成。

經濟思想是以自由經濟爲主導，所以雖有與此思想對立的理論出現，如法國社會主義理論者聖賽門（1760～

*　淡江大學美國研究所專任教授兼所長

1825）、英國社會改革家羅伯·歐文（1771～1858）等人之學派，即便這些人很努力地朝著社會主義前進，但仍無法遏阻自由經濟思想的發展。在美國經濟學家亞瑟（1877～1959）出現之前，人們質疑市場機制能否解決一切的經濟問題，包括公用事務的缺乏、生意上的盈虧週期、貧富不均的問題等，是以亞瑟鼓吹福利經濟的概念。此概念綜合應用主義、馬歇爾的經濟原則以及政府的干預等經濟理論，用此一概念嚐試解決自由經濟所無法解決的經濟難題。

凱恩斯（1883～1946）將 1930 年的經濟大蕭條歸因於有效需求的匱乏，所以，市場機制如何調整皆可，但仍無法合理分配資源，使其達到完全就業的理想目標。然而，失業是一自然現象，故凱恩斯從經濟觀點來看，解決 1930 年經濟大蕭條的方法，最重要的是政府的因應對策，如羅斯福總統所提出一連串政府政策一般。像挪威等北歐國家，即是以凱恩斯之主張來推動國家福利政策。所以，政府要管制經濟發展到何種程度呢？是需要衡量現有之經濟狀況，以作爲因應方案之參考。

東方陰陽調和觀念與天人哲學，即已蘊含此一問題的答案了，在今日二十世紀資本主義衰退的時代，或許新的經濟模式與東方思想有著密切的關聯性存在。

The Chinese Principles of Economics: New "Principles of Economics" with ChineseCharacterization

Wei Wou

Abstract

Adam Smith (1723-1790), founding father of economics and classical economic theory, in *The Wealth of Nations* (1776), and Alfred Marshall (1842-1924), in *The Principles of Economics* (1898), emphasized the ability of the market function to solve the principal issues of human economic existence: how to produce, what to produce, and for whom to produce. Macroeconomics theory covers production, consumption, exchange, and distribution.

In 1898, British economist Marshall used "price is determined by demand and supply" to analyze human behavior. Thus began Neo-Classicalism. Economic thought was dominated by the free economy, and, although theories emerged in opposition to the spirit of the free economy, the efforts of the French socialist Saint Simon (1760-1825), English social reformer Robert Owen (1771-1858), French utopian socialist Charles Fourier (1772-1837), French anarchist Joseph Proudlon (1809-1865), and German Communist Karl Marx (1818-1883) could not change society's march toward a free economy.

Before the arrival of American economist Arthur C. Pigou (1877-1959), people doubted the market function could solve all economic problems. The "invisible hand " did not solve problems of externality, lack of public goods, business cycles, and unequal distribution of wealth. Pigou promoted the concept of welfare economics, a combination of Jeremy Bentham's (1748-1832) utilitarianism, Alfred Marshall's economic principles and government intervention, in an attempt to resolve economic difficulties the market function could not conquer.

John M. Keynes (1883-1946) attributed the Great Depression of the 1930s to insufficient effective demand. Adjustment of the market function could not make full use of the resources necessary to accomplish total employment. Unemployment was a natural phenomenon. Keynes thought the best economic solution for the Depression was government fiscal policies, President Franklin D. Roosevelt's New Deal for example. Scandinavian countries later used Keynesian concepts to implement their social welfare policies.

To what degree should the government control economic development? The answer is related to the current stage of economic development. The Oriental value of the Harmony between Yin-Yang and the philosophy of Heaven and Human nature can give the answer. This is the evidence of the collapsed of the Communism and the declined of the Capitalism in the 20th century. Perhaps, the third model economic development of the oriental value will be the main stream of the economic development in the 21 century.

中國資本論不是馬克思（Karl Marx, 1818-1883）的「資本論」。馬克思的《資本論》（Das Kapital,1867）❶確實是一部甚富學術性的著作。它的經濟思想是反西方主流思想的西方思想。馬克思的思想曾經在這個世界上怒潮澎湃了一個多世紀。既往矣！它的功過只有讓歷史學家去評斷。

中國資本論旨在把握中國經濟主流思想精髓，並且輔之以經濟「拿來論」的要義❷，來開創二十一世紀的中國經濟。

東方思想的哲學基礎是「天人合一」，這與西方思想「神人分離」的看法不同❸。東方經濟思想是重視市場經濟、政府經濟與文化經濟等「三隻手」的功能性❹。此外，倫理、民主和科學等「三元一體」的經濟發展模式也不是西方「二分法」辯邏輯的經濟分析所能解釋的❺。「易理經濟學」是重視經濟「文化調和」，以避免「文化衝突」所衍生的經濟「痛苦指標」。西方經濟思想獨領了世界兩百多年的風騷，這他們莫非要拜「基督新教」所創造的西方經

---

❶ 馬克思的《資本論》第一卷於一八六七年出版，第二卷於一八八五年出版，第三卷於一八九四年出版。其中第二卷、第三卷是馬克思去世之後，由恩格斯整理出版的。因此馬克思的「資本論」難免受恩格斯思想的影響。

❷ 魯迅，〈拿來主義〉《中華日報·動向》，一九三四年六月七日。該篇論文是以霍沖爲筆名發表的。文載於《魯迅選集》第四卷（北京：人民文學出版社，一九九五年）頁26～31。

❸ 西方思想也有「天人合一」的多神論者，但其並非其主流思想。此情況正好與東方思想相反。

❹ 魏萼〈經濟中國三隻手的思考〉，見「中國的崛起與世界的格局國際學術研討會」，北京大學國際關係學院主辦，一九九八年五月五日。

❺ 同前註。

濟文明所賜。然而戰後五十年來東方經濟發展表現傑出，已突顯了東方思想的價值所在。因此兼顧經濟發展與社會正義的東方價值觀已普遍引起世人的關注❻。可是二十一世紀末東亞金融危機也多少令人懷疑東方思想的永恆性❼。韓國的「外在型」文明衝突與印尼的「內在型」文明衝突等皆非東方價值觀的代表。❽面向二十一世紀的東方思想與世界經濟發展的相關性，甚值經濟學家們的思考。

一、前　言

中國現代化是要走自已的道路的。兩百多年來西方現代化的模式移轉型中國後，必然先產生「文明衝突」而後「文明調和」的「拿來」過程❾。換言之，西方的民主政治和市場經濟模式等均只能選擇性的「拿來」成爲中國現代化模式的一部份。否則將造成中國的傷害，特別是西方的政黨政治和公民投票等模式移植到中國後，將造成中國的大災難，萬萬不可行。西方自由市場經濟的資本主義模式亦與中國文化水土不合。一昧的崇洋媚外，將使中國陷入混亂和不安。這是西方野心家的期望，他們怕中國富強，以爲國中國富強

---

❻ 林蔭庭譯，Naisbitt,John原著，《亞洲大趨勢》（Megatrend Asia），（台北：天下文化出版社，一九九六年）頁30～50。

❼ 東方價值的現代化理論模式，在實踐上有偏差，因而產生了「文化衝突」。

❽ 印尼的「盤查西拉」（Pancasila）文化是爪哇本土文化與伊斯蘭教文化結合，在理論上是重視和協的，此乃印尼一九四六年蘇卡諾政權以後的立國精神。

❾ 魯迅，同註❷。

了後會威脅世界，所以他們在大戰略上不斷的要推銷西方那一套自由、民主、人權等觀念。我們要走出以中國特色的自由市場經濟，民主政治和社會制度。具體的說要以中國文化振興中華，以民主政治再造中國和以市場經濟重建大陸。具體的意義是要提握倫理、民主和科學等「三元一體」的中國現代化理論模式。這也與今日北京大學的校訓「愛國、進步、民主、科學」在某些意義上多少是相一致的。

中國文化、中國民族、中國宗教基本上是具有「容他性」的，這與西方希臘、羅馬以及希伯來宗教文化的「排他性」是不同的。中國在二十一世紀壯大過程中，中國文化、民族、宗教等將逐漸從「衝突」過程中趨於「調和」。此結果將是圓滿的，但過程中是陣痛的。尤其是中國基督教、中國天主教、中國伊斯蘭教等的發展至爲重要。而中國佛教、中國道教將參與中國「文藝復興」的盛事。這個新文化、新啓蒙將與未來中國的興衰息息相關。富有中國特色的「政教合一」與西方歷史上的「政教合一」，在意義上則完全不同，此有助於中國的富強與國家的現代化。

中國歷史上的黃河、長江等不知有多少水患，但正常的黃河、長江等是東流黃海、東海。有如這個古老的中國曾歷經苦難，尤其是執政方向偏離中國文化的航道時，其必然帶來了中國的災害，此與洪水氾濫一樣均非常態。中國仍然是中國、中國永遠是中國、中國終將回歸中國文化的中國。所以一九七八年以後的中國現代化道路走對了，中國自然趨於富強。不止中國，蘇聯及東歐等國家亦復如此，他們也逐漸恢復古老俄羅斯、歐洲應走的道路與方向。在亞洲的蒙古、北朝鮮、柬甫寨、越南等等地區的發展亦不會離開此一軌跡，因爲這是一個規律。這也將就是二十一世紀世界新經濟秩序的重建❿。

「馬列中國化」的道路是一九七八年以後鄧小平功在中國的作爲。這與從前的「中國馬列化」思維方式完全不同。「馬列中國化」是中國共產黨回歸中國文化的正確作法，它儘力擺脫任何意識形態的拘絆，重視實事求是的政策方針；其邁向理性，重視知識的國家發展方向已使中國奠定二十一世紀國家富強、民生樂利的基礎。其逐漸重視「知識就是權力」而非「權力就是知識」的現代化觀念將可媲美「漢唐盛世」重視中國文化與儒學的楷模。

二、「馬列中國化」的經驗

由此可見郭沫若（1892～1978）的「馬克思進文廟」，此見解至爲深遠⓫。而富有中國特色社會主義中「社會主義初級階段論」，是要把康有爲「大同書」的內涵推向儒學「禮運大同篇」的境界⓬。此亦可把馬克思的眞義與中國儒家文化貫串起來。清末康有爲「大同書」所談論的據亂世、升平世、太平世等的「三世論」或許與春秋公羊的「三世說」的內涵不甚一致，但其面對現實的看法與作法，

---

❿ 東方價值的一體多元化模式，當中各國均有其特色，但其所標示的文化價值座標大致相同。

⓫ 郭沫若〈馬克思進文廟〉，見《現代中國文學：小說》。該篇作品於一九二五年十一月十七日初次發表。

⓬ 中國特色社會主義實施的步驟。此亦可喻爲社會主義初級階級到社會主義成熟階級。孫中山先生也曾說民生主義就是共產主義。

甚值欽佩⓭。康有爲的「三世論」是依據中國現實環境循序漸進的進化觀念，即文明未開、漸入文明、大同世界等「三世論」作爲政治變革理論階段，甚爲務實可行⓮。中國國家建設的長遠目標應是理想的社會主義，亦即西漢戴慎禮記的儒家「禮運大同篇」的理想⓯。換言之，也可以看到馬克思文化到中國後從與中國「文明衝突」到「文明調和」的過程，而馬克思文化終將成爲中國文化的一個元素。「大同書」也是富有中國特色社會主義初級階段的具體意義⓰。此乃面對現實擺脫西方資本主義和社會主義紛爭而有利於中國邁向小康、富裕之道路。

二十一世紀的中國，中國人溫飽問題基本上可以解決，但其所面對的是精神面的「新扶貧」工作。這是另一階段的攻堅工程。中國國民道德的重建至爲重要。中國人的民族劣根性正是腐朽儒學的表徵，其又臭又硬。國家富裕了，國人不懂得生活的意義與人生的價值，這是另一類的貧窮。這正是「新扶貧」工作的重點，極爲艱鉅。

「路見不平就怒吼，該出手就出手」，這兩句話說得好.這代表對正義、眞理與公平的呼喚⓱。曾被宮刑的西漢大儒，太史公司馬

⓭ 康有爲《戊戌奏稿》，卷七，第一頁，卷二十一，第二頁。或參閱汪榮祖〈晚清變法思考析論〉，《後現代中國思想人物論晚清思想》（張灝等著）（台北：時報出版公司，一九八八年）頁99～102。

⓮ 同前註，第100頁。

⓯ 同前註。

⓰ 中國文化的特色是具有其包容性的。外來文化終將被中國文化所吸收，然後變成中國文化的一部份。

⓱ 一九九七年臺灣與大陸均甚受歡迎的電視連續劇《水滸傳》的片頭語，這兩句話也是當時儒家思想的一個表徵。

遷（西元前一四五年～西元前九〇年），爲了申張正義，眞理與公平替武帝大將軍出擊匈奴，兵敗被俘的李陵講了話，但他被漢武帝認爲是司馬遷針對著其愛將李廣而言，被認爲此乃不但藐視皇上的尊嚴，並且也被認爲最反對朝廷的行爲⓲。司馬遷被宮刑後保全了生命完成了其春秋之筆照耀千秋的偉大著作：史記⓳。「史記」誠如司馬遷之心願，是「通古今之變，究天人之際，成一家之言」的史學巨著。史記凡五十二萬六千言。人生自古誰無死，死有重於泰山，或有輕於鴻毛。司馬遷完成「史記」後，自稱人生無憾，於是投河自盡了。司馬遷的儒生風範，有儒氣、有骨氣、有才氣、有俠氣、有義氣，還有幾份讀書人的傲氣與狂氣，正是中國知識份子的典範。

二十一世紀的中國一定會富強，中國人當可揚眉吐氣頂天立地有尊嚴的站起來。當前中國現代化過程其方向雖然正確但問題千瘡百孔、滿目瘡痍，何況中國天災人禍勢將頻仍，此有待有良知的知識份子在「邦有道則仕」的原則下爲國家有所獻替，不論在朝或在野，知識份子及學術智庫應發揮「國家之干城」和「學術之重鎮」的功能。

中國人醜陋嗎？評論家柏揚的觀點多少是正確的⓴。中國人的醜陋源自中國人的貧窮、無知和世俗儒家的猖獗。國人富裕之後是否能變成爲「驕傲的中國人」呢？有待觀察。嚴復所說中國人的問

⓲ 〈史記的故事〉，見《中國文史名著故事精粹》（台北；添翼文化出版社，一九九四年）頁468～472。

⓳ 同前註。頁2～5。

⓴ 柏楊《醜陋的中國人》（台北：林白出版社有限公司，一九八五年）頁24～28。

題在於貧、愚、弱、貪等問題。㉑柏楊也說中國人的髒、亂、吵、窩裡鬧等等㉒。中國是文明的禮義之邦，但國人所表現的行爲卻有相當落差，有人形容國人在行爲表現上是蠻愚之人，深值警醒㉓。百年來中國人的崇洋媚外，不守信用、不守秩序、不重衛生、陽奉陰違、鄉愿投機等均非常態。所以在社會上經常有所謂劣幣驅逐良幣的現象㉔；好人不見得可以出頭，這莫非是肉腐而後蛆生的必然現象。因此某些經常高喊誠信、無愧、無憾的善良人士，卻經常是各行各業失敗者。這或許魯迅小說集「吶喊」中最優秀作品「阿Q正傳」（於一九二一年十二月撰）講得對。日本統治臺灣的第四任總督兒玉源太郎當時總督府民政長官後滕新平（一八九六年二月就任）曾說在臺灣的中國臺灣人，其民族性是畏威而不懷德，因而採取軟硬兼施的懷柔政策等，均值國人警惕。中國要富強，中國人要頂天立地的站起來，還要切實面對醜陋中國人的某些民族劣根性，以迎接二十一世紀。

所謂亞洲的價值觀，其實乃是東方的價值觀，具體的說就是儒家思想的價值觀。此價值觀的代表國家是東北亞的日本與東南亞的星加坡，而中國是東方思想泉源國家，何以不能做爲代表呢？因爲中國仍然貧窮㉕。我們還要學學日本。二十一世紀我們擔心中日難

㉑ 吳相湘〈孫逸仙近代思想與鄭觀應、容閎、嚴復之比較〉，「紀念孫中山先生誕辰130週年學術討論會」，廣東省中山市，一九九六年八月。

㉒ 柏楊，同註⑳。

㉓ 同註㉑。

㉔ Weber Max,The Religion of China:Confucianism and Taoism ,New York：Free Press,1951。

㉕ 直至西元二〇〇〇年，中國仍是開發中國家，其年平均國民總生產仍排行在全世界第一百名以外，何況還有「中國威脅論」的西方疑慮。

免還會發生嚴重的摩擦。爲了亞太的和平、安定與繁榮。「師日長智以制日」可能是未來階段性的一個方向，因爲它比「師夷長技以制夷」的看法實際㉖。

費正清等人所謂的中國通，其實他們不懂中國。西方的許多所謂權威中國問題專家經常誤解了中國㉗。例如著名的韋伯（Max Weber）教授也誤解了中國文化與宗教，他把世俗腐朽的「病儒」視爲「眞儒」㉘；哈佛大學費正清（John Fairbank）教授亦復如，他以爲儒家文化的僵硬性，其與封建思想、權威主義相結合，這是錯誤的認知。因此其所分析的「東方專制論」和中國問題當然是不正確的，這也是杭廷頓（Samuel H.Huntington）教授「文明衝突論」的由來。㉙二十一世紀的中國知識份子另一重要工作要使西方人士眞正認識眞正的中國，並且尊重中國文化的價值。

三、尋找亞洲的價值

幾百多年來，西方經濟學人才輩出，但觀念分歧，其中有重農主義、重商主義、古典學派、新古典學派、歷史學派、洛桑學派、

㉖ Weber Max,The Protestant Ethics and the Spirit of Capitalism, New York, Free Press,1958。

㉗ 狄百瑞 （William T.de Bary）〈中國知識份子的角色與地位〉，見《中國歷史轉型時期的知識份子》（余英時等著）（台北：聯經出版社，一九九二年）頁2～23。

㉘ 同註㉖。

㉙ Huntington Samuel P，The Clash of Civilization and the Remaking of the World Order,Simon and Schuster, N.Y. 1996,PP.20-30。

斯德哥爾摩學派、凱恩斯學派、制度學派、劍橋學派、芝加哥學派等等經濟思想。史密斯（Adam Smith）、李嘉圖（David Ricardo）、馬爾薩斯（Thomas Malthus）、瓦拉斯（Lawrence Walras）、彌爾（James Mill）、馬歇爾（Alfred Marshall）、熊彼得（Joseph Shumpter）、凱恩斯（John Keynes）、韓森（Alvin Hansen）、韋伯（Max Weber）、馬克思（Karl Marx）、羅賓遜（John Robinson）、席克斯（John R.Hicks）、薩慕爾遜（Paul E.Samuelson）、費里德曼（Milton Friedman）等大學者層出不窮㉚。他們的學術思想獨領風騷二百多年影響世人至為深遠。

中國歷史三千多年來的道家、儒家、法家、墨家、兵家、釋家等經濟思想相當豐富亟需作一個整理的工作。禹貢、管仲、范蠡、孔丘、孟軻、墨翟、荀況、李悝、商鞅、韓非子、白圭、司馬遷、桑弘羊、耿壽昌、王莽、王符、楊炎、王安石、丘濬、徐光啓、王夫之、魏源、孫中山、鄧小平等經濟思想皆有其代表性。如何凝聚中西經濟文化的菁華以尋找到世界性的共同價值。這莫非人類之福。

若欲研究馬克思必需認識馬克思（Karl Marx 1818-1883）的原意。過去所謂的傳統共產主義一再曲解馬克思的基本思想。其已禍害了世界㉛。因為馬克思是人道主義者才會撰寫「資本論」等等偉大的著作。馬克思「資本論」等雖是所謂的科學社會主義，其仍屬

㉚ 陳榮貴譯，日本近代經濟學研究會編，《世界十五大經濟學》（台北；志文出版社，一九八五年）頁1～14。

㉛ 馬克思的思想不但被曲解，也被政客所誤用。最典型的模式是史達林時代（一九二八～一九五三）共產主義經濟發展的策略。

反西歐古典學派經濟主流思想的一個環結。其與東方的哲學思維方式也是裁然不同的[32]。

「資本論」旨在描述資本的生產、流通、總運動、總形態等過程，其重點是剩餘價值的生產、流通、實現，分配以及其所採取的各種具體形式的過程。[33]「資本論」是以西方唯物論和辯證法爲中心的思維方式爲出發點，其指責資本家的剝削和社會的非正義。馬克思「資本論」共有三卷，其實應有四卷，分別於一八六七年、一八八五年、一八九四年、一九〇五～一九一〇年出版。其中第一卷由他自己出版，第二卷、第三卷是恩格斯根據馬克思的手稿整理出版；第四卷則由孝茨基（M.Kautsky）整理而以「剩餘價值學說史」爲中心分成三冊出版。馬克思的著作甚爲豐富[34]。譬如說政治經濟學批判大綱（一八四四年）、神聖家族（一八四五年）、關於費爾巴哈的提綱（一八四五年）、德意志意義形態（一八四六年）、哲學的貧困（一八四七年）、共產黨宣言（一八四八年，恩格斯合撰）、關於自由貿易的演說（一八四六年）、雇用勞動與資本（一八四九年）、政治經濟學批判（一八五九年）、哥達綱領批判（一八七五年）、反杜林論（一八七八年）等等重要著作均有代表性[35]。中國資本論的撰寫是站在東方思想的哲學思維方式，而且是以東方的主流經濟思想爲出發點。

---

[32] 這也可以從蘇聯解體以後俄羅斯以及東歐等國家一昧否定史達林共產主義模式的作法看出。中國自從一九七八年以後的政策方向則另有特色。

[33] 蕭灼基主編，《哲學社會科學名人名著辭典》（張家口：河北人民出版社，一九八七年）頁30～35。

[34] 同前註，頁31。

[35] 同前註，頁5～30。

中國資本論也是基於社會正義及人道、人性、人本主義等的立場；以互助合作取代階級鬥爭，以仁受取代仇恨，促成資本家與勞動者的合作、政府與人民的合作，並且主張以「藏富於民、民富國強」的中國傳統經濟思想等爲主軸。馬克思的「資本論」缺乏通俗性因而被許多政客們所誤解，甚也被政客們所蹂躪。中國資本論正是要補此一缺失，它不僅希望使中國富強，也希望對東方價值觀有所貢獻。因爲中國資本論竭力要促使中國資本財和技術之增加，以提高勞動生產力和產品的附加價值。這是經濟發展的具體表徵。然而藏富於民、均富思想是中國濟思想中的社會主義與西方馬克斯「資本論」撰寫期間資本家剝削勞動者時的理論完全不同㊱。

中國資本論是有關二十一世紀中國經濟的著作。中國要富強一定要走中國人應走的道路，西方的「國富論」、「資本論」或「一般理論」等鉅著，僅足可選擇性「拿來」做爲經濟政策工具，但其絕非不易的萬靈丹。其實二百多年西方重農主義、重商主義、古典學派、新古典派、新經濟學等經濟思想在先秦諸子的經濟思想中均可尋找得到，就以西漢司馬遷的史記中「貨殖列傳」爲例，它的市場經濟與生產、消費經濟，就有其代表性㊲。司馬遷的經濟思想似有史密斯「國富論」與凱恩斯「一般理論」的精神。但這些中國文化寶藏本是救人類、貢獻世界的經典之作，但卻鮮爲人知，實在太可惜了。二十一世紀富強的中國，另一個歷史性的使命是研究與發展中國傳統經濟思想，並給予新的生命力和時代任務。

㊱ 孫中山先生的經濟思想即是中國文化的產物。

㊲ 韋葦《司馬遷經濟思想研究》（西安：陝西人民教育出版社，一九九五年，頁310～320。

四、大陸不改革，中國沒希望—兩岸不交流，臺灣沒出路

中國資本論希望能有三卷，這是第一卷。其他的二卷，也希望能夠完成㊳。中國資本論的撰寫旨在為臺灣找出路，為大陸找發展，為中國找希望、為中國人找前途，為華人找福祉，和為亞洲找價值。這部著作是要站在中國的立場說話。希望中國人能眞正頂天立地而且有尊嚴的站起來。因此認為「一體多元化」的歷史中，目前的臺灣與大陸關係而言，我們認為「若兩岸不交流，臺灣沒有出路」，「若大陸不改革，中國沒有前途」。還有只有強大而富裕的中國，那裡會有分裂的臺灣呢？換言之，中國不強大，臺灣必分離呢？中國資本論旨在使臺灣、大陸與港澳兩岸三地在經濟上、政治上、社會上、文化上的發展趨同㊴。

若欲使中國富強，魯迅（1881-1936）的「拿來主義」最令人玩味。魯迅強調「拿來主義」不是「送來主義」㊵。面向二十一世紀的中國，閉關自守是不可能的，而外來的文化、思想、經濟、政治、科技等等在所難免，而且亦有需要。這些「舶來品」要我們主動的

㊳ 這是一個嘗試，仍需大大的修正與充實。

㊴ 一九八〇年代初擔任德國總理的施密特先生於一九九八年十一月訪問臺灣，並於十一月一日在台北圓山飯店以「德國領導人物之任務與展望」為題發表演講。另有關施密特談話，請參閱《海峽評論（96）》，（台北，一九九八年十二月號）頁16。

㊵ 魯迅，同❷。

而且理性的去取、去拿，而不是外國人蓄意送來的[41]。過去英國人送來鴉片，法國人送來香水，日本人送玻璃絲襪、美國人送來好萊塢電影片等均不是我們所需要的，更不是我們的自願的。這些都是外國人侵略我們用強迫，用騙術送來中國的。這些「送來主義」的具體例子，我們要設防[42]。面向二十一世紀的中國，西方人士大量推銷他們的自由、民主、人權等到中國，這都得檢視其是否合於我們的國情。若他們蓄意「送來」取代了我們主動「拿來」，則會引起國家的混亂與不安。這種水土不合的現象或許是西方人士居以其自身利益而有所作爲的，這姑且不論。我們最擔心的是來自他們是別有用心的「陰謀論」，那就更危險了。「拿來主義」是我們居以中國自身發展的需要，有選擇的吸收外來的東西，這包括「硬體」的科技與經濟，也包括「軟體」的政治與文化。「送來主義」是指中了西方國家的毒計，或因崇洋媚外的情勢下，使中國不得不接受西方人士任意送來的擺佈[43]。「送來主義」不是我們意願的，此必有害中國的發展，我們必需審慎注意。

魯迅的「拿來主義」論，甚爲傳神，這已表達了中國確實面對西方應有的看法。中國是閉關自守，這包括一九七八年以前中國的「閉門主義」在內。甚至於經常有所謂發揚國威的「送去主義」一說。根據魯迅的敘述，中國人爲了「發揚國威」而將國寶不斷往國外展示，這好象是尼采（F. Nietzsche, 1844-1900）自詡爲太陽，不斷往外發光、發熱，只是「發電」式的給予而不是「充電」式的吸

---

[41] 同前註，頁28。

[42] 同前註，頁29。

[43] 同前註，頁30。

收㊹。魯迅說得好，尼采後來發瘋了。他比喻中國不是太陽，然而尼采更不是太陽，雖然他曾是「唯意志論」和「超人」哲學的鼓吹者㊺。中國不但要門戶開放，並且要發揚並推動「黃色文明」與「藍色文明」的結合，使之成爲中國現代化的動力。

從「拿來主義」的意義來看，西方經濟思想應只能做爲中國經濟思想的注解而已，而不能喧賓奪主將西方的經濟思想成爲中國經濟二十一世紀的主文化。僅管中西經濟思想的基本哲學有許多相關性。易學思想中「陰陽論變」的內涵就是將中西經濟思想中找到調和之處。

易學是中國文化之源，也是中國文化中道家、儒家、法家、兵家、墨家等學術思想相貫通。甚至於與東方文化代表性之一外來的釋（佛）家學術思想相通。若能將易學的生命力與現實環境，特別是國家現代化的觀念想結合，則更有意義。西漢對周易經傳的重新解釋，給予周易新的生命力和現代化的使命。此代代薪火相傳的學術生命力。可是仍然有所謂占卜、摸骨易理之周易熱。此爲人卜卦、相命等經常產生歪風，並且爲不法之人找利謀取錢財之機會。所以中華易學史上也有所謂反愚蠢和迷信之論戰。易學以儒、釋、道三位一體爲中心的學術思想，它是中國傳統文化的精隨所在，也是中華民族的精神靈魂。它可以在政治學、經濟學、社會學甚至於在國際關係方面的應用，當然也不離開做人做事，人事管理、企業管理、公司理財等等範圍的用。易經所謂天地人的理性三結合意義和奧妙

㊹ 同前註。尼采是德國哲學家，「唯意志論」和「超人」哲學的鼓吹者。

㊺ 同前註，頁31。

就在其中。其在修身、齊家、治國、平天下的道理可以將自然科學與人文哲學相結合。若能體會到易理的精髓所在則能通曉人情與世故。因此也有智慧（方向）而且足以掌握世事的哲學（道路）和科學（車馬）意義；這是一個大的戰略。易學的研究在中國歷朝歷代均有其特殊的時代需要而有所發展的規律，可是唯心、唯物相調和是中國文化的基本精神永恆不變。總之，易學的研究早已離「易圖說」停留於考證的思維方式階段，而傾向於多采多資豐富的現代文明建設新方向。而以實驗與檢驗的過程中，尋求在「拿來主義」的眞理與價值。

五、結論：西方資本主義的沒落

歷史學家湯恩比（Aronald Toynbee 1889-1975）曾說，十七世紀至十九世紀是歐洲科技文明統治世界的時代，二十世紀以後是非歐洲將依靠自己的文明來抵抗歐洲文化的時代㊻。西方文明是以個人爲中心，而以人類欲望爲出發點的西方價值將帶來世界生態環境失衡，這相對的顯示東方價值觀的世界意義。東方宗教文化中的佛教和道教文化以及儒家文化都不是立於個人的自私基礎之上，而重視人本思想的教化、站在高高的角度上重視社會整體利益的調和。這與源自希臘羅文化的笛卡爾式(Rene Descartes，1596-1650)的思維

㊻ Toynbee,Aronald,Civilization on Trail,（Collected essays），Oxford University, Press,1948，P.85。亦請參見梅原猛〈以稻作文明拯救地球〉，見《中日東方思想研討會論文集》（上海：三聯書店，一九九七年）頁1～16。

方式不同㊼。雖然西方也有思想家崇尚東方思想的價值觀，有如史瓦慈（B. Schwartz），他研究中國思想家嚴復的思維方式而且贊同嚴復思維中集體意識的價值觀，這個看法與德國哲學家康德（Immanuel Kant 1724-1804）重視道德情操以制衡只追求欲望爲理性的哲學，本質上的看法是相同的，但他們並非西方主流思想㊽。日本明治維新理財專家澀澤榮一所撰述的「論語與算盤」正是東方思想的代表著作之一，因爲它是經濟和道德的結合。日本在十七世紀江戶幕府將儒教爲國教，而當時日本的儒教是以王陽明的理學爲主。日本明治維新後，雖然儒教不再爲國教，雖然重視西方的思想與文化，但王陽明儒學仍被朝野人士所尊重。特別是忠孝、仁愛、勤儉、信義等倫理道德被視爲維繫民間社會秩序的主要力量。日本明治維新以後重視對外文化經濟科技的交流，這也是日本造經濟創造奇蹟的原因之一㊾。中國歷史上的漢朝與唐朝的富強與對外文化經濟文流也有相關的。漢朝的陸上絲綢之路，唐朝的海上絲綢之路等皆是具體的例子。鴉片戰爭以後又是另一階段的中西交流；過去一百五十多年的對外開放經驗過程是難苦的，其先經過中西文明的衝突，然而逐漸步東西文明的調和。若從長遠看，中西文化經濟「拿來」之後必然帶來中國富強，再造「中華盛世」於世界。

㊼ 魏萼、謝幼田《中國經濟文化史論》（台北：五南出版社，一九九六年）頁28～30。另同註㉝，頁181～182。

㊽ Schwartz,Benjamin,In Search of Wealth and Power：Yan Fu and the West,Harvard University Press,Cambridge Massachusetts,1964,PP20-25。另同註㉝，頁190。

㊾ 同註㊻。

從中國歷史觀察，任何一個朝代或政權若違背中國文化的政治軌跡，該朝代或政權必然不會持久。相反的，「大漢天威」或「大唐天威」不但其回歸了中國文化的歷史傳承，同時也階段性融合了各種民族文化而孕育出一個中國文化的新生命力。這就是消化外來文化，深化中國文化的意義㊿。這充實顯示太史公司馬遷所言通古今之變，究天人之際而且能成一家之言的具體意義。

鴉片戰後，中國文化面臨史所未有的西方文化大衝突。這個「文明衝擊」的過程是嚴峻的。中國必然淪入苦難，中國人難逃陷入悲慘。洋務運動、自強運動、新政、戊戌維新變法、辛亥革命、「五四」新文化運動、軍閥割據、國共合作、抗日戰爭、內戰、國民黨的敗退、共產黨的執政、臺灣經濟發展的奇蹟、中國大陸的改革與開放、台海兩岸的交流互動與文化趨同。這個從「文化衝突」發展到「文化調和」的過程中，東西文化撞擊後所產生的火花，帶來了中國經濟的敗壞：生產凋敝、失業嚴重、通貨膨脹、貧富懸殊等等，使民不聊生，這個代價是相當高的。此際，中國政治與社會不安自不言而喻。

> 中國經濟發展的路向是什麼？魯迅所說的「拿來主義」或許是解決這個問題的答案。中國要尋找「富強」之道要吸收西方現代化國家的經驗。然而西方經濟思想發展過程中亞當·史密斯的「國富論」、卡爾·馬克斯的「資本論」、約翰·凱恩斯的「一般理論」等改變世界經濟的偉大著作均有其時

㊿ 牟宗三〈中國文化中義理開創的十大爭辯〉，台北《中國時報》第八版，一九八七年五月十五日。

代背景的。在西方每當經濟環境時過境遷後，新的經濟環境終需新的經濟思想來配合。何況在中國呢，本著作乃是一個大膽的嘗試。五十年來，中國大陸因爲政治、經濟、社會等主客觀環境的變化，中國大陸經濟發展模式已從「以俄爲師」演變到「以俄爲鑑」；對於馬克思「資本論」的偏好程度也已從一九七八年以前的「資本論」第一卷（階級關係爲主要）到一九七八年以後的「資本論」第二卷（生產關係爲主要），而一九九二年以後則必然又轉移到「資本論」的第三卷（市場關係爲主要）[51]。馬克思「資本論」因被曲解雖已禍害了世界，已如前述，但其階段性的學術價值仍將永垂不朽。然而超越此一階段，二十一世紀的中國經濟發展模式，應該是邁向一個富有中國特色的新「資本論」[52]。

---

[51] 中共黨校也有同樣的看法。請參閱台北《聯合報》第十三版，一九九八年十一月二十三日。

[52] 中共黨總書記江澤民先生於一九九七年九月十二日在中央第十五次全國代表大會上主要講話，甚有時代性。一八九八年有康有爲、梁啓超的戊戌變法，而一九九八年中國大陸上的一些變革如村民自治、法制改革、輿論開放等有人譽之爲「戊寅變法」。稍前也有所謂朱鎔基灑淚爲商鞅的美譽、佳談。

1839 年到 1895 年間的日本、鴉片戰爭與不平等條約

柯塞北*

摘　要

1841～1842 年的第一次鴉片戰爭是中國近代歷史的一個轉折點。在任何一個關於中國歷史的著作，鴉片戰爭的地位是無可爭辯，標誌著近代中國歷史的開始。但是，如果進一步研究中國十九世紀歷史，就會發現對當時的統治階層和很多知識界來說，鴉片戰爭不一定有什麼重大意義。大於鴉片戰爭的邊疆戰爭是屢次發生的，而清政府十九世紀四十年代所簽約的「不平等條約」並不是沒有前例的。其實，清政府與現在位於烏茲別克斯坦的一個汗國在一八三〇年代已經簽了兩個條約，其內容與南京條約和虎門條約很相似。對通商口岸制度和不平等條約的全國性興

*　日本金澤大學東洋系研究生

論和反抗，到十九世紀末才出現。

鑒於上述情況，有意思的是，日本一直密切注視中國大陸的趨勢。鴉片戰爭的爆發，不僅使日本幕府對鎖國政策進行調整，也引起了日本知識界的注意。因此，美國東印度艦隊司令培理一八五三年到江戶灣要求幕府放棄鎖國政策，日本人已有心理準備。幕府於一八五八年被迫簽約的「日美友好通商條約」激起了日本武士階層的極大憤怒，引起了倒府運動。一八六八年奪權的明治政府將條約改正列入政治議程的首位，使它與日本現代化互相配合。

本文探討中國和日本對鴉片戰爭和不平等條約的不同反應，進行初步分析。

關鍵詞　中日關係　鴉片戰爭　不平等條約　中國近代史　日本近代史

The Japanese, the Opium Wars and the Unequal Treaties 1839-95

Pär Cassel

Introduction

The First Anglo-Chinese War of 1839-42 or the "Opium War," as it is commonly known, remains one of the defining events in modern Chinese history. The Opium War has a given place as a *the* turning point in any standard work on Chinese history and in Mainland Chinese historiography, the war invariably marks the beginning of modern Chinese history (*jindaishi*). However, a closer study of the period around the Opium War shows that the war was not regarded as a historical watershed by most contemporary Chinese and that a systematic anti-imperialist and nationalist response to the legacy of the Opium War did not emerge until the late 19th century. Given the tardiness of the Chinese "response to the West" it is very interesting to note that the Opium War and subsequent events on the Asian mainland were closely watched by the Japanese and the development in China had many direct and indirect consequences on the development of Japanese nationalism. In this paper I will try to explore what kind of impact the Opium War had on Japanese politics and intellectual trends in the middle of the 19th century onwards and I will make some general comparisons to the same period in Chinese history.

The Chinese and the Opium War

For an observer at the end of the 20th century, it is obvious that the Opium War is a significant turning point in modern Chinese history. It is, if you will, one of the most important events in China's entire recorded history. For the next hundred years, China would gradually loose control over its sovereignty through a series of humiliating military defeats and resulting treaties, a process which culminated when China was plunged into a war against Japan in the end of the 1930s. The beginning of the colonial era also opened China to the challenges of modernisation, exposing China to an unprecedented influx of new ideas, institutions and innovations, ultimately threatening many of the fundamental institutions that had supported Chinese society through the millennia. But sometimes the significance of the Opium War is overstated or simplified to the effect that we tend to ignore the importance of Sino-Foreign relations prior to the war.

Although the activities of foreigners in China were rigorously regulated and most of the maritime trade was limited to the southern port of Canton, the Qing court and the Chinese political elite were by no means ignorant of the West or the progress that was taking place in European science and industry. On the contrary, from the middle of the 17th century the Manchus increasingly drew on Jesuit expertise in order to correct deficiencies in the Chinese lunar calendar and to cast cannons, for instance. Jesuit translations of Western scientific literature was to remain a major source for knowledge about the West and many of the scientific terms that were coined by Matteo Ricci and his successors are still in use in both Chinese and Sino-Japanese.❶

The Jesuits also provided the Manchus with diplomatic know-how in their first dealings with the Russians. Even after the Yongzheng Emperor banned the Christian mission in 1723, he and his successors continued to consult the foreign experts. It has sometimes been suggested that the failure of the Macartney mission to secure diplomatic relations with the Celestial Empire in 1793 was as much due to the fact that Macartney represented a protestant nation, as the supposed claims of world political primacy on the part of the Qing emperor.❷Indeed, the Great Qing Empire had already made important concessions to Russia in the treaties of Nerchinsk (1689) and Kiakhta (1727), effectively agreeing to diplomatic equality with Russia.

Neither were the "unequal treaties" that the Qing court concluded with Britain and the other Great Powers something unprecedented in Chinese history or something that the European imperialists had simply forced on China unilaterally. Quite on the contrary, most of the concessions that were granted to the Great Powers in the 1840s were based on concessions already made to the Uzbek Khan of Kokand between 1831 and 1835. One of the most important elements of the

---

❶ Cf. Federico Masini, "The Formation of Modern Chinese Lexicon and its Evolution towards a National Language: The Period from 1840 to 1898," *Journal of Chinese Linguistics 6* (Berkeley 1993), pp. 57ff.

❷ See for instance Tom Bartlett's contribution to H-ASIA on July 27, 1999. Cf. http://www.h-net.msu.edu/~asia as of August 30, 1999.

unequal treaties, the principle of exterritoriality, was a time-honoured tradition among Muslim traders and from the Chinese point of view, the extension of this privilege to Western traders did in no way compromise the sovereignty of the Qing Empire.❸

For Chinese living in the middle of the 19th century the war against the Taiping Heavenly Kingdom in the 1850s and 60s, which would devastate the Empire and claim millions of casualties, was surely a much more significant political event than the "pacification of English rebels" on China's southern maritime frontier. It is true that the defeat in the Opium War would prompt a number of astute intellectuals such as Lin Zexu (1785-1850), Wei Yuan (1794-1857) and Xu Jiyu (1795-1873) to explore the sources of Western strength. But the outcome of the war did in no way shake the confidence of the regime and the literati in the superiority of Chinese culture. Too strong an interest in things Western could often become a liability in this political environment. For instance, Xu Jiyu's deep involvement with Western studies and frequent contacts with Westerners would eventually lead to the ousting from his position as governor of Fujian province.❹Only the Arrow War 1856-60, or the "Second Opium War" as it is also known, and the subsequent occupation of Peking by British and the French forces in 1860 would bring about a serious attempt to learn from the West. In 1861, a foreign office called *Zongli Yamen* was established by the Qing government and the following year *Tongwenguan* was launched, a school devoted to the study of Western languages.

From the point of view of the Manchus and the Chinese political

---

❸ Cf. Denis Twitchett & John K. Fairbank (ed.), *The Cambridge History of China*, vol.10, *Late Ch'ing 1800-1911* (Cambridge University Press, 1978), pp. 375-85.

❹ Cf. "The Formation of Modern Chinese", p. 33.

elite, the Opium War was a short, albeit painful affair, that did not challenge established diplomatic practises enough to prompt any fundamental reassessment of Qing foreign policy. The British were integrated into an already existing system of Qing frontier policy and when the Manchus realised that the British were more interested in trade than in territorial gains they were only happy to negotiate peace with them.

Given the tardiness of the Chinese "response to the West" it is quite interesting to note that the developments on the Asian mainland were followed closely by the Japanese and that the outcome of the Opium War would have a direct influence on both Japanese intellectuals and policy-makers. To understand why, we first have to take a brief look at Japanese society.

The social setting in Edo Japan

Unlike China, which had been run by centralist governments for most of the time since Qin Shi Huangdi unified China in 221 BC, Japan had seen a gradual fragmentation of its political and social structure since 10th century. The warrior class, spearheaded by local feudal lords, appropriated more and more power from the imperial court in Kyoto and when the first military government (*bakufu*) was established in 1185, the emperor had been reduced to a mere figurehead, whose main function was to confer legitimacy to the *shogun*, the head of the bakufu. The Edo period (1600-1867), which roughly coincided with the Qing dynasty, represented the pinnacle of Japan's feudal period. The Tokugawa family, which resided in Edo, controlled lands that yielded one quarter of the country's entire rice production and instituted a sophisticated system of control known as "alternate attendance" (*sankin kôtai*). The approximately 260 feudal lords (*daimyô*) were largely free to run their own local affairs, but were required to stay in Edo for six months every year and had to leave their families behind when back on duty in the domain. The emperor was still kept as a symbol of legitimacy, but his movements were closely monitored by Edo. The territorial fragmentation of Japan was matched at the social level by a strictly regulated class system. The population was divided into four main classes, warriors, peasants, artisans and merchants, to which every member of society had to be affiliated. Social mobility between the classes was not encouraged.

The experience of the "Christian century," during which Portuguese and Spanish Jesuit missionaries managed to convert hundreds of thousands of Japanese to Christianity, had convinced Japan's rulers that contacts with foreign countries should be kept at a minimum in order to safeguard social stability and the survival of the regime. In four edicts beginning in 1613, Christianity was banned, the missionaries expelled, Japanese subjects forbidden to travel overseas and the "Southern barbarians", i.e. the Spanish and the Portuguese, were denied entry to Japan. The climate that followed persuaded most other foreigners that it was time to leave and by the middle of the century, only Dutch and Chinese remained in the Southern port of Nagasaki, where they were allowed to practice trade under strictly controlled forms. The foreigners that resided there had to pledge that they would abstain from preaching the Christian faith and most of the contacts with them were handled by interpreters appointed by the *bakufu*. In order to alert the authorities of possible threats from abroad the foreigners were obliged to submit regular reports (*fûsetsugaki*) on the situation in the world. The information was handled with great secrecy, but the authorities themselves paid only scanty interest to the contents of the reports.

Although the trade was brisk for most of the 17th century, the significance of the trade declined steadily and by the end of the next century only one Dutch ship and ten Chinese a year were permitted to land at Nagasaki.

In short, Japan was hardly a country that we would expect to show active interest in the outside world or respond to international changes any more than their confident neighbour on the Asian mainland. Yet, beneath the surface important changes had taken place throughout the 18th century, which would eventually outgrow the political system. The constant pilgrimage to Edo by a significant part of the population, which the system of alternate attendance had give rise to, strengthened the trade between different parts of the country. Agriculture was gradually commercialised and a class of wealthy peasants came into existence. The spread of literacy among commoners and the expanding publishing industry made it more difficult for the authorities to control the exchange of ideas. The society that emerged by the beginning of the 19th century was far more urbanised and commercialised than Japan had ever been and the supposedly subordinate merchant and agricultural classes could claim a substantive part of the output of the country. The ruling classes had also changed and become more internally polarised. Many of the samurai who were tied to the castle towns in the domains were becoming increasingly pauperised and dependent on moneylenders. On the other hand, the prolonged periods of stay in Edo of the upper echelon of the warrior class had created a national elite which identified more with the whole country than with their native territorial states. After a couple of generations, most of the feudal lords and their retainers were born in Edo.

Intellectual transitions in the Edo-period

For most of the Edo period Chinese learning remained the scholarly ideal of the Japanese literati. Ever conscious of the need to stabilise the country and eager to divert the samurai class from too much martial pursuit, the *bakufu* established Neo-Confucianism as the official doctrine during the first decades of the 17th century. A Confucian academy, known as the *Shôheikô*, was founded in Edo to promote Chinese studies, which had been in decline since the beginning of the feudal period. It became fashionable to compose Chinese poems and to write in "pure" Classical Chinese (*jun kanbun*) instead of the various forms of Sino-Japanese idioms that had flourished previously. Imported Chinese books were coveted commodities at the book markets. In fact, Chinese books constituted a significant part of the trade in Nagasaki, especially since other commercial activities had started do decline in the 18th century.

The Neo-Confucian doctrine perfected by the Song philosopher Zhu Xi did however not satisfy most Japanese scholars intellectually. The fall of the last native Chinese dynasty Ming in 1644 was a profound shock to many and the political upheaval on the Asian mainland both reinforced the Japanese feeling of vulnerability to threats from abroad and boosted the sense of superiority in relation to the Chinese. Many started to ask themselves whether the Chinese had not strayed too far from the Way of the Ancient Sages. A number of prominent scholars tried to reconstruct the "real" meaning of the Chinese classics, without relying on the Song commentaries or Japanese *kun* renderings. Some even went so far as to say that China, where even a peasant like could dethrone the emperor and become emperor himself, had lost its right of primogeniture to

Confucian civilisation. Instead, Japan, where the ruling dynasty had prevailed since time immemorial, was the true centre of civilisation.

The calling in question of Confucianism also paved the way for a negation of Chinese culture altogether and by the end of the 18th century a nativist school of thought, *kokugaku*, was gaining wide popularity. Through studies in ancient Japanese literature, the prominent nativist scholar Motoori Norinaga (1730-1801) came to the conclusion that there was an unbridgeable gap between the Japanese heart (*yamatogokoro*) and Chinese heart (*karagokoro*). He also rescued the long neglected mythical Japanese history book *Kojiki* from oblivion and became a celebrity when he published elaborate work on it. Although the early nativist scholars were politically quietist and mainly preoccupied with philological and literary pursuits, the nativist movement would become increasingly political in early 19th century. The studies in Japan's pre-feudal past led to a rediscovery of the imperial institution and many identified the emperor as the only legitimate political authority, thus implying that the ruling Tokugawa family had usurped their power.

The impracticality of a complete denial of Japan's Chinese heritage led to the emergence of a number of other schools that tried to combine nativist thought with Chinese learning. In the Mito domain became home to one of the more influential political schools of the early of 19th century, which emphasised "reverence of the emperor, expulsion of the barbarians" (sonnô jôi). The proto-nationalist Mito school would make its influence known through the feudal lord of the domain, who belonged to one of the collateral houses of the Tokugawa family and thus was an important political operator in Edo.

In 1720, the ban on foreign books was relaxed, which spawned a new guild of "Dutch scholars" (*rangakusha*), who were studying and translating mainly Dutch works on medicine, chemistry, astronomy, mathematics and military sciences. The influx of new ideas had a deep impact on many Japanese intellectuals. Student of medicine discovered that Western works on anatomy were far more accurate than the traditional Chinese works that had been consulted until then. The Japanese, who had been defining themselves in relation to China for thousands of years, began to realise that there were other alternatives to Chinese learning and Chinese civilisation.

Foundations of national isolation challenged

However, the changes in Japanese society had failed to produce any corresponding changes at the political level. The financial burden of the non-productive warrior class, which was dependent on official stipends, and the lavish life style of the feudal lords were beginning to consume the financial resources of the authorities. By the end of the 18th century famine and rural unrest was further destabilising Japanese society. Pressed from many directions, the *bakufu* saw its authority and freedom of action gradually reduced and beginning in the Kansei era (1789-1801), it embarked on a series of conservative reform programs in order to strengthen the agricultural and fiscal basis of its rule. Through a number of measures it sought to impose a more frugal lifestyle on the population and endeavoured to limit commerce. Part and parcel of the reforms was a strengthening of the Neo-Confucian doctrine and in 1790 a ban on heterodox doctrines (*Kansei igaku no kin*) in official schools was imposed.

It was during this period uninvited foreign ships started to appear in Japanese waters again, further increasing the feeling of crisis and undermining the authority of the *bakufu.* A number of incidents involving Russian and British ships occurred in the first decades of the 19th century, which prompted a renewed debate on the foundations of national isolation. Until then *sakoku*, "closed country," had not been regarded as a systematic or unchanged policy of isolation, but merely the product of a series of edicts limiting foreign intercourse to a minimum for the sake of national stability. The term "sakoku" was not even an indigenous Japanese term, but had entered the Japanese language through translations of foreign works on Japan. Although foreign trade was limited to China, Netherlands, Korea and island kingdom of Ryukyu, there was nothing in principle that excluded other nations from trading with Japan except, of course, for the two kingdoms of the Iberian peninsula, which had disqualified themselves through their zealous mission during the "Christian century." The fact that the Dutch had been able to clung to their position in Nagasaki was more a consequence of their colonial possessions in East Asia than anything else and their influence was steadily waning and being replaced by the British.❺

The famous "Expulsion edict" (*Ikokusen Uchiharai Rei*) which was issued by the *bakufu* on February 18th 1825 was a product of this renewed debate on *sakoku*, during which the expulsionist Mito domain had asserted itself. The immediate cause of the edict was an incident with British whalers the preceding year and according to the new policy all foreign ships that ventured into Japanese waters should be fired on "without thinking twice" (*ninen mo naku*), the only exception being Dutch and Chinese ships landing in Nagasaki.

❺ For a further discussion, cf. Bob Tadashi Wakabayashi, *Anti-Foreignerism and Western Learning in Early-Modern Japan"* (Cambridge, Mass.: Harvard University Press 1985).

The Expulsion edict was zealously supported by the scholar Aizawa Seshisai (1782-1863), who submitted his famous memorial *Shinron* ("New Theses") to the lord of Mito domain the same year. In *Shinron*, he sketched his understanding of the challenges Japan was facing and made concrete proposals for reform in the domain in order to "expel the barbarians." Seishisai was by no means a primitive xenophobic scholar and the text testifies amply to the fact that he was one of the first Japanese that understood that Japan was facing an unprecedented threat.

The strengthening of the national isolation policy did however not enjoy universal support and some scholars expressed their reservations against shutting the country off from foreign influences in the years immediately preceding the Opium War. After the American ship *Morrison* had been driven away by force in 1837, the painter and Dutch scholar Watanabe Kazan (1793-1841) wrote an essay, *Shinkiron,* in which he criticised the expulsion policy. Although the essay was never published, it was discovered during purge against Dutch scholars in 1839 and Kazan was sentenced to house arrest and later committed suicide. If he had written *Shinkiron* one or two years later, he might have been spared from that fate.

The *bakufu* and the Opium War

There is no reliable information as to exactly when the Japanese first became aware of the Opium War, but we may safely assume that the news first reached Japan through the foreign traders in Nagasaki. Many of the initial reports were grossly exaggerated, claiming that China was soon be swallowed by the British Empire like India. We do not know whether the *bakufu* believed these rumours or not, but they were clearly alarmed by the news and in 1840 they ordered the Dutch to submit a full account on the war. Apparently the account that eventually reached the *bakufu* was incomplete, partially due to the fact that the translations had been carried out in great secrecy, only allowing the individual translators to see parts of the material.❻ But the war was to go on for another two years and Japan's rulers would get more reliable information in due course.

The Opium War did not bring about any substantial revision of *sakoku* initially, but in order not to precipitate a similar conflict with foreign countries, the regent Mizuno Tadakuni (1794-1851) repealed the expulsion edict in July 1842, as it happened, one month before the Treaty of Nanking was concluded. The new ordinance decreed that foreign ships that had been driven to the Japanese coast by hurricane or other special circumstances should be offered provisions according to their needs and only fired on if they then refused to leave.❼

The new situation created by the Opium War must have encouraged those who wished to see an end to sakoku altogether, for in 1844 William II of Netherlands took the unusual step of sending a letter directly to the shogun urging him to open Japan to the world. In his letter, the king welcomed the new ordinance offering kind treatment to ships in distress, but asked "What will be done with vessels that come for other and friendly reasons to visit the Japanese coast? Are these to be repulsed by force or unfriendly treatment? Will quarrels arise? Quarrels lead to war, and war leads to destruction." The king warned the shogun that what had befallen China recently may happen to Japan in the near future and added "We hope that wisdom will make the Japanese Government

---

❻ Cf. Masuda Wataru, *Seigaku tôzen to Chûgoku jijô* (Tokyo 1979), pp. 56-7.

❼ *Shôsetsu Nihonshi Shiryôshû* (rev. ed. Tokyo 1999), pp. 229-30.

realise that peace can only be maintained through friendly relations, and that theses are only created by commercial relations". ❽

The reply of the bakufu, which was sent to the Netherlands the following year was not signed by the shogun himself, but by four senior councillors (*rôjû*), thus implying that the relation between Japan and Netherlands was not one between equals. The letter begins with stressing that the trade that has taken place between the two countries up to then has been a manifestation of good will on the part of the shogun and expresses gratitude for the gifts that had been enclosed with the royal communication. It then proceeds to say:

> Although the suggestions offered are worthy of adoption, there are reasons why this can not be. When the founder of our dynasty entered upon his career, intercourse and trade with countries beyond the sea were in an unsettled condition. Later when the time came for determining with what countries intercourse should be permitted, intercourse was limited to Korea and Loochoo [Ryukyu], and trade to Your Excellencies country and China. Aside from these countries all intercourse was entirely disallowed. If now it were desired to extend these limits, it would be in contravention with the ancestral law. …… Although this may be discourteous, such is the strictness of the ancestral law, that no other course is open for us.❾

❽ As quoted in D.C. Greene, "Correspondence between William II of Holland and the Shôgun of Japan A.D. 1844", in *Transactions of the Asiatic Society of Japan*, xxxiv (1907), pp. 112-3.

❾ *Ibid*. pp. 121-2.

The Japanese intellectuals and the Opium War

If the *bakufu* resisted further positive action by reiterating the somewhat misguided idea that national isolation was part of an unchanged policy since the early beginning of Tokugawa rule, other circles in Japanese society were quick to respond to the new situation. Although the restrictions on overseas intelligence were still severe in the 1840s, the news of the Anglo-Chinese war soon leaked out and gave birth to a significant literature, which was circulated among intellectual elite in manuscript form. One of the earliest examples of this literature is the *Ihi Hankyôroku*, which is an account of the course of the war from July 1840 to the peace treaty in 1842. The book reproduces several documents from both the contending parties, but it is not known when, where or by whom the book was compiled. Although it is possible that the book was first produced in China and then exported to Japan, no copies of the book are known in China, neither is the name of the book known to have occurred in any Chinese work.[10]

Wei Yuan's famous works *Haiguo Tuzhi* and *Shengwu Ji* were imported to Japan in the early 1850s and became best selling handbooks on geography and foreign learning for many years to come. Copies of the two books constituted a large proportion of the literature imported from China in 1850s, in proportion to which the prices of these books also rose rapidly. Records show that people from the upper echelons of the *bakufu*

[10] *Seigaku*, pp. 66-7.

and the Confucian school of Shoheiko were big purchasers of the books.⓫

It is very interesting to note that Confucian scholars were among the most productive authors on the Opium War, which is perhaps reflection of the fact that the ancestral country of the civilisation which they had devoted their life to study appeared to be threatened by the Western onslaught. It is, however, important to not exaggerate the importance of that fact since many young men had become Confucian scholars more because of career considerations rather than of real conviction. The Kansei ban on heterodox teachings had made it impossible to get a government appointment for people who been trained in other schools than the officially sponsored Zhu Xi school.

The Shoheiko scholar and poet Saitô Chikudô (1815-1852) could be described as one of these "conventional Confucians." According to his biographer, Chikudo was very interested in foreign studies and deplored the fact that many of his colleagues wanted to ban foreign books as heretical. In 1843 he wrote the interesting essay *Ahen Shimatsu* ("Origins and Outcome of the Opium War"), which is a short account on the opium trade and the course Opium War.⓬The essay is quite rich in facts and details about the war, but it also reproduces some clearly fictive elements, such as the alleged capture of "Third Princess of the English barbarians."

According to Chikudo, there were three princesses in England, one who was the reigning queen, one who was a general, both whom were in England, and a "Third Princess", who was an admiral. The "Third Princess" was feared for her courage and cruelty in the war against China and was captured by the Qing forces during the war, which reportedly led to some diplomatic complications between the English and the Manchus.⓭ The same anecdote appears in many of the other Japanese

---

⓫ *Ibid.* pp. 32-3.

⓬ Reprinted in *Nihon Kaibô Shiryô Sôsho* (Tokyo 1932-33), vol. 3, pp. 203-210.

⓭ Cf. *ibid.*, p. 206, Masuda pp. 79-80 and R.H. van Gulik, "Kakkaron: A Japanese

accounts on the Opium War and it is not clear where it originally came from.⓮But the persistence of the legend testifies to the fact that the eagerness of the Japanese to learn more about the war also made them vulnerable to rumours and distorted accounts.

Chikudo is clear on the moral issues, the English barbarians ought to be condemned for their smuggling of opium and their invasion of China, but in the concluding remarks he bursts out:

> After pondering this question repeatedly, I concluded that English victory and Ch'ing [Qing] defeat, English cleverness and Ch'ing ineptness, had nothing to do with (the moral issue of) opium. Instead, the crux of the matter lay in a more commonplace, everyday attitude of long standing. Namely, there are many countries in the universe, and each differs from the others. Who can say that one of them is civilized, and the rest, barbarian. But China (*Kando*), presumes itself Middle Kingdom civilization (*Chûka*) and considers other peoples despicable animals, mysterious beings devoid of spirit. They know nothing of the Westerners' shrewdness or of highly sophisticated machines because they have never considered these valuable as such… When the Chinese (Kan) devise strategies to ward off Western incursion, they simply rant 'barbarian, barbarian.⓯

This is a very damning indictment coming from someone who has been raised in the Confucian tradition and it gives us an idea how alienated many Japanese had become from China and Chinese culture in

Echo of the Opium War,", *Monumenta Serica* 4 (1939), p. 506 for a short English translation.

⓮ Cf. *Seigaku*, pp. 90ff.

⓯ As quoted in *Anti-Foreignerism*, pp.139-40.

the pre-modern era. It is hardly surprising that Chikudo was never able to get this essay printed and it did not appear in printed form until the 1920s.

In the 1840s and 50s a number of books and pamphlets were published by officials such as Nagayama Kan and Confucian scholars like Shionoya Tôin (1809-1867), who managed to get his impassioned pamphlet *Kakkaron* printed in 1859.⓰ A brief look at many of these books suggest that the writers keenly quoted, copied and even plagiarised each other's works and that they also drew on earlier proto-nationalist literature. For instance, when Toin warns of the dangers of not checking evil tendencies in time in the first chapter of *Kakkaron*, he quotes the same passage from *Yijing* as Aizawa Seishisai had done in *Shinron* some thirty years earlier:

> Treading on hoarfrost. The strong ice will come'……This means that if sinister things are not suppressed when not yet in full bloom, they develop into a most extraordinary monster……Deep indeed is the meaning of these words, warning to guard against the growing of small things! When I now observe the Opium Calamity that befell the Manchu Dynasty, did it not originate because the warning implied in 'treading hoarfrost' was not heeded? For the Opium Calamity began already when the various foreign barbarians settled down in Macao.⓱

Although Tôin lashes out at crude Sinocentrism several times later

---

⓰ Translated in "Kakkaron," pp. 478-575.

⓱ Ibid., p. 517. For the reference to Yijing cf. Imai Usaburô et al (ed.), *Nihon Shisô Taikei*, vol. 53 (Tokyo: Iwanami Shoten 1973), pp. 69 and 388, see also Wakabayashi, p. 169.

in the text, he also directs sharp criticism against the failure of the Qing dynasty to expel the foreigners from China, which is evident from the paragraph above. This reference must have been aimed at the *bakufu* as well, which had just signed one of the notorious unequal treaties with the United States. Since the political climate was very charged in Japan in the 1850s, Toin took a great personal risk when he spread these views and after *Kakkaron* he never spoke up on political subjects again.⓲

Two of the most interesting commentators on the Opium War are Sakuma Shôzan (1811-1864) and Yoshida Shôin (1830-1859), both of whom were deeply influenced by the Opium War and devoured any book they could find on it.⓳ Shozan was a retainer from Shinano who experimented with modern gunnery and took great interest in other branches of Western studies. He tried to learn the Dutch language and at one point he even tried to publish a Dutch dictionary. Like many others, Shozan was deeply upset when he first heard about the Opium War and in 1843 he submitted a "Eight Point Memorial on Naval Defence," in which he warned that if the *bakufu* did not pay more attention to coastal defence Japan would risk meeting the same fate as China.⓴His advice went unheeded, but he continued to write memorials and kept a small circle of students. One of them, Yoshida Shoin, took his teacher's criticism of *sakoku* seriously and tried to board one of Commodore Perry's "black ships" in 1854 in order to go America and learn more about the West. Shozan got involved in the affair and was sentenced to

---

⓲ "Kakkaron," p. 499

⓳ Cf. *Seigaku*, pp. 38ff.

⓴ H. D. Harootunian, *Toward Restoration – The Growth of Political Consciousness in Tokugawa Japan* (Berkeley: University of California Press 1970), pp. 149ff.

house arrest. Yoshida Shoin later set up his own school in his home domain, a school that would train many of the leaders of the Meiji restoration.

One of Sakuma Shozan's most interesting works is *Seikanron*, which was written after he was released from confinement and in which he summarises many of his ideas on Western studies and coastal defence. He also relates how impressed he was with Wei Yuan's *Haiguo Tuzhi* when he first found it and takes special joy in noting that his memorial on naval defence and *Haiguo Tuzhi* were completed only four months apart the very same year. Being born in different countries and without knowing about each other beforehand, he felt that he had found a "kindred spirit" (*dôshi*) in Wei Yuan. But he does not let this coincidence befuddle his judgement and proceeds immediately to direct scathing criticism against Wei Yuan for being superficial in his understanding of naval affairs and foreign affairs. Shôzan concludes that Wei Yuan's Sinocentric conceit prevented him from seriously studying Western languages and military techniques himself.㉑

Perry's arrival

So, despite the thriving debate on the developments in China, the *bakufu* lacked any clear policy to counter the foreign threat, which was looming on the horizon. As has already been pointed out, several lukewarm attempts to open Japan had been made to prior to Perry's arrival. Britain, France and Russia had all tried to challenge Japan's self-

㉑ Cf. Satô Shôsuke et al (ed.), *Nihon Shisô Taikei,* vol. 55 (Tokyo: Iwanami Shoten 1971), pp. 251 and 415f. See also Harootunian, pp. 150ff.

imposed isolation, but they were all too preoccupied with in commitments elsewhere. Neither could the value of the trade with Japan justify a costly military adventure.[22]

It fell on the United States, which had no colonial concerns at the moment, to open Japan with "gunboat diplomacy." The United States had just opened a window to the West in California and foresaw the possibility of a profitable trade over the Pacific Ocean. The Americans had also an important whaling fleet in the Pacific, which sometimes needed to call at an intermediary port in order to obtain food and fuel. The ill treatment of some American castaways in Japan the 1840s had alerted the United States to the fact that *sakoku* clashed with American interests in the Pacific. Fully aware of the fact that the Japanese obtained intelligence through the Dutch, the Americans announced publicly in 1851 that an expedition would be undertaken to open Japan.

Since the *bakufu* clung to the idea that national isolation was an unchangeable ancestral law, Commodore Matthew Perry's determination to deliver his letter from the American president with force, if necessary, in 1853 triggered something of a constitutional crisis. The *bakufu* realised that a conclusion of a treaty with a foreign power would have serious political implications. The abortive Tempô reforms also meant that the *bakufu* enjoyed low prestige and had little room to manoeuvre. Trying to reach consensus, the regent Abe Masahiro (1819-57) took the unprecedented step to circulate Perry's and President Fillmore's letters and requesting advice, not only to the *fudai daimyô*, the "inner lords", but also to the *tozama daimyô*, "outer lords" who were traditionally

---

[22] Cf. W.G. Beasley, "The Foreign Threat and the Opening of the Ports," *The Cambridge History of Japan,* vol. 5 (Cambridge: Cambridge University Press 1989), pp. 261-9.

excluded from *bakufu* politics. The response Abe Masahiro received from the feudal lords was inconclusive, but he had no other choice than to sign a treaty with Perry when he returned to Japan in 1854 to receive the *bakufu's* response to the communication from the American president. The treaty which was signed the same year allowed for the new opening of a few ports of refuge for American ships, established an American consular office in Japan and gave the United States most favoured nation treatment. The Great Powers followed the American example and in the following years a number of Western countries signed similar treaties with Japan.

As the Japanese had managed to exclude the open ports from trade in the first treaty, it was not deemed satisfactory by the American public. When the first American consul general Townsend Harris (1804-78) arrived in Shimoda in September 1856 to take up his post, one of his orders was to negotiate a more comprehensive treaty with the Japanese on the Chinese model. When he entered into negotiation with the new regent Hotta Masayoshi (1810-64) in Edo the following year, Harris did not hesitate to use the example of the Arrow War to warn the Japanese of what could happen if Japan did not abandon its policy of seclusion. If Japan failed to sign a commercial treaty with the United States, Britain would certainly be willing to employ its fleet to force its will on Japan as soon as it had disengaged from the war with China. Such a danger could best be averted if Japan signed a more favourable commercial treaty with the United States, which would set the framework for subsequent treaties. As the United States was not interested in the opium trade it could be banned in the treaty, forcing other nations to follow suit, Harris promised. Eventually Harris and Masayoshi agreed on a proposal for a treaty in February 1858, which included the gradual opening of eight ports to trade, consular jurisdiction for American citizens, fixed tariffs and a ban on opium trade.㉓

When the terms of the proposed treaty were circulated among the feudal lords, upheaval ensued. By acceding to most of Harris' demands, Masayoshi had clearly transgressed the boundaries of the frail consensus which his predecessor had tried to build up. Seeking to mollify his critics, Hotta Masayoshi then turned to the imperial court in Kyoto to secure an imperial sanction, but was snubbed by the court, which hinted that he would have to unite the country before he could expect any sanction from the emperor. This was not only a consequence of the young Kômei emperor's well-known opposition to the treaties, but also an expression of the political discretion of the court, which had learnt to survive through the centuries. Hotta Masayoshi was dismissed in disgrace and replaced as regent by the Ii Naosuke (1815-60), the lord of Hikone domain. By the summer of 1858, news of the Treaty of Tianjin which had just been concluded, reached Japan through Townsend Harris. He warned the *bakufu* that a huge British fleet now was expected and that Japan's must sign the treaty or risk a disastrous confrontation with the Great Powers. Ii Naosuke gave in to Harris' threats and signed the treaty without imperial sanction on July 29th, a move that would produce national outrage and cost him his own life two years later.㉔

By the beginning of the 1860s the West had managed to force a treaty port system on Japan according to the model established in China. But the consequences would be very different. Trying to build a consensus by consulting the feudal lords and the imperial court, *bakufu* had only succeeded in bringing the political divisions in Japanese society into the open and strengthening the political image of the emperor. The

---

㉓ *Ibid.* pp. 271ff. Se also W.G. Beasley *Select Documents on Japanese Foreign Policy 1853-1868* (London: Oxford University Press 1955).

㉔ *Ibid.* pp. 283

signing of the Harris Treaty in 1858 precipitated a process that would eventually end with the overthrow of the *bakufu* itself and the nominal restoration of imperial rule in 1868.

Treaty revision

The spectre of a colonised and enslaved China continued to haunt Japan and the first eyewitness reports Japanese brought back from China only strengthened their resolve to redress the national humiliation of the unequal treaties.㉕ To secure treaty revision became one of the top priorities of new regime after 1868. When the Meiji oligarchs realised that the Great Powers were unwilling to concede equal relations with Japan unless Japan developed a modern judicial system, they put a lot of efforts into the reforming of the political and judicial system of Japan. Political reformers outside of the government also used the existence of the unequal treaties skilfully as a lever to press for constitutional and legal reform.㉖ Five years after Japan had adopted its first modern constitution, Britain finally signalled that it would be willing to revise the treaties and the other treaty powers soon followed suit. By 1899 Japan had achieved diplomatic equality with most of the Great Powers and was free to embark on its own imperialistic adventures in Korea and elsewhere.

In China, however, it seems that the unequal treaties were a not major concern of the ruling classes, neither did the constant concessions

---

㉕ Cf. Feng Tianyu, "Riben mufu shituan suojian 1862 nian zhi Shanghai," *Jindaishi Yanjiu*, no. 3, 1999.

㉖ Cf. Tsuda Mamichi, "Gômon ron no ichi," *Meiroku Zasshi* no. 7 (1873). Reprinted in Meiroku zasshi (Tokyo: Iwanami Shoten 1999), pp. 259-262.

of the Qing court to the colonial powers provoke any national outrage of magnitude until the end of the 19th century. Foreign affairs were held in low esteem and service in the foreign affairs was not an attractive career option for most aspiring Chinese youth. Even though a number works on Western science were published in Chinese from the middle of the 19th century, very few Chinese did preoccupy themselves with the challenges the new world order posed to the Chinese way of life. Instead, many of the books got a larger readership in Japan. Henry Wheaton's *Elements of International Law,* which was published in 1864 as *Wanguo Gongfa* under the auspices of the newly established Tongwenguan, became something of a Bible to many of the young Meiji leaders and was republished in Japanese editions several times. When the Japanese statesman Ôkuma Shigenobu argued with British and French diplomats over treaty revision in the 1880s, he always kept a copy of the book at hand.[27] Incidentally, he would later be known in China as one of the originators of the infamous "21 Demands."

The existence of the treaty ports and the increasing number of unruly foreigners exempt from Chinese jurisdiction were indeed a source of political conflict and social unrest for most of the 19th century. But it was not until after the defeat in the Sino-Japanese war that the support of the Manchus started to decline in earnest among the Chinese literati. An increasing number of Chinese began to regard the Qing dynasty not only as a generally corrupt and incompetent government, but also as a "court of foreigners," making unreasonable concessions to the Western powers and being utterly lacking in concern for the Chinese people. This was only compounded by the fact that the Qing court was not ethnically Chinese, but of Manchu stock, and by the turn of the century anti-

---

[27] *Seigaku*, pp. 4-6.

Manchuism had become an important element in the growing nationalist movement. The fact that many Chinese students were sent to Japan and could witness with their own eyes the progress made under the Meiji government and its successes in revising the unequal treaties also gave a strong impetus to the nationalist movement in China. Demands for treaty revision would grow stronger at the inception of the Republican Era and culminate in the May 4–movement in 1919, which erupted in response to the treatment China had fared in the Versailles peace conference.

China would remain unsuccessful in addressing the issue of the unequal treaties for most of the first half of the 20th century. The Great War 1914-19 and the political convulsions in the wake of the depression left the imperialist powers to busy with their own problems and the political record of the weak Nationalist government in China did not seem to justify a reconsideration of the treaties. Not until the 1940s, when Chiang Kai-shek's nationalist government was needed as an ally in the war against Japan were the Great Powers willing to consider a revision of the treaties. But the Nationalists were never able to reap the benefits of the new situation after World War II, for in 1949 they lost the Chinese civil war and was exiled to the island of Taiwan. It fell on China's new Communist dynasty to remove the last politically significant remnant of the Opium Wars and secure the return of Hong Kong to Chinese sovereignty on July 1st 1997.

Some conclusions and observations

One of the first things that struck me when I researched this paper was the contrast between Japanese alarmism and Chinese complacency. The news of imperialist incursions in China or the sight of foreign ships in the Japanese archipelago often provoked almost hysterical reactions in Japan and the image of colonial India was often invoked to highlight the dangers Japan was facing. Yet, most of the Great Powers were too bogged down by their colonial possessions elsewhere and were unwilling to commit their resources to large territorial conquests in East Asia. As long as the balance of power between the different parties was not disturbed, they were more interested in trade and contented themselves with a limited presence in the form of the treaty port system. Furthermore, the trade with China was by far the most lucrative and Japan only merited limited interest. Ironically, it was Japan's own victory against China in 1895 that would eventually bring about the "scramble for China" threatening the country of being "cut up like a melon."

It seems that one important reason for this Japanese alarmism was the deep-rooted feeling of vulnerability that runs through Japanese history. For instance, the unification of China under the Sui and Tang dynasties and the fall of Japan's Korean ally Paekche in 663 brought the Japanese face to face with the prospect of being incorporated with China. The speed and the urgency of the reforms in Japan in the 7th and 8th centuries are in many ways reminiscent of the changes that Japan would undergo some eleven hundred years later.[28]

Another factor that worked in Japan's favour was the fact that Japanese society had already come quite far in the development of pre-modern nationalism at the time of the Opium War. Increased contacts between different parts of the country and semi-permanent residence in the important political arena of Edo had welded the Japanese elite

---

[28] Cf. Delmer M. Brown (ed.), *The Cambridge History of Japan*, vol. 1, *Ancient Japan* (Cambridge University Press, 1978), pp. 30ff.

together and enabled it eventually to overcome local rivalries in the face of the foreign threat. Although the *bakufu* was no less impotent than the Manchus were in dealing with the "red haired barbarians," the fact that strong, increasingly independent political forces existed outside of the *bakufu* would quickly readjust that imbalance. To the same degree as the Perry and Harris treaties became national issues the *bakufu* lost the initiative in favour of the growing anti-*bakufu* camp. The existence of an imperial house, albeit with only symbolic authority, provided an alternative focus of legitimacy around which a anti-*bakufu*, restorationist and nationalist movement could be effectively rallied.

In contrast, the complacency on the part of the Manchus and the Chinese literati would be disastrous for China. Millennia of central rule and a splendid civilisation, which had once dominated the Eastern Hemisphere, would prove to be a heavy luggage to carry into the modern era. China had far more experience in dealing with foreign countries than Japan and the defeat in the Opium War did not constitute a sufficiently strong impetus to abandon already existing models of foreign relations. The fact that the Manchus were not ethnic Chinese made them reluctant to appeal to the Han Chinese masses to resist the foreign invaders. After all, the Manchus were "foreign invaders" themselves and too strong an appeal to national and ethnic feelings could pose threat to their own rule.

China's defeat in the Sino-Japanese war fifty years later was not only a result of the unsuccessful Tongzhi Restoration and the Self-Strengthening Movement. It was also a consequence of the failure of the Manchus to mobilise the Chinese people in the war. The war was merely treated as a local affair by the Qing government, a fact that contemporary Japanese observers with fresh memories from the feudal era did not fail to take notice of.[29] The ignominious defeat in the war and the seemingly imminent threat of partition and national extinction, would cause the Chinese political elite to question not only the mandate of the Manchus to rule China, but eventually the value of Chinese culture itself. Thus by the beginning of the 20th century the Chinese were plunged into a painful process of self-questioning and reappraisal at same time as they were forced to deal with increasingly aggressive foreign threats. In Japan, the corresponding process had already been initiated under much more peaceful conditions from the 18th century onwards.

The Chinese students' encounter with the successes of late Meiji Japan was another factor that galvanised Chinese nationalism and it reminds us in many ways of the "pilgrimage" that local elites made to their respective mother countries in the colonial era, which Benedict Anderson has described in his seminal work *Imagined Communities*.[30] Although I have not been able to establish this sufficiently, it would not surprise me if the movement against the unequal treaties that gained momentum after the turn of the century was largely inspired by and modelled on Japan's successful movement to revise the treaties. In which case, to a certain extent we are entitled to say that modern Chinese nationalism is not so much a product of the so-called "response to the West" as the "response to Japan".

A study of Sino-Japanese relations from the Opium War onwards is a very fruitful way of approaching the development of nationalism and a

---

[29] Cf. the quote of Yamagata Aritomo in Marius B. Jansen, *JAPAN and CHINA: from war to peace 1894-1972* (Chicago 1975), p. 17.

[30] I this respect, I disagree with Mitani Hiroshi's assertion that Anderson's model of nationalism does not apply to China. Cf. Mitani Hiroshi, *Meiji Ishin to nashonarizumu* (Tokyo 1997), p. 21.

modern political consciousness in both and China and Japan. The sometimes too strong focus on the role of Western imperialism in East Asian history runs the risk of ignoring domestic forces in East Asia and the interaction between the different countries in the region, which a could block our understanding of the respective countries on their own terms.

Conceptual Challenges Facing the Student of Popular Literature in Mainland China and Taiwan

Marja Kaikkonen*

Abstract

The various political, social, material and cultural changes that have taken place in China during this century have all left their mark on the Chinese vocabulary. This applies even for the vocabulary used to describe literary phenomena. It is only when trying to penetrate to the core meanings of such terms that they reveal the complicated relationships they bear to historical contexts, while seemingly synonymous glosses turn out to command crucially different concepts.

While the large number of works on 20th century Chinese

* 蓋瑪雅，瑞典斯德哥爾摩大學中國研究學系

literature has eased the confusion when it comes to elite literature, the student of Chinese popular literature is still today confronted with a huge array of terminology, where several different interpretations - of history, including literary history, of literary ideology, and of social change -vie with each other. Even basic questions such as “what is ‘popular’?”, “who is popular?”, and “what is popular literature?” all get different sets of answers and even different Chinese wordings - when these different views are being applied to them. No wonder the history of 20th century Chinese popular literature still remains to be written!

This paper wants to take a closer look at the key concepts of the popular literary field, and, by analyzing the historical, political and literary historical settings that they have grown out of, it wants to illustrate the complicity and depth of the ideas involved and discuss the difficulties that are often experienced when using the concepts - difficulties which often have to do with the sets of values attached to the original historical contexts.

Keywords: Chinese vocabulary, literary phenomena, popular literature, terminology.

The various political, social, material and cultural changes that have taken place in China during this century have all left their mark on the Chinese vocabulary. This applies even for the vocabulary used to describe literary phenomena. It is only when trying to penetrate to the core meanings of such terms that they reveal the complicated relationships they bear to historical contexts, while seemingly synonymous glosses turn out to command crucially differing concepts.

While the large number of works on 20th century Chinese literature has eased the confusion when it comes to elite literature, the student of Chinese popular literature is still today confronted with an array of terminology, where various interpretations—of history, including literary history, of literary ideology, and of social change—vie with each other. Even basic questions such as "what is 'popular'?", and "what is popular culture?" or "what is popular literature?" all get different sets of answers—and even different Chinese wordings—when these various views are being applied to them. No wonder the history of 20th century Chinese popular literature still remains to be written!

In this paper I have tried to trace some key terms/concepts of the popular literary field, and, by analyzing some of the historical, ideological and literary settings that they have grown out of, I have wanted to illustrate the complicity and depth of the ideas involved and discuss the difficulties that are often experienced when using the concepts—difficulties which often have to do with the sets of values attached to the original historical contexts.

But this situation is not surprising. These terms are by no means easy to define, and I certainly do not want to suggest that they would have been clearly defined in the West. Quite the opposite. There is no straightforward definition of these terms to be found in either *Encyclopedia Britannica* (1997) or 1999 *Encyclopedia Americana.* The reason is, of course, that these terms are perhaps impossible to define, as their connotations, and/or the attitudes of the world toward these phenomena, have shifted continuously for at least a century—as long as they have been described at all. My aim here has not been to fill these gaps, but rather to show that they exist. It has not been possible to always treat popular literature on its own, as it is a part of a larger complex, popular culture, which many commentators choose to address as a whole.

Liang Qichao was perhaps the first intellectual in modern China to express a theoretical interest in popular literature. For him, popular culture, especially fiction, appeared as an important channel through which the growth of the "new citizenry" could be promoted.❶ He viewed popular literature as a didactic means to a patriotic end, and joined thus the Confucians of old who agreed that writings and, consequently, also reading should be useful (*wen yi zai dao*). He was concerned with what popular literature could be, or ought to be, not what it was. Liang Qichao's type of "potentialist" vision came to dominate Chinese views of popular literature for decades, both among radicals, leftists and rightists alike.

A great upsurge of interest in folk literature occurred in China in the late teens. A number of scholars at the National Beijing University, including Liu Fu (Liu Bannong), Zhou Zuoren, and Gu Jiegang set up in

---

❶ See Liang Qichao, "Xiaoshuo yu qunzhi de guanxi" (On the relationship between fiction and popular sovereignty), *Xin xiaoshuo* No.1, 1902. On Liang Qichao's views on this question, see also Milena Dolezelova-Velingerova, *The Chinese Novel at the Turn of the Century*. Toronto 1980, pp. 27-29; and C.T. Hsia, "Yen Fu and Liang Ch'i-ch'ao as Advocates of New Fiction", in Adele Austin Rickett, ed., *Chinese Approaches to Literature from Confucius to Liang Ch'i-ch'ao*. Princeton 1978, pp. 221-257.

1918 an office for collecting folk songs, and in 1922 they started the journal *Geyao zhoukan* (Folksong weekly) to publish them in. This journal attracted much attention, and resulted in the Fengsu diaochahui (Custom Survey Society) being established in 1923. Newspapers and journals started carrying special columns on folk literature, and the interest in folklore gradually spread to many parts of China, forming a whole movement.❷

Several terms were used for folk literature ever since the early 20th century: *minjian wenxue* (literature among the people), *minzhong wenxue* (literature of the masses of people), *pingmin wenxue* (literature of common people), *minsu wenxue* (folk customs literature). *tongsu wenxue* (literature common among the vulgar?, literature of common customs?). Or the word "*wenxue*" (literature) was replaced in these compounds with the word "*wenyi*" (literature and art). Even the terms *dazhong wenxue* (people's literature?, the great masses' literature?), *nongmin wenxue* (peasants' literature), *xiangtu wenxue* (rural literature, country literature), *kouer wenxue* (literature of mouth and ear), *koubei wenxue* (?), *jiangchang wenxue* (told and sung literature), or *dazhongyu wenxue* (people's language literature) were used of folk literature.❸ Lou Zikuang, another pioneer of Chinese folk literature studies and later very active in Taiwan, recommended the term *su wenxue* (vulgar literature) as late as 1968.❹ In the People's Republic of China, folk literature was given the connotation *minjian wenxue*, a term that is still in consequent use within the study of folklore.

---

❷ Chang-tai Hung, *Going to the People: Chinese Intellectuals and Folk Literature 1918-1937*. Cambridge, Mass. 1985, p. 1.

❸ Lou Zikuang and Zhu Jiefan (eds.), *Wushi nian lai de Zhongguo su wenxue* (Fifty years of Chinese vulgar literature), Taibei 1963, p. 1

❹ Ibid.

What these terms were used for early this century was naturally nothing like today's popular literature, nor did it even refer to the urban popular culture of the time. It was a term reserved for rural folklore. Lin Fu made the distinction by terming the Shanghai fiction he studied *xiadeng xiaoshuo* (low grade fiction, low class fiction). Folklore had come to function as an ideological eye-opener for Chinese intellectuals with modern orientation just as it had been for European intellectuals somewhat earlier. The acceptance of the idea that the cultural products of a lower social group had a value of their own and made a difference in the society as a whole was a definite step toward a more modern, egalitarian view of society and of different social groups.

In their enthusiasm over a renewed outlook on society and an ernest wish to share the best of folk literature with Chinese readers, many adherents of this view acquired a highly idealized and romantic vision of Chinese rural life and peasants, stereotyped as a pastoral idyll inhabited by intuitively Daoist peasants who went about their everyday chores and lived their sound life enjoying its simplicity.❺ This vision acquired nationalistic overtones from the 1920s, when folk literature－the culture of the idyllic peasants－was found to be "the crystallization of the national spirit", and therefore a method for national salvation.❻ This view has had a strong and lasting influence in China. It has unfortunately played an equally strong obstructing role for the reception of modern popular culture, which by comparison certainly has appeared less national and more foreign, and therefore, by implication, unpatriotic and practically traitorous.

That even the acceptance of folk literature was an ideologically

❺ For an account of the romantic idealization of rural life in the folk literature movement, see Chang-tai Hung, pp. 10-17.

❻ Chang-tai Hung, p. 17.

controversial issue is revealed by the fact that it continued to meet with opposition. While Qing laws had forbidden women to sing folksongs, Republican Chinese governments considered it equally natural to suppress folk culture on various pretexts, such as its "vulgarity" and its "corrupting influence on public morals". The Guomindang government in Nanjing continued this tradition on even harsher lines from 1928-29, launching campaigns called *Pochu mixin yundong* (Superstition Destruction Movement), which were to eradicate local customs that were considered unsuitable. This caused severe setbacks to the folk literature movement.❼

Among the early folklorists only Liu Fu showed an interest in urban popular culture. He even conducted some unique very early studies on popular literature in Shanghai,❽ but it seems that he was met with disinterest and discontinued the work. Consequently, he concentrated on collecting folk songs.

The large scale radicalization of Chinese intellectuals after the May Fourth movement in 1919 caused a massive challenge of many established views. However, this did not apply to popular culture. The radicalism of this period included the idea that literature ought to accomplish ideological awakening among the people, and thus patriotically participate in the modernization of the country with national salvation as the final goal. This echoed Liang Qichao's 1902 call for "new fiction" for nation building purposes, and thus meant a continuation, not a break, in tradition. Literature in general was divided into "old" and "new", the new being the kind that would be produced from then on in accordance with patriotic needs (but which did not exist yet). In this light, the existing popular literature could only be condemned: negative views

---

❼ Chang-tai Hung, p. 160.

❽ Liu Fu, "Zhongguo zhi xiadeng xiaoshuo", in *Zhongguo xin wenxue daxi.* Shanghai 1935, vol. 2, pp. 358-76. Liu's article was written as early as in 1918.

prevailed on both traditional popular literature, considered "feudal", and modern popular literature, seen as "Western" and "commercial", the modern kind being even worse as it was not a natural part of China's history, which the "feudal" type was.

In line with the idealization and nationalization of peasant culture, a differentiation was made between folk literature and popular literature. Among the radicals, this was done by Mao Dun and Zhou Zuoren. Zhou termed folk literature *yuanshi wenxue* (primitive literature),❾ thus excusing it from intellectual criticism.

In 1921-22, Mao Dun and Zheng Zhenduo lead a ferocious attack against urban popular literature, describing it with the title "mandarin ducks and butterflies" literature, which now acquired a derogatory tone. ❿ Such literature was seen as pernicious, it poisoned the minds of its readers and kept them from reading more useful literature.⓫ Even the

---

❾ Zhou defined popular literature as written by the literati, and found two categories: *caizi jiaren* (stories of talents and beauties) such as *Hongloumeng*, and *xiayi* (stories of knights-errant) such as *Shuihuzhuan*. See Chang -tai Hung, pp. 5-6, and Zhou Zuoren, "Guanyu tongsu wenxue", *Xiandai* Vol. 2, No. 6, pp. 795-797.

❿ Much of these polemics was published on the pages of *Wenxue xunkan* , and reprinted in *Yuanyang hudie pai wenxue ziliao*, 2 vols. Fuzhou 1984, vol. 2, pp. 726-752. For other relevant articles see pp. 710-725. See also Perry Link, "Traditional-Style Popular Urban Fiction in the Teens and Twenties", in Merle Goldman, ed., *Modern Chinese Literature in the May Fourth Era*. Cambridge, Mass., 1977, pp. 327-349; and E. Perry Link Jr., *Mandarin Ducks and Butterflies*. Berkeley 1981.

⓫ Lu Xun, whose views were given a monopoly of interpretation of the literary field of the May Fourth era in Mao's PRC, joined the critics by slandering entertainment literature in numerous essays and even in his influencial work *Zhongguo xiaoshuo shi lüe* (A Brief History of Chinese Fiction), which uses various derogatory terms for popular literature since late 19th century. The book was published in 1930 but written 1923-24 as university lectures. See Lu Xun,

commercialism of its writers was unbearable: instead of thinking of earning money, writers were to work unselfishly for the best of their own nation. At the same time, the critics were filled with indignation over the degenerate state in which they found Chinese urbanites. With their attack they hoped to prompt a literature that would revolutionize the Chinese masses. But in order to be influenced by the new literature, the masses needed to read it. This was the big problem.

Ever since the May Fourth movement and for almost two decades to come, the discourse on popular readings centered on the question of what the new literature should look like in order to live up to its ambitions and to be well received. Below the surface loomed the question of how to make the masses like the things they ought to like and read the things they ought to read. These debates certainly meant ruthless criticism of the writers who tried so hard (—this is what research into this period has very much concentrated on), while nothing was done in the way of analyzing the contemporary popular literature itself, it was seen as simply too backward. From a popular point of view, the critics seemed to be saying: if we, elite writers, are patriotic enough to write for the needs of the common people, then the common people should [be grateful enough to/in the name of equality] read these products to become patriotic as well.

One of the most caustic critics of the May Fourth writers and literary products was Qu Qiubai, Marxist theorist and one-time leader of the CCP. He was extremely critical of the writers' attempts to near the "popular", attempts which he considered totally inadequate and

---

Zhongguo xiaoshuo shi lüe. Beijing 1973. A critical appraisal of Lu Xun's views expressed in the book can be found in V.I. Semanov, Lu *Hsün and his predecessors*. White Plains 1980,pp. 56-74.

superficial.⓬ Qu was an exception among his contemporaries in that he did not allow his own value judgements or aesthetical preferences to blind him for the importance of the cultural forms that the common people actually supported. He could even visualize workers and peasants in the future being schooled to the point where they were able to write their own literary works.⓭ But he was too much May Fourth and too Marxist to allow cultural matters to develop in their own way－they were to be improved through political and social means, as soon as possible. The working class of his day could still not produce its own literature, it had to be done by "intellectuals who possessed a 'genuine' proletarian consciousness".⓮

This view reveals how elitistic, patronizing, and condescending the attitudes of even the leftist radicals remained: certain people ("intellectuals with proletarian consciousness") could see the needs of the common readers ("working class") and consciously choose to produce works to agitate on their behalf and to enlighten the readers, who apparently lack the visions of the writers and cannot see which things lie in their own interests.

As the politicization of Chinese cultural life deepened, it is interesting to note that radical May Fourth generation writers had something very much in common with the Nationalist government: their abhorrence of urban popular culture. While leftist writers and critics were busy arguing about how to "popularize" their literature

⓬ On Qu Qiubai's criticism and attitudes to popular culture, see Paul G.Pickowicz, *Marxist Literary Thought in China: The Influence of Ch'ü Ch'iu-pai.* Berkeley: University of California Press, 1981, especially pp. 147-167.

⓭ Pickowicz,pp. 150-53, and *Qu Qiubai wenji*, 4 vols., Beijing 1954, vol. 2,pp. 874, 885-6, 891-2.

⓮ Qu Qiubai wenji, vol 2, pp. 875-78. See also Pickowicz, p. 149.

(*dazhonghua*), the Nanjing government launched in 1934 the New Life Movement (*Xin shenghuo yundong*), with custom reform (*fengsu gaige*) programs not just to curb superstition and demolish temples,[15] but also, for example, to ban public dancing in Nanjing[16] and to ban popular music from being broadcasted.[17]

The debate on *puluo wenxue* and particularly Qu Qiubai's ideas appear to have had a certain impact on Mao Zedong's thoughts on how to develop culture. Mao came to express his views in his "Zai Yan'an wenyi zuotanhui shang de jianghua" (Talks at the Yan'an conference on literature and art) in 1942,[18] which was to have an unreasonably strong influence on mainland Chinese cultural life for decades. Unfortunately, Mao was much more rural than Qu Qiubai, and therefore could not understand Qu's ideas on the importance of modern urban popular culture. This may be one of the reasons why Mao talked very little about popular culture, and when he did, his ideas appear very conventional, old-fashioned and unsophisticated, with a dogmatic view of the urban "*xiao shimin*" as the only consumers of decadent urban popular culture, and a hierarchic view of "elementary literature and art" as needed by the broad masses (*jin ri zui guangda qunzhong suo zui xian xuyao de chuji*

---

[15] Chang-tai Hung, p. 160.

[16] A.C. Scott, *Literature and the Arts in Twentieth Century China*, London 1965, p. 53.

[17] See Andrew Jones, "Nie Er, Mass Music, and the Politics of Phonographic Realism", unpublished article presented at the Berkeley China Seminar 9 Nov., 1999, pp. 21. See also "Zhengli guangbo jiemu zhi banfa", *Yule zhoubao*, 11 July 1936, p. 531.

[18] For the text of this talk, see e.g. [Mao Zedong], *Mao Zedong lun wenyi*. Beijing 1992,pp. 34-68. For a annotated translation and a discussion, see Bonnie S. McDougall, *Mao Zedong's "Talks at the Yan'an Conference on Literature and Art": A Translation of the 1943 Text with Commentary*. AnnArbor 1980.

de wenyi).[19] On the other hand, someone that understood urban culture very well was of course Jiang Qing, Mao's wife. Perhaps it was her very understanding and experience of modern urban popular culture that made Mao entrust her with running PRC culture during the cultural revolution.

Zheng Zhenduo cemented the usage of the term *su wenxue* for non-elite literature in his work *Zhongguo su wenxue shi* (The history of Chinese vulgar/popular literature),[20] published by Shanghai shudian in 1938. What he wrote about were various traditional literary forms since antiquity. Inspired by egalitarian views on culture and critical of the narrow literati view on belles lettres, Zheng wanted to legitimize folk culture through serious scholarly work, and did it by proving that most literary forms, no matter how high their status is today, in actual fact have their roots deep in folk cultural forms. He contrasted *su wenxue* (synonymous with *pingmin wenxue*) with *ya wenxue* (elegant literature, i.e. elite literature), but equated *su wenxue* with what we now understand with folk literature: created among the common people [*dazhong*], anonymously and collectively created, and orally produced.[21] It was only gradually when more professional knowledge of the science of folklore was spread that this view was revised.[22] This means that in many writings for years to come su wenxue and folk literature were treated synonymously, and the view survives even today.

The scholarship of Zheng's work was seen as scientific proof of his

---

[19] *Mao Zedong lun wenyi*,pp. 51-52. McDougall, p. 72.

[20] The translation of this title is problematic: earlier the term "vulgar literature" was actually used in many contexts as the English equivalent of su wenxue. This is probably illustrative of the way many contemporaries understood the title.

[21] Zheng Du [Zheng Zhenduo], *Zhongguo su wenxue shi*, 2 vols. Taibei: Taiwan Shangwu yinshuguan, 1967, vol. 1, pp. 3-6.

[22] Chang-tai Hung claims, however, still in 1985 that the term *minjian wenxue* (folk literature) has never been defined by Chinese folklorists. Hung, p. 1.

ideas, which were by no means new in China.[23] Such as support was enthusiastically received by radical and leftist intellectuals, and came to have a profound, if not normative, influence on PRC literary historical writing all through the 1980s.[24] That Zheng's views also appealed to Nationalist scholars on Taiwan is shown by the fact that his book was printed by Taiwan Commercial Press in 1967, although under another name, Zheng Du.[25]

From a modern point of view, however, the problem with Zheng's ideas was that he did not bother about today's world. He requests appreciation of folk culture because it digests the world into wonderful source material for the literati to work on; this view accepts and perpetuates the hierarchies of traditional society, but it does of course remind the readers - intellectuals - of values other than their own. Still, folk culture is not so important for what it is, but for what others will

---

[23] The idea that all literature has its origins in folk literature can be traced to Xu Jiarui. He presented in his book *Zhonggu wenxue gailun* (An introduction to medieval literature) in 1924 the theory that in Medieval China, folk literature was much more important than aristocratic literature. This view was received with enthusiasm by Hu Shi and many others, and incorporated in much theoretical writing of the 1920s and 1930s. See Chang-tai Hung, pp. 7-8.

[24] Particularly appealing to leftists was the idea that folklore was collectively created and collectively consumed. It seems that this was later taken to prove that common people were prone to collective action, had homogeneous taste, and were anti-individualistic, all qualities that Mao Zedong, for example, cherished and needed for the feasibility of his theories.

[25] Neither *Zhongguo xiandai zuojia biming suoyin* (Index of modern Chinese writers' pseudonyms) (ed. by Sichuansheng zhongxin tushuguan weiyuanhui, 1980?), Chu Pao-liang, *Twentieth-Century Chinese Writers and Their Pen Names* (Boston 1977), nor Austin C.W. Shu, *Modern Chinese Authors: A List of Pseudonyms* (East Lansing 1969) recognizes Zheng Du as one of Zheng Zhenduo's pseudonyms. That seems to mean that this name was made up only to disguise the [leftist] identity of the author.

make it into. Zheng Zhenduo explains history. Therefore, the individualism of the modern man in modern popular culture cannot be accommodated within Zheng's theory, and therefore it could not explain the development current in his time.

The debates of the 1920s and 1930s focussed at times on certain terms to such an extent that they still seem to carry the stigma of history today. Terms such as puluo wenxue (proletarian literature), geming wenxue (revolutionary literature) and dazhong wenxue (literature of the masses) all seem to belong to this category. Puluo wenxue became anachronistic very soon, whereas *dazhong wenxue* was significantly employed by Mao Zedong, and the communist cultural establishment continued to use it even after 1949. Since at least 1949, popular book series like Dazhong wenyi congshu (Popular literature and art series), Dazhong wencong (Series for the masses), etc. were published. *Dazhong* was also used with the connotation "popularized": Dazhong yuwen congshu (Language series for the masses, 1950), *Dazhong yuwen xuexi shouce* (The masses' handbook for language study, 1957). That the term *dazhong* had definitely been appropriated by the communists is perhaps best shown by the fact that in the midst of the cultural revolution in 1969, a certain Dazhong wenyi bianjibu edited and published leftist books in even Hong Kong.

Terms with a leftist stamp became naturally taboo in the Nationalist and Taiwanese discourse, as can be seen on propaganda writings denouncing mainland Chinese cultural policy and proposing a "*xin de wenyi fuxing yundong*" (new cultural renaissance movement) with "*minzhong wenyi*" (culture and art of the masses of the people).[26]

---

[26] Ding Miao, Zhong Gong gong-nong-bing wenyi (The CCP's worker, peasant and soldier culture and art). Hong Kong: Yazhou chubanshe youxian gongsi, 1955, pp. 141-164.

The expression tongsu was first utilized in compound terms such as *tongsu yanyi* (popular history), *tongsu xiaoshuo* (popular novel) during the 19th century, and its connotation was "understood by the commoner", or "[written] in the colloquial language".[27] After the debates and communist policies involving *dazhong* in the 1930s and 1940s, it was also employed in the connotation "popularized". Since thc early PRC we consequently find books, pamphlets, and book series on various topics, and even publishing houses, called something with tongsu, e.g. *Tongsu shehui kexue jianghua* (Popular introduction to social sciences, 1949), *Tongsu baokan yu xiezuo tongsuhua wenti* (Popular newspapers and journals and the question of popularized writing, 1951),[28] *Tongsu xiao cidian* (Popular pocket dictionary, 1952), *Tongsu duwu chubanshe* (Popular readings publishing house, 1950s), and the usage has continued to these days: *Tongsu junshi zhishi* (Popular military knowledge, 1983), *Tongsu renkouxue* (Popular demographics, 1987).

For the longest time, Chinese dictionaries have not treated the word *tongsu* as a word, *ci*. Instead, it has apparently been understood as a phrase, "something that penetrates to the vulgar [layers of society]". The Taiwanese *Zhongwen da cidian* (1962-68) recognizes the modern word tongsu only in the compound *tongsu jiaoyu* (popular education), but still describes *su wenxue* as "*liuxing minjian zhi tongsu wenxue*". Much more surprisingly, the mainland encyclopaedia *Zhongguo da baike quanshu/Zhongguo wenxue* compiled in mainland China in the mid-1980s contains no mention of *tongsu wenxue* or anything else *tongsu.*[29]

---

[27] See Mao Dun, "Tongsuhua, dazhonghua yu Zhongguohua" as quoted in Wang Chungui and Liu Bingze, *Zhongguo tongsu xiaoshuo gailun*. Taiyuan: Beiyue wenyi chubanshe, 1993, p. 1.

[28] Gao Jianmin, *Tongsu baokan yu xiezuo tongsuhua wenti*. Guangzhou 1951.

[29] *Zhongguo da baike quanshu: Zhongguo wenxue*, 2 vols. Beijing 1986.

Neither does it contain the terms *su wenxue* or *dazhong wenxue*.[30] Quite remarkably, the work manages to negate not just the entire leftist debate heritage, but also most of 20th century popular literature by leaving out *yuanyang hudie pai, zhentan xiaoshuo* (detective novel) etc. It stands as a monument over its contributors' elitism that had survived the cultural revolution.

It is only in the 1990s that *tongsu* seems to have become a word. Since tongsu was never the object of any specific debate since the 1920s, it was apparently conceived of as neutral. This was an important qualification in the post-Mao period, when the value-laden words of the Maoist jargon were questioned. *Tongsu* seems therefore to have been adapted for the generalizing connotation of popular literature. It is possible that this was done in Hong Kong and/or Taiwan even earlier than the 1980s. In the PRC the term came into common use because of the very conspicuous "popular literature fever" of the early 1980s. This fever happened to coincide with the spread of postmodern ideas among PRC critics, ideas through which the understanding of popular culture is reconsidered and elaborated.[31] My experience is, though, that both in Taiwan and in the PRC, the postmodern ideas have seldom been received among traditional scholars of Chinese literature or history. Through the 1990s, therefore, the scholarly understanding of *tongsu wenxue* has, quite surprisingly, still largely been either the late 19th century approach of it being the equivalent of *baihua wenxue*, or the Zheng Zhenduo interpretation of *su wenxue* as all the historical literary forms that have had popular origins.

---

[30] The only compound with *dazhong* is the mention of *Dazhong wenyi congkan* (Masses' literature and art journal),a communist journal in Hong Kong 1948.

[31] For a general review of these theories, see e.g. Dominic Strinati, *An introduction to theories of popular culture*. London: Routledge, 1995.

If we try to distance ourselves from the details above, we can perhaps visualize the development of attitudes toward popular culture as a story of the reception of the egalitarian idea, a story of how people have mentally adapted to the idea of equality through a systematical exploration of its various tenets and practical consequences.

A hundred years ago, the idea of the popular as being something more than a lack of positive elite qualities was still new. When modern ideas were introduced in China, one of these was the egalitarian view that all humans have a similar basic value. Traceable to many thinkers of the past and finally concretely substantiated by Darwin, this view naturally met with much opposition everywhere, but also support. The academic/ scientific communities, certainly representative of the elite in each society, went out of their way trying to invalidate the claims to equality by measuring the sculls, noses and ears of criminals, beggars, "wilds" and others whom the scientists had a hard time seeing as their peers, in search of differences.㉜ When no significant physiological differences could be found, they turned to other than biological factors. Even if all humans had similar bodies, their groupings (read: states) and their cultures (read: cultural accomplishments) were obviously not equal, they seemed to say, clearly judging by their own set of values only. Therefore, with the help of scholars, ethnic groups/nation states started "discovering" their national cultural histories and heritages, and challenged each other in finding the most ancient origins to their own particular culture, as if the oldest or richest culture would win a game. The contest was often acted within the fields of folklore and archaeology. Thus even folk culture became an area of focus, of national significance.

㉜ Still in the 1980s, Chinese reference works described Finns as a people with "large, round heads".

When it was shown that each folk had an ancient and unique cultural tradition and could therefore be seen as equals,[33] it still remained puzzling that individuals within the same nation could show such striking differences in accomplishment: how could they be equals? This gave rise to social/behavioral sciences: the study of the behavior of individuals or groups was hoped to solve the question, and perhaps disprove the idea of equality in the end. These studies brought focus on social strata and revealed that all of them, even the poorest urbanites, did have a culture of their own, a culture which was not just a lack of elite culture or a degenerate version of their traditional folk culture,but an intricate system that corresponded to their specific needs. This is where the study of popular culture and popular literature fits in. —But why is it then almost non-existent, and why has it been so controversial?

I think we need to place popular culture/popular literature not just within this sketchy "historical" framework, but also to focus on the elite vs non-elite dichotomy as a struggle over influence in a modernizing society—in order to explain the controversiality of popular culture. Popular culture has never needed any preachers, integrated as it is in the economic, material and conceptual world of its producers and consumers. The economic development during this century has improved the living standards of a huge number of individuals and created in most countries a large middle class wealthy enough to consume plenty of popular cultural products. This has meant that the traditionally more prominent

[33] It is interesting to note that this conclusion coincides with the growth of international cooperation; we can see the forming ot the League of Nations and the United Nations etc. as a way in which people in the world have taken the consequences of the stated lack of fundamental differences between nations. The next step is the elimination of the nation as a significant unit—that is why we are today talking about globalization.

elite culture, which disseminates elite interests through elite values, has gradually been marginalized, while various more popular cultural forms have taken over. It is the proponents of the elite culture (often symbiotic with so called traditional culture) that have found their authority and legitimacy questioned, and who, consequently, have refused to accept the state of things and protested aggressively by slandering popular culture/literature.

臺灣與大陸對於兩岸關係定位之認知比較——「特殊國與國關係論」的意涵、反應與影響

潘錫堂*

摘　要

我們如果不能在兩岸進行政治性議題的談判以前，先將自己的定位做好，恐怕上了談判桌後再做就太遲了。

政府宣佈「特殊國與國關係論」的方向是正確的，但是時機稍嫌粗糙。事實上自一九九一年起我們陸續宣佈結束動員勘亂時期、修憲、建立國統綱領以來，我們對兩岸的地位一直採取比較保守的措辭。在一九九一年前後江丙坤對兩岸關係的各種解釋只是告訴中共：中華民國的國際人格並沒有因爲一九四九年我們喪失對大陸的有效管轄、

*　淡江大學中國大陸研究所副教授

也沒有因爲一九七一年我們退出聯合國而有任何的喪失，我們照樣擁有許多只承認台北卻不承認北京的邦交國。過去我們對兩關係的定位雖然很模糊，卻依然處處受到中共在國際外交上的打壓，尤其九八年張京育擔任陸委會主委時中共曾發表的三光政策：也就是把我們邦交國挖光、把國際政治生路堵光和未來在國際政治桌上的籌碼賭光。其後，就我與唐樹備兩次碰面的經驗，他告訴我大陸方面沒有這樣的想法，在國際上互搶邦交國是事實，所以最多只有一光政策，另外兩光是臺灣自己的推測。無論如何，國內非常在意中共在國際上打壓我們，九八年我們和東加王國的邦交因中共而斷、後來我國和馬其頓建交、再演變到金援科索伏和巴紐建交的生變引起國內對務實外交的檢討和質疑，也讓執政當局感到在一個中國的框架下，我們務實外交難以推展的困境。另一點就是我方也感受到汪道涵來訪之後，由政治性對話導入政治談判的腳步會加快，事實上辜振甫九八年十月訪問北京和上海與錢其琛和江澤民的對話難道沒有涉及政治議題嗎？可是我們卻稱之爲建設性對話。事實上在六月二十九日陸委會副主委吳安家在美國，正當陸士達二度提出中程協議，我方將其解讀爲事務性協商時，其實美方已有某種程度的不滿。事後吳在接受媒體訪問時曾說，九八年辜訪問大陸其實就是政治性的對話。所以我們如果不能在兩岸進行政治性議題的談判以前，先將自己的定位做好，恐怕上了談判桌後再做就太遲了。雖然這次時間選在汪道涵訪台前夕也許快了點，但是我們在正式談判前，對自己做出明確的政治定位確有必要。其實這次政治性宣示的重點不在於強調兩方都是國家，而是在強調兩方是對等的。中共常表示在涉及到一個中國的政治性談判時，一定不會以他們是中央，我們是地方的態度來對待。但是我們所要的不是只有談判桌上形式化的對等而已，我們要的是在談的形式、談的過程與談的可能的協商過程和結果都有對等的實質。我剛參加大陸的一個學術研討會回來，大陸的學者和官員都不解李如果要發表「特殊國與國關係論」，爲何不選在汪訪台之後，那時發表雖然也會有衝擊，但是不至於像現在這樣，連汪會不會來都不確定。以我的推測，大陸權衡這整件事情的利弊得失後的反應應該只會停留在一系列的文批上，還不至大肆武嚇，因爲中共還是會考慮美國的態度。雖然美國一再重申一個中國的政策，但是也堅持兩岸的問題要以和平的方式解決。同時中共也在觀察中華民國是否會做出較和緩的解釋，尤其是辜振甫的反應，像他們就說李先生以前好像常說錯話，但是這次好像有很多官員替他背書，所以中共這次很在意辜振甫的反應。如果我們此次沒有在大陸政策上做結構性的改變，而只做政治性的宣示，中共的反應應會漸趨和緩。至於汪道涵訪台應會採拖延暫緩的方式，二○○○年下半年，我想最後還是會成行，因爲汪道涵的訪台是目前兩岸深度政治性協商的唯一推手。

關鍵詞　特殊國與國關係論　事務性協商　三光政策　一個中國　務實外交

The Impact of the State-to-State Doctrine onCross-Strait Relations

Pan Hsi-tang

Abstract

I think that if we don't establish our position before we begin negotiation of political issues, it will be too late when we're already at the table.

I think that the government's announcement of the state-to-state doctrine is going in the right direction, but I think the timing could have been better. In fact, since 1991,we have one after another announced the end of the Period of Mobilization for the Suppression of the Communist Rebellion, amended the constitution and established the National Unification Guidelines. And we have been quite careful in choosing the wording regarding the status between the two sides. Around

1991,P.K.Chiang was essentially telling China through various measures: our independent and sovereign status has in no way been compromised neither by our loss of control over China in 1949 and nor by our having to pull out of the U.N. in 1971-there are still a number of countries that formally recognize Taipei and not Beijing. Although we had a very ambiguous way of defining our relationship to China, we continued to have to deal with pressure exerted by Beijing internationally-especially when Chang King-yu was chairman of the Mainland Affairs Council and China had its policy of stripping Taiwan on three fronts: wresting a number of our diplomatic allies, blockading all routes of political survival for Taiwan, and taking away any of our remaining international bargaining chips. Later, I spoke with Tang Shubei on two occasions and he said that isn't the way China was thinking. It's true, he said, that China had a policy of luring away Taiwanese diplomatic allies, but the other two policies existed only in the minds of Taiwanese. No matter what the actual policy was, Taiwanese people pay a lot of attention to any pressure exerted on Taiwan by China internationally, Last year, we severed ties with the Kingdom of Tonga because of China, and later we established ties with Macedonia, which evolved into suspicion of our pragmatic motives when it came to giving aid to Kosovo and establishing diplomatic relations with Papua New Guinea. I think that if we don't establish our position before we begin negotiation of political issues, it will be too late when we're already at the table. Perhaps this announcement was made too soon before Wang Daohan's visit, but it is necessary that we spell out our political position clearly before formal negotiations. In reality, the stress of the recent announcement isn't on the fact that both parties are countries, but that they are equal. Now it isn't even certain that Wang will come. I would guess that China's reaction after all will be U.S. continues to reiterate its adherence to the one-China policy, it also persists in wanting to find a peaceful resolution to cross-strait problems. At the same time, China will also be looking to see if we offer a toned-down explanation-Koo Chen-fu's reaction will be particularly important. In the past, President Lee seemed to make mistakes once a while, but many officials now appear to be offering their endorsements… so China will pay special attention to Koo Chen-fu's reaction. If we don't make structural changes to our China policy-if we only make political pronouncements-then the Chinese reaction will be attenuated. Wang Daohan may delay or postpone his autumn visit, but I think the will come in the end since a visit from him is the only way for both sides to deepen the level of cross-strait negotiations.

前言

李總統登輝先生於一九九九年七月九日接受「德國之聲」專訪時，提及兩岸關係的定位是「特殊的國與國關係」❶，隨後海基會董事長辜振甫亦論及海協會會長汪道涵訪台係「國與國的會談」❷，引發中共各界強烈批判為「製造兩個中國」、「破壞兩岸關係」、「兩會交流、對話之基礎已不復存在」❸，形成氣氛上已造成兩岸關係的緊張。本文要探討的是究竟李總統「特殊的國與國關係」的提法有何理論依據？其眞實意涵係維持追求統一目標不變抑或恰恰相反？中共的反應與因應策略如何？對於美「中」台關係有何影響？在在值得進一步研究。

一、「特殊國與國關係論」的意涵

首先是李總統一九九九年七月九日講話之理論依據，係在於德國於二次大戰後分裂以來，東西德各擁國際空間，到良性互動，迄於重歸德國再統一的過程所型塑的「德國經驗」，這在傳統國際法與主權、國家理論上形成一種新的型態與詮釋，易言之，一個原先主權獨立的國家因國際勢力介入的國際政治背景因素，使得一分為

❶ 台北《中國時報》，第一版，1999年7月10日。

❷ 台北《聯合報》，第二版，1999年7月10日。

❸ 海外版《人民日報》，第一版，1999年7月10日。

二，這兩個政治實體各在國際強權之支持下，各擁完整國際人格與國際法人地位，不僅各以主權獨立國家呈現於國際社會，各有獨立自主的內政、外交、國防，尙且各擁邦交國、型塑對兩德之雙重承認，而且還以「平行參與」方式同時參與國際組織包括聯合國在內，惟兩德處於分裂分治各擁國際空間之狀態，也由對立到互動，卻絲毫沒有影響兩德追求德國再統一的最後目標，而德國終究也完成其夢寐以求的國家統一。❹

準此以觀，兩德統一過程型塑二次大戰後對國家與主權理論之衝擊的所謂「分裂國家模式」或「分裂主權說」，不僅造成德國分裂後主權由東西德各享或共享，治權分屬，甚至還型塑國際上對兩德之雙重承認，及兩德參與國際組織之「平行參與模式」，在在均爲二次戰後分裂國家由尙未統一、各擁國際空間，到良性互動，邁向最終統一，樹立了極佳的經驗典範❺。令人印象深刻的是，當年西德布朗德政府先有政策，然後再去修憲，提出著名的「屋頂理論」。我們認爲它爲分裂國家邁向最終統一過程提供了良好的借鏡，即是統一前彼此各自擁有主權，對等分治，可以良性互動、雙重承認與平行參與，透過在國際上之相互扶持，消弭分歧與降低敵意甚至共建互信機制，爲國家之統一攜手並進。

然而中共植基傳統國際法及傳統之國家與主權理論，堅持主權不容分裂、主權與領土完整不可分割，國家當然不能分裂，認爲不

---

❹ 潘錫堂：〈從兩德經驗看李總統講話之意涵〉，台北《中華日報》，第四版，1999年7月10日。

❺ 包宗和等主編：《爭辯中的兩岸關係理論》(台北：五南圖書公司，1999年3月)，頁77。

能接受「分裂國家模式」或「分裂主權說」，在中共眼中，迴避了兩岸分立分治、主權與治權有所區隔之現實，拒斥了中華民國所倡議之較爲含蓄與中性之兩岸關係定位的提法，舉凡歷來諸如「一國兩府」、「以一個中國爲指向的階段性兩個中國」、「一個中國，兩個對等政治實體」、「一個分治中的中國」、「主權共享，治權分屬」等等提法皆遭中共解讀爲「製造兩個中國」、「製造分裂」、「明統暗獨」、「爲『獨台』包裝」、「悖離『一個中國』原則」。由此可見，中共基於一九四九年取得對大陸地區之有效管轄，加上一九七一年十月在聯合國「中國代表權」之爭上取得勝利後，自認對原中華民國已享有「主權全面繼承」，堅持國際社會已承認中華人民共和國是中國政府的唯一合法代表，漠視中華民國仍存在並擁有二十多國之承認，拒斥雙重承認與平行參與，甚至透過片面界定之「一個中國」原則遂行對台外交圍堵，意圖抹殺中華民國之國際人格，以利於實現「和平統一、一國兩制」的目標。

中華民國領導高層有感於將兩岸關係定位予以模糊化，中共既不接受而對台遂行圍堵仍未鬆緩，反而造成自己本身國際地位定位之混沌不明，在推動務實外交拓展國際空間時飽受國際與國內各界之質疑，在經過深入沙盤推演後，認爲反正如何含蓄模糊地詮釋臺灣在兩岸關係的定位，中共都不會接受反而自陷外交困境無法突破，再者將自我定位明確化亦有利於未來不可迴避要進行兩岸政治談判時，爭取提前將自我定位明確化以利政治談判之優勢地位與籌碼。由是之故，李總統一九九九年七月九日講話根本不會如當年西德布朗德政府去進行修憲，我們無意改變現行大陸政策與台海穩定情勢，既不可能進行修憲來反映「國與國關係」，亦不會修改國統綱領與兩岸人民關係條例，一切均維持不變，中華民國在意的僅是本身定位必須明確化以確保追求統一前必須相互尊重與對等分治相待，不能再坐視中共漠視中華民國政治地位之情事。

二、中共的反應

李登輝總統自一九九九年七月九日提出「特殊國與國關係論」以來，其後續效應可分三個階段：一爲中共文批階段，二爲中共透過美國對台施壓階段，三爲中共武嚇、文批及國際孤立之齊頭並進階段，目前顯然已進入第三階段。究竟現階段中共因應「特殊國與國關係論」之策略何在？如何迫使臺灣放棄「特殊國與國關係論」？「特殊國與國關係論」之「美國因素」何在？臺灣之因應對策爲何？在在值得深入探究。

首先是「特殊國與國關係論」提出後，獲得臺灣官方正式背書，其中以七月十二日陸委會之說明最具代表性❻，大陸方面乃展開黨政軍與媒體之大加撻伐，諸如❼：中共兩台辦發言人所謂「拒絕統一、蓄意分裂，不得人心，注定失敗」；中共外交部發言人所謂「中國統一是大勢所趨，李登輝必須懸崖勒馬」，新華社亦發表評論員文章，評李登輝的分裂言論，尤其海協會常務副會長唐樹備強調「臺灣當局應立即停止對兩岸關係的破壞」，汪道涵會長對辜振甫董事長有關兩岸會談是「國與國會談」提法深表驚訝，是爲「文批」階

❻ 台北《中國時報》，第一～二版，1999年7月13日。

❼ 海外版《人民日報》，第一～二版，1999年7月10日～13日。

段；迄柯林頓、江澤民熱線電話起，美方主動宣示「一個中國」政策，惟在國會質疑下，為扭轉「傾『中』壓台」刻板印象，行政部門乃派遣亞太事務助卿陸士達與美國在台協會理事主席卜睿哲分赴兩岸進行「預防外交」，傳達柯林頓「一中、兩岸對話、和平解決」之所謂兩岸政策「三大支柱」的底線，並呼籲兩岸自制，是為中共透過美對台施壓的階段。然而北京透過華府對台施壓，要求放棄「兩國論」並重返「一個中國」原則，本以為可以奏效，惟自七月三十日、三十一日美方發布對台五億五千萬美元軍售案❽，復以美方不僅未如北京所願達成對台施壓效果，尚一再強調維持台海穩定係美一貫政策，致使北京懷疑華府是台北「特殊國與國關係論」之背後奧援，為避免美方強力介入台海情勢，中共新華社宣稱八月二日成功試射東風卅一型遠程飛彈，再加上中共因不滿辜振甫董事長七月三十日「談話稿」❾，其中央軍委會已下令福建沿海軍隊進入二級戰備。由此顯示，當前兩岸已進入武嚇、文批兼國際孤立之多重階段。

據一九九九年夏中共北戴河會議之決議，現階段中共因應「特殊國與國關係論」之策略包括：㈠繼續觀察、保持政軍壓力：即「一批、二看、三準備」；㈡主觀上要制定兩岸統一時間表，但客觀操作上卻很難；㈢認定「特殊國與國關係論」得到美暗中支持；㈣加強對台戰備：共軍高度戒備，準備一系列軍事演習；㈤重新定位「中」

---

❽ 台北《聯合報》，第一～三版，1999年7月31日、8月1日。

❾ 潘錫堂：〈評海協會拒收海基會函稿之意涵〉，台北《中華日報》，第三版，1999年8月2日。

美關係為「戰略性競爭關係」：即「鬥而不破」。準此，中共如何迫使臺灣放棄「特殊國與國關係論」，應該有五個途徑與方法：㈠伺機與美恢復有關中共加入WTO之談判，俾能儘速加入WTO並藉其盟友阻撓臺灣入會；㈡繼拒絕接受海基會來函與辜振甫「談話稿」後，全力批駁陸委會八月一日「說帖」中之「一個中國，各自表述」，要求確認「一個中國」之共識❿；㈢加緊對臺灣國際空間之打壓，包括入聯、參與國際組織及維持邦交國數量；㈣形式上關閉兩會對話之門，實則不輕易取消汪道涵訪台以為籌碼，但無限期延宕汪道涵訪台時程，以迫使臺灣在當前或明年新總統上台後調整「特殊國與國關係論」；㈤加緊對台正面之軍事施壓。

然而實際上，中共之逼迫策略能否奏效？值得商榷。理由是㈠中共要阻撓臺灣先中共而入會，雖可奏效，但要完全阻絕臺灣入會，係違反WTO「四大支柱」之共識，應不會成功；㈡只要臺灣持續詮釋「一個中國，各自表述」係「特殊國與國關係論」植基之兩岸統一前的內涵，應可逐漸獲得華府之理解或諒解，符合美方「『一個中國』內涵應由雙方共同去界定」之認知，使得中共在經歷一段時期之強烈反應後，也會無可奈何；㈢會加劇兩岸外交競逐之態勢，而台北未必會就範，北京也未必能獲利；㈣預期臺灣明年總統大選，無論誰當選，「特殊國與國關係論」都不可能收回，至多只會低調處理。只要臺灣不修憲、不修法，持續強化「一個中國，各自表述」訴求應為兩岸政治對話與談判之基礎，則研判汪道涵在二○○○年五月二十日新總統就任以後還是會訪台，否則中共會喪失對台「促

---

❿ 香港《文匯報》，第二版，1999年8月2日。

談」之主要切入點；㈤中共對台軍事增壓會持續到二○○○年總統大選後，但應不至於昇高為武力犯台，或重演九六年對台三波軍事試射飛彈。

三、中共的因應策略

中共全國台辦主任會議於一九九九年八月十八日在北京就如何因應臺灣的「特殊國與國關係論」做成決議，確定將兩岸政治與經濟分開處理，繼續針對臺灣當局進行鬥爭，但不以政治分歧影響兩岸的經濟合作⓫。此種政經分離的對台兩手策略，將對兩岸關係產生深遠的影響。

值得注意的是，此項中共全國台辦主任會議，係李總統提出「特殊國與國關係論」以來，中共對台系統的一次「統一口徑」會議。

本次中共全國台辦主任會議之重申繼續貫徹一九九八年的工作部署，意味著在歷經九九年中共北戴河會議「以武維和，以武逼統」的爭議而獲致「一批、二看、三準備」(繼續觀察、保持政治軍事壓力)之決議後，明確訂定「以戰制獨，以談促和」的策略，並對臺灣目前這種「似獨非獨」，還之以「似戰非戰」。

尤有進者，台辦會議表明，要繼續推動兩岸人員往來與經濟文化等各方面的交流，更證明中共因應「特殊國與國關係論」的策略仍採一貫的「和戰兩手」，一手強硬的對臺灣當局進行大加撻伐與政治鬥爭，一手鬆軟的以經濟合作爭取臺灣民心與台商的支持。

⓫ 北京《人民日報》，第二版，1999年8月19日。

由此可見，中共一貫擅於運用「軟要不改既定原則立場，硬要不致造成雙方破裂」的軟硬兼施之和戰兩手策略，其中鬆軟的一手係意圖將對台經貿合作提高到「祖國統一」的戰略層次，二來拉住台資並吸引臺灣大財團赴大陸投資，從而使臺灣對大陸經濟產生高度依附，俾使對台經貿合作對促進「和平統一」發揮關鍵性作用。中共總書記江澤民嘗言，多做臺灣大中型企業家的工作，使兩岸經濟「你中有我，我中有你」，在經濟上將臺灣拖住，以遂其「以台引台，以台促台」的目的⑫。

準此以觀，中共原先和平解決「臺灣問題」之「寄希望於臺灣當局，更寄希望於臺灣人民」之所謂「兩個寄希望」，在李總統提出「特殊國與國關係論」及其後臺灣當局不願放棄「特殊國與國關係論」之後，只好全面動員涉台人員及文宣系統予以強力批判，意圖迫使台北就範而最終可能難以如願；在無法寄希望於臺灣當局之情況下，也只好寄希望於臺灣人民，傾全力強化對台民間交流以拉住臺灣，而兩岸經貿交流與台商投資大陸則扮演舉足輕重的角色。

例如：因「特殊國與國關係論」的提出，先是取消而又恢復之中共國台辦召開的台商協會負責人會談，出面會見的中共國台辦副主任李炳才八月二日即表示，不管兩岸關係發生什麼情況，中共都繼續貫徹執行鼓勵台胞赴大陸投資的相關政策，認眞執行「臺灣同胞投資保護法」和即將頒布的實施條例，不斷改善投資環境，確實依法維護台商和其他台胞的一切正當權益⑬。中共外經貿部長石廣

⑫ 潘錫堂《中共外交與兩岸關係》(台北：五南圖書公司，1997年4月)，頁317～325。

⑬ 海外版《人民日報》，第三版，1999年8月3日。

生於八月五日更進而強調，兩岸經貿合作符合歷史潮流，符合兩岸人民利益，因此絕不允許兩岸經貿合作受「特殊國與國關係論」的衝擊而倒退⓮。再者，同年八月十八日閉幕的前述台辦主任會議也決議，將繼續鼓勵台商投資，維護台商的正當權益⓯。

儘管中共不樂見兩岸經貿合作與台商投資受到「特殊國與國關係論」的影響，惟近來兩岸關係因中共文攻武嚇而緊張，原本熱中登陸投資的台商也逐漸降溫，已知目前有幾個大型投資計劃都已取消，兩岸貿易有衰退跡象，值得密切關注。

四、「特殊國與國關係論」的美國因素

美國在台協會理事主席卜睿哲於訪台兩天期間，密集會晤了包括李登輝總統在內的中華民國高層首長，並與中華民國外交部、陸委會首長舉行工作總結會議，傳達美方立場並聽取中華民國對「特殊國與國關係論」的完整說明，於一九九九年人七月二十五日會晤海基會辜振甫董事長交換對汪道涵訪台及兩岸對話等問題，隨即赴機場發表美方立場的離華聲明後，結束台北之理解「特殊國與國關係論」之旅⓰。

無獨有偶的是，美國亞太助卿陸士達與白宮國安會亞太資深主任李侃如亦於同時銜命前往北京，與包括中共外長唐家璇在內的外

⓮ 香港《文匯報》，第二版，1999年8月6日。

⓯ 北京《人民日報》，第二版，1999年8月19日。

⓰ 台北《中國時報》，第一版、二版，1999年7月25日、26日。

交部官員作了一系列「建設性會談」，其中包括了「臺灣問題」的發展⑰。隨即陸、李飛往新加坡與美國國務卿歐布萊特會合，爲七月二十五日中午展開自北約轟炸中共大使館事件以來美「中」首度的外長級會談鋪路。究竟美方在「特殊國與國關係論」引發兩岸緊張情勢中扮演何種角色？美方分派特使前往兩岸將可發揮何種功能？此舉對美「中」台三邊關係會產生什麼影響？在在均值得高度關注。

在卜睿哲來訪前，雖然美方行政、立法部門甚至輿論對「特殊國與國關係論」評價不一，惟華府已感受到北京之強烈反應，大陸內部「不惜軍事威懾」之聲甚囂塵上，華府實在不願一九九六年台海危機重演迫使美方必須做出政治外交與軍事上之適當反應，這在業已跌入谷底的美「中」關係現狀而言，是極不樂見的事。復以二〇〇〇年是美國總統大選年，民意與國會之看法不容忽視，一度暫緩對台軍售及延緩軍事人員赴台交流之舉，均爲美國國會（尤其是眾議院）視爲華府傾斜北京而向台北施壓之明證。是以白宮與國務院有必要派遣特使分赴北京與台北斡旋，發揮「預防性外交」作用，一則向北京保證恪遵「一個中國」政策，袪除北京對華府從中暗助台北「特殊國與國關係論」之疑慮，同時呼籲中共和平解決兩岸分歧包括透過對話協商，切勿輕忽美國根據相關法律（指「臺灣關係法」）維護台海穩定安全的決心；再則亦向台北清楚傳達美國對兩岸政策之四項基本要素（「一個中國」政策、履行「臺灣關係法」有關安全與軍售之承諾、支持兩岸對話、和平解決歧異），惟在深入瞭解台北「特殊國

---

⑰ 北京《人民日報》，第一版，1999年7月24日。

與國關係論」僅限於口頭政治宣示而不致於觸及修憲修法之後續行動層次，仍期望台北在回覆海協會及辜振甫之說明上能體現大陸政策不變及邀訪汪道涵之誠意，用以紓緩緊張氣氛並製造中共有台階可下之契機。

準此以觀，美方此次在「特殊國與國關係論」風波發揮了某些穿梭外交之效益。華府宣示其兩岸政策之「三大支柱」，既是提醒北京自我克制、避免因誤判而反應失控，又敦促台北做出周延完整的澄清，避免刺激北京而使汪道涵訪台之兩岸對話大門關閉。由是之故，筆者有理由深信，中共在經過一段時間的「文攻」及對臺灣當局「聽其言、觀其行」後，發現臺灣方面側重於對本身政治地位之「對等分治」與「平等談判」要求之凸顯，而並非在具體行動上要把事實上之「獨台」定型化與恆久化，則短期內中共即使不會在文宣上減緩對臺灣「特殊國與國關係論」批判之力道與強度，惟在因應對策上不僅不會採軍事手段避免重蹈九六年美方做出軍事上必要反應之覆轍，尚會明確回應美國「和平解決、兩岸對話」之倡議，俾能積極爭取自北約轟炸中共大使館事件以來雙方關係低迷之改善良機。筆者研判，北京發現台北已很難祛除辜汪台北會晤之兩會政治性對話，才會急於推出「特殊國與國關係論」作政治對話前之自我「對等」定位，因此在世紀之交，為把「臺灣問題」之解決導入「促談（政治對話與談判）、促通、促統」之框架，汪道涵訪台，乃勢在必行，否則將淪喪催促兩岸政治對話與談判之主要切入點，這對中共而言是不利的。惟在具體操作上，北京會以汪道涵訪台做為籌碼，適時、適度作時程上之展延，一來逼台北就範重返「特殊國與國關係論」提出前之原點，並且力促由兩會深入政治性對話儘速導入政治性談判之程序性商談階段，二來亦可據此向美方討價還價，側重華府切勿把台北納入TMD之考量。

儘管北京推延汪道涵訪台之合理時機，應在二〇〇〇年臺灣總統大選後，尤其是新任總統五月二十日就職後其大陸政策框架明確化。然而中華民國之大陸政策既不因「特殊國與國關係論」而有變，當然也不存在有因美方施壓或因中共逼迫而重返原點之可能。尤有甚者，雖「特殊國與國關係論」提供了美「中」加強對話、俾能恢復雙方有關中共加入WTO談判甚至改善關係之途徑或契機，美「中」關係之諸多障礙包括TMD、人權、間諜案等問題，仍不易透過近來彼此之許多對話來逐一解決，即便有新加坡之美「中」外長級會談亦是如此。

總之，臺灣「特殊國與國關係論」之提出，其遠因係受到九八年柯林頓上海宣示對台「三不」之影響，使得自此華府之兩岸政策向北京一邊傾斜且壓縮臺灣之國際空間⓲，近則受到華府一九九九年六月底重新詮釋「中程協議」之影響，使得台北已強烈感受到兩岸政治對話與談判之壓力，惟此種華府無意介入兩岸談判之促談壓力，並非台北獨有，北京也有，只不過台北較欠缺「抗壓」能力。尤其美國爲避免捲入類似九六年台海危機，以軍售力挺臺灣並提醒北京不可造次，但仍高度期盼兩岸復談，使得促談壓力如影隨形，面臨國會「傾『中』壓台」之指責，美行政部門既無法勉強臺灣放棄「特殊國與國關係論」，則面對臺灣委婉提出之「一個中國，各

⓲ 潘錫堂：〈從柯江北京會談到辜汪會晤論兩岸復談策略〉，「第二屆孫中山與現代中國學術研討會」（台北：國父紀念館，1999年1月5日～7日），頁2～3。

自表述」解釋，似乎是華府尚難明確反對之底線。

五、「特殊國與國關係論」對美「中」台關係的影響

柯江紐西蘭高峰會談於九月十一日在奧克蘭舉行，柯林頓總統重申美國之兩岸政策「三大支柱」不變，江澤民雖強調對台政策仍維持「和平統一、一國兩制」立場，惟一旦有外國介入或獨立則不承諾放棄用武，雙方並達成重開中共加入WTO談判之共識⑲。時值美「中」關係陷入低潮，兩岸關係因「特殊國與國關係論」緊繃之際，此項自九八年六月柯林頓訪問大陸以來首次召開的APEC會外柯江會談所凸顯之意涵與影響，深值高度的關注。

僅管華府規劃柯林頓參與美「中」高峰會談，具有降低兩岸的緊張關係、尋求恢復美「中」雙邊關係的動力，及恢復與北京之WTO入會談判等三項目的，惟在華府的考量中，紓緩兩岸關係及恢復美「中」之北京入會談判等二者均有其時間上之急迫感與緊急性，若不能在近期內一方面要安撫北京已被撩撥之激情，一方面透過口頭宣示一再重申「一個中國」政策，袪除北京懷有對華府「暗助」或「默許」臺灣提出「特殊國與國關係論」之疑慮，再方面立足美台相關法律強調美方有售台防禦性武器及期盼中共與臺灣對話、反對動武之明確「戰略」立場，則北京有可能因誤判華府之反應而動手「懲罰」臺灣，此為美方所不樂見之結果，亦悖離美國的國家利益。

---

⑲ 臺北《聯合報》，第一～三版，1999年9月12日。

當然，華府亦察知，北京一直在試探一旦「有必要」必須使用軍事手段「懲罰」臺灣則何時動手？以那個目標切入？動手至何種程度？方不致重挑美方採取軍事反應予以介入？迄今，美方在柯江會之態度，仍是「中共一旦對台動武，將會有嚴重後果」，凸顯美方「戰略明確，戰術（策略）模糊」之立場，易言之，柯江會後北京仍拿捏不出華府能容忍北京對台「動手」之底線，此爲華府處理因「特殊國與國關係論」引發中共激烈反應之技巧性手法。準此，在柯江會前，僅管江澤民提出「汪訪台二條件說」希望臺灣收回「特殊國與國關係論」，復以會前美方並未對台具體「保證」不會提出「第四不」，然而可能經過自一九九九年七月以來臺灣方面不斷地闡述「特殊國與國關係論」的眞實意涵，美方可能已理解該項宣示雖不爲中共所接受，但可作爲兩岸對話之實質議題，因此柯林頓在高峰會中雖應景式的稍提「特殊國與國關係論」使美「中」關係之處理有所困難，但並不認爲有宣示對台「第四不」之必要，反而認爲重申「一個中國」政策、兩岸對話、和平解決等所謂兩岸政策之「三大支柱」即已足夠涵蓋。

與消弭兩岸緊張關係同樣具可操作性的，在美方看來還有恢復美「中」之北京入會談判。本來北京遲不恢復入會談判，用以作爲迫使美方在北約轟炸大使館事件上賠償道歉讓步⑳，如今該事件之處理已有重大進展，如果美「中」有關北京入會談判再不迅速恢復，則損及的不僅有中共，還包括美國的利益，因此，恢復中共入會談

---

⑳ 潘錫堂：〈民族主義——一刀兩刃〉，《國魂月刊》第645期，（1999年8月號），頁19～21。

判議題已不再是北京先前考量中之籌碼，反而對美「中」雙方而言是「雙贏」的結果，此亦足說明一九九九年九月五日美國亞太事務副助卿謝淑麗公開表示，中共應現在立即善待臺灣，而非打壓臺灣，而一再提出諸如「一國兩制」之未來統一遠景，對臺灣人民是沒有誘因的，即可顯露出美方在柯江會談中不會對中共做出太大讓步以及柯江會談不會有太讓臺灣意外之結果㉑。

然而值得注意的是，柯江會談達成之美「中」重開中共入會談判之共識，是否眞的讓低迷已久之美「中」關係有所改善？更是一個頗值省思的課題。美「中」自從一九九七年十月柯江華府會談建構「建設性戰略夥伴關係」以來，雙方關係朝著消弭分歧與增進合作的大方向邁進，迄九八年六月柯江北京會談柯林頓在上海宣示對台「三不」，美「中」台三邊關係已明顯朝北京傾斜而不利於台北，幸好柯林頓宣示的對台「三不」所具有對臺灣壓縮國際空間之效應並未發酵，九八年十一月江澤民訪日，小淵首相只口頭宣示對台「一不」，即可見一斑㉒。惟自九八年八月起，中共祭出對台「三光策略」（邦交國數量、國際政治生路、政治談判籌碼之挖光），意圖藉由柯林頓「三不」宣示進而窄化臺灣國際空間。惟適值此時美「中」關係急劇惡化，人權問題、西藏問題、核子擴散問題、間諜案、貿易逆差、TMD、加入WTO等問題盤根錯節，再加上九九年之北約轟炸使館事件、考克斯報告，益使美「中」關係雪上加霜，正好七月

㉑ 台北《中國時報》，第二版，1999年9月6日。

㉒ 潘錫堂：〈辜汪會晤後兩岸恢復協商策略之比較〉，第二屆「國軍軍事社會科學學術研討會」（台北：劍潭，1999年5月27日），頁34～37。

初碰上了「特殊國與國關係論」效應，北京期盼透過華府迂迴向台北施壓以收回「特殊國與國關係論」，結果是台北不僅沒收回「特殊國與國關係論」、更進而將「特殊國與國關係論」意涵打入國際社會（包括「入聯」提案訴求）及列入國民黨十五全二次大會決議文，尤令北京不滿的是，華府還在「特殊國與國關係論」效應沸騰之際仍執著宣布對台軍售與不排除提供臺灣TMD，可見華府欲透過柯江會藉由恢復中共入會談判來修補進而拉抬美「中」關係，惟實際成效可能不彰，美「中」關係之本質雖有「戰略夥伴關係」之框架，惟其內涵仍多分歧與糾葛，夾雜著衝突與合作之辯證型態關係。

至於柯江會談對兩岸關係有何影響？㈠北京在拿捏不準華府對北京動手懲罰臺灣之容忍底線，仍不致輕啓對台動武，惟近期一段時間應會持續舉行共軍聯合作戰演習以示中共之不滿反應，㈡江澤民雖提「汪訪台二條件說」，其實仍在藉機對美作態故示「有與臺灣對話之誠意」，實則意圖迫使臺灣「特殊國與國關係論」改弦更張，或正在等待臺灣給予「下台階」，臺灣只要不斷重申隨時歡迎汪道涵訪台及不將「特殊國與國關係論」入憲與修法之立場，則中共自會在二○○○年臺灣新總統就任而大陸政策明朗化之後選擇適當時機作爲推動汪道涵訪台「促談」之切入點；㈢兩岸關係之「美國因素」持續加重，柯江會後北京對華府的兩岸政策保持「勿須擔心但又不太放心」之模糊，對於「特殊國與國關係論」效應衝擊下之兩岸關係將逐漸產生紓緩與回穩之功能。

尤有進者，臺灣之因應對策，持續強調歡迎汪道涵訪台進行對話，應是制衡中共「文攻武嚇」之最佳訴求，惟臺灣尚不僅止於此，下一階段採取推動國際宣傳及新的入聯合國案以爲因應。

惟聯合國總務委員會卻於一九九九年九月十五日第七度封殺臺灣友邦所提中華民國參與聯合國案，美、英、法、俄、中共等五個常任理事國聯手發言反對提案，尤其美國一改過去六年不介入立場，首度表態支持「一個中國」政策，不支持臺灣參與聯合國㉓。此舉是否意味「特殊國與國關係論」效應之兩岸外交攻防將漸趨激烈？臺灣如何有效因應？均值得高度關注。

自從「特殊國與國關係論」提出以來，中共強烈反應，運用文攻、揚言武嚇，並迂迴假手華府向台北施壓，意圖迫使台北收回「特殊國與國關係論」。在台北堅持「特殊國與國關係論」在於陳述兩岸對等分治之客觀現實，根本毫無收回之必要，更何況強調不入憲與不修法之前提下，台北的大陸政策不變，同時重申歡迎大陸海協會會長汪道涵訪台之一貫立場，使得北京對台北施加文攻武嚇之力道與正當性漸趨弱化，是以北京要遏止臺灣「特殊國與國關係論」國際效應之發酵，乃寄望於一九九九年九月十一日的柯江紐西蘭會談與同年九月十五日的聯大總務委員會審議臺灣入聯提案之攻防上。

首先是臺灣的十二個友邦國常駐聯合國大使，於九九年八月中旬聯名提出中華民國參與聯合國案，此爲臺灣自一九九三年以來連續第七年由友邦提案推動參與聯合國。由於九九年提案適值李登輝總統宣示「特殊國與國關係論」餘波盪漾之際，此舉具有何種意義，頗值高度關注。

自李總統七月九日宣示「特殊的國與國關係」政治定位以來，

㉓ 台北《中國時報》，第一～二版，1999年9月16日。

北京預期台北下一波訴求手段爲國際宣傳，而且除鎖定美國，台北宣示「特殊國與國關係論」基調之主戰場爲聯合國。同時也意識到在國際上封殺「特殊國與國關係論」的迫切性，已將聯合國體系視爲壓制台北「特殊國與國關係論」的首要戰場，展開最強烈的反制動作。

準此，臺灣改變往年在聯合國大會開議前，由友邦提出中華民國參與聯合國案之作法，由於預期北京將施重壓，臺灣極其謹愼地促使友邦將提案時間破例後延，即期盼能在兩岸攻防戰中凸顯「對等分治」地位之國際訴求。易言之，過去六年臺灣推動參與聯合國一向立足於「一個中國，兩個政治實體」之基調；惟九九年提案在兩岸定位上，則更強調「對等」及兩岸由兩個「不同且分離的」政府統治，甚至首度並列兩岸國名，稱呼中共爲「中華人民共和國在大陸」，有別於「中華民國在臺灣」，不僅少提「一個中國」，也已不再強調「一個中國下的兩個對等政治實體」，從而充分體現「特殊國與國關係論」之精神。

總體看來，臺灣九九年的提案並非意圖向中共挑戰，而是運用符合兩岸客觀事實之現狀，一面爭取中華民國「對等存在」之權利，一面開創兩岸良性互動與平等談判之雙贏新機。由是之故，在九九年提案核心部分「決議草案」中，也一改過去二年要求「撤銷」二七五八號決議文中關於將中華民國排除在聯合國之外的部分決議，而要求在九月中旬開議的五十四屆聯大設立工作小組，審視中華民國臺灣被排除在聯合國體系外的特殊情況，並作出適當建議，尋求有效解決。

値得注意的是，九九年提案的第二部分「解釋性備忘錄」中陳述近五十年來兩岸分別由「不同且分離」的政府所統治，而不再提九八年訴求的「兩個政府一直統治著中國的兩個部分」或九七年強調的「中國境內同時存在著兩個政府」。尤有甚著，九九年「解釋性備忘錄」著重「在臺灣的中華民國與在大陸的中華人民共和國於兩岸共存，互不受對方統治」之說理性，並針對九八年、九七年所強調之傳統國際法中「政府繼承」的概念不適用於中華民國的提法，略而不提。

由於二○○○年係美國總統大選年，復以民主黨的柯林頓政府爲回應美參眾兩院要求，進而扭轉行政部門過於傾「中」壓台之刻板印象，柯林頓總統在柯江會談中，僅重申「一個中國」政策，不但沒有宣示對台「第四不」，連九八年六月在上海表述的對台「三不」均未提及；尤有進者，柯林頓政府不但未應江澤民之請而同意中止對台軍售，同時還呼籲北京勿對台訴諸武力，否則將有「嚴重的後果」。華府的想法在於向北京重申「一個中國」的承諾，用以祛除北京的疑慮，同時以「兩面光」的手法，一面勸阻北京切勿反應過度對台「動手」，避免讓華府不得不軍事介入，一面附和式表態並不同意台北「特殊國與國關係論」，用以彰顯華府固守「一個中國」政策立場，並有效地促使北京能自制。在北京無法透過柯江會談測試出華府對北京一旦「懲罰」臺灣之容忍底線，華府又不願向台北施壓以便收回「特殊國與國關係論」，則如何讓江澤民雖不滿意但勉可接受的平衡點，可能即是美方一改過去六年不介入之立場，起而宣示美之「一個中國」政策，不能支持臺灣參與聯合國之立場，一面體現華府言行如一之承諾，並遏阻「特殊國與國關係論」國際效應之擴散，一面安撫北京不滿情緒並期許以對話取代對抗。

儘管台北參與聯合國之提案，七度受挫，但此次聯大總務委員會審查臺灣十二友邦提案登記發言，不論是發言國家數目或發言時間，均創下有史以來最高記錄，顯示台北參與聯合國在聯合國內仍維持相當的動力與熱度，反映出國際社會對台北入聯案與日俱增的興趣與重視。尤有甚者，自「特殊國與國關係論」宣示以來，北京已把聯合國視爲打擊台北的主戰場，以使全面壓縮其國際效應之擴散。台北應審慎衡量情勢，提出有效因應對策，包括：持續呼籲汪道涵訪台展現推動兩岸對話之誠意，強化與國際重點大國之雙邊關係，用以爭取支持台北參與經濟與科技性國際組織，並且多方參與國際或區域多邊對話機制（論壇），以迂迴漸進方式，達成最後入聯的目標。

六、結　論

基本上，李總統所謂「特殊的國與國關係」提法，係植基於突破務實外交困境與爭取未來與中共對等政治談判之有利籌碼等兩大戰略因素考量，並非突如其來之舉。換言之，台北揚棄兩岸軍事對抗及不再與北京競逐於中國正統之爭而邁入兩岸民間交流之舉，卻迄未獲致北京承認「對等分治」的正面回應，北京反而認爲㈠由於一九四九年取得對大陸地區之有效管轄，㈡對中國主權的全面繼承，㈢主權與領土完整不容分裂，㈣在一九七一年聯合國通過「2758號決議案」後已取得國際對北京擁有「中國代表權」之承認與勝利，因此即使台北對本身在兩岸關係的定位採「模糊性」提法，也無法爲北京所接受。而隨著台北務實外交政策的開展，北京祭出所謂「一個中國」原則遂行外交圍堵，兩岸外交競逐加劇，然而北京挾「大國外交」優勢，一面與周遭強權建構「戰略夥伴關係」，一面卻也包抄壓縮台北的國際政治空間，台北務實外交遭逢嚴峻之挑戰與困局。

其次，台北研判，若汪道涵九九年內順利來訪，恐怕經由兩會高層台北會晤後政治性對話勢難避免，準此，則兩岸進入政治性談判或其程序性商談之步伐將加速，台北認爲若一再迴避政治性對話或政治性談判之程序性商談，則以北京對復談之底線堅持來看，兩岸要恢復協商機制，勢必難上加難。爲爭取兩岸政治性談判前先行作自我明確「對等」定位之先機，台北重提二次戰後「德國經驗」，希望能在理論上強化「分裂國家模式」適用於兩岸關係之說服力，從而爭取北京接受「雙重承認」與「平行參與」，俾能發揮對等相待、良性互動與邁向統一之作用。

然而北京以兩岸分裂背景與國際承認「一個中國」原則爲由，實則難掩「成王、敗寇」之心態，拒斥了「兩德模式」之適用，甚至連兩岸分立分治之現實亦不容口頭上表述，其唯恐不僅促統不成，反而讓事實上之「獨台」更加鞏固或定型化。因此自九九年七月九日以來中共反應相當強烈，無論官方、學界、媒體均齊一口徑口誅筆伐，認爲嚴重破壞兩岸關係，揚言「兩會交流與對話之基礎已不復存在」。惟據筆者研判，北京目前的對策有兩條戰線，一爲在國際視聽上，爭取以美國爲首的認同與支持，期望透過美國的「關切」對台施壓，要求台北在立論上澄清或改弦更張，另一爲凸顯事態的嚴重性，包括暫緩推動汪道涵訪台，迫使台北能收回「特殊國與國關係論」。

惟在華府看來，不樂見美「中」關係陷入谷底之際，又因「特殊國與國關係論」而益形疏離，更何況維持台海情勢之穩定及堅持兩岸和平解決分歧，係美國一貫的兩岸政策，顯然在經過美國白宮、國務院及柯江熱線，甚至華府派遣陸士達、卜睿哲分別赴北京、台北遂行「預防外交」，傳達華府希望兩岸儘速透過對話而非武力解決歧見之立場，並向北京保證遵守「一個中國」政策，期盼北京在反應上自我節制，同時亦欲聽取台北之當面澄清，包括說詞上之和緩。可見美方會再度彰顯其兩岸政策「戰略上明確，戰術上模糊」之一貫立場的意涵。

筆者認爲，只要台北僅止於口頭之政治宣示，而不採法理上調整之後續配套措施（包括修憲、國統綱領與兩岸人民關係條例之修訂），則北京當會逐漸由激情回歸理性，二〇〇〇年下半年應仍會推動汪道涵訪台，避免喪失催促兩岸政治對話之主要著力點。尤値注意的是，受到「特殊國與國關係論」之衝擊，臺灣依然維持兩岸經貿「戒急用忍」與不宜立即「三通」之立場，台商投資大陸之意願在短期內受到消息面緊張氣氛之影響會稍作觀望，惟大陸當局卻不願因而影響兩岸經貿關係，仍宣示歡迎台商赴大陸投資之一貫立場未有絲毫改變。

從玉臺新詠到全唐詩看舞者之形象轉變

陳大道*

摘　要

唐代是中國舞蹈的高峰期。當時的舞蹈可分爲健舞與軟舞兩種。軟舞的舞姿柔美，通常是一種娛樂表演。健舞則顯得健康許多，可被視爲一種以運動爲目的的舞蹈。

在集合六朝宮體詩之大成的《玉臺新詠》一書中，大部分的舞蹈場面都是柔美的軟舞。到了唐代，我們可以從《全唐詩》之中發現許多精彩的健舞場面，其中杜甫的〈觀公孫大娘舞劍器行〉就是一例。

舞者在傳統中國的社會地位不高。史書記載，孔子曾與當時所謂的優人發生衝突，孔子稱他們熒惑諸侯。甚至

---

* 淡江大學中文系助理教授

因爲齊人送女樂予季桓子，桓子三日不朝，憤而離職。然而，孔教並不是始終主宰中國文化，尤其在國家分裂的時代以及外族佔領時期。而南北朝時期就是屬於這種階段。以娛樂爲主要目標的軟舞，提醒世人，舞蹈藉由肢體傳達性的訊息。

關鍵詞　玉臺新詠　宮體詩　舞蹈　軟舞　健舞　唐代文化

The Change in the Depiction of Dancers from the *Yu-t'ai hsin-yung* to the *Ch'uan T'ang-shih*

Chen, Ta-tao

Abstract

Chinese dance reached its high peak in the T'ang dynasty when Chinese and foreign choreographers practiced their dancing skills in one of the greatest empires in world history. The dance contained two categories, one was named *ruan wu* 軟舞, the soft or delicate dance usually performed for entertaining purposes, and the other was *chien wu* 健舞, more akin to a health exercise but practiced as a sport.

In the poetry anthology of Palace Style Poetry 宮體詩, *Yu-t'ai hsin-yung* 玉臺新詠compiled in late Six Dynasties, *ruan wu* predominated the poetic imagery of dance. *Chien wu* 健舞 appeared in the *Complete T'ang Poetry, Ch'üan T'ang-shih* 全唐詩 which included the famous *A Song of Dagger-*

dancing 觀公孫大娘舞劍器行 by Tu Fu.

According to historic records there were conflicts breaking out between Confucius and entertaining dancers. Confucius accused them of leading the feudal lords astray. However Confucian values have not always been linked strongly with Chinese Civilization, especially when civil wars took place or during the non-Chinese tribes' occupations of which the Northern and Southern Dynasties was one of these episodes. Thus *ruan wu* often appeared in Palace Style Poetry, creating imageries, and perpetuated the awareness that sexuality and dance share the same instrument-the human body.

Keywords: ruan wu, chien wu, Place Style Poetry, Yu-t'ai hsin-yung.

The poems compiled in *Yu-t'ai hsin-yung* 《玉臺新詠》are generally known as Palace Style Poetry, *kung-t'i shih* 宮體詩 which became the mainstream of poetry writing towards the end of southern dynasties.❶

---

❶ "It was to be over two centuries, however, before the potential of 'regulated verse' to achieve this perfect coordination of form and content was realized in practice. Its more immediate result in the end of the Six dynasties period was to encourage a development that most later critics regarded as pernicious; the immediate preoccupation of writers with the formal techniques of versification encouraged poetry as a technical exercise and intensified a tendency toward the composition of erotic verse as emotional outlet. The bifurcation of the old Chinese social conception of poetry opened the door for the making of verse that had meaning *only* as articulation of pure emotion, a verse without moral-allegorical import and thus shorn of its traditional relation to society. Known

Dance was one of the major subjects in these poems, and the dancers are mostly female. It has been said Palace Style Poetry depicted women either as objects of admiration or of pity.❷ As a dancer, it was the woman's duty to present herself as an object to be admired and desired. Thus the dancing girls' inviting and tempting gestures prompted the poets of Palace Style Poetry to depict them down. Such poems are not only literature works but also testimonies to the awareness that sexuality and dance share the same instrument-the human body.❸

Conventionally imagery of sexual intimacy in these poems is common. Their readers soon comprehend that the main purposes of the dances are to charm the audience to stay longer. *The Dancer*, *yong wu*

---

usually as *kung-t'i shih** (palace-style poetry) and gathered in the sixth-century anthology *Yu-t'ai hisn-yung,** this poetry was condemned by the Confucian critics of later centuries as frivolous and licentious because it appropriated and expanded the old images of sexual love while abandoning their traditional moral-political associations (Hightower, 1950, pp. 46-47; Watson, 1971, pp. 90-108)." William Nienhauser (ed.). (Taipei: SMC publishing), 1988, *The Indiana Companion to Traditional Chinese Literature*, p. 68.

❷ "The obsession with women and their affairs is perhaps the aspect of palace-style poetry most objectionable to later generations of critics influenced by Confucianism. Typically, women were objects either of admiration or of pity; in either view they were mere objects of yung-wu scrutiny. A new court favorite would attract the poet's fancy in the sway of her robes, the disarray of her coiffure, or the nuance of an eye-brow. Alternatively, the abandoned wife or once-favored now-neglected courtesan, aging alone in her ironically ornate chamber, provided the theme of tristesse upon which the poet could lavish mannered expressions of opulent grief." *Ibid.* , p. 517.

❸ "Using the signature key of sexuality, essential for human survival and desirable for pleasure, dance resonates universal behavioral needs and particular concerns." Judith Lynne Hanna, *Dance, sex and Gender,* (Chicago: the University of Chicago), 1988, Overture p. xiii.

ji<詠舞妓> by Ho Hsun 何遜is an example.

> 管清羅薦合，弦驚雪袖遲。逐唱回纖手，聽曲動蛾眉。凝情盼墮珥，微睇託含辭。日暮留嘉客，相看愛此時。

The Dancer❹

Pipes blow clear, silk seats move closer,
Strings sound anxious, snowflake sleeves adagio.
Following sung rhythms slim hands interweave,
Answering the melody moth eyebrows move.
Numb passion notes his dropped earring,❺
Narrowed eyes confide eloquent secrets.
Sunset delays her honoured guest,
She looks at him in this hour of love.
——Translated by Dr. Anne Birrell

This poem starts with music and dances, then depicts the hands, eyebrows, ears and eyes of the dancer, and eventually focuses on describing the beginning of a love affair. After a series of physical description followed by the hint of an affair, the reader will finally realize that "dance" in this poem might somehow become a euphemism for sexual foreplay.

Chinese dance reached its high peak in the T'ang dynasty. Apart from the traditional ones there were many foreign dances arriving.❻

---

❹ Translated by Anne Birrell, *New Songs from a Jade Terrace-An Anthology of Early Chinese Love Poetry, Translated with Annotations and an Introduction,* (London: George Allen & Unwin),1982 , p.154.

❺ The word "his" might be "her".

❻ Kao Ian & Li Wei 高琰&李維, Chung-his wu-tao pi-chiao yian-chiu 中西舞

Chinese Choreography of the T'ang dynasty comprised of two categories of dance, one was named *ruan wu*軟舞 the soft or delicate dance usually performed for entertaining purposes and the other was *chien wu*健舞, more akin to a health exercise but practiced as a sport. It is clear that the dances described in *Yu-t'ai hsin-yung* belongs to the first category, *ruan-wu.* When the Six dynasties was replaced by the Sui, followed by the T'ang dynasty latter, *ruan wu* still played an important role in those poems depicting dances. However there were poems describing various forms of *Jian wu* as well. Of the kinds of dances described, the Sword dance, *chien wu* 劍舞, was one of them and the Foreign Whirling Dance, *hu-shuan wu* 胡旋舞 was another. The poems depicting them can be found *Complete T'ang Poems, ch'uan t'ang-shih*《全唐詩》.

The T'ang poets who focused on depicting the healthful and virile dance showed the influence of the martial spirit, *shang-wu jing-shen* 尙武精神, both in positive and negative ways. For example, from the positive point of view in Tu Fu's *A Song of Dagger-dancing, kuan kung-sun ta-niang wu chien-ch'i hsing*〈觀公孫大娘舞劍器行〉, a heroin-like female dancer was highly praised. Her Sword Dance not only drew numerous audiences but also inspired her contemporary, the well-known master of calligraphy Zhang Hsu 張旭. Nevertheless Po Ch'u-I in his *Dancing Girl of the Foreign Whirling Dance, hu-xuan nyu* 〈胡旋女〉 described the ardently turning and whirling dancer without admiration but criticized this type of dance for enticing the emperor away from ruling the country. It also mentioned that the notorious Empress Yang 楊貴妃 and the turncoat An Lu-shan 安祿山 were both known for their grand skill of dancing the Foreign Whirling Dance. Empress Yang, wife

---

蹈比較研究, (Taipei: Chung-yang wen-wu kung-ing shih 中央文物供應社,) 1983. pp. 54-57.

of the Emperor Hsuan-tsung 玄宗 and an exquisite beauty, was accused of being distracting Hsuan-tsung from attending imperial court sessions. The rebellion of An Lu-shan plunged the country into chaos.

This paper is a study of dance imagery transformation depicted in poems from the southern dynasties to the T'ang. Poems studied in this paper are from the two influential books *Yu-t'ai hsin-yung* representing the Southern dynasties, and *Ch'uan T'ang-shi* representing the T'ang. This paper consists of three sections. The first section is devoted to *juan-wu* describing poems of the Southern dynasties, the second section is concerned with *chian-wu* describing poems of the T'ang dynasties. The influence of Confucianism on dance is mentioned in the third section.

Poems depicting *juan-wu* dance in the *Yu-t'ai hsin-yung*

Poems collected in the anthology *Yu-t'ai hsin-yung* was named *ian shi* 豔詩 and the style named *kung t'i* 宮體. They had been translated into English in the book *New songs from a jade terrace: an anthology of early Chinese love poetry* by Dr. Anne Birrell in 1982. Seemingly " New songs from a jade terrace "is a translation of the title *Yu-t'ai hsin-yung* according to its Chinese meaning and "love poetry" is Dr. Anne Birrell's version of *ian shi* 豔詩. There are ten volumes of 870 poems in the well-collated new edition of *Yu-t'ai hsin-yung* published by Zhong-hua Shu-ju 中華書局in1985.❼ However there are only 656 poems in Dr. Anne Birrell's book and so Dr. Birrell's translation, this would lead the readers to think that the original anthology had been fully translated.❽ Professor

❼ 徐陵編，穆克宏點校*Yu tai xin yong jian zhu*《玉臺新詠箋注》, (Beijing: zhong hua shu ju 北京：中華書局,） 1985.

❽ "This book is a translation of a medieval Chinese anthology of love poems called *New Song from a Jade Terrace.* It was compiled by a court poet, Hsu Ling, in about the year AD 545. It consists of 656 poems in the ten volumes

Lin Wen-yue 林文月 believed that the edition adopted by Dr. Birrell's was published in the Sung dynasty. She proclaimed that there were poems mixed into the anthology after the Sung, she also praised the decision of using the Sung edition, however neither Professor Lin nor Dr. Birrell made any comments on this edition.❾

Dr. Birrell neither mentioned the Chinese edition nor juxtaposed the English translation with its original Chinese poem. I have no intention of criticising Dr. Birrell's translation, in fact, by comparing her work with the edition published by zhong hua shu ju, it is easy to find which poems have been translated and which poems haven't, because her interpretations are reasonable clear. Furthermore looking on the side of introducing Chinese poetry writing of Southern dynasty to the world, her achievement is truly remarkable. Her translations were cited in this section.

Amongst Dr. Birrell's translation only titles of the poems mentioning dance will be introduced, although dances were depicted very often in various occasions in *Yu-t'ai hsin-yung*.

梁簡文帝*The Dance* 〈詠舞〉

可憐初二八，逐節似飛鴻。懸勝河陽妓，闇與淮南同。入行看履進，轉面望鬟空。腕動苕華玉，袖隨如意風。上客和須起，嘑烏曲未終。

How sweet, just sixteen!
Her rhythm likes a gliding swan

---

arranged in chronological sequence " Anne Birrell, *New Songs from a Jade Terrace-An Anthology of Early Chinese Love Poetry,* p. 1.

❾ Lin Wen-yue 林文月, 'Book View' <書評>, *Chinese Studies* 《漢學研究》, Vol. 1:1 一卷一期, Taipei, 1983. pp. 317-325.

Is far better than Hoyang entertainers,
Is sultry like Huainan dance.
I see her feet approach in the line,
I watch her chignon vanish with a turn of the head.
On her arm moves Chao Hua jade,
Sleeves follow winds fancy-free.
'Honoured guests don't get up!
My Sobbing crow tune is not ended!' [10]

We can find the conventional pattern of dance performance in this poem. The dancer and her dancing skills were depicted in the beginning and at the final couplet the guests were asked to stay longer.

徐陵 *The Dance*[11] 〈奉和詠舞〉[12]

十五屬平陽，因來入建章。主家能教舞，城中巧旦妝。低鬟向綺席，舉袖拂花黃。燭送窗邊影，衫傳峆裏香。當關好留客，故作舞衣長。

At fifteen she belonged to the Princess of P'ingyang
And so came to enter Chienchang Palace.
The Princess's house taught well the art of dance,
The city perfected the craft of dawn make-up.
With lowered coiffure she nears the silk mat,
With raised sleeves brushes on floral yellow.
Candles cast shadows near the window,
Her dress spreads perfume in her wardrobe.

---

[10] Anne Birrell, *New Songs from a Jade Terrace*, p.198.

[11] *Ibid.* p.226

[12] *Harmonizing with Hsiao Kang's.*

The reason she attracts guests so well must be
That she makes her dance gown deliberately long.

The " Princess of P'ingyang" in the first line is also known as the Master of Yang-e 陽阿主. She was the famous patron of performing arts in the West Han dynasty, and she owned many singing and dancing girls. The well-known concubine of Emperor Wu-ti 漢武帝, Lady Li 李夫人 was introduced by her. The other Wu-ti's beloved concubine Wei tzu-fu 衛子夫 was also from the Princess of P'ingyang's palace. Wu-ti was beguiled by Wei Tzu-fu's voice during a visit. In addition to Lady Li and Wei tzu-fu, the success of Empress Chao Fei-yan 趙飛燕, who began as dancing girl, later captured emperor Ch'eng-ti's heart and eventually became the most influential woman of the dynasty, proving that the Princess of P'ingyang's palace can be regarded as the best private performing arts institution.⓭

The proceeding poem starts with the introduction of the dancer's schooling, and then her make-up and figures. Finally, as usually, it reveals the dancer's intention of asking the guests to hang around.

梁武帝 *The Dance*⓮〈詠舞〉

腕弱復低舉，身輕由回縱。可謂寫自歡，方與心期共。

Arm delicately lift and drop,
Her body light keeps twirling.
If you mean this to tell of desire,
You must come and join your sweetheart!

⓭ Kao Ian & Li Wei 高琰&李維, *Chung-his wu-tao pi-chiao yian-chiu* 《中西舞蹈比較研究》. pp. 49-50.

⓮ Anne Birrell, *New Songs from a Jade Terrace.*p.282

The last two lines of this short poem make a clear statement to having an intimate time after the dance. In other words the delicate dancer passed a message of sexual desire, and the poet emperor Wu-ti spoke it out.

江洪 *The Dancer* ⑮〈舞女〉

腰纖蔑楚媛，體輕非趙姬。映洤闐寶粟，緣肘挂珠絲。發袖已成態，動足復含姿。協精若不眄，當轉復遲疑。何慚雲鶴起，詎減鳳鸞時。

Slim of waist, but not a Ch'u lady,
Light on body, but not a Chao girl,
Her sparkling collar strewn with jewel seeds,
From her elbows pearl tassels swing.
With loose sleeves she perform her pose,
Move her feet in different positions.
Her eyes slant, seem not notice you,
She goes to turn, then pretends to withdraw.
Why should she blush to soar with cloudy storks?
Is she less lovely than phoenix in alarm?

Comparing to previous poems this poem pays more attention on choreography. In the beginning couplet it emphasize that the dancer was "slim of waist" and "light on body". These two characteristics seem to be the standard requirement of a dancer in traditional Chinese dance.

Readers can easily follow the paces of the dancer when the poet depicts her moves in detail. Nevertheless, one can still find the sexual

⑮ *Ibid.* p. 148.

reference in the final line. The "phoenix" is usually cited as the symbol of coupling.

庾信 *The Dance*⑯〈奉和詠舞〉⑰

洞房花燭明，燕餘雙舞輕。頓履隨疏節，低鬟逐上聲。半轉行初進，飄衫曲未成。回鸞鏡欲滿，鵠顧市應傾。已曾天上學，詎似世中生。

In cloistral rooms floral candles bright,
Spoils of Yen, two dancers light
Stamp their heels in time to staccato rhythms,
Lower coiffures on the high notes.
Half a pirouette, step back to position one,
Whirling gowns, melody lingering on,
Paradise birds turn, the mirror will soon be full,
Geese look back, the town will surely fall.
Trained long ago to the dance in heaven,
Aren't they like dancers not borne of this world?

This poem does not follow the conventional type; the sexual reference does not take place in the final couplet. If the imagery of the "cloistral rooms", *tung-fang* 洞房, doesn't remind readers the wedding night, there are no sex references in this poem.

The poet Yu Hsin leads readers to first see slim dancers dancing in a dance in the cloistral room, then, in the second couplet, to follow the rhythm as the dancers do. In the following couplet, the dancers hold back a bit but is fully presented in the next couplet. The poet praises the

---

⑯ *Ibid.* p.222

⑰ Harmonizing with Hsiao Kang's

dancers to be not borne of this world. High praise to them indeed.

The poet has no intention of encouraging the readers to fantasize. And in this poem choreography becomes important and to be respected as an art form.

梁簡文帝Dance⑱ 〈賦樂府得大垂手〉⑲

垂手忽苕苕，飛燕掌中嬌。羅衣恣風引，輕帶任情搖。詎似長沙地，促舞不回腰。

Lowered hands suddenly soar, soar,
Fejiyen enchanting on his palm.
Her silk dress lures wayward winds,
Her light sash sways with passionate surrender.
It's not like the land of Ch'angsha
Where dance steps don't make waists whirl.

This poem also ended with no sexual reference. After two couplets depicting the elegant dancing poses, it cited a historic reference in the final couplet referring to the prince of Ch'angsha of the Han ching-ti period. According to historic records, Prince of Ch'angsha was not satisfied with the allotment of his feudal land. Once he danced in front of his emperor father, he with rigid hands pretended to be unable to turn around. His father felt strange and asked he about his odd gestures. He replied that his territory was too small to turn around. The emperor was amused, and promised him more land.

In Dr. Birrell's book I found six poems with title concerning dance. In the version published by zhong hua shu ju, there are more poems, for

---

⑱ Anne Birrell, New Songs from a Jade Terrace. p. 197.

⑲ *Assigned the Folk-Song theme Major Dance Gestures*

example *Dance, Responding to the Emperor*, *ing-ling yong-wu* 〈應令詠舞〉 written by Liu Tsun 劉遵, and the other poem with the same title by Wang Hsun 王訓, both in the eighth chapter.⓴ They all follow the conventional pattern, female dancers' gestures depicted in the beginning and most of the poems and the expectation of intimacy taking place in the final lines.

Poems with *chian-wu* dance themes in the T'ang poetry

In the popular Anthology of T'ang Poetry, *Three Thousand Poems of the T'ang Dynasties, t'ang-shih san-bai shou* 《唐詩三百首》, there is a poem combining choreography and martial arts named *A Song of Dagger-dancing (with preface),* guan gong-sun da-niang wu chian-ch'i hsing (bing-hsu) 〈觀公孫大娘舞劍器行〉(並序) written by Tu Fu. It is one of Tu Fu's great works of *yueh-fu* 樂府 poems.

〈觀公孫大娘舞劍器行〉(并序)

(序)大歷二年十月十九日，夔府別駕元持宅見臨潁李十二娘舞劍器，壯其蔚跂。問其所師，曰：「吾公孫大娘弟子也」。開元三載，余尚童，記於郾城觀公孫氏舞劍器渾脫，㉑瀏灕頓挫，獨出冠時。自高頭宜春梨園二伎坊內人，外供奉舞女，曉是舞者，聖文神武皇帝出，公孫一人而已。玉貌錦繡衣，況於白首，今茲弟子，亦匪盛顏。既辨其由來，知波瀾莫二。撫事慷慨，聊為劍器行。往者吳人張旭，善草書帖，數常於鄴縣見公孫大娘舞西河劍器，自此

⓴ *Yu tai xin yong jian zhu* 《玉臺新詠箋注》, pp. 370-371.

㉑ Hun tuo 渾脫 is one of the chian wu dances. *Chuan-tang-shi chong di yueh-wu tsi-liao* 《全唐詩中的樂舞資料》, Zhong-guo wu-dao i-shu ian-jiu-hui 中國舞蹈藝術研究會, (Beijing: In-yue 音樂出版社), 1958. p. 139.

草書長進。豪蕩感激，即公孫可知矣。

昔有佳人公孫氏，一舞劍器動四方。觀者如山色沮喪，天地爲之久低昂。如羿射九日落，矯如群帝驂龍翔。來如（末）雷霆收震怒，罷如江海凝清光。絳脣珠袖兩寂寞，況有弟子傳芬芳。臨潁美人在白帝，妙舞此曲神揚揚。與余問答既有以感時撫事增惋傷。先帝侍女八千人，公孫劍器初第一。五十年間似反掌，風塵傾動昏王室。梨園子弟散如煙，女樂餘姿映寒日。金粟堆南木已拱，瞿唐石城草蕭瑟。玳筵急管曲復終，樂極哀來月東出。老夫不知其所往，足繭荒山轉愁疾。

A Song of Dagger-dancing㉒

(On the 19th of the Tenth-month in the second year of Ta-li, I saw, in the house of the K‘uei-fu official Yuan T’e, a girl named Li from Ling-ying dancing with a dagger, I admired her skill and asked who was her teacher. She named Lady Kung-sun. I remembered that in the third year of K‘ai-yuan at Yen-ch’eng, when I was a little boy, I saw Lady Kung-sun dance. She was the only one in the Imperial Theater who could dance with this weapon. Now she is aged and unknown, and even her pupil has passed the heyday of beauty. I wrote this poem to express my wistfulness. The work of Chang Hsu of the Wu district, that great master of grassy writing, was improved by his having been present when Lady Kung-sun dances in the Yieh district. From this may be judged the art of kung-sun.)

㉒ Trandslated by Witter Bynner, *Three Thousand Poems of the T‘ang Dynasties 618-906* 《唐詩三百首》, (Taipei: Ren- ren Shu-chu 人人書局), 1971, pp. 166-167.

There lived years ago the beautiful Kung-sun,
Who, dancing with her dagger, drew from all four quarters.
An audience like mountains lost among themselves,
Heaven and earth moved back and forth, following her motions,
Which were bright as when the Archer shot the nine suns down the sky,
And rapid as angels before the wings of dragons.
She began like a thunderbolt, venting its anger,
And ended like the shining calm of rivers and the sea. ...
But vanished are those red lips and those pearly sleeves;
And none but this one pupil bears the perfume of her fame,
This beauty from Ling-ying, at the Town of the White Cod,
Dancing still and singing in the old blithe way.
And while we reply to each other's questions,
We sigh together, saddened by changes that have come.
There were eight thousand ladies in the late Emperor's court,
But none could dance the dagger-dance like Lady Kung-sun.
... Fifty years have passed, like the turning of a palm;
Wind and dust, filling the world, obscure the Imperial House.
Instead of the Pear-Garden Players, who have blown by like a mist,
There are one or two girl-musicians now- trying to charm the cold Sun.
There are man-size trees by the Emperor's Golden Tomb. ....
I seem to hear dead grasses rattling on the cliffs of Ch'u-t'ang.
... The song is done, the slow string and quick pipe have ceased.
At the height of joy, sorrow comes with the eastern moon rising.
And I, a poor old man, not knowing where to go,
Must harden my feet on the lone hills, toward sickness and despair.

Although the title of this poem tells that this poem is about Dagger-dancing, (translated by Witter Bynner) or Sword dance, only the first four of its thirteen couplets depict the weapon dance scenes. The other lines mainly speak of the degeneration of the Pear-Garden, *li-yuan* 梨園, from the splendor of the year of K'ai-yuan to that of when poet Tu Fu watched the dance again. Emperor T'ang Hsuan-tsung had established Pear-Garden where he gathered and trained performers. Obviously Lady Kung-sun was one of the best dancers. The splendid time ended when the rebellion of An Lu-shan started. To the poet Tu Fu, after fifty years when he was old and the golden era could never come back again, one of Lady Kung-sun pupils who had danced in front of him evoked an overwhelming nostalgia for the past glories.

The dance performance depicted in the beginning was fierce and powerful. It was absolutely different from the dances depicted in *Yu-t'ai hsin-yung*. In the preface of *A Song of Dagger-dancing* the poet cited an anecdote about Chang Hsu 張旭, the great master of grassy writing *ts'ao shu* 草書, said that Chang Hsu was improved by watching Lady Kung-sun's dances. It was said that wearing military uniforms became a trend, girls loved Lady Kung-sun's sword dance, and the poet Ssu-kung T'u in *The Sword*, *chien ch'i* 劍器wrote,

樓下公孫昔擅場，空教女子愛軍裝。

Downstairs used to be Lady Kung-sun's playground,
In vain, girls love to dress military uniforms. ㉓

In the final couplet, readers are left with the imagery of an old man who could not find his way home, implying that he was loosing his memory. This old man was an example of having been defeated by the transience of time. It explains that the poet not only wanted to describe

---

㉓ Wang K'e-fen 王克芬, 'Chung-kuo ku-tai wu-tao shi-hua' <中國古代舞蹈史話>, *Chung-kuo ku-tai wu-tao shi* 《中國古代舞蹈史》(Taipei: Lai-t'ing蘭亭書局), pp. 22-23.

an excellent performance of dance, but also spoke of the passage of time.

The next poem Dancing Girl of the Foreign Whirling Dance, hu-hsuan nü 〈胡旋女〉 written by Po Chü-i, was one of Po's well-known group of poems, New Yüeh-fu 新樂府. This poem and other poems of the New Yüeh-fu contain social criticism. Po Chu-i and his contemporary Yuan Chen 元稹 promoted feng-yu shi 諷喻詩, and New Yüeh-fu was an example. This ideology of poetry writing was characterized by the belief that poetry should serve as a vehicle for the expression of moral values㉔, or that poetry could effect social and political changes.㉕

胡旋女，胡旋女，心應弦，手應鼓。弦鼓一聲雙袖舉，迴雪飄飆轉蓬舞。左轉又轉不知疲，千匝萬週無已時。人間物類無可比，奔車輪緩旋風遲。曲終再拜謝天子，天子爲之微啓齒。胡旋女，出康居，圖勞東來萬里餘，中原自有胡旋者，鬥妙爭能爾不如。天寶季年時欲變，臣妾人人學圜轉:中有太眞外祿山，二人最道能胡旋。梨花園中冊作妃，金雞障下養爲兒。祿山胡旋迷君眼，兵過黃河疑未反。貴妃胡旋惑君心，死棄馬嵬念更深。從茲地軸天維轉，五十年來制不禁。胡旋女，莫空舞，數唱此歌悟明主。

Hu-xuan girl, Hu-xuan girl, your mind follows the string-instrument rhythms and you Hands move in response to the drums.

Songs of the string-instrument and drums come together and your hand raised,

Like the whirling snow flakes you dance.

Turn to the right, turn to the left, you don't feel tired.

㉔ William Nienhauser, *The Indiana Companion to Traditional Chinese Literature*, p. 859.

㉕ *Ibid.*, p.949.

Turning hundreds and thousands times non-stop.
Nothing in the world can compare with you,
The wheels of running carts are slower than you, the whirlwind.
When the music stop you bowed to the emperor,
And the emperor smiled.
Whirling dance girl is from Kang-ju,
Emptiness, you traveled eastwards for more than a thousand li,
In Central Plains we already have Hu-xuan dancers,
They are so excellent and skillful that you can't compete.
At the end of Tian-pao year, the government was close to collapse,
Courtiers and emperor's concubines all practiced whirling dance.
Tai-zhen in the court and Lu-shan in the frontier were the best dancers.
She was conferred as empress in the pear-blossom garden
He in the Gorden-chicken tent became the adopted son of the emperor
Lu-shan's whirling dance obscured the emperor's vision,
The rebellion troops marched across the Yellow River were still unawared.
Empress Yang's whirling dance seduced the mind of the Emperor,
When she was killed and abandoned on the Ma-wei hills he loved her more.
Since then the earth and heaven pillars turned and tumbled,
For fifty years there were no laws stopping the whirling dance.
Whirling dance girl, don't dance with emptiness,
Sing the song to the bright ruler again and again!

This poem starts with an excellent dance performance. Then the best dancers of the Foreign Whirling Dance, Empress Yang and General

An Lu-shan were invoked to warn the emperor of the day of the dangers of excess. The way this poem depicted dance scenes, followed by stories telling is similar to the pattern of the previous poem by Tu Fu.

The poem criticized the emperor for being distracted by the dancers from ruling his country. Further in the final couplet the poet reminded the dancer to warn the emperor. Obviously he was also warning the dancer not to follow the steps of the bad examples of the formal times.

Kang-ju, present day Samarkand, one of the major trading posts on the Silk Road in central Asia where the dancer was from, was also the birthplace of the Hu-hsuan Dance. When dancers of the Hu-hsuan danced, they turned and spun fast, and "turning and spinning" is what the the word *hsuan* 旋 stands for. This dance had various forms, a solo dance, a double, a triple or four people dancing together. Female dancers were more common than male.㉖

The next poem, the *Foreign Leaping Dance Hu-t'eng wu* 〈胡騰舞〉, written by Li Duan 李端, is also a *chian wu*. According to *Chuan-tang-shi chong di yueh-wu tsi-liao* 《全唐詩中的樂舞資料》, this dance originated from Tashkent, and dancers of this dance were mainly male.㉗

〈胡騰兒〉

胡騰身是涼州兒，肌膚如玉鼻如錐。桐布輕衫前後卷，葡萄長帶一邊垂。帳前跪作本音語，拾襟攪袖爲君舞。安西舊牧收淚看，洛下詞人抄曲與。揚眉動目踏花氈，紅汗交流珠帽偏。醉卻東傾又西倒，雙靴柔弱滿燈前。環行急蹴皆應節，反手叉腰如卻月。絲桐忽奏一曲終，嗚嗚畫角城頭發。胡騰兒，胡騰兒，故鄉路斷知不知。

㉖ *Chuan-tang-shi chong di yueh-wu tsi-liao,* 《全唐詩中的樂舞資料》 p. 144.

㉗ *Ibid.* . p.145.

The Hu-t'eng young man is from Liang-chou,
His skin is as white as snow and his nose is like an awl.
The tails of his thin gown of *t'ung* cloth are curled up in the front and back,
Long belt with grape shape hangs on one side.
He knelt down and addressed in his native tongue,
Then grasps the cuffs of his sleeves and dances for you.
The former chief administrator of the An-ci chou stopped weeping and watch,
The poet from Lo-hsia wrote the song and handed it out.
The dancer raises his eyebrows, lifts his eyes and tramples on the flower carpet.
He perspires all over his red face and his hat leans to one side.
Like a drunken man he bends backwards, to the right, and to the left,
Lamps light his two soft boots.
He circles and kicks fast to staccato rhythms,
He stands with arms akimbo like the old crescent moon.
The sound of string-instruments suddenly rises and the play of music ends,
Wu, Wu, the noise of horns come from the top of the city wall.
Hu-t'eng young, Hu-t'eng young,
Do you know or not your way home has been blocked!

This poem depicts the choreography of the vigorous Hu-t'eng dance. Trampling, bending, circling and kicking he dances. Amongst many female dancers this dance preformed by male is comparatively uncommon. Nevertheless, he is not a bad dancer and his dancing skills evoke the performance of *chian-wu*.

Apart from scenes of dancing, the dancer's status is also described. His skin color, prominent nose, his language and his birthplace indicated his ethnic background, which was not of the Han Chinese but the minority tribe of the western area. Before he danced the former chief administrator of his hometown cried, and at the end of this poem, noise of the horns warning that there were battles taking place in the western area of the empire. Although the dance scenes were excellent, readers can surely realize that this young dancer is becoming a refuge of a crucial war.

There were still more *juan-wu* than *chian-wu* practiced in the T'ang dynasty. Some of the T'ang poem depicting *juan-wu* dance were just like the palace style poems. For, example, in *Watching the Singing Girl in Chang the Tenth's Residence During a Rainy Day in Yang-chou* 〈揚州雨中張十宅觀妓〉 written by Chang Wei 張謂,[28] the female entertainers held their audience spellbound.

> 夜色帶春煙，燈花拂更燃。殘妝添石黛，豔舞落金鈿。掩笑頻歆扇，迎歌乍動弦。不知巫峽雨，何事海西邊。
>
> This night is covered with the mist of spring,
> The wick of the lamp after being cleaned burns stronger.
> Remaining adornments covered by new cosmetics,
> Enticing dances and falling golden filigrees.
> Covering laughing lips with ceaselessly swaying fans,

[28] The dates of Chang Wei's birth and death are unknown. He earned the*chin-shih* distinction in the second year of T'ien-pao reign, 745 AD.. Mang Liang-ch'un 馬良春 & Li Fu-t'ien 李福田(eds.). *Chung-kuo Wen-hsüeh Ta-tz'u-tien* 《中國文學大辭典》*(Zhongguo Wenxue Dacidian)*. （T'ienchin: T'ienchin Jan-min Ch'u-pan-she 天津人民出版社）, 1991. p. 5602.

To match the song the string instruments are surprisingly stirred again.
I do not know why the rains of the Wu Gorge,
Come to the western seaside.

The last couplet refers to the legend of the King of Ch'u 楚王, spending a night with the goddess of the Wu Gorge.㉙ In this context it is implied that the entertainers will bestow sexual favors upon their audience after the gathering is over.

Dance and Society

The majority of the dancers were praised in the poems. Their exquisite dancing skills provided audiences with impressive experiences whether or not there were sex implications involved. The only dancers being criticized were Empress Yang and General An Lu-san both of whom were accused of being responsible for the nation's turmoil and the downfall of the Emperor Hsuan-tsung's reign, or the High T'ang period.

Nevertheless the dancer who entertained people for living has low social status in ancient China. The archeological finds of the noble's tombs dating back to the Sang dynasty （商朝 1800-1400 B. C.） suggested that there were dancing girls and female musicians buried alive to accompany their dead masters.㉚ According to documents entertainers could never change their status, which is passed on to their offsprings. They generations, were not allowed to marry ordinary citizens, and their

---

㉙ The story can be found in *Shen-nü Fu*〈神女賦〉, and in the preface of *Kao-t'ang Fu*〈高唐賦〉by Sung Yü 宋玉, Hsiao T'ung (ed.). *Wen Hsüan,* 《文選》 c. 19, pp. 265～68.

㉚ Wang Ke-fen 王克芬, Chong-kuo Ku-dai Wu-tao-chia de ku-shi 《中國古代舞蹈家的故事》, (Taipei: Lant'ing 蘭亭), 1986, pp. 2-3.

were identified as different from farmers.[31]

They were mostly trained performers and danced for their masters. The poem *The Dance* by Hsu Ling 徐陵 mentioned previously contained such an example. Its third line says"主家能教舞" which Dr. Birrell translated as " The Princess's house taught well the art of dance". Even though the word "主" according to the context surely means "Princess", its literal meaning is master, and the dancers were taught in their master's place. Dancing girls were objects to be traded, exchanged as presents, cast out when they were old or less favored. The Chinese tradition of training dancing girls in their masters' places has a long history. Robert Hans Van Gulik described this situation saying,

> At this time （later in the Chou 周period 1100-77 B.C.） princes and high officials maintained not only harems but also their own troupes of *nu-yueh,* trained dancing girls and female musicians who entertained at official banquets and private drinking bouts. These women, mostly slave girls and prisoners or war, were subject to be sold or offered as presents. This class became the forerunner of *kuan-chi,* "official prostitute", who attained important positions in subsequent Chinese social life.[32]

nu-yueh is 女樂 and kuan-chi is 官妓.

In some cases entertainers became victims of political conflicts, for example a group of performers were decapitated in a meeting of the country lord Ch'i-kung of Ch'i, 齊景公and the lord Ting-kung of Lu 魯定公 who was escorted by Confucius. Confucius accused them the

---

[31] "一沾此色，累世不改，婚姻絕於士庶，名籍異於編甿。" *Ibid*. p. 3.

[32] Judith Lynne Hanna, *Dance, sex and Gender,* p. 60.

entertainers of leading feudal lords astray.㉝ Nevertheless, after four years a group of *nu-yueh* caused Confucius's resignation according to the Confucian *Analects,* Liu-yü 論語.㉞ The *nu-yueh* group was given as present to Chi Huan-tzu 季桓子, the chief minister of Confucius' home country Lu 魯, by the neighboring country Ch'i 齊. When Chi Huan-tzu received the group, he stopped attending the daily court meeting for three days. Thus Confucius resigned. This record can also be found in *Shi Chi* 史記.㉟ Conflicts between Confucius and the entertainer helped to keep the latter's status low in Chinese society.

Confucian values were not always linked strongly with the Chinese Civilization, especially when civil wars broke out or during the non-Chinese tribes' occupations, and Northern and Southern Dynasties was one of these episodes.㊱ As a result when the Anthology *Yu-t'ai hsin-yung* was completed, and the dancing girls were given appreciative

---

㉝ "（孔子）曰：「匹夫而營惑諸侯者罪當誅！請命有司！」有司加法焉，手足異處。" Ssu-ma Ch'ien 司馬遷 (ed.). *Shih Chi*《史記》, c. 47, （Beijing: Chung-hua Shu-chü 中華書局）, 1972. p. 1915.

㉞ 「齊人歸女樂，季桓子受之。三日不朝，孔子行。」《論語》〈微子第十八〉。

㉟ Ssu-ma Ch'ien 司馬遷 (ed.). *Shih Chi*《史記》, c. 47, p. 1918.

㊱ "To Han Confucians the public function of literature bad been to assign praise and blame to those who governed, to encourage virtue and criticize corruption; its private function was to express personal sentiments, but such sentiments were seen primarily as reactions to prevailing political and social mores. The value of the expression of such sentiments was that through them the condition of society and the moral nature of the poet would be made manifest. These attitudes were certainly not a fertile ground for a great imaginative literature, but they were immensely compelling in that they provided a legitimate position for literature in the Confucian state. In the Northern and Southern Dynasties these ties with Confucian values and the literary and cultural past were almost broken. " Stephen Owen, *The Poetry of the Early T'ang,* (New York: Yale University), 1977, p. 3.

mentions. Stephen Owen described the poetry writing of this epoch saying,

> Disillusionment with Confucian literary values and the ideal of the Scholar-official had appeared strongly as early as the early third century. At first the dissociation of poetry from the state and its consuming ethical standards proved to be liberating: poetry found a wealth of new themes in the act of rejection itself. Eremitic poetry, landscape poetry, Taoist philosophical and imaginative poetry flourished.[37]

Conclusion

Although the dancer's social status was low they did not lead an isolated life. Once they became famous they would have the opportunity to perform in front of influential people and their skills would become much better after constant practices. Under some circumstances they would have the opportunities to enter the status of aristocracy. As mentioned previously Chao Fei-yan 趙飛燕, originally a dancing girl, became the Empress. Despite the fact that the dancing girls were given away as present, they could carry missions which no others could do. For example according to the tradition the beautiful His Shi 西施, the famous singing and dancing girl given by the defeated King of Yueh Kou Chien 越王句踐 to his conquer the King of Wu Fu Ch'ai 吳王夫差, was an agent for her mother country. She completed her mission of distracting Fu-ch'ai, resulting in the demise of the Wu ruler. Although the downfall of the Wu was said to be due to the beautiful Hsi Shih, there were different view points, such as the one by T'ang poet Lo Yin 羅隱

[37] Judith Lynne Hanna, *Dance, sex and Gender*. pp. 3-4.

in the poem *Hsi Shih* 〈西施〉, saying

家國興亡自有時，吳人何苦怨西施。西施若解傾吳國，越國亡來又是誰

The downfall of a family and a country are predestined.
Why do the Wu people bitterly complain about Hsi Shih?
If Hsi Shih is the reason for the downfall of the Wu?
Who is responsible for the subsequent downfall of the Yüeh?

From the view point of Confucius himself, and later Confucianist such as the T'ang poet Po Chü-i in *Dancing Girl of the Foreign Whirling Dance,* there were dancers whose performance were regarded as immoral and sinful. However Lo Yin's *Hsi Shih* reminded us these dancers were not all guilty, and the audience had to take some responsibilities too. In those periods in Chinese history when Confucian ethics disappeared momentarily, the views of Hans Van Gulik's as expressed in *Dance, sex and Gender* by Judith Lynne Hanna might be true "the Chinese did not regard prostitutes with contempt; rather considered the visitation of prostitutes a legitimate pastime for man."[38]

---

[38] *Ibid.* p. 60.

韓中詩學比較研究
——李朝李德懋與清朝王士禎詩學關係

宋永珠*

摘　要

韓中詩學比較的對象是韓國的李朝後期人李德懋（號炯菴）與中國的清士人王士禎（號漁洋）。本論文的研究重點是詩學淵源與傳承的關係中，一個國家原來的理論，到另一個國家文化的傳統，其間如何接受，變化之歷程之探求。

本文之構成分爲三部分：第一，王漁洋詩學與李炯菴的關係。主要是關於李炯菴對王漁洋文集的接觸與給李朝

*　韓國江原大學中語文學科教授

文壇紹介過程。第二，時代性執著問題。當時朝鮮詩壇與一百餘年前明末清初的詩壇的形勢相仿，漁洋爲了糾正當時詩壇流弊，炯菴也爲了打破當時宗唐模倣，蹈襲的偏弊觀念。兩人任詩壇的地位，處境類似。第三，詩之要諦論。二人在詩歌創作之法上，論詩的觀點相似，作詩的關鍵在妙悟，其所謂意境是妙悟中自得之境。炯菴要求詩的理想境界，是觀照事物本性與一切現象，體會造化之妙，與自然合爲一體。這點是與漁洋所謂「詩禪一致」相同，也可說在李炯菴的詩學上，有漁洋神韻說的影響。

關鍵詞　王士禎　李德懋　李朝文壇　妙悟　意境　詩禪一致　神韻說

一、前　言

在韓國漢學史上，李德懋（號炯菴）被稱爲李朝後期四家詩人中一位，是一代詩壇的領導者。

在中國文學史上，王士禎（號漁洋）被稱爲神韻說的倡導者，是清代詩壇的一代正宗。

二人沒有直接的面識，然而在李德懋所著書籍中，卻可找出他接觸王士禎文集的事實，所以本文在尋求其傳入過程及其緣由，探討王士禎詩論與李德懋文學的關係如何。

二、漁洋詩學與炯菴的關係

李炯菴（一七四一～一七九三）比王漁洋（一六三四～一七一一）晚百餘年誕生。這時正是中國清代雍正至乾隆年間。漁洋則於順治、康熙年間主盟詩壇，當時聲望如日中天。到了雍、乾時，批評他神韻說的人越來越多，有沈德潛的格調說、袁枚的性靈說、翁方綱的肌理說。

王漁洋的神韻說傳入朝鮮文壇，並非在王氏生前，而是在他卒後的四、五十年之後。李炯菴是在當代詩壇的領導地位，建立新詩觀，並主導當時風氣的人。

炯菴對王漁洋文集的接觸與給文壇介紹如下，他說：

> 《陶谷李相國集》，始見《蠶尾集》，王士禎著，而不知其詩之如何。李槎川嘗得邵子相選本三冊而爲帳中之秘，故槎川之詩，能脱凡陋之習，良有以也。槎川沒後數十年，其書流落爲薑山所藏。《帶經堂全集》之來東，纔二十餘年，而藏之者不過二三家，亦不識其爲何人。余嘗從人借讀，洋洋巨視，目瞠舌呿，自恨相見之苦晚。於是有詩曰：「好事中州空艷羡，堯峰文筆阮亭詩」遂詫張夸震於冷齋、薑山、楚亭諸人，舉皆咀嚼濃郁，耳濡目染，流波所及，能知有王漁洋於天壤間者，亦稍稍相望也。今僅五、六年，其表章之功，余亦不讓焉。❶

---

❶ 李德懋，《青莊館全書》卷三十四，《清脾錄》卷三，〈王阮亭〉。

在朝鮮，漁洋的名氣是來自《陶谷集》，他所著書《蠶尾集》則只有詩題，而無內容。直到康熙辛卯年間（一七一一年），漁洋卒年所刊行的《帶經堂集》在一段時間之後，至炯菴當時才介紹傳入朝鮮。炯安是朝鮮文人中，最早接觸到漁洋文集中的一個。

炯菴一見到漁洋的詩，便大受感動，並感欽慕。立刻開始向四家稱讚推薦，對漁洋無限傾倒。同時他也逐漸向朝鮮文壇介紹漁洋，並普及對漁洋的認識。於此可知炯菴對漁洋文集接觸的積極，並大力予以傳播。

炯菴第一次接觸漁洋文集，大概是他二十六歲以前，這是由他的《耳目口心書》中有關於漁洋之文，推測出來。炯菴第一次面對漁洋的詩文，即感覺到其魅力，不管其書之龐大，遂手不釋卷，落入讀書三昧之境。同時，他對漁洋的詩風，文體的新傾向，充滿感動，這由他的〈秋日讀帶經堂集〉詩中可以探知。他說：「沉寥秋令樹先知，任忘喧涼做白痴，壁靜萬蟲勤自語，簾虛一鳥慣相窺。拋他錢癖如將浼，呼我書淫故不辭，好事中州空艷羨，堯峰文筆阮亭詩。」❷

炯菴對漁洋在知識、文學方面的印象和見解，散見於其著作中。他說：

> 王漁洋名士禎，字貽上，一號阮亭，濟南人。官至尚書，其詩和婉沉鬱，爲清初第一大家。且淹雅好古，著書皆傳。❸

又說：

---

❷ 同上，卷十，〈雅亭遺稿〉二。

❸ 同上，卷六十三，《天涯知己書》，〈筆談〉。

> ……善爲詩，大率清秀閒雅，澹靜流麗，淹洽宏肆。其老來諸作，尤磊落槎牙。爲海內詩宗者，迄今百餘年，無一人異辭，尊敬之極，書尺筆話漁洋二字，必跳行而書。❹

炯菴以爲漁洋爲清初第一大家，其聲望足以奔走天下，聞響繼續到炯菴當時，這點與事實有出入，似嫌誇張。他於後代人對漁洋的酷評不予置理，他的文集中，只記載趙執信與王峻對王漁洋之批評事實，但炯菴仍然不改變它尊重漁洋的態度，可知他對漁洋傾倒的程度。炯菴對漁洋作品之評價，有「和婉沉鬱」、「淹雅好古」、「清秀閒雅」、「澹靜流麗」、「淹洽宏肆」、「磊落槎牙」等之語。他說：

> 余酷嗜貽上詩，常以爲非徒有明三百年無此正聲，求諸宋、元，亦罕厥儔。雖上躋唐家極盛之際，必不下於岑、儲、韋、孟之席，知詩者亦不以為過也。❺

可知炯菴認爲漁洋的詩風，不以進入「詩必盛唐」之風爲榮，推重宋、元之作風，漁洋詩的水準可與岑參、儲光羲、韋應物、孟浩然齊。

炯菴更以爲漁洋論詩，不拘於「詩必盛唐」，他有取於宋、元，且能博其旨趣，他認爲漁洋如此的觀點，才是公平。他說：

> 王漁洋論詩絕句「鐵崖樂府氣淋漓，淵穎歌行格儘奇。耳食

---

❹ 同上，《清脾錄》，〈王阮亭〉。

❺ 同上。

紛紛說開寶，幾人眼見宋、元詩。」余嘗愛此詩之公平雅博。暮秋穫稻南部，歸路雨中，入白雲山中，謁本菴，龍村在坐。……余於袖中出詩卷，一一讀之，兩長老有時頷可，讀到「痴人談古詩，善斥元明代，何如是元明，茫然失所對。」本菴微哂曰：「政道吾輩也。」顧謂龍村曰：「何如是元明？」龍村即對曰：「格律非唐配。」本菴曰：「何如非唐配？」龍村呵呵而笑曰：「茫然失所對。」余詩偶與漁洋相符，而兩長老雅謔，足使余詩發光一時。❻

漁洋表彰元代楊維楨、吳萊樂府歌行，對不同的藝術風格都能欣賞，而炯菴常強調兼師眾長，盛唐格調以外，宋元詩也有其價值，所以炯菴是贊成漁洋的這種態度的。也可知炯菴與漁洋論詩之旨趣闇然相合。

炯菴對漁洋這種打破時代限制的詩觀，認爲是建立在公平博雅的基礎上。因此，炯菴的詩評，常以「公平」爲出發點。如他的《清脾錄》，就是公平爲選詩和評詩的標準。柳得恭就曾經在《清脾錄》序中說，炯菴選詩準於「題品平允」、「不執偏見，取其所長」。炯菴認爲不拘時代、對象，只要公平博雅，自能在各人的詩作品中，找出他們的價值。炯菴對漁洋在文集中，提及朝鮮文人清陰金尚憲的詩文，倍感興奮。他說：

阮亭《池北偶談》載清陰先生詩十餘聯，甚稱美之。今見阮亭《帶經堂集》，有戲效元遺山論詩絕句三十六首。自建安至崇

---

❻ 同上，〈漁洋論詩〉。

> 禎末歷敘詩人。第三十三詩曰：「澹雲微雨小姑祠，菊秀蘭衰八月時，記得朝鮮使臣語，果然東國解聲詩。」注曰：「明崇禎中，朝鮮使臣，過登州作云，蓋首二句，清陰詩也。」❼

除此之外，漁洋在《池北偶談》的〈朝鮮採風錄〉條及《感舊集》八卷中，都曾鈔錄清陰的若干詩篇。炯菴也都一一闡述。

炯菴接觸漁洋文集後，發現漁洋文集中，作詩方面，漁洋有清秀閒雅之新面貌，即不因襲前人崇唐，而論詩方面，也推重詩歌之新變，表彰宋、元詩之價値。漁洋這種特色之旨趣與炯菴自身之詩趣相當符合。炯菴在朝鮮詩歌發展上，主張新變。透過漁洋文集，他像是得到了相當的支持，並且因此在朝鮮積極傳播王漁洋的詩學成就。炯菴的這種作法，李薑山曾為詩云：「俗子雌黃巧索瘢，風懷蕭颯不成看，中州勝事誰空羨，愁殺東鄰李懋官。」❽

炯菴將漁洋的詩學傳介入朝鮮詩壇後，李薑山承繼了這樣的新風格。炯菴說：

> 薑山明澹且妍哀，僞體詩家別有裁，眉宇上升書卷氣，漁洋流派海東來。❾

由以上的敘述可知，炯菴脫離前代的傳統古典詩學思想，接受新的詩學觀念，並以僞體、別裁的方式表現。同時，他接觸漁洋文

---

❼ 同上，卷之五十三，《耳目口心書》卷六。

❽ 同上，眷三十四，《清脾錄》卷三，〈王阮亭〉

❾ 同上，卷十一，《雅亭遺稿》三，〈論詩絕句有懷篠飲雨村蘭垞薑山冷齋楚亭〉。

集後，發展出他自己的詩學理論。

三、時代性執著問題

在李朝，看當時的文藝思潮背景，宣祖以來，支配文壇的是唐詩風，被人稱讚的文章標準是「詩則盛唐」。朴趾源云：「我見世人之譽人，文章者，文必擬兩漢，詩則盛唐也。」❿

大體上，壬辰之亂以後，詩壇盛行唐詩學、唐詩風。朝鮮文壇以「文必兩漢」、「詩必盛唐」爲主流，學明七子盛行擬古派。隨著擬古派明七子王世貞、李攀龍的作詩格調，模仿、因襲古人之詩的惡習，日益嚴重。爲了擺脫這種流弊，以炯菴爲中心的北學派詩人，開始自覺。炯菴認爲應該打破整個文壇缺乏個性的詩風格，主張：

> 見人詩文，不與我同一意致，則必大生疑忌，公然勒定曰：「敗世道、壞心術也。」嗚乎！如此之人，眞是敗世道、壞心術也。詩文如其面之不同，何必強而同之。⓫

炯菴認爲每篇詩文，都應各具自己的面貌，強迫自己因襲模仿他人，而缺少自己的性情，這種作法是遠離心性，遠離作詩之道的。因此他主張作詩應隨著時代、隨著個人的不同，而有各自的風格，並且認定凡是模仿的、因襲的詩，都是虛假的、造作的。他說：

---

❿ 朴趾源，《燕巖集》，〈贈左蘇山人〉

⓫ 李德懋，《青莊館全書》卷二十八，〈士小節〉中〈士典〉二。

代各有詩，人各有詩，詩不可相襲，相襲、贋詩也。⓬

炯菴之前，朝鮮文人中，擺脫蹈襲中國詩，創出新理論的第一人是蛟山許筠。他說：

我國自羅麗以來，局於聞見，雖有逸才，只蹈襲一套，其自謂文章，絕不可見。惟許端甫創出新論若徐袁輩，奇哉！⓭

許筠是宣祖時人，當時詩風流於學唐，但許筠反對固守崇唐之正統詩學，主張獨創性文學⓮。然當時的人不接受許氏之主張。至英、正祖時，以李炯菴爲中心的北學派文人之間，喚起了對許氏見解之發展與擴散。炯菴反對模仿盛唐李杜，而重視自己的面目。他的〈論詩絕句〉中云：

各夢無干共一床，人非甫白代非唐，吾詩自信如吾面，依樣衣冠笑郭郎。⓯

可知炯菴反對剽竊古人、古法，而重視個人創見風格。他以爲時代已非盛唐，時人也非李、杜，一味追求舊時代風格，以剿襲爲

⓬ 同上，《雅亭遺稿》三，〈楚亭詩稿序〉。

⓭ 同上，《青莊館全書》卷五十一，《耳目口心書》六。

⓮ 許筠，《惺所覆瓿□》卷二十一，〈文部〉十八，尺牘，〈與李蓀谷〉云：「翁以僕近體爲純熟嚴縝，不涉盛唐，斥而不御，獨善古詩爲顏謝風格，是翁膠不知影也。古詩雖古，是臨榻逼眞而已。屋下架屋，何足貴乎？近體雖不逼唐，自有我造化。吾則懼其似唐似宋，而欲人曰許子之詩也。毋乃濫乎？」

⓯ 李德懋，《青莊館全書》卷五十三，《耳目口心書》六。

復古，務為牽合，棄目前之景與個人獨創之情感，是不當的觀念。又云：

> 文章不必專主一門，隨地從心。⑯

烔菴既注重廣泛向前人學習，又主張文章應當源於作者對環境遭遇的體驗與作者自己具有的眞心。

烔菴之子光葵在〈先考府君遺事〉中提及，有人問烔菴，歷代詩中，何者最好？烔菴作了以下的答覆：

> 或問歷代詩何者最好？曰：蜂之釀蜜，不擇花，蜂若擇花，蜜必不成。為詩亦猶是也，為詩者，當泛濫於諸家，有所裁度，則吾詩各具歷代體格。今之人曰唐、曰宋、曰明，各有所尚，非言詩之鐵論也。⑰

可見烔菴認為各個時代都有優秀作者，各有成就，不能以某一時代和一種風格為極限。如只標榜一格，學習某家，絕不能創成自己一家之風，而廣泛地向唐、宋、明諸家學習，體悟它們詩學之優點，才能獨自成家。

此語是烔菴針對當時詩壇「詩必盛唐」的模仿剽竊作風，一針砭的批評。他說：

> 學古而泥，非眞古也，酌古斟今，今眞古也。⑱

---

⑯ 同上，卷六，《嬰處雜稿》二，〈觀讀日記〉。

⑰ 李光葵，《刊本雅亭遺稿》八附錄，〈先考府君遺事〉。

⑱ 李德懋，《青莊館全書》卷五十三，《耳目口心書》六。

炯菴承認學習古代、古人，但古今的文學在演變，創作必須隨時代而變化與發展。

隨著時代的變化，自然改變文風，才能產生新時代的作品。他雖主張改革，但只排斥盲目崇古，卻並非認爲要放棄學習古人。他主張酌古斟今，仍然肯定文學之繼承性與創作之嚴肅性。他又云：

> 文章之藝，其多方乎哉！代代而殊，倫倫而不相侔也。⑲

他主張文學不必限於一家一代，因新變的文學，各有其特色與成就。炯菴主張應兼取眾長的原因之一，是因當時詩壇捨本逐末，只知墨守成規，片面的追求詩必盛唐的觀念，摹擬的濫調形成風氣。爲改革這種詩風，挽救這種弊病而主張改革。爲了糾正時代的流弊，炯菴主張這種新的觀念，有漁洋詩論的影響。

在清，王漁洋一生論詩，標舉神韻，爲了糾正詩壇之偏弊。

先看清初詩壇之情況，有明末崛起的公安、竟陵派的威勢，和前後七子的擬古風兩大潮流。這擬古與反擬古兩派，在當時詩壇互相攻擊、論爭。《四庫全書總目》云：

> 詩自太倉、歷下以雄渾博麗爲主，其失也膚；公安、竟陵以清新幽渺爲宗，其失也詭。學者兩途並窮，不得不折而入宋，其弊也滯而不靈，直而好盡，語錄史論，皆可成篇。於是士禎等，重申嚴羽之說，獨主神韻以矯之，蓋亦救弊補偏，各明一義。」⑳

---

⑲ 同上，卷三，《嬰處文稿》一，〈甲申除夕記〉。

⑳ 《四庫全書總目》卷一九〇，集部·總集類五，〈唐賢三昧集〉。

可知漁洋標舉神韻，亦爲了求弊補偏而提出。

在當時，主張雄渾豪健的前後七子，主張清新幽渺的公安、竟陵派，都各有缺陷，漁洋因此主張不限一格，兼取所長，以救其弊，他的詩論三變，也與當時詩壇的弊端有密切的關係。其三次變化，早年宗唐，中年崇宋，晚年復宗唐，這點引起漁洋生前的弟子們，和對漁洋詩學之研究者，相當的爭論。

但他標舉神韻的基本立場，則始終一貫，只是隨著詩壇潮流之弊，隨時提出不同的看法，而有所謂「三變」。這是只爲了糾正詩壇之偏弊，並未改變自己標舉之神韻理論的主意。

漁洋對他生前不同時期流行的不同詩風，曾在〈高津草唐詩集序〉云：

> 三十年前，余初出，交當世名輩，見夫稱詩者，無一人不爲樂府，樂府必漢「鐃歌」，非是者弗屑也；無一人不爲古選，古選必「十九首」、公讌，非是者弗屑也。余竊惑之，是何能爲漢、魏者之多也？歷六朝而唐、宋，千有餘歲，以詩名其家者甚眾，豈其才盡不今若耶？是必不然。故嘗著論，以爲唐有詩，不必建安、黃初也；元和以後有詩，不必神龍、開元也；北宋有詩，不必李、杜、高、岑也。二十年來，海內賢知之流，矯枉過正，或欲祖宋而祧唐，至漢魏樂府古選之遺音，蕩然無復存者，江河日下，滔滔不返，有識者懼焉。㉑

這裡漁洋說明三十年以前，詩壇都傾向宗奉漢魏盛唐，不規撫宋元

㉑ 王士禎，《池北偶談》卷上，〈施宋〉條下。

以下，而二十年以前詩壇變了，都放棄漢魏盛唐之音，而倒追宗兩宋之音，詩壇偏向之流弊仍然存在。可知漁洋之三變，不是欲祖宋而祧唐，欲宗唐而棄宋。他的意思是，欲突破詩壇片面宗奉特定時代的狹隘界限。他原不是反對漢魏盛唐，只是企圖兼取宋元。俞兆晟〈漁洋詩話序〉中也曾有他的自述：

> 吾老矣，還念生平論詩凡屢變，而交遊中亦如日之隨影，忽不知其轉移也。少年初筮仕時，惟務博綜賅洽，以求兼長，文章江左，煙月揚州，人海花場，比肩接跡，入吾室者俱操唐音，韻勝於才，推爲祭酒，然亦空存昔夢，何堪涉想。中歲越三唐而事兩宋，良由物情厭故，筆意喜生，耳目爲之頓新，心思於焉避熟。明知長慶以後已有濫觴，而淳熙以前俱奉爲正的，當其燕市逢人，征途揖客，爭相提倡，遠近翕然宗之。既而清利流爲空疏，新靈寖以佶屈，顧瞻世道，惄焉心憂，於是以大音希聲，藥淫哇錮習，《唐賢三昧》之選，所謂乃造平淡時也。然而境亦從茲者矣。

由此可知漁洋詩論三變的理由，與當時詩壇末流之弊病。漁洋之宗唐、越三唐而事兩宋、復歸於唐的變化，是隨著潮流而變，並爲補救潮流而變。如他糾正盛唐之膚，公安、竟陵之詭，兩宋之滯而不靈等。

漁洋所主張的原則，就是各時代有各時代的長處，文風可隨著時代而變化。他對這種隨著時代而變化的特色，作下面這些評語：

> 近人言詩好立門户，某者爲唐，某者爲宋，李、杜、蘇、黄，

強分畛域，如蠻觸氏之鬥于蝸角而不自知其陋也。㉒

初盛有初盛之眞精神面目，中晚有中晚之眞精神眞面目。㉓

李滄溟詩名冠代，祇以樂府摹擬割裂，遂生後人詆毀，則樂府擬爲其變，而不可以字句比擬也，亦明矣。㉔

唐人尚文選學……亦是爾時風氣。至韓退之出，則風氣大變矣，蘇子瞻極斥昭明，至以爲小兒強作解釋，亦風氣遞嬗使然耳。㉕

詩，騷以下，風會遞遷，乃自然之理，必至之勢。㉖

後人之不能取漢魏，猶漢魏之不能風雅，勢也。㉗

漁洋喜歡兼取所長，不拘於一代一格，故於歷代詩作皆有所取，因各代有各代之眞精神眞面目，所以不可以字句比擬模仿。

自有詩以來，詩隨著時代而有各種變化，這叫風會遞遷。這種遞變的原則，是循著自然之理，非人力所能阻止，是必至勢。也因此各代才有各代特殊的色彩、特殊的風格。因此，漁洋口號神韻，提出補救詩壇偏弊之論，對於推崇特殊一代固執者，下一針砭，主張該脫離偏向性學習及作詩。

反而至於李朝炯菴，他也認爲各個時代都具有自己的特色和其成就，炯菴曾吟幾句話，他說：「難齊萬品整而斜，色色璁瓏日炙

㉒ 《帶經唐詩話》卷二十七。

㉓ 同上，《居易錄》。

㉔ 《詩清話》，《師友詩傳錄》。

㉕ 同上。

㉖ 同上。

㉗ 《帶經堂詩話》卷一，〈池北偶談〉。

霞。喫著雖殊元一致，蠶家未必哂耕家。」〈論詩絕句〉可知炯菴以爲各時代皆有好詩，有各樣特色，豐富多彩，不必以一格一律論優劣。他主張摒棄「詩必盛唐」的狹小性，於歷代詩作皆有所取，皆可學習。

但當時擬古派詩人，對炯菴矯正時弊的新詩論，大肆批評。炯菴對自己年輕時，企圖糾正詩壇末弊，與其他具有相同主張的文友，共同推展文學活動的回顧，曾說：

> 吾儕二十年前，汎覽百家，亦云富有。……發爲詞章，亦以別裁僞體，多師爲師，相與約誓。蓋自《三百篇》、《騷》、賦、古選、漢魏六朝、唐宋金元明清、羅、麗、本朝，以至安南、日本、琉球之詩，上下三千年，縱橫一萬里，眼力所湊，不遺錙銖。自謂不敢多讓於古人，而間嘗隨其所好，種種仿傚，一試為之，放蕩遊戲。㉘

炯菴以別裁僞體，自創新路，即暗示他欲脫離當時「詩必盛唐」的潮流，開闢詩的新境界。同時，炯菴所學，也不限於唐，他廣博涉獵各時代，各地域特色，採其價值，博其旨趣。

炯菴除了他對當時朝鮮詩壇「詩必盛唐」的口號，對於反對七子，卻又一味傾倒袁中郎的態度，也表示反對。他反對公安派過度貶低漢唐傳統，追求庸俗的主張，他說：

> 或曰：「今若有李雪樓，左擁王元美，右攜張肖甫，驅謝茂秦、徐子與輩，來問於子曰：『文當擬《左傳》、《國策》、

㉘ 《刊本雅亭遺稿》卷七，〈與朴在先齊家書〉。

《史記》、《漢書》，而韓柳以下不論。詩當擬建安、黃初、開元、天寶，而元白以下不論。或敢脫此法律而出它語，皆非吾所謂文章也。』子當何答？」

曰：「我當曰拘也。……文章一造化也。造化豈可拘縛而齊之於摹擬乎？夫人人俱有一具文章，蟠鬱胸中，如其面不相肖。如責其同也，則板刻之畫，舉子之卷也，何奇之有？亦余豈曰盡棄古人之法也？非子之所以縛於法而不能自恣也。法自具於不法之中，豈曰棄也？……」

或曰：「又若有袁柳浪，左擁徐文長，右攜江進之，驅曾退如，陶周望輩，來問於子曰：『文章安有定法哉？理何必先民所恆訓，語何必前賢所恆道？當快脫粘縛，直段步武，門戶則特立，而洞天則別開也。或掇拾古人字句？豈曰文章各世哉？』子當何答？」

曰：「我當曰拘也。……然天下之才，非超脫而止也。有典雅者，有平易者，壹皆責之以別創新奇，或恐反喪其本然，而日趨于高曠超絕之域，不亦敗道乎？振作多士之文章，豈一律而已哉？無乃局乎。人才奇正，自有可觀，抑揚與奪，正規暗諷，順導反說，其變化也無涯。但不使之太剶削其渠之本然與天真，去其滲滓腐穢而已矣。且古人軌轍，不可拘束，亦不可專然拋棄也……」

或曰：「子奚取焉？」曰：「集二子而各棄其酷焉，可也。……」㉙

㉙ 《青莊館全書》卷四十八，《耳目口心書》一。

因此可知，炯菴並不是完全反對漢魏盛唐的格調，也不完全忽視公安派的理論，而是主張取長棄短，包羅所有的理論。像七子那樣盲從古人之法，一味模仿的陳腐論調，像公安派的無視於古法，流於喪失本然的主張，炯菴都不以爲然，而主張法自具於不法之中，認爲以才調可救七子之弊，以典雅可救公安之失。

炯菴的理論是爲打破當時宗唐法古、模仿、蹈襲的狹隘觀念，而主張博取歷代之長、調和折衷，以救偏向性的末弊。

當時朝鮮詩壇與清代詩壇之趨勢是不相同的。中國已經脫離了前後七子、公安、竟陵的爭論，漁洋詩學也走向衰退之路。然朝鮮詩壇與一百餘年前明末清初的詩壇的形勢相仿。

漁洋的詩論特性在突破漢魏盛唐的界限，博取宋元，此點與炯菴的詩論主張相同。而漁洋爲了糾正當時詩壇流弊，在詩論主張方面，歷經三變，炯菴也爲了矯正當時詩壇宗唐的偏弊，成爲新變詩學的領導者。兩人任詩壇的地位，處境類似。

四、詩之要諦論

炯菴對學詩的過程，主張應該熟讀歷代各家之詩。另外一方面，在詩歌的創作方法上，提出所謂「妙解透悟法」。他在論〈文章之定法〉一文中云：

> 且古人軌轍，不可拘束，亦不可專然拋棄也。自有妙解透悟法，在人人各自善得之如何耳。㉚

㉚ 《青莊館全集》卷四十八，《耳目口心書》一。

炯菴反對任何定法，重視自得之境。

他主張詩歌創作的特性在妙解透悟，詩人必須超越「法」的限制，而應善用自得、自悟。炯菴與金錫汝論文章，借他的話云：

> 文章無悟解處則不可，如東坡諸公，得妙悟法，故多有可觀，楞嚴及莊子，不可不一覽。又有一種病根，作文者不到精熟地位，而反以減字爲先務，故意思不得流注。譬如初學詩人，不先學精神意趣之如何，而區區於格律高低，反不如放意為之之時耳。㉛

又云：

> 文章有悟處，然後立脚，勿以中郎爲末季怪品侮之。齋心靜會，必透得玲瓏竇。一轉眼則萬物皆吾文章也。㉜

由此可知，炯菴主張文章必須有悟解處。學詩、作詩都應有一種基本態度——對悟有自覺。他認爲學詩者對詩的基本特性要具備確實的認識，並先學習精神意趣的運用。他對初學詩者，對詩本質及特性的認識不夠，而只注意字句與格律的追求，表示反對。他強調詩創作最重要的是「悟」。悟的特點，是不假理論的造作與思索的活動，直接的感受對象之審美現象，內包心靈感應之因素。這一點與性靈說有相通之處，所以炯菴不排斥袁中郎之文學批評的識見與旨趣。炯菴認爲一旦齋心靜會，掃除一切，進入得心應手的頓悟境界，此時之悟境，就是「達到詩歌創作上運用自如、豁然無礙的境界。」

㉛ 同上，卷五十一，《耳目口心書》四。

㉜ 同上，卷十六，《雅亭遺稿》八，〈內地朴稚川，宗山〉。

㉝道則無所不在，「隨遇皆道，觸處可悟。」㉞都合於自然，所以烔菴說「一轉眼則萬物皆吾文章也。」

烔菴採用妙悟法的詩道，也同時肯定了佛家、道家與詩學的淵源。

詩道與禪道的關係，在唐代時已經盛行。到了宋代，蘇東坡將作詩與參禪相比，宋人將詩禪相提並論，也更常見。

嚴羽之「大抵禪道惟在妙悟，詩道亦惟在妙悟」的詩論是借自禪宗，他受到佛家之影響，遂集詩禪互通說之大成。詩與禪的共通點在於「悟」，也成為一般人普遍接受的觀念。嚴羽之「妙悟說」對於後世詩歌批評發展甚有貢獻。借禪語論語以後，妙悟一詞是詩學理論中重要關鍵之一。妙悟是指在創作時的特殊心理現象，也就是持一種審美認識。

更仔細地尋找「妙悟」的意味，則陳伯海所云：

> 「妙悟」是人們從長時期潛心地欣賞，品味好的詩歌作品中養成的一種審美意識活動和藝術感受能力，它的特點在於不憑藉理性的思考而能夠對詩歌形象內容的情趣韻味作直接的領會與把握，這種心理活動和能力構成了詩歌創作的原動力。……今人有把「妙悟」當作靈感，就其不假思索的活動方式而言，可能包含靈感的因素在內，但它本身是一個有意識進行積累的過程，和靈感的來不可遏，去不可止，藏若景

㉝ 郁阮〈嚴羽詩禪說析辨〉（學術月刊，一九八一年，第七期）轉引黃景進《嚴羽及其詩論之研究》。

㉞ 《傳燈錄》卷十。

> 滅，行猶響起，顯然是不容相混的。也有人認為「妙悟」相當于今天所謂的形象思維，就其極力強調藝術活動的特殊性來看，確實觸及形象思維的某些重要內涵，但它帶有非理性的玄學色彩，又使它不可能等同于形象思維的科學概念，倒比較近似于西方美學家所講的「藝術直覺」，而又結合了中國古典美學中對興象、韻味等的探索和追求。「妙悟」說的眞正思想淵源，應該是佛教禪宗學說。㉟

可知「妙悟」不是靠理性的思考活動，是於一種「直覺」的思維方式。「妙悟」的境界是指不經過理智的思索，由完全沒有用意的心理狀態下，產生的直接的認識。這時的悟境，是一種極高的警覺狀態，具有直接認識事物更深本質的能力。」㊱

妙悟說之思想淵源，來自禪宗，禪宗所說之悟是本來不假理性的思維之推理，是憑直覺察照。

炯菴論詩，也接受佛家借悟言詩的基本觀念，認為詩道非邏輯判斷，非推理演繹，而是直覺的心靈感應。他認為了作詩時，應該掃除一切雜念，努力於進入自得自悟的境界。

炯菴認為理會自得處即所謂妙悟，詩的本質有妙解透悟的審美意識。而妙悟的重點是自得，是與「法」無關的。

炯菴平時生活，以典型的儒家規範作為實踐目標，因此對佛、道有偏狹的排斥心。這種矛盾心理，經常在他心中造成衝突。

㉟ 陳伯海，〈妙悟探源——讀《滄浪詩話》札記之二〉，社會科學戰線，一九八五年第一期。

㊱ 黃景進，《嚴羽及其詩論之研究》。

而炯菴的佛老思想對他的文學活動及思想的影響，使他脫離了儒家理論的狹隘性。他說：

> 心溪宗姪光錫，衷襟炯然，言入虛無，幾陷佛者之學。余甚憂之，近者猛下工夫，爲聖賢之學，入孝出恭，越有規矩，眞可敬也。然其所唫哢者，□出尋常，多有悟解，人皆不知，余獨知其頭頭皆道。時箴其太僻者而嘗笑曰：「君詩宛是讀楞嚴經者口中語，非讀大學人口中語。」遂歛手而對曰：「心無所累，語或灑脫，何害吾道！」㊲

他雖借的是心溪的話，其實是他自己的想法。他的基本生活態度是儒家的，但他也同時肯定佛老的形而上之學。他曾說「多有悟解」「頭頭皆道」，都可見他傾心禪道的痕跡。他的詩學理論根柢，是來自禪學。所以他認爲詩道、禪道的共通之處在「悟」，妙唔處全仗天機偶到，合於自然。詩禪均需到達「自得之境」。

炯菴以爲觀察景物，體悟宇宙間造化與天機，使外在之物，與內心感情能合而爲一，將天地間至妙、至化之理融入詩中。

再至漁洋，他以禪禪觀禪境入詩，追求詩的境界超越言語所能表達，進入外之精神，貫通一切事物之眞相，而能以自然合一。此爲神說的理想境界。兩人都以「明心見性」的態度，品嘗，宇宙天機爲兩人的共通點。

漁洋以禪論詩的用意如下：

㊲ 《青莊館全書》卷四十八，《耳目口心書》一。

> 唐人五言絕句，往往入禪，有得意忘言之妙，與淨名默然，達磨得髓，同一關捩，讀王、裴《輞川集》及祖〈詠終南殘雪詩〉，雖鈍根初機，亦能頓悟。㊳

又云：

> 嚴滄浪以禪喻詩，余深契其鋭，而五言尤爲近之，如王裴輞川絕句，字字入禪……妙諦微言，與世尊拈花，迦葉微笑，等無差別，通其解者，可悟上乘。㊴

又云：

> 嚴儀卿所謂如鏡中花，如水中月，如水中鹽味，如羚羊掛角，無跡可求，皆以禪理喻詩，內典所云「不即不離，不黏不脫」，曹洞宗所云參活句是也，熟看拙選唐賢三昧集，自知之矣。㊵

漁洋借禪語以論詩，價值在詩語意外之，他重視的是「得意忘言」、「妙諦微言」。他以爲文字背後隱藏的無窮之詩趣，正是透過體悟入禪，即詩與禪二者都需要體悟。詩與禪以體悟見機，與世尊拈花、迦葉微笑等無別，二者皆有體悟成份內在之重要性，此即是二者相連貫之處。以禪理喻詩，禪理全融入了詩境，靜觀自得，超然物外，物我兩忘，達到絕對的境界。此種詩與禪機全然契合，

㊳ 王士禎，《帶經堂詩話》卷三，〈佇興類〉。

㊴ 同上，〈微喻類〉。

㊵ 同上，卷二十九，〈答問類〉。

即是「不即不離，不黏不脫」之意境。

漁洋以禪論詩，是通禪於詩，以禪義入詩，禪通詩，詩通禪，工夫在悟上面，使禪學與詩學合一。他說：

> 捨筏登岸，禪家以爲悟境，詩家以爲化境，詩禪一致，等無差別。㊶

漁洋所謂詩禪一致，換言之，即詩是禪，禪即是詩。禪之經驗與詩之經驗相同，二者皆出於同一本源之心。此時，禪與詩沒有區分，乃屬於絕對的、自由的悟性，因心已不受理智的驅使。即禪與詩的最高境界是「不能以文字傳達，但在妙悟的內光中呈現的奧秘」㊷，是超乎理性與感覺，不受理性與感覺束縛。體悟的頂點是圓融無礙，不偏於某一方，一切歸源於一，屬於絕對的自性，「一切即一，一即一切」的意境。此時的狀態，以禪的立場看爲思想的最高境界。以文學的立場看，是藝術的最高境界。豁然頓悟的瞬間，明徹一切事物眞相，把握宇宙萬物之玄機及人生的樂趣。此時，禪與詩無分，禪通於詩，詩通於禪，所以漁洋說「捨筏登岸，禪家以爲悟境，詩家以爲化境。」

在炯菴的詩論中，已述其以妙語爲重視，作詩的關鍵就是在妙語，其所謂意境是妙悟中自得之境，可知漁洋與炯菴之論詩觀點相似。

炯菴之文學，是全然基於體悟，不只限於文字上。他以爲在詩

㊶ 同上，卷三，〈微喻類〉。

㊷ 劉若愚，《中國詩學》，頁一三三。

作活動上，重要的是齋心靜會、靜觀、理會自得。此法，是指不靠理語之造作與思索活動，直接進入自我的覺醒，把握內心之自得。靜觀開悟之時，與自然凝合，消除物我之對立感，與宇宙合一，與萬物爲一，自然得到明徹宇宙之究竟。炯菴以詩的境界爲目標，明徹一切事物之眞相，而表達宇宙萬物之本體眞實性。

從王漁洋、李炯菴論詩主張的重點來看，他們都主張澄心、靜慮、觸境成機，天動神解，自然而得，爲二人的共通點。這也是因爲他們都以此爲詩境界的目標。他們所嚮往的詩的理想境界，是明徹一切事物的眞相，把握宇宙玄機的至妙，而與自然合一。這也就是漁洋所謂「詩禪一致，等差無別」，與炯菴所謂「文章有悟處，然後立脚」的基本論調。

五、結　言

炯菴是朝鮮文人中，最早接觸到漁洋文集中的一個。炯菴第一次對漁洋詩論之新傾向，即對他頗爲傾倒。炯菴接觸漁洋文集後，認爲漁洋是不因襲前人崇唐，而表彰宋元詩壇之價値，即是建立在「公平博雅」的基礎上。

炯菴發現漁洋這種詩學特色之旨趣與他自身之詩趣相當符合，因此，炯菴的詩評亦以「公平」爲出發點。炯菴在朝鮮詩歌發展上，已討厭前代的傳統古典詩學思想，嘗企圖求新求變，透過漁洋文集，他像是得到了相當的支持，發展出他自己的詩學理論，並且由此，在朝鮮積極傳播王士禎的詩學成就。炯菴認爲漁洋有清秀閒雅之新面貌，故賦與他「清初第一大家」之稱呼。

炯菴主張擺脫宗唐、學宋之狹隘觀念。因當時朝鮮詩壇盛行擬古，因襲盛唐之風，他提出博取歷代之長，補救詩壇偏弊之論。當時朝鮮詩壇似乎與明末清初詩壇形勢相彷彿。漁洋也爲了矯正當時詩壇之流弊，成爲新變詩學的領導者，兩人在詩壇上的處境類似。炯菴所嚮往的詩的理想境界，是明徹一切事物的眞相，與萬物內在本性之天機，全然契合。他主張詩人以絕對出自本性的眼目，感知宇宙變化，關照事物本性與一切現象，體會造化之妙，與自然合爲一體。這即是與漁洋所謂「詩禪一致」相同。兩人以「明心見性」的態度，品嚐宇宙天機，爲兩人的共通處。

「鐵屋」中的個人——中國大陸當代文學中「自我」的品格

陳邁平*

一、大陸當代文學中「自我」的再出場

在中國文學史上，「自我」作爲審美活動的主體曾扮演過非常風光的角色。「文以載道」固然成爲一種正統，但是，歷代文人墨客，不論入世出世，不論顯達隱逸，都講究以詩言志抒情，營造有我之境，形成中國文學一貫傳承的文風文品。因此，中國古典文學，包括戲劇，與西方古典文學相較，顯然更富主觀性、抒情性和表現性，而史詩和敘事文學在中國不是未登廟堂，就是發展較晚。進入現代，尤其在五四新文化運動時期，個人主義張揚，「自我」之地位更得到提昇，對現代詩歌、小說、話劇的發展有過很大影響。

在後來的一個相當漫長的歷史時期，尤其是在大陸的文化大革

* 瑞典斯德哥爾摩大學中國研究學系講師，筆名萬之

命中，由於民族危機和社會變亂等種種原因，民族主義和集體主義壓倒個人主義，東風壓倒西風，因此「自我」幾乎從當局劃定的文學舞台上消失。她被冷落、被貶斥、被驅逐、被禁錮、被禁止出場，被那些仍想登上舞台的作家們拋棄。只有在官方劃定的文學舞台之外，在地下、在一些年輕的叛逆者當中，她還有一些秘密的追求者。

毛澤東逝世之後，隨著毛的幽靈逐漸退場，當局劃定的文學舞台逐漸坍塌，冰河解凍，禁錮被打破，這個「自我」的幽靈才重新獲得自由，重新出現在中國文學的場景之中。時過境遷，現在她成了越來越多的作家追求的理想、熱戀的目標、崇拜的偶象，甚至被推到了主宰一切的地位，成爲文學唯一的女神。人們爲她寫作，歌頌她、擁抱她、爲她撒野、爲她發狂。我們常常聽到一些作家聲稱，他們要通過寫作尋找他們曾經失去的「自我」，要在文學中表現「自我」，標揚「自我」，爲「自我」創造一個自由呼吸的心靈空間。毫無疑問，這種爲「自我」的文學，是文化革命後的中國大陸文學的一種主要傾向、一種潮流、一種時髦。

在這種具有個人功利的寫作被強調的同時，社會功利性的寫作，包括當局所規定的政治性寫作，遭到了很多作家的貶低或抵制，甚至反映社會現實生活的寫作也被認爲沒有必要或不可能。對標揚「自我」的作家來說，如果文學是一面鏡子，那麼它也只是讓人看見自己，而不是客觀的世界。那種巴爾扎克式的爲歷史做筆記的寫作被認爲是過時的，甚至受到某種嘲笑。至於純粹商業性的寫作活動，除非出於無奈，自然絕不爲之。不但如此，基於文學應該是個人活動的立場，有些作家甚至完全拒絕了爲讀者的寫作。所謂「純文學」的主張，大致也是在這樣的語境中提出來的。爲「自我」的文學寫作意味個性、意味獨特、意味自由想像和主觀色彩，意味著文學的世界不再只是一種一成不變的風景，而是在各個作家不同「自我」的視野裡呈現各種姿態。因此，大陸的文學在文化大革命後不論在內容和形式上都發生了相當巨大的變化，文學發展的方向、速度和不斷出現的新的結果都已經變得和毛澤東逝世前的文學大不相同，從單一陳舊變爲豐富多樣，面貌一新。我們甚至可以說，「自我」在大陸文壇上發動了又一場除舊佈新的文學革命。詩人顧城說，「新詩之所以新，是因爲它出現了『自我』」❶。

大陸文學的這種新面貌是和「自我」的再出場分不開的。但本文的目的不是對大陸文學中這種「自我」的頌揚，而是對其品格的分析和批判。在我看來，大陸文學雖有進步，但還是顯得侷促、步履艱難，原因之一恐怕就是很多作家還過於沉溺在對這個「自我」的迷戀中，而「自我」事實上還被侷限在魯迅當年在《吶喊》自序中所說的那種「鐵屋」中。

二、「自我」和個人主義及「現代性」

雖然中國大陸當代文學非常推崇「自我」，但是這個「自我」的含義卻依然展示得很模糊。我們很少看到作家對他們要表述的「自我」作明確和具體的交待和分析。在使用「自我」這個字眼的時候，這些作家好像認爲它的含義已經是眾所周知不言而喻的了。

---

❶ 見顧城：〈請聽我們的聲音〉，《墓床》，作家出版社，北京，1993，第172頁。

然而，我們的「自我」眞那麼簡單嗎？如果我們注意作家們使用這個字眼的不同語境，我們會發現顯然不同的含義：有時它是指作家的主體或本體，有時是指可以失而復得的個性；有時是指作家的血肉之身，有時只是指一種意識或是心理狀態；有時是指創作的出發點，有時是指創作的終極。這種模稜兩可常常給人留下很多疑問。如果一個作家說他的寫作是從「自我」出發，而他又要通過寫作找到「自我」，那麼，聽起來有些騎驢找驢的味道了。只有一點大概還是比較明確的，也是反映這些作家比較共同的看法，那就是這些作家都把「自我」看成是一個單獨的個人，都表現出強烈的個人主義的意識。因此，這種「自我」在大陸當代文學中的再出場，也可以看作是個人主義在中國的復興。

當然，個人主義即使在西方其實也是面目靈活多樣的，有時它的概念外延可能伸展至自我主義(Egoism)或者利己主義(Egotism)。在當代中國知識份子身上，我們也看到理性個人主義和非理性個人主義這樣截然不同的傾向。如果說劉再復可以算是理性個人主義的一個重要代表，那麼劉曉波就是標榜非理性個人主義的一個先鋒。不管有怎樣的區別，個人主義無疑是毛澤東逝世以後中國社會的最主要最普遍的思潮之一。在這個時期，中國知識份子的「自我」意識重新覺醒，普遍表現出了對個人主體的強烈關懷，對個人確證、個人權益和個人價值的熱烈訴求。他們的一個比較共同的特點是將個人定爲價值判斷的座標，將個人和群體，和社會，和國家民族等對立起來，強調個人或者「自我」對群體，對社會，對國家民族的超越。

按照劉禾提出的見解，在毛澤東逝世之前的幾十年的中國大陸文學主導話語是所謂「民族國家文學」❷。我認爲，這類「民族國家文學」話語目前在大陸仍有增強的趨勢，但是，隨著「自我」角色的活躍，而這種「自我」又以個人主義爲基礎，所以在大陸當代文學中比較活躍的文學主導話語是一種和「民族國家文學」話語分庭抗禮的「個人主義文學」。

杜維明把「現代性」歸納爲政治上的民主制度，經濟上的自由貿易和思想文化上的個人主義❸。這種歸納是否恰當還可以進一步討論。但是，我至少同意這種看法，即個人主義是「現代性」最重要的標記之一。在這種意義上，「自我」在中國當代大陸文學中的重新出場可以和「現代性」的重新出場聯繫起來，而「自我」發動的這場文學革命也可以因此稱之爲現代主義文學運動。這和中國社會整體向現代社會的轉型也是一致的。

無須諱言，在中國，不論是「自我」意識的重新覺醒，還是個人主義的復興或者所謂「現代性」的出場，都是受到西方現代文化的影響。當代中國的個人主義話語本身是來自西方的舶來品。表示單個個人的「自我」和「個人」等詞彙在中文中最早出現大約是在本世紀初，比較明確的個人主義則是由陳獨秀、胡適、魯迅、李大釗、周作人等知識份子作家在「五、四」運動前後從西方翻譯介紹過來，並在當時造成過巨大影響。當代推崇「自我」的中國作家和這一歷史發展往往有不可否認的淵源關係，他們多有閱讀上述作家

---

❷ 見劉禾：〈文本，批評和民族國家文學〉，《今天》，1992年第一期。

❸ 這裡是引述杜維明先生在一九九三年六月十日至十四日瑞典斯德哥爾摩大學中文系和亞太研究中心聯合舉辦「國家、社會、個人」國際學術討論會的發言。

作品的經驗。當然，這還是一種比較間接的資源。實際上，中國作家常常更願意把他們的個人主義觀念和西方啓蒙時代以來的個人主義直接聯繫起來。當被問及他們所受的影響時他們常常願意直接提到西方現代作家的名字。有些西方評論家以爲文化革命切斷了中國大陸知識份子和西方文化的聯繫。事實是，即使在文化革命的危險條件下也有青年知識份子想方設法搜求西方現代文學的書籍，例如多多曾經談到他和朋友們偷偷閱讀和討論洛爾迦、惠特曼、波德萊爾、聶魯達的詩歌和薩特的小說❹。據我所知，文化大革命中後期，有一本英國人寫的被譯成中文內部出版的哲學書叫作《開放的自我》，曾經在很多年輕人手中傳抄，成爲這一代人的一本啓蒙讀物。在中國當代個人主義作家的話語中，我們還經常聽到充滿西方個人主義精神的一些術語，比如「獨立意志」、比如「個人尊嚴」、比如「自決權利」，比如「獨特個性」，比如「自我確證」，如此等等。由於某種歷史的原因，「現代性」和「西方性」在中國常常被一些人當做同義語。「現代的」等於「西方的」，「現代化」等於「西方化」，所以，像方勵之和劉曉波等知名人物甚至提出如果中國要全面地「現代化」就要「全盤西化」，其實也不足怪。

由於這樣一種語境，在一些批評家看來，中國大陸當代文學中的「自我」幽靈純粹是個外來的入侵者。大概出於對西方文化霸權的警覺，一些批評家站在一種「民族國家文學」話語的立場上，強調中國文學應該有中國文學的自己的獨特品格。以此爲批評的尺

❹ 見多多：〈一九七〇—七八年的北京地下文學〉，《今天》，1991年第三／四期。

度，他們對這個外來的「自我」幽靈及其推動的文學革命的成就和價值表示懷疑。他們批評那些崇拜這個「自我」的中國作家，是在西方文化霸權的陰影下創作，不光是在移置和翻版西方文學的「現代性」的話語，甚至是在模仿、複製、甚至抄襲西方現代主義作品。有些批評家甚至認爲這個「自我」連入侵者也算不上，只是一個沒有自身生命的傀儡。八十年代中期在大陸出現的關於「僞現代派」文學的爭論，就是以此爲背景。這個「僞」不僅是表示「眞僞」之「僞」，也是表示漢奸賣國求榮的「僞軍」之「僞」❺。

在西方，也有一些文學批評家持相似的觀點。例如，一位瑞典評論家在談他自己閱讀北島的詩歌的感受時說，雖然北島的詩寫得很出色，但是他讀時總有似曾相識之感，好像看到了一輛西方早就發明而今天又在中國被複製的自行車❻。說得直接了當一點，就是他認爲北島詩歌具有「複製」西方現代詩歌的特點。另一些西方學者則認爲中國作家出於一種想獲得全球影響的「焦慮」，在創作時力求趨近西方文化霸權控制下的世界美學價值標準❼。他們的言外之意是，爲了贏得世界的承認，中國作家在爲西方批評家和讀者的口味寫作，因此中國當代文學的「現代性」也許只是在西方現代強

❺ 參閱李陀：〈也談僞現代派及其批評〉，《北京文學》，1984年第四期。

❻ 見約然·格萊德：〈甚麼樣的自行車〉，《今天》，1990年第一期。

❼ 見 Steven Owen: "The Anxiety of Global Influence: What Is World Poetry?", The New Republic, 1990, No. 19. 以及 Bonnie S. McDougall, "The Anxiety of Out-Influence", Inside Out : Modernism and Post Modernism in Chinese Literary Culture, edited by Wendy Larson and Anne W-Wedellsborg, 崎Arhus: Aarhus University Press, 1993, 第102-3頁。

勢文化壓迫下食人牙慧的結果。

三、話語資源和利用環境

查爾斯·泰勒（Charles Taylor）的《自我探源》（Sources of the Self）一書是對西方「現代性」品格的深入而富有說服力的調查。受他的啓發，我以爲關於中國大陸當代文學中的「自我」或者「現代性」的討論應該越過所謂證「僞」的階段而進入對品格的更爲認眞的分析和批判，也應該一看其話語資源構成，二看那些資源的現實利用環境，以一種尊重事實的歷史學家的態度代替那種只追究眞僞的藝術收藏家的態度。需知，即使是一種以假亂眞的複製，由於複製材料的來源、複製的過程及複製時的環境是獨特的，是原品生產時所不具有的，因此複製品也會有自身的特點，作爲一種歷史的存在也必然有它自身分析的意義。何況，我也不認爲中國當代文學中的「自我」或「現代性」就僅僅是模仿西方文學的複製品，所謂「全盤西化」是不可能的。它們的話語資源、它們發展起來的歷史語境和語位，實際上遠比人們所想像的複雜和特殊，因此它們的品格和西方文學的「自我」或「現代性」的品格既有相似之處，又不可混爲一談。實際上，作爲已經進入中國當代人文景觀的眞實具體的一種話語，它們已經獲得自己的生命，已經有自己的獨特品格。

就中國當代文學中的「自我」和「現代性」話語的資源構成來說，西方現代人文思想雖然是其中最重要的一個部分，但不是唯一的部分，中國自己的強厚的人文資源也占據了相當的比例。如果正如泰勒所指出的那樣，西方文學的「現代性」和西方的人文傳統有著千絲萬縷的聯繫，那麼，根據同樣的道理，我們也可以看到中國當代文學中的「自我」和「現代性」和中國的人文傳統之間的千絲萬縷的聯繫。例如，已經有些作家和批評家指出，在中國當代文學中的「自我」和中國傳統的群己觀念有密切的關係。還有評者認爲，中國作家身上瀰漫著中國傳統文化獨特的「隱逸」精神❽。我甚至認爲，統治中國幾十年的官方話語和中國當代文學中的「自我」意識也有些糾葛。關於這種聯繫，後面將進一步分析。

就中國當代文學中的「自我」和「現代性」話語資源的現實的利用環境來說，即使來自西方的資源，在中國的特殊的社會人文環境中也會被製造成不同的產品。就像泰勒所描述的那樣，同樣的精神或觀念資源，是經常會在不同的時代、不同社會的歷史上下文中出現的，它們的意義可能也會因此不同，今天我們仍然聽得見席勒時代的號角，然而它的意義、它的形象，卻可能和席勒時代完全不同。這正如中國官方的話語生產，雖然這種生產有西方馬克思主義作爲主要的資源，但是它也結合了中國傳統文化的資源，並在中國的特殊利用環境中製造出特殊的政治產品。鄧小平提出的「中國特色的社會主義」，其實就是一個例子。

因此，不能以資源的來處來判斷產品的性格，因爲資源來自西方就斷定中國當代文學中的「自我」和「現代性」僅僅是複製西方。一種話語可能只是一個框架，一個既是實體但又是理念的容器。所

---

❽ 參閱高行健：〈《靈山》及其它〉，《今天》，1992年第二期以及高健平：〈中國傳統繪畫中的隱逸精神〉，見作者在一九九三年六月十日至十四日瑞典斯德哥爾摩大學中文系和亞太研究中心聯合舉辦「國家、社會、個人」國際學術討論會的發言。

謂「自我」、「個人主義」和「現代性」這些話語眞可以像集裝箱一樣裝載不同資源的觀念和思想，像一只潘多拉的盒子藏盡現代日常生活的各種奧秘。事實上，這種箱子本身的製作材料和樣式也不一定有甚麼一成不變適合一切社會條件的規定標準，也是可以因地制宜，千變萬化的。因此，雖然從話語資源來說，它們是來自西方，但它們裝載的東西卻不一定是西方的。

在我看來，使用來自西方的話語也無須看作對西方文化霸權的屈服。我們完全不必害怕使用這些話語，因爲我們不一定要把它的內涵簡單地界定在西方的所指範圍之內。有些話語是可以描寫屬於全人類的普遍文化現象的，不應該以一種弱勢文化心態去加以抵制，而應該用國際化的立場來對待，這樣，不論它們是西方還是東方發明的話語，都可以坦然地拿來採用。好比攝氏溫度表或經緯線雖然是西方發明的測溫或地理定位標準，但全世界都可以用來測溫或標取地理方位。同樣，即使「自我」、「個人主義」或「現代性」這些話語是屬於西方的一種專利，但個體觀念和「自我」意識的發展，現代社會的產生，並不是西方社會的獨有現象，因此這些話語也可以用來描寫把其它文化中發展起來的類似現象，而不用把它們視爲複製品。我個人的看法是：人類社會從傳統向現代過渡是因爲人本身的個體觀念和「自我」意識的發展，它的發展結果就是人類對自然、對傳統文化和傳統社會制度的認識的改變，因此重新調整個人和自然或者和傳統文化和傳統社會的關係，從重視神權到重視王權最後進一步落實到人權，現代社會於是誕生。從歷史看，「神—王—人」的過渡幾乎成爲各個不同文明社會發展的一種共同模式，至少一種廣義的「個人主義」是人類社會從傳統向現代過渡時一種普遍的現象。區別也許只在過渡有快有慢而已。例如，在我看來，個人觀念和「自我」意識本來在中國文化傳統資源中並不缺少，中國文化本身有過獨立發展出個人主義或者「現代性」的可能性，只是這種時機大概在明末就被歷史錯過了。❾在這方面，西方是捷足先登了，但先登不等於獨有。

四、中國個人主義發展的歷史語境和本世紀中國作家的「鐵屋」心態

中國當代的個人主義者身上往往暴露出一種複雜矛盾的品格。一方面，他強調個人或者「自我」的超脫性或者可剝離性：可以超越黨派、民族、國家，可以從社會團體剝離出去。另一方面，在面對西方文化的強勢壓力的時候，爲了保持個人的身分，他往往不自覺地採取民族文化的立場，表現出強烈的群體意識，甚至不惜放棄個人主義的身份和利益。這時，他就會積極投入群體活動而不再超脫。要是加入了某個政治黨派，就服從黨團的利益，並且頗有犧牲了個人的氣概。我以爲這種矛盾，這種不得兩全的尷尬和痛苦是中國個人主義品格所獨有的。

我們不妨將中西方個人主義觀念作一下比較：在西方的個人主義觀念中，個人和社會群體或黨派的關係不一定是衝突的，個人不過是組成社會群體或黨派的一個最基本單位，因此一個個人主義者

❾ 參閱 Chen Maiping,「Xu Wei and Modernity in Chinese Literature」, Stockholm Journal of East Asian Studies, 1993年第一期。

同樣可以積極參予黨派活動而不失獨立的個人的身份和自由。在中國的個人主義觀念中，一個個人往往必須無黨無派才算得上是獨立自由的個人，因此很多個人主義知識份子拒絕加入政治黨派和民主團體，甚至要在心理上和整個社會保持距離、脫離關係，也就是所謂「自我流亡」、「超越」或者「隱逸」。

中國個人主義和西方個人主義這種品格上的差別首先是因爲他們的歷史語境不同而造成的。這種語境的特點是兩種危機並列交織的存在：一是民族危機，反映民族文化和西方文化的矛盾；二是社會的危機，反映個人和社會的矛盾。用毛澤東的話語就是又要反帝又要反封建，用李澤厚話語就是所謂又要救亡又要啓蒙。這兩種危機、兩種矛盾，實際上是互相衝突干擾的，造成個人主義發展的一種困境。一個中國知識份子又要在第一種危機中採取民族的立場以對抗西方，又要在第二種危機中站在個人的立場對抗傳統，也就是靠攏現代、靠攏西方。他既要考慮整體，又要考慮個人，眞是進退兩難。

我們不妨也將中西方個人主義發展的歷史情境也作一下比較。在西方，從歷史來看，個人主義沒有是被用來當做民族復興的武器，借倡導個人權利而富國強兵，它基本上也不是用來作爲對抗社會的武器，不是用來顚覆控制社會的價值體系。西方個人主義的發展最早是從人道主義立場出發，突出了人權和神權或王權的矛盾，是把人從不平等的社會等級制下解放出來，當時和個人主義相應的文學寫作往往是針對教會、專制暴君和貴族，或者歌頌生命、愛情和自由。在個人主義的理想，基本上通過種種途徑付諸實踐的西方現代社會，關於個人權益的條文明確地寫在各個民主國家的憲法和宣言中，個人主義本身成爲西方現代社會運作法則和道德倫理的一大基石。因此，我們可以說，個人主義在現代西方基本上是處在一種如魚得水的社會環境中。社會就是個人的集合，個人可以自由地、也是自覺地生活在社會群體之中，被鼓勵在其中奮鬥。在這種情況下，個人和社會之間基本上是一種正面的關係而不是互相衝突的兩極。個人並不因爲在社會中而不成爲個人，換言之，他不用因爲害怕失去個人的身份而把自己抽離出社會去「隱逸」。相反，他會積極地參與社會活動，強調個人的民主權利，因爲社會進步，個人同樣得利；社會出錯，個人也受影響。我們當然看到西方當代知識份子對社會的失望和批判，但這不是一種個人主義者對非個人主義社會的失望和批判，而往往是對個人主義本身的失望和批判，或是對一個曾經向個人有過種種許諾而沒有兌現的個人主義社會的失望和批判。不論怎樣的失望和批判，我們看到的還是個人對社會的參與感。在中國，個人主義者主要是對付一個充滿敵意的社會生存環境，用魯迅當年在其小說集《吶喊》自序中所用的象徵來說，就是「一間鐵屋子，是絕無窗戶也萬難破毀的」，裡面的人也都要很快悶死了。我認爲，這種「鐵屋」心態是本世紀標榜個人主義的中國知識份子的典型心態。首先，他是面對一個在傳統倫理觀念上壓制他的個人主義的頑固的社會，他曾經被視爲洪水猛獸而遭到批判；其次，他是面對強調民族國家危亡高於個人利益的戰亂社會，不得不犧牲個人，「先天下之憂而憂」；到了共產主義極權控制時代，如果個人理念和統治者的意志格格不入，那就不但幾乎沒有實施個人理念的可能，甚至不允許個人理念在頭腦中存在。所以，它的社會環境始終是困難的、敵意的、險惡的。我們可以看到，從魯迅寫〈狂人日記〉的時代開始，接受了個人主義觀念的現當代中國知識份子就把中國的社會看成是一個「吃人」的社會，而這個被吃的「人」當然是所謂「個人」，而不是傳統意義上的「人」。關於傳統中國社會的「吃人」，一直是影響著當代中國思維模式的一個神話。在這種「鐵屋」心態的影響下，個人和社會之間基本上是一種對立的互相衝突的關係。面對這樣的一個社會，爲了避免個人被吃掉的命運，中國的個人主義者必須採取和社會對立的立場，不是爭取個人從這一社會的剝離或者解放，就是要把這個社會推翻或打碎。強調個人和社會的敵對，這就是中國個人主義和西方個人主義在品格上最主要的區別。當代作家和魯迅時代的作家相比有所不同的是，如果魯迅還強調參與和抗爭，要拆毀鐵屋，是吶喊和喚醒民眾，當代大陸作家則常常強調逃避或超越，是只求自救自保自娛，其發出的聲音更多是呻吟、是私語、是夢囈。

中國個人主義品性最獨特突出之處就是它的這種對立觀念：它不是把個人和社會看成可以相容甚至和諧的一體，而是把個人置於和社會對立的另一極端，或者和其它概念（如民族、家族、國家、群體、公家等等）對立的另一極端。在這種定義下，兩個極端之間的關係是緊張對立和不可調和的。因此，不是爲了社會、群體、民族、國家、公家而犧牲個人，就是爲了個人而放棄。

中國個人主義者同時感受著西方文化的壓迫，因此要重建民族意義上的尊嚴。更具體地說，在這種歷史語境中，個人主義的提倡表面上有人道主義的背景，比如爲了反抗封建禮教的束縛，提倡個性解放，但同時也是爲了民族復興的目的。個人主義在中國最先被倡導時恰值國家處於受難危亡之秋，知識份子起先是爲了尋求救國之道才選中個人主義的，因此它從一開始就被挾裹到民族主義中，被當成改善民族文化的手段，同時符合了傳統文化中「國家興亡、匹夫有責」的道德標準，於是這種個人主義從一開始就演變得有些不倫不類，似乎不是信仰，而只是工具。我們因此看到，中國早期的個人主義者同時也是熱烈的民族主義者，盡管這兩種立場在實際中往往使他們陷入自身的矛盾。到了日本侵略、民族危機加深的時候，那些早期提倡個人主義的中國知識份子就紛紛改變了主義，放棄了個人主義的立場。這就是李澤厚總結的「救亡壓倒了啓蒙」。後來的專制極權也往往是以國家和民族大義來壓制個人自由，迫使個人主義者就範。

就以文學來說，毛澤東對文學爲甚麼人的問題做出過明確的規定：文學應當是爲了所謂「工農兵大眾」的，也是爲政治服務的。在他發動的文化革命中，他更把這種規定推到了一個極端，使作家完全發不出個人的聲音，更談不上表現「自我」了。作家的「自我」不僅在文學中遭到壓抑，而且在實際社會生活中屢受摧殘，因此個人的悲劇和苦難意識日益擴張漫延，如地層下的熔岩一樣聚集著爆發的力量。那麼，一旦當這種個人被壓抑的情緒到了極點，社會危機再次出現，歷史鐘擺就自然向相反方向運動：在思想上是從文化大革命的專制主義向個人主義回擺，在文學上是從「民族國家文學」向「個人主義文學」回擺，從爲「工農兵大眾」擺向爲作爲個人的「自我」。

當代作家重新提倡個人主義，並且以此重新定位個人和民族或國家的關係，提出「超越」民族和國家的口號，似乎在這一點上比「五、四」時期的作家徹底。然而，他們中不少人在思想上仍然沒有擺脫個人情結和民族情結的內在衝突，也沒有越出東西方文化衝突的框架，一但感到所謂西方霸權文化的壓力，就很快暴露出一種非個人的「類」意識和一種民族主義的立場。就以當代的文學創作和批評來說，尋根文學的出現，對漢語純潔性的追求和捍衛，以及反對西方文化霸權，拆除西方語言影響的努力，往往都不是個人意義的行爲，而是站在民族文化主義的立場，擺出民族文化主義的姿勢。我想，有一本叫作《現代漢詩》的詩歌雜誌就是這樣問世的，它的宗旨既是追求現代性，又是追求所謂「漢詩」的民族語文特點。大概正是因爲這種曖昧的立場和姿勢，我們的「個人主義文學」常常可以被讀解成民族的寓言。一個個人的受難故事常常變成了民族的受難故事。

當代文學中「自我」再出場的社會環境基本上是歷史的一次重複。如果我們回顧歷史，我們會發現當代文學的個人主義傾向和本世紀前期「五、四」新文學運動有驚人的相似之處。捷克漢學家雅・普契克評論「五、四」新文學運動至抗戰的中國文學時總結說：「毫無疑問，從一九一九年的五、四到抗戰爆發，中國文學的最大特點是伴隨著悲觀主義和生活悲劇感的主觀主義和個人主義。」⑩以我看，他的這個總結幾乎可以原封不動地搬來描述毛澤東逝世以後的中國當代文學。需要補充的只是，那種他所說的悲觀主義和生活悲劇感在當代文學中逐漸被幽默化了。如果說在當代文學的早期發難

---

⑩ 見 Jaroslav Prusek: The Lyrical and the Epic, Studies of Modern Chinese Literature, edited by Leo Ou-fan Lee, Bloomington: Indiana University Press, 1980, 第3頁。

者，比如「朦朧派」詩人那裡，我們還能看到這種悲觀主義和生活悲劇感的沈重，看到緊張的姿勢和英雄色彩，那麼，到了八十年代末，我們在一批標簽不同的新小說作家那裡看到了某種輕鬆和自信，看到了類似莎氏比亞悲劇丑角的那種隨意和機靈。這自然不是向樂觀主義的轉向，而是作家在充分看到個人的現實境況或者自我實現的非現實性之後，反而以一種調侃的態度來對待自我。

五、「個人」概念結構的錯位

中國個人主義特殊品格的形成還不僅是由於它所處的特殊社會背景和歷史語境，也是在它的概念結構（Conceptual Structure）本身有著較爲複雜的資源，值得進一步分析。在這一方面，我是受到了美國漢學家查德・漢森的啓發。他曾經指出，由於中國傳統哲學中人的概念結構和西方個人主義的概念結構是如此不同，因此中國傳統文化中不存在也不可能發展出西方意義上的個人主義。根據他的分析，中國傳統哲學中，不論儒家、道家還是佛家哲學思想，人的概念結構基本上是一種「部分—整體」的模式，而西方個人主義的概念結構則是「個體—群體」的模式，這兩種概念模式相去甚遠。⓫且不論漢森關於中國傳統文化不會發展出個人主義的論點是否有理有據，他關於兩種不同概念結構的分析還是有啓發性的，給我們

⓫ 見Chad Hansen: "Individualism in Chinese Thought", Individualism and Holism: Studies in Confusican and Taoist Value, edited by Donald Munro, the University of Michigan Center for Chinese Studies, 1985, 第35-36頁。

指示了認識中國個人主義品格的一條路徑。

根據漢森在西方個人主義的概念結構模式中，社會被看成群體，即個體的一種集合，因此個體是和群體搭上關係的。在這種模式中，個體的存在是重要的前提，群體只是容納個體並努力體現多數個體的意志。不論怎樣，個體總是獨立的，是可以從社會群體剝離的，盡管這種剝離常常沒有必要或沒有意義，相反，個體要留在社會群體中才能更好地充份發揮個人的作用，體現個人的價值。因此，至少在理論上，個人和社會兩者之間並無你死我活的矛盾。這種關係就好比聯合國的成員國和聯合國的關係：聯合國是一個由個體成員國組成的群體，加入這個群體，也並不意味著個體成員國被吃掉，相反能更好地充分發揮個體成員國的作用，同時，每個成員國又都可以隨時退出。不論退出還是留在其中，成員國的個體性獨立性的存在都沒有受到影響。再如現代民主社會，在理論上，它也是具有獨立意志的個人的集合，因此個人無須對這樣的社會產生害怕和敵視的情緒。如果對社會狀況不滿，可以批評、可以參與改造的工作，無須把自己剝離出去。正因為這樣，我們可以看到，西方個人主義知識份子的參與意識普遍比中國個人主義知識份子強烈。

在中國傳統哲學的概念結構模式中，社會被看成整體，個人是作爲部分的人存在於整體之中，因此一個人是和整體搭上關係的。在理論上，部分和整體是不能夠分離的，就像一個人的手腳身體不能分開一樣。這種關係就像聯合國機構和聯合國的關係一樣，聯合國各個機構都是構成聯合國的一部分，是不能脫離聯合國而獨立存在。在這種「部分—整體」的模式中，如果我們以西方意義的個人主義來觀察作爲個體的人在社會中的獨立性，當然就會發現個人作爲一個部分離不開社會整體，因此好像沒有了獨立性，好像是被整體吞沒了，是被關在「鐵屋」之中了，所謂中國傳統社會「吃人」一說大致也就是這樣建立起來的。

這時引進西方個人主義，無疑是「個體—群體」模式對「部分—整體」模式的衝擊或者解構，原來是「部分」的人要轉變成「個體」的人，要取得從「整體」剝離出去的可能和自由。但是，概念模式的結構錯位於是就產生了。因爲在這時「整體」的中國社會還沒有相應地轉化成爲「群體」，依然在整體主義控制下，還不存在西方意義上的「群體」這樣一個個人意義上的集合或現代民主社會，甚至大多數中國知識份子本人在概念上實際也沒有脫離中國傳統哲學的整體主義概念結構模式的影響。在外患當頭的時候，他們仍然以「整體」概念看待國家和民族，那麼，舊的概念模式被打亂後就重新組合成一種「個人—整體」概念模式。

正是在這種新的「個人—整體」概念模式中，中國個人主義顯出了不同於西方個人主義的獨特的品格，有了一種尷尬痛苦的姿勢。一方面，他要維持概念結構模式本身固有的相依性，要搭上關係，所以他離不開依然是一個整體的社會，他沒有脫離這個整體；另一方面，他又面對原來兩種結構模式都沒有的結構內的衝突，作爲個人，他的對方已經不是可以容納他的群體，而是要吃掉他的整體了。而他要不被吃掉，要成爲單獨的個人，就不能繼續留在這個結構模式裡，就要拼命從作爲整體的社會剝離出來，就要超越和隱逸，就要想方設法打破或逃出「鐵屋」。 我把中國個人主義這種自身矛盾的品格描述爲一個「鐵屋」中的個人，或者整體陰影下的個人：個人既要從「鐵屋」（整體）中剝離出來，要逃到「鐵屋」之外，又離不開「鐵屋」，念念不忘「鐵屋」，因此始終越不出「鐵屋」的陰影。這一點也可以從歷史得到證明，早期倡導個人主義的中國知識份子，後來大多數捲入整體主義的社會革命活動之中。一九八九年「六四」事件前後一些中國知識份子的表現，也可以說明在中國個人如何落入進退維谷的矛盾狀態。不是捲入，就是逃避，這兩種姿態總是被經常交替使用。

六、官方話語和社會期待心理的影響

中國當代個人主義的資源可能是多樣的。除了西方個人主義，除了傳統的整體主義的思維方式，是否還有其它資源，也值得我們思考。根據一種流行已久的比較公認的看法，大陸的統治是專制性的，它扼殺個性，壓制人的「自我」意識的，它只能引起個人的反叛，而當代個人主義的復興，尤其是「自我」意識的覺醒，正是個人對抗專制社會的結果。但是，事實恐怕不盡如此。我以爲大多數年青的個人主義者並非天生的反叛者，他們曾經多少接受過官方的信仰，有些甚至是這種信仰的狂熱信徒，在他們身上，我們還是會發現官方話語的影響留下的印記。

大陸官方話語基本上是提倡「集體主義」的，我在此使用引號，是由於「集體主義」這個詞語義不明，實際上也常常被混同於「整體主義」。在這種話語統治下，一個個人是「集體」的一部分，他要以「集體」利益爲重，不惜犧牲個人的利益，實際上是要個人奉獻自己給黨的事業，成爲其中的一個部分。表面上，這種官方話語是排斥個人主義的，但實際上它不完全排斥人們考慮個人和「自我」。這是一個比較複雜的問題。官方話語帶著「整體主義」的色彩，又結合了封建等級觀念，所以，一些人可以成爲高級部分，而另一些人則只能是低級部分。一些人可以做主軸，而另一些人只可以做螺絲釘；一些人做頭腦，而另一些人只可以做手和腳。在大陸專制制度下生活過的人，對官方統治方法有過親身體驗的人，都會了解共產黨的先鋒隊理論，都會體會到官方對人們的個人或「自我」意識的巧妙利用。例如，在社會的各個層面各個空間，官方每年都要搞所謂的先進個人評比，樹標兵、插紅旗等等。這不光涉及個人的榮譽感，甚至帶有許多特殊的政治和經濟利益。因此，以「忘我」的姿態達到自我的目的，以「犧牲個人」的表現來表現個人，所謂吃小虧佔大便宜，這種做法同樣可以使一些個人被突出，雖然沒有逃出整體的控制，卻可以從一個人員比較廣大的低級部分被抽離到人員較少的高級部分，同樣可以培養出優越的「自我」意識，讓一些人覺得自己是先鋒份子而優於其它人。

正是在這一點上，大陸官方話語和當代個人主義所強調的超越性和脫離性有些合拍了。雖然這樣抽出的「自我」不是個人主義意義上的獨立的人格，但這種做法爲這種帶精英意識的個人化的「自我」留下了表現的機會和渠道。文化大革命的混亂當然造成了不少曾經有過這樣的「自我」優越感的人的失落，正是這種失落感，爲官方造就了他們自己的最早的一批文學反叛者。但是，這些反叛者之所以訴諸文字的方式來表現「自我」，往往也是別無選擇的結果。

從官方話語的這種影響來看，我想進一步說明的是：個人的活動不一定是根據個人的價值取向，也可以是根據一個群體或者整體（有時也就是官方）所規定的價值原則。這主要是指在公共性的活動中，個人似乎仍然存在選擇的權利，可以出於個人的意志和目的做決定，但是價值取向卻是由公共意志決定的。所以，這是一種群體壓力或者整體陰影下的個人活動。

現代心理學也告訴我們，有強烈「自我」意識的人，在一個群體的場合下，常常爲了表現「自我」，也是爲了滿足一種群體的期待，而有所謂超常的「自我」表現。例如，有關交通事故的報告證明，一些明明是平時開車十分小心謹愼的年青人，在車上有年青朋友的情況下，只要這些年青朋友都期待他開快車，他就會因爲擔心同伴的譏笑，爲了表現勇敢而超速。根據同樣的道理，當我們的社會期待著造反者的時候，許多的造反者就是這樣誕生的。社會的期待心理，是我們中國當代社會造就了無數非常著名但又非常平庸的人物的一個重要原因。社會期待心理構成了一種壓力，就是在這種壓力下，個人的表現實際上順從的是群體的意志和價值，並非是個人的要求。在這種情況下的表面的個人活動實際上成爲米蘭·昆德拉所譏諷的「媚俗」。

當代大陸文學所表現的「自我」，有時也多少有這種「媚俗」的味道，表面是個人的活動，實際並未逃離整體的陰影，甚至是一個整體的造物。比如，盡管有些作家強調表現「自我」才是更爲「純粹」的文學，但是，爲了實現「自我」的寫作其實還是涉及寫作之外的目的，因此使得他們經常陷入自相矛盾之中。他們一方面強調寫作應該有單純的個人化的性質，拒絕爲讀者寫作，甚至高傲地把讀者推開。在他們的寫作中，不是羅蘭·巴特爾所說的「作者已死」，而是唯有「作者永生」。另一方面，他們還是在歷史的舞台上表演，需要觀眾的喝彩，比任何時代的作家都更依賴讀者的認可和評價，更需要聽眾和掌聲，因此常常被時代的潮流所席捲。在中國，標榜「自我」，好像是對社會的宣戰，他們先要推開公眾跳上台去才能顯出了「自我」，但是「自我」的意義又必須依賴公眾的存在才顯示出來。由於這種特點，我們看到大陸所謂表現「自我」的寫作，往往既是孤芳自賞的寫作，想再造一個僅屬個人的世界，同時又是針對社會的寫作，是一次公開的演講。這就好比在舞台上表演的自白，它像是說給自己聽的，實際又是說給觀眾聽的。

七、「自我」在文學世界的錯位

羅伯特·黑格爾指出，文學中的「自我」，實際上可以分成兩種：「被揭示的自我」（the Revealed Self）和「被創造的自我」（the Created Self）⓬。「被揭示的自我」是作家本人的「自我」或者所謂「本我」在作品中的再現，例如陀斯妥也夫斯的《賭徒》或郁達夫的《沉淪》等作品中的主角，基本是作家的「被揭示的自我」。而「被創造的自我」則是作家根據一定的價值取向和需要創造出來的藝術形象，他們和作家的「自我」有聯繫但並不重合，有時，其品格甚至恰恰相反。這是因爲作家在把自己放入作品之時，往往會出於一種心理的或者審美的需要，根據一種個人的理想創造出高於自身的藝術化的「自我」，雖然作者以爲這個「自我」代表自己，但兩者實際的品格會有相當大的差距。作家和這兩種「自我」之間

⓬ 見 Robert E. Hegel, “Introduction”, The Self in Ming Literature, edited by R. Hegel, The Michigan University Press, 1990, 第28-32頁。

的關係有些像戲劇藝術中演員和角色的關係，他們可以非常接近，也可能有很大的距離或反差，就好比慷慨的劇作家兼演員莫里哀可以創造並且扮演一個一毛不拔的吝嗇鬼阿巴公，同樣，一個平庸的演員也可以扮演英雄，一個食盡人間煙火的俗人可以扮演超凡脫俗的聖人。

就本人的閱讀經驗來看，當代大陸文學中的「自我」以「被創造的自我」居多，很少是「被揭示的自我」。其原因大概是後者強調對自我的分析和批判，以一種現實主義的精神表現個人沉淪的痛苦，而前者幾乎完全以正面肯定的態度推崇「自我」，是用一種浪漫主義的姿態和英雄意識向壓迫個人的社會挑戰。有些西方評論家認爲當代中國詩歌讓人回想到歐洲上個世紀的浪漫派，自然是有些道理的。正是由於這種傾向，中國大陸當代文學仍然缺乏用現代的科學和理性精神對「自我」的分析和交待。他們常常不問「自我」是甚麼，只問作品中有沒有「自我」。記得曾經有一位作家批評我的小說落伍。這當然是一個有很多根據的事實，不過這位作家批評我的根據，僅僅是他在我的作品中再也看不到我。換言之，對我的這位批評者來說，一個作家應該在作品中展現「自我」，不僅要讓自己看見，也要讓別人看見。可見，有沒有「自我」構成了一種文學的價值判斷標準，達不到這個標準，將不能進入時代，不能進入文學的殿堂。

由於這種對「自我」的厚愛，我們在大陸當代文學中看到的更多的是一些自我擁抱自我，自我和自我做愛的文學場景，看到的更多的是自戀自愛和自誇自大，較少見到當代西方文學中常見的自嘲自噱和自我批判。文學表現「自我」的口號至少對一些人來說已經成爲創作的某種準則，某種終極目標，某種至高無上、不可置辯的文學圭臬，也可能是馳騁文壇時通行無阻、無往而不勝的護照或護身符，一種萬能的靈藥；它既是寫作的出發點，同時又是方向，是寫作的終極目的，還是文學評價的惟一的尺度，是「純粹」文學的唯一標志。它會不會過於萬能反而把我們引入另一種困境呢？

我無意否認文學可以展現「被創造的自我」，但是，我對大陸當代文學中的這種浪漫精神和英雄意識早有一種憂慮和懷疑，它在表面上呼應我們這個時代的需要，實際上卻和這個時代的沉重混亂不合拍。當這種傾向被過份強調的時候，我甚至擔心文學表現「自我」這個本來美好的主張可能會起一種不美好的作用，正如我們已經看見「民主」被用作一種壓迫他人的權利，「自由」被當成干涉他人思維的枷鎖，新時代的思想者們手握「眞理」也像手握利劍，在他們前進的中途總要在身後留下鮮血和尸體。

更令人憂慮和懷疑的是一些作家把「被揭示的自我」和「被創造的自我」混爲一談，就如戲劇中把演員和角色混爲一談，而其中的品格反差又構成明顯的自身矛盾，於是作品就顯得華而不實，缺乏藝術眞實的震撼力，於是那種浪漫精神和英雄意識就顯得可憐可笑。它們只提供一種幻覺。這種幻覺就像戲劇中斯坦尼斯拉夫斯基表演方法製造的幻覺，不過，斯坦尼斯拉夫斯基要演員進入角色，忘記自己是個演員，而現在的這種幻覺是演員忘了自己是角色，以爲演的就是自己。

爲了說明這種「自我」的矛盾，我可以把黑格爾的論點進一步發展，也就是把文學中的世界也分成兩種：「被揭示的世界」（the Revealed World）和「被創造的世界」（the Created World）。「被揭示的自我」是和「被揭示的世界」也就是現實世界相應的，「被創造的自我」則存在於「被創造的世界」。現在，一些作家以爲通過文學可以表現和拯救在現實世界的整體中被吞食的「自我」，給「自我」提供一個家園。於是他們把「被揭示的自我」和「被創造的自我」混爲一談的同時，又以爲「被揭示的世界」和「被創造的世界」可以區別開，以爲這時「被揭示的自我」可以擺脫現實世界，進入「被創造的世界」，得到充份自由的表現，得到超越和解放。他們沒有意識到這裏發生的錯位，沒有意識到在「被創造的世界」中出現的實際只是「被創造的自我」而並不是作家的「被揭示的自我」。

八、結　論：
陷入「自我」的悖論還是走出「鐵屋」

總結以上的分析，我們可以看到，雖然「自我」的再出場爲大陸文學發展帶來新的動力，但是，正如我們這個時代其它的一些時髦口號一樣，爲「自我」的文學這種主張也未能避免陷入某種悖論。這種悖論的最大特點就是思維的出發點往往等同於思維的歸宿或結果，就是結論往往被等同於前提、論據和論證本身，就是評判的尺度往往被等同於尺度的評判。具體地說，就是把文學可以表現「自我」當成表現「自我」即是文學，就如過去官方話語的悖論把文學是一種宣傳當成宣傳即是文學。在衡量文學價値的天平上，持「自我表現論」的作家在一端放上「自我」，在另一端也放上「自我」，而希圖其中的一端會把另一端高高托起。

最後，讓我用一個簡單的比喻來討論個人主義的兩種不同的言說形式，借以進一步說明當代中國個人主義和「自我」的悖論問題。假定在我的手中握有一把白色的圍棋子，它們構成了一個白子的群體或整體，就看我們以哪種概念結構來觀察它。我可以強調其中的每一粒白子都是一個個體，它可以獨立地存在，可以留在這個群體中，也可以拿出來，拿到我的另一個手裏，不論怎樣，它都不失獨立性，仍是一個個體。同時，每個白子也都有自己作爲一個白子的權益。而且，請注意，我要強調每一個白子又完全不同，在太陽光下會閃耀不同的色彩。我以爲，這樣言說的人，可以是一個個人主義者，而且是一個符合人本精神的個人主義者。但是，也有人只注意到了「白子」這個概念的類的意義（一種整體主義的看法），他覺得，這樣的一顆白子，無法和其它白子有個性的區分，一個白子的個性就被抹掉了，「我」就不是「我」了，即使它可以和其它白子分開，獨立地存在，比如說，單獨地放到我的另一個手裏，它仍然只能是一個白子，是白子整體中的一個。於是，要使這粒白子具有個性，最好的辦法就是把它塗黑，使它成爲白子中的一顆黑子，對白子作一次徹底的反叛，這樣才能鮮明地把自己作爲一個個體從整體中分離出來。這樣言說個人主義的人，大概也算是一個個人主義者。

當代中國的個人主義者，包括那些強調文學表現「自我」的作家，大部分是採取後一種言說形式的人。對於他們，「自我」必須是一顆黑子（一個被創造的自我），必須和其它白子有所區別。只有這樣，「我」才能成爲「我」，和其它人才能兩樣，「我」才能有「我」的語言，「我」的形式，「我」的個人的故事和形象。當代中國文學的「現代性」，基本上就是這樣的一種品性。

問題是，黑子仍然可以是一種整體主義的類的概念，因爲一個黑子，不管它是天生地黑還是後來塗黑的，仍然會屬於黑子這個「整體」。同時，黑子的存在意義，恰恰是由於白子的對比的存在才顯示出來的。因此，要顯示一個黑子的獨特性，實際上還是不可能脫離白子。不論怎樣，只要我們維持一種整體主義的看法，我們的個人主義者都沒有擺脫「自我」的悖論，擺脫個人的困境，擺脫整體的陰影，擺脫「鐵屋」心態。所以，我們可以也必須追問，如果大陸作家不擺脫這種「鐵屋」心態，那他們的「自我」，還是眞正的「自我」嗎？它還能眞正走出「鐵屋」嗎？

臺灣地區語言政策的跨世紀省思

盧國屏*

摘　要

不論從那個角度來看臺灣過去百年的歷史，其所呈現的都必然是複雜的、多元的與變動不居的。尤其過去一百年，臺灣歷經了日本殖民時代、國民黨政府遷台戒嚴及解嚴時代，不但政治複雜，本地的社會變遷、文化衝突、族群融合等也都充滿了矛盾與詭譎。而臺灣這些問題的歷史過程及未來發展，語言的觀察，就提供了許多重要的線索。

語言的本質，雖是自然約定俗成的溝通工具，但當政治、社會、文化起了人爲因素的衝突與矛盾時，語言就經常成爲「被管理」與「被約制」的對象，而形成了一種人爲控制主導下的溝通工具，不再是純然的約定俗成。因此欲觀察一個地區或一個社會的各種歷史，則語言其實是最

---

*　淡江大學中文系副教授

直接的管道之一，臺灣就是一個典型的例子。

本文從語言政策、語言計劃、及語言教育三個方向著手，省思臺灣的過去與未來，即是由上述角度出發的研究。也藉以表示，在進入新世紀時對這塊土地的關懷。

Abstract

The history of Taiwan in the past centuries, viewing from various angles, is completx, plural, and transitional. Particularly during the last hundred years, Taiwan has been through Japanese colonization, Nationalist take-over, Martial Law period, which results in contrariety among political, social, cultural, and ethnical groups. The observation of language provides important sources of the historical process and the future development in Taiwan.

Although the essence of language is to communicate, language sometimes becomes an object to be manipulated into certain tool of communication. Hence, to observe the history of a society or region, language is one of the most direct aspects. Taiwan serves as the typical example.

This essay will survey three dimensions including language politics, language plans, and language education. By so doing we reconsider the past and further problems of the land we love.

一、前言：語言政策與臺灣

在語言理論的體系中，所謂「語言政策」指的是：「國家或社會團體為語言的學習、使用、建設、發展，而採取的態度和措施」。在社會語言學的研究對象中，語言政策是極其重要的一部分，它的內涵，又必須具備為有效控制語言或文字的變化，以適應溝通需要而訂出的種種「語言計畫」、及配合計畫實施的「語言教育」始能成功❶。

臺灣是個多語的社會，多語社會的語言政策，本來就是困難度較高、且不易執行的。更何況其中又牽涉到臺灣複雜的政治、社會、文化、族群，及其歷史變遷，使得本地的語言政策代有不同，又必須隨時進行。這從一七二八年清朝雍正皇帝對福建、廣東督府所下的一道推行官話的諭令便可看出：

> 諭內閣：官員有蒞民之責，其語言必使人人易曉，然後可以通達民情，而辦理無誤。是以古者六書之例，必使諧聲會意嫻習語音，所以成遵道之風……朕每引見大小臣工，凡陳奏履歷之時，惟有福建廣東兩省之人，仍係鄉音，不可通曉……

---

❶ 「社會語言學」指研究語言與社會多方面關係的學科。它與社會學、人類學、民族學、心理學、教育學等學科有密切關係。研究範圍大致有兩類：一類是宏觀社會語言學，包括語言政策、語言計畫、語言規範化、語言和民族等；一類是微觀社會語言學，研究語言的各種社會變體。〈語言新學科〉，《中國語言學大辭典》（江西：江西教育出版社1992年2月），頁633。

此兩省之人，其語言既皆不可通曉，不但伊等歷任他省，不能深習下民之情，既伊等身爲編氓，亦必不能明白長官之意，是上下之情扞格不通……應令福建廣東兩省督府，轉飭所屬，遍爲傳示，多方教導，務期語言明白，使人通曉。

當時臺灣是福建的一個府，臺灣的族群除了福建移民外，還有內地派駐的官員、士兵，當然也包括九大族的原住民，他們各自使用著自己的語言，造成了溝通不便，雍正這個推行官話的政策，在臺灣更是重要。

過去一百年來，臺灣又歷經了政治上的大變動，從中國的領土成爲日本殖民地、再從殖民地成爲國民黨政府遷台主政下的區域；直到今天，本土意識抬頭，又開始了新的政治、族群、社會的權力角力。這百年來的語言政策，顯然是要與這段歷史息息相關的。

如今，新世紀即將到來，爲強調本世紀與二十一世紀的跨世紀歷史意義，本文將以過去一個世紀的時代變遷爲討論縱線，各時期的政治、社會背景、語言政策爲討論橫線；先檢視過去這段歷史中的語言政策得失，再提出邁向新世紀適合臺灣語言政策的新方向。

二、1895—1945 日本殖民時期的語言政策

㈠、語言政策與教育

⑴限制國語（漢語）的措施

西元一八九五年，清朝光緒二十一年，日本進據臺灣，同年六

月十七日舉行臺灣總督始政典禮，當天成立學務部。學務部長伊澤修二，給樺山總督提出《臺灣教育意見書》說：「臺灣的教育，第一使新領土的人民，從速學習日本語。」從此便展開了所謂的國語（日語）政策，這個政策一直執行到臺灣光復，從沒有鬆懈過，教育目標，始終以這個政策爲重心，設法消滅臺灣的方言和國字❷。

當年日本的方法是採取逐漸加緊的步驟，初期只是推行日語，並不限制漢文，並且也不限制臺灣人前往大陸，讀書人可以任意到福建讀書，參加考試。一八九七年，光緒二十三年，福建巡撫會同禮部奏請清廷「凡臺灣士子，可以自動內向福建應鄉試及北上會試。各於場中設『至』字坐號，定有舉人進士的中額。」日本人所辦的日日新報，有漢文欄，公學校也有漢文科。一九〇三年，固定人口，禁止中國圖書入境，一九三七年，學校取消漢文，並禁止學生說中國話，同年六月，報紙期刊漢文欄也被取消，社會上就完全日語化了❸。

⑵皇民化的溫床——公學校

自一八九五年學務部成立，制定日語教育的語言政策後，首先他們設了三種課程不一樣的學校：小學校，給日本人讀的，和日本本土的課程完全相同；公學校，給漢人讀的，與日本本土的制度不同，不完全限制漢文，畢業生可以去日本讀醫校或日語學校；番人

❷ 參張博宇《臺灣地區國語運動史料》，上篇第四章〈保衛國語〉（臺灣商務印書館一九七四），頁十三。

❸ 同前註❷。

公學校，給原住民讀的。這一切，都只是同化臺灣人的初步而已❹。

一八九八年，臺灣總督府便斷然施行「臺灣公學校令」，規定以地方經費設立的六年公學校，取代原先的「國語傳習所」。因其認爲，臺灣的日語教育，爲配合皇民化的同化目標，應爲義務教育之一，宜以公學校廣收臺灣人爲主，以奠定日語環境基礎，於是國語普及教育正式展開。自此以後，公學校就成爲主要的日語推行機構。

⑶國語（日語）普及運動的推展

一九一八年，明石原二郎就任臺灣總督，揭示以同化主義爲施政方針。翌年一月，頒布「臺灣教育令」標榜臺灣教育目的在「培養忠良之國民」，藉口台人「皇化」未久，修習日語仍爲困難，所以仍保持差別教育❺。但在施行三年後，被認爲此舉可能遭致本地人疑慮，在統治上產生不良效果。遂由繼任的首任文官總督田健治郎，進而實行「內地沿長主義」，他認爲：

> 臺灣構成帝國領土的一部分，當然爲從屬於帝國憲法統治的版圖，……因此，其統治方針，概以此大精神爲出發點，而從事各種事業與經營，使臺灣民眾成爲純粹的帝國人民，忠誠於日本朝廷，且須予以教化與指導，使涵養對於國家的義務觀念。❻

❹ 矢內原忠雄：《日本帝國主義下之臺灣》（帕米爾，1985年），頁149-153。
❺ 種村保三郎：《臺灣小史》（台北武陵，1991年），頁203。
❻ 同註❹，頁172。

至此，已不再將臺灣視爲特殊的區域，而主張完全同化臺灣人爲日本人，使臺灣日本化，這就是「內地沿長主義」。

在全面同化的政策下，普及日語遂成爲最大的教育目標。爲了徹底培養日本精神，增進兒童的日語能力，學務部門建議廢除漢文，唯時勢不易，並未強制。直到一九二二年，新「臺灣教育令」公佈，將漢文改爲選修科目，許多公學校爲配合政策，或奉承長上，逕行廢除漢文科，引起了許多臺灣人反國語運動的推行❼，但是，國語（日語）普及運動，也因此進入了新的階段。

⑷國語普及網及國語家庭

一九二〇年代以後，日本帝國主義對內極權、對外侵略擴張的態勢日益高張，臺灣是其南進的基地，無可避免的首當其衝。臺灣總督府一方面強化對台統治，一方面力求台人的同化。一九二二年，新「臺灣教育令」公佈，解除了以往臺灣人教育程度低於日本人的差別，只在初等教育以小學校收容常用漢語者，公學校收容不常用漢語者做爲分別，中等程度以上的學校則實施日人、台人的共學制❽。

表面上，臺灣人受教育的機會與日本人平等了，但是其目的則仍在國語普及網的建立和台人的同化上。一九三〇年終於禁了臺灣的私塾，而私塾一向便是臺灣人用漢語讀文言文的地方。一九三七

---

❼ 見下文。

❽ 《臺灣省通誌》卷五〈教育志.制度研革篇〉（台北：臺灣省文獻會），頁71。

年爲了要讓臺灣人完全使用日語，廢除了各級學校的漢文科，禁止學生說臺灣話，並且報紙期刊漢文欄也被禁止，這些措施的目的，都在積極的同化臺灣人❾。

當時的配合方式，便是對「國語家庭」獎勵，或給予獎金補助，或是公開表揚。到了這個階段，日語教育的運動，已經積極推行到全島，通過學校、官方、非官方的機構，日本殖民政府到一九三〇年已經成功的發展出一個普及網，一九三二年臺灣人會日語的有23%，到一九四二年已經有 51%，到一九四四年這個比例增加到 71%❿。雖然一般人離開官府、教室用的還是母語，但單以會說日語來評估日本的殖民地語言政策，大致上可以說是成功的。

㈡、殖民地語言政策之檢討

既是殖民地的語言政策，則強制被殖民者改變母語系統，進而造成同化的殖民心態，是可以理解的。雖然其手段諸如壟斷媒體、控制學校等，並不人道，但日本在臺灣推行的國語運動，使 71%的人會日語，基本上是頗成功的。不過，就會日語而言，與日本原先所設計的皇民化的同化目標，其成效並不成比例。因爲在殖民時代，臺灣人反抗日語教育的努力，其實未嘗停頓，從以下的幾件事，便可看出殖民地語言政策之成效，是要打折扣的：

---

❾ 同註❷。

❿ 李勤岸：《語言政策與臺灣獨立》頁2，1997.7.17刊於台獨聯盟論壇網站 www.wufi.org.tw

⑴臺灣人對日語的仇視心態

日人在台推行日語，最早設立的學堂是一八九五年設在士林芝山巖學務部內。當時招收二十一名學生為練習生，分甲、乙、丙三組，甲組是最早入學，略通日語的學生；乙組是年齡稍長，漢文素質高，不懂日語的學生；丙組則是年齡最輕，漢文也無基礎的學生。日人一進入臺灣就設立此學堂，很明顯是要積極的先訓練出一批通日語的臺灣人，以作為最初的溝通人才與管道。

臺灣人對這所學習日語的學堂非常憎恨，於第二年就與學務部發生衝突，不但搗毀了學堂，且殺死學務部官員六人、軍夫一人⓫，這是保衛母語、排斥日語最積極的一次行為。雖然此事發生在日人據台之初，爾後的抗爭，也轉為非武力的消極方式，但因此許多人不敢把子弟送到日本人辦的學校去，形成日語推行的很大阻力。也因此種下了本省同胞，對日語潛在的仇視與反抗，直到光復。

⑵私人自費學習漢文

日據時代，有錢有勢的本地士紳，多在家庭教授子侄漢文，如清水貢生楊澄若先生，親自教他的子嗣楊肇嘉先生；鹿港秀才洪月樵先生，教他的子嗣洪炎秋先生頌讀經史，從月樵先生的一首七言古詩，可以看出他的心情與態度：

時勢變遷一至此，讀書今已無種子。仁義道德等籧篨，糞土五經二四史。吾兒閉門讀典墳，吾與汝作羲皇人。世風不染

⓫ 同註❷頁14。

歐非美，時事遑知魏晉秦。⓬

這首詩可算是是當時一般文人的寫照，爲了闡揚儒家思想，維繫中國固有文化於不墜，寧願自己或請人在家裏教子弟，如霧峰林獻堂、台南連雅堂等都是當時著名的塾師。多數人在初期，都不願把子弟送入日本人辦的學校，這便是對日語教育的最直接反抗。

⑶書房的漢文教育

「書房」是私人興學的學校，日據時代稱爲書房，是文人保衛漢語的重要基礎。日據初期，臺灣約有書房一七二七所，學生數二九八七六名，可見當時書房之多、學生之眾，幾乎所有文人都擔起了保衛漢語的擔子⓭。遺憾的是，日人對書房的限制也日趨嚴格，一八九八年所頒布的書房義塾規程大要如下：

1.加授日語的書房，予以補助金。

2.印發大日本史略、教育敕語述義、訓蒙窮理圖解等日本書籍的漢譯本，以爲教材。

3.禁止採用當時我國出版的教科書，如清末出版的小學國文、修身、歷史教科書，以及幼學瓊林等。

4.獎勵使用公學校漢文讀本。

5.舉辦書房教師講習會。

其基本態度是鼓勵日語，削弱漢語。而後，且經常派出憲警，對不合規定者加以查封，到一九三三年，全省的書房只剩一二九所，學

⓬ 同註❷第四章〈保衛國語〉第三節〈保衛國語的組織〉頁15。該詩無題。

⓭ 王詩琅：《日本殖民地體制下的臺灣》（台北：眾文圖書公司，1980年）。

生約四千人⓮，可見書房受到的嚴厲打壓，即使有書房，課程的內容也不以國語爲主了。但從這段歷史也可知，臺灣人保衛其母語的用心，是不絕如縷的。

⑷詩社、文社

臺灣詩社、文社的組織，在清朝時期便有十餘社，到了日據時代，增加到約二百多社⓯，社中的有志之士，成了非武裝反抗殖民帝國、保衛漢語文化與民族精神的重鎮。其中組織最大、影響最深的是林痴仙、林幼春、賴紹堯於一九〇二年成立的「櫟社」，鹿港施梅樵、台南連横、霧峰林烈堂等都是該社社員。一九一一年，梁啓超先生甚至遠從大陸應詩社之邀，來台遊歷，留台期間共得詩八十九首，現收於其《飲冰室文集》卷七十八中，⓰足見詩文社與文人們，對臺灣民族思想的貢獻。

一九三一年，櫟社成立三十週年時，鑄了一座紀念鐘，上刻銘文：「小叩小鳴，大叩大鳴。願我多士，雅韻同賡。振聾發聵，勿墜清聲。」其維繫清聲（漢語文），使之勿墜，恢復漢民族儒道傳統的理想、職志是顯而易見的。

特別的是，大陸內地旅台文人對臺灣漢語文運動，也深具影響。除前述梁啓超先生外，章太炎先生更早在一八九九年，便來到臺灣，擔任日日新報的漢文欄主筆。後因經常撰文激發臺灣人的民族思

⓮ 同註⓭。

⓯ 臺灣銀行經濟研究室：〈古今臺灣詩文社〉，《臺灣文獻》卷11第2、3期。

⓰ 傅錫祺：《櫟社沿革志略》，臺灣銀行經濟研究室編臺灣文獻叢刊一七〇種。

想，引起日人不快，遂於第二年返回大陸。但是除了章氏在台詩輯《太炎詩錄》外，以後仍不時的給臺灣期刊寫文章⓱。可見臺灣雖淪爲殖民地，但臺灣文人與大陸內地文人，在精神與做爲上是一脈相連的。日人的語言政策與同化目的，眞正算起來，恐怕是失敗的了。

三、1945—1990 國民政府遷台及戒嚴時期的語言政策

㈠、七〇年代以前規範化的語言政策

⑴國語推行委員會的成立

一九四五年十月，中國政府收復了臺灣，結束了日本在台長達半個多世紀的殖民統治。在殖民期間，日本對臺灣實行嚴密且有計畫的奴化教育，到四〇年代初期，國語、甚至是方言，在臺灣幾瀕於滅絕的境地。因此，語言建設，成了臺灣光復後社會重建的當務之急。

光復初期，臺灣地區通曉國語的人很少，推行國語所需要的大量人才只好從大陸選派。當時的教育部就先後派出魏建功、何容等一批專家來台，並陸續調進一批國語教師與國語推行人員。魏、何二先生來台後，開始籌建推行國語的專責領導機構，在一九四六年正式公佈「臺灣省國語推行委員會組織規程」在當時省政府教育處

⓱　同註❷第四章〈保衛國語〉第三節〈保衛國語的組織〉頁20。

下成立了「國語推行委員會」簡稱「國語會」，這是臺灣光復後第一個專業、專責的國語政策領導及推行機關⓲。

在「國語會」成立以後，爲了落實國語推行及紮根之工作，又陸續在各縣市政府下設立了「國語推行所」，甚至偏遠的花蓮縣、台東縣亦不例外。這個由上到下的國語推行機構，在光復後的臺灣語言政策中，扮演了極爲重要的角色，幾乎所有重要的國語推行工作，皆由「國語會」所開展。

⑵國語會的國語推行業務

隸屬臺灣省教育處的「國語推行委員會」，在一九四六年成立後，便積極展開各項國語推行之工作。當時國語會的國語政策與工作方向，由其組織規程中，便可窺見梗概，根據「臺灣省國語推行委員會組織規程」第四條，國語會下設四組，分別是調查研究組、編輯審查組、訓練宣傳組及總務組，除總務組負責一般庶務外，其餘三組職掌如下：

調查研究組：

①關於國語及本省方言系統之調查事項
②關於國語及本省方言之聲音組織研究事項
③關於本省語文教育之研究設計事項
④關於高砂族同胞語文教育之研究設計事項⓳

⓲ 同註❷下篇第一章〈臺灣光復後的國語運動〉第三節〈人員的邀約和機構的成立〉頁28。

⓳ 高砂族又稱高山族，今稱「原住民」。

⑤其他有關國語及本省方言之調查研究事項

編輯審查組

①關於國語教材教法之搜集審查事項
②關於國語教材之編輯事項
③關於國語書報及字典辭書之編輯事項
④關於國語書籍標準之審查事項
⑤其他有關國語教材之編輯審查事項

訓練宣傳組

①關於各級國語師資之訓練事項
②關於各級學校語文教育之視導事項
③關於高砂族同胞語文教育之推行事項
④關於民眾識字推行事項
⑤關於推行國語之指導考核事項
⑥關於利用社會教育方式傳播國語事項
⑦其他有關國語訓練及宣傳事項[20]

綜合這些業務項目來看，當時推行國語的工作重點，是從研究、教育及大眾媒體三方面著手，多管齊下，「國語會」確實是光復後，國語政策的主要設計者與執行者。

⑶國語教育

任何語言政策的推行，教育是成功的必要條件，光復後的國語

---

[20] 同註[18]。

教育亦然，自高等教育至社會教育，乃至軍中國語教育，皆環環相扣，與後來國語政策的成功有很大的關係：

①高等教育方面

高等教育初期以培育國語師資爲目標，故自一九四七年起，教育部便在國立臺灣大學文學院內，附設了二年制的國語專修科，隔年起，顧及專業教育，又改由臺灣省立師範學院接辦㉑。這個國語專修的學制，到一九五一年停辦，將國語的教育普及到師大的各科系課程中，使中學的各類師資均能具備國語能力，不止是之前少數專修科學制之師資而已。目前各師範大學及學院均設有「國文系」、「語文教育系」，以國語文的教學師資爲主，其由來已久。

②基礎教育方面

光復初期，臺灣人普遍不會講國語，小學生亦然。因此光復後爲使國語迅速往下紮根，便於各師範專科學校下設置實驗小學，進行國語教學法和注音符號教學法的實驗。歷經十多年的嘗試及許多實驗的累積，直到一九六三年，教育部修正公佈了國民學校課程標準，其中教科書的編寫方式有了重大突破，國民小學的低年級課本，全部採用了注音符號；中年級的國語課本只附注音生字表、其他課本注音；高年級課本則全部不注音，完全以國語及漢字教學㉒。從課本的設計與使用看來，一般小學生已能接受國語的注音系統，成立近二十年的國語會，其推行國語的成效至此已獲得重大成果了。

㉑ 今國立臺灣師範大學。

㉒ 同註❷下篇第四章〈國語教育的實施〉第二節〈國民教育〉。

③社會教育

日據時代，日人想盡辦法消滅方言，所以一般青少年及青年，都不認識國字，也不能完全用方言表情達意，對國語及國字可說是「既啞且盲」。光復後，由臺灣省國語推行委員會所主導的社會民眾識字教育，就在此情況下產生。民眾識字教育，在臺灣普遍推行始於一九五〇年，由國民學校辦理民眾補習班。據調查，當時全省各縣市失學民眾共計一百四十一萬三千五百六十九人，從三十九年到四十三年，在國民學校中共開了約兩萬班次，讓失學民眾全部接受補習教育㉓。

姑且不論成效如何，從數字上看來，基本上已完成了一般民眾的識字教育，而後配合六年義務教育的推展，臺灣地區的文盲至今已很少見。甚至目前在各地區國民中學、小學中，失學民眾的補習教育，依然實施者，使很多光復後的失學民眾，取得了國中、小學歷。這段語文補習歷史，對臺灣的國語政策推行顯然是助益良多的。

任何語文教育，從實施到有具體成效，通常是頗耗費時日的。光復後的國語政策，從四〇年代到六〇年代二十年間，成果是很顯著的，這的確與教育政策、單位的積極有密切關係，從當時的軍隊也積極的從事國語教育，就可窺知一二。遷台以後的軍隊士兵，許多是在台的本地兵源，其國語教育與社會民眾同等重要，當時新兵入伍後，便安排有注音符號的課程。一九六二年起，更規定新兵入伍後，均須有五週的國語訓練，一律以國語直接教學，以利軍令的

㉓ 同註❷下篇第四章〈國語教育的實施〉第三節〈社會教育〉。

執行與各種溝通[24]。從此看來，由高等教育到役男教育，以推行國語爲主的語言政策，在教育部份可說是滴水不漏了。

⑷國語日報社

國語日報是臺灣地區人民耳熟能詳的一份報刊，多數光復後在臺灣受教育的人，在小學階段的國語文教育中，都受到國語日報的啓發與指導，至今仍然出刊。

顧名思義，國語日報是爲國語而設，一九四八年三月教育部長朱家驊、次長田培林赴台視察國語教育，當時的臺灣省國語推行委員會，便要求在臺灣辦一份注音的報紙，以利推行國語。於是教育部便在台北設立「教育部國語推行委員會閩台辦事處」之機構，主要任務便是以此機構名義開辦「國語日報」，主事者是當時國語會專委何容先生，同年十月二十五日國語日報創刊號便正式出刊[25]。

國語日報的出版，目的在普及語文教育，尤其是國語注音符號的使用，這對光復後初期的國語推行運動是很重要的。當時整個臺灣物力維艱、經濟貧困，要以國語書刊的傳佈使人民學習國語，既缺乏經費也緩不濟急。因此簡易的報刊型式，彌補了此些困難，許多民眾，尤其是小學生課後，是依賴國語日報上的注音來增進國語能力的。另外，國語日報社還出版了「古今文選」單元，初期目的在推行注音之學習，而後其中所選文章，還成了中上學校和社會自

---

[24] 同前註[23]。

[25] 《臺灣省通誌》卷五〈教育志.教育設施篇〉（台北，臺灣省文獻會），頁250。

修青年的讀物與課本，對國語文的推展有著莫大貢獻。

㈡、八〇—九〇年代語言政策之遷變

經過二十多年的堅持推行，到了六〇年代，國語在臺灣已算普及。但在生活語言的某些領域中，方言勢力仍然很強，甚至是主流。以閩南語爲母語的多數人，放學下班後，仍然以閩南方言作爲生活溝通的主要方式。同時，國語推行委員會的諸多政策也逐漸疲乏，教育部在一九七三年，遂又公布了新的「國語推行辦法要點」，以加強國語推行的力度。當時新聞局規定，電視台每天的方言節目，不得超過一個小時，而且晚間六點半以後的黃金時段，閩南語節目要限台限時播出。一九七六年又通過法令，規定國內廣播電台以國語發音的比例，電台不少於55%、電視台不少於70%㉖。這些政策，都仍是國民政府遷台前期推行國語運動的延續。

進入八〇年代以後，推行國語的基本方針和政策沒有改變，一九八二年教育部公布了一項「加強推行國語文實施計畫」，具體實施事項中包括「研定加強國語重點工作，在學校機關，及公共場所須使用國語。」該計畫把排除方言干擾、強化國語推行，作爲提高國語文能力的一項重要措施㉗。這個時期值得注意的是「台語熱」的不斷升溫，強調「本土文化」，開展「母語運動」，甚至號召「講媽媽的話」。語言問題泛政治化，影響語言態度的社會因素也日趨複雜化。

㉖ 參林進輝：《臺灣語言問題論集》（臺灣文藝雜誌社，1983年）。

㉗ 仇志群：〈臺灣五十年來語文規範化述略〉，《語文建設》第9期（1996年）。

到了九○年代，臺灣的語言政策又有兩項重大調整。一是教育部一九九三年四月三日宣佈「將母語教育列入中小學正式教育範疇」，這個政策一般認爲是臺灣語言政策的劃時代轉變㉘。另一項是新聞局「刪除廣播電視法第二十條有關電台播音語言以國語爲主的規定」，自此以後，「國內電台對播音使用語言將擁有充分自主權」㉙。這兩項調整，對臺灣語言社會產生了深遠影響。借著傳播媒體的力量，方言尤其是閩南語，成了官方語言外，使用最頻繁的語種了。

㈢、國語推行運動之成效檢討

「普及化之成果」及「本土化之迷思」可說是半世紀以來，臺灣語言政策的兩項顯見的結果。

就前者言，國語的推行及普及，是臺灣半個世紀來語言規範化工作的成就，這項龐大的社會語言體系建構工程，經過幾十年努力，有了很好的成績。在今天，臺灣人不懂國語的已是非常少數，這對一個組成份子複雜，背景差異性大的語言社會來說，是極不容易的。

九○年代以後，臺灣開始了方言在內的雙語教育，是各種「本土化」意識與實際表現中的一項。電視台、廣播電台對方言也不再設限，甚至許多節目是國台語雙聲發音的。回顧臺灣本土化意識之形成，其實有其複雜的政治、社會、歷史因素，但單就政府來台後的國語政策一項言，方言意識的抬頭，表面上是與政策不符的，但

㉘ 《聯合報刊》，1993年6月13日。

㉙ 《中央日報》，1993年7月16日。

實質上卻也是阻擋不住的潮流。今日生活在臺灣的人若不通閩南語，在社會上有時便成了少數異類，甚至造成不便，這恐怕也是當初國語推行政策所始料未及的。

語言使用本來是一種社會習慣、約定俗成，但越是語系複雜的區域，語言政策又不可或缺，所謂「本土化的迷思」其衝突也就展現在此。姑不論語言政策是否必須調整，其實目前臺灣面臨最大的語言問題，是如何確定語言規範的標準。臺灣一直沒有像中國大陸那樣明確的提出國語的標準，但實際上以北京音爲標準音、以北方方言爲基礎方言，也就是臺灣標準國語的標準。臺灣從一九四九年以來與大陸長期隔絕，形成一個封閉的漢語言環境，雖然堅持以國語爲標準語，但臺灣的國語形式，自然地靠向了南方官話痕跡頗重的五〇年代前的現代漢語書面語，也可以說靠向了一個歷史的靜態的標準。

在口語交際方面，臺灣的日常交際、大量的商業活動以及基層的社會活動，多數還是使用以閩南語爲主的方言，在此情況下，一種臺灣化國語逐漸形成。臺灣的國語，有大量的臺灣社區詞語㉚，有語音、語法、語用的一系列特點，這種國語被認爲是臺灣通行的國語形式。雖然臺灣式國語已是一個事實，但其實仍處在一個變動不居的狀態中，那些是臺灣國語的語音、詞彙、語法的特點，還沒有明確、全面的描寫。而臺灣的這一語言現狀，也使臺灣的語文規範化更難定位。

㉚ 特定社會環境裏產生的地區通用語。

四、二十一世紀臺灣語言政策的宏觀思考

㈠、共同語的使用

一個國家或一個民族內部通用的交際工具稱為「共同語」，前者又叫「國語」、後者又叫「民族共同語」。以在臺灣的中華民國而言，組成國家的是漢民族，漢民族目前的共同語，包括中國大陸、新加坡皆是以北京話為中心的北方方言為基礎所形成的。在臺灣，此民族共同語也就是國語，這是過去半個世紀的具體語言現象，就語言政策而言，推行的也就是這個系統。

臺灣地區現行的共同語系統，其使用狀況普遍也穩定，並無立即之改變因素出現。但是潛在的變異因素也不是沒有，那就是出現於世紀末期的「本土意識」之抬頭。目前臺灣本土化的呼聲與具體行動，除了政治訴求外，文化、歷史乃至語言訴求，皆是本土化意識的一環。以語言而言，普遍使用於臺灣共同語之外的，便是閩南方言及客家方言，尤其閩南語系更為民間交際語言之主流。激進的本土化支持者，不但以政治為訴求主軸，更以語言之改變為輔，希望達到以政治獨立為中心的全盤改變。

因此在世紀末的此時，若干民間團體的集會語言、大眾傳播媒體的語言取向，往往已轉變為使用閩南語或客家語，而捨棄現行的國語。例如以臺灣獨立為黨綱的建國黨，便以閩南語作全面的發音，以求符合其定義的完整的本土色彩。甚至在非官方場合的各種形式中，閩南方言成了不可或缺的表達工具，且在某種程度上是必須的

潮流，例如，電視節目中的戲劇節目，就經常刻意的在一個單元中「雙語發音」；熱門的政治選舉活動，也更是須借助方言的凝聚力量，以求本地閩南族群、客家族群乃至其他族群的認可。這些本土語言意識之抬頭，甚且形成潮流，對未來的語言政策，將形成一定程度的影響，是不容置疑的。

臺灣因爲地理環境與中國大陸遠隔，百年來與大陸地區之政權也互不隸屬，加以本地族群複雜，遂也導致語言使用上之主觀爭議。再加上政治的不確定因素，遂使共同語的標準有了潛在的異動因素。其實臺灣地區人民應有宏觀的語言觀念，以面對此問題，縱然未來政治情勢有所改變，語言也不應是政治角力下的圖騰，畢竟沒有阻礙的溝通方式，才是各族群間應採取及思考的方向。

語言的使用雖是約定俗成，但共同語的制定，往往取決於政治力量。以北京方言爲基礎的近代官話系統，之所以形成民族共同語，便因北京在過去建都八百多年[31]，一直是中國政治文化的中心。北京話所屬的北方方言，在漢語各方言中一直佔者優勢，形成民族共同語、乃至今日臺灣的國語，也是自然。而且因爲此共同語使用近千年之久，歷代的語音資料、拼音方式，留存最多的也以此語言系統爲主，成了與漢字對應最爲人接受的系統[32]。若要驟然改變，並非易事，也不是上策。尤其是國語運動在臺灣推行五十年，有其顯

---

[31] 金、元、明、清四代建都北京，從西元一一一五年至一九一一年。

[32] 例如元以後的歷代韻書，流傳較廣、影響較大的，多與現代國語系統相近。如元代周德清《中原音韻》四聲中的入聲已經消失，和國語一樣只有陰平、陽平、上、去四聲。又如明代蘭茂《韻略易通》二十個聲母中，全濁聲母消失，和國語的二十二聲母已十分接近。

著成效與持續力，短期內，北方方言系統的國語，仍應是本地的語言主流，在政策的轉變上，應有更宏觀的思考，逐步而循序才是。

㈡、方言與共同語的文化兼容架構

支持共同語的最重要因素是政治，它是官方的工作、宣傳語言，在社會語言生活中有一定的權威性，因而在共同語與方言並存的情況下，共同語常處於優勢之地位。

但語言又是文化的載體，尤其在多元族群、多元文化的區域中，方言更是其個別文化的表徵，甚至是命脈㉝。就多元文化的社會而言，共同語反映全民社會的主流文化，而方言則反映地域文化。比較起來，方言的文化蘊涵在某些地區，如臺灣，甚至比共同語更久遠、純厚些。反映本地文化的方言，較之共同語更具有獨特的魅力。共同語追求規範、標準，使它在一定程度上帶有「人造」的性質，而代表臺灣方言主流的閩南語，在表現地域文化方面的優勢，從近年來電視節目的方言比重增加，到學校教育中方言教育的法制化，便可見一般。

這種方言優勢，相當程度反映了地域文化的抬頭及歷史淵源。其實仔細思考，這對本地的共同語而言，原非壞事。就交際功能之角度而言，臺灣的國語共同語是全民通用的交際工具；閩南語及其他方言則是地域性交際工具。前者具有廣泛的傳意作用，帶有規範意義；而後者則更具親和作用。共同語是社會開放條件下的交際工具，反映了人際關係和人群關係在廣度上的擴展；方言則體現了社

㉝ 比如臺灣原住民語言的逐漸消失，也將帶來其文化的沉積。

會的封閉性，但它使人際方面具有更親近的凝聚力，它的親和力反映了人際關係在深度上的延展。

因此，在臺灣這個既用共同語又用方言的雙語社會中，兩者其實有著不同的語境適應性。國語多用於公眾交往，方言多用於家庭、鄉黨等場合，未必衝突，而且長久以來，不同族群的臺灣地區民眾其適應程度也未見嚴重分裂，這是可喜的現象。

不過在邁入二十一世紀的此時，以下針對本地共同語與方言間融合架構的應變、思考方向，卻是必須的：

第一、必須進一步加強方言語言結構包括語音、詞彙、語法的研究，建構方言與共同語間的結構轉換機制。尤其要重視詞彙、語法，甚至二者相對應的漢字間的轉換與適應，以減少相對的疏離感[34]。

第二、從政治與語言的關係來說，目前的國語是語言政策之主流，但未來應創造一種更寬鬆的語言環境，防止過去的語言高壓政策，避免方言與國語間的泛政治化矛盾對立，這在政治環境、情勢多變的臺灣，尤其重要。

第三、從文化與語言的關係而言，則須給臺灣各方言以適當的生存空間，包括原住民語、使方言充分發揮其表現區域文化的優勢。長久來說，保存本地文化、語言，其實另一方面也就加強了政治不確定性之外的區域安全團結，未嘗不是好事。

㈢、多元文化社會的語言教育

人類透過語言助長思考，更借助語言理解自身存在的世界。人

---

[34] 例如閩南語〝Huam-muan〞與國語漢字「顢頇」之對應。

類個體在運用語言的同時，以意識的自我反省作爲社會認知和意義建構的基礎。在社會中經由語言活動使存有的意義不斷展開，語言和文化的關係也愈加密切；換言之，語言和文化的關係是精緻且複雜的交互作用的歷程。浸潤在某語言環境中的人，通常能自然的通曉其語言的內涵，並遵守該語言的習慣和規律，因此語言的教育，也就蘊藏著該語言所屬的文化教育。

臺灣未來的語言教育，應有宏觀的社會文化目的。因爲多元的文化環境中，語言常成爲爭論的主要議題，過去十多年，臺灣的語言使用就經常出現此種爭議㉟。其實臺灣的多元文化社會，是既存之事實，島內各族群及個人均有其文化特質，因此成熟的多元文化價值所包含的尊重與包容胸懷，是必須有的素養。就語言而言，提供多樣選擇的語言教育政策，便應是建立此種素養的必要模式，而不應再有如從前般的單一語言政策。

近年來，臺灣社會急速變遷，民主及本土意識強烈發展，社會中大量的次級團體，形成眾多次級文化，對教育的質量需求其實越來越高。現今及未來社會，可預見的語言教育形態，是除了國語教育外，也重視母語教育、外語教育、鄉土教育。此種發展明顯反映了本地多元文化社會的語言需求，也正是語言和社會文化相融的具體表現，是一種潮流，也是一種語言交際本質的體現。因此就維繫與穩定臺灣多元社會的急速變遷而言，此種多元語言教育的方向，是必須且正確的。

㉟ 如閩南語與國語間使用的爭議，表現在會議、問政乃至課堂授課中，皆曾出現。

但是令人擔憂的是，目前臺灣地區的母語文化意識，與實質方言母語使用、教學，其目的經常是主觀意識強烈的本土色彩所引起，形成了局限性；意即要求正視方言母語的目的，在達到一些政治或鄉土文化維護之訴求後，便缺乏更高更廣的理想性。例如從政者在公開正式場合以方言發音，其目的常常只在突顯個人本土政治色彩的表象，而非語言政策的轉變或理想，如此的心態是不切實際且危險的。

因此，在邁向新世紀之時，語言的教育除以照顧母語文化為目標外，更應擴展島內人民的文化視野，以本土化與國際化的前瞻觀念，培養世界公民為理想才是。也就是說應避免沉溺於母語文化的眷戀，而是教育民眾從母語文化出發，肯定自我並了解其他的語言文化，進而尊重多元社會中的異文化。這才是成熟的多元文化社會，應有的語言教育政策。

㈣、重視語言感情培養正確語言觀

就語言理論而言，「語言情感」指使用某一種語言的社會集團成員，對自己的母語所具有的強烈情感㊱。這是一種社會心理現象，其心理狀態表現在兩方面：一方面，這個社會集團的成員，在不以其母語為主流的社會環境中，強烈的希望要用母語彼此交際；另一方面，任何一個社會集團的成員，雖然能掌握另外一個社會集團所使用的語言，但在一般情況下，他總認為只有使用母語，才能最準確、流暢的表達思想、情感，因而一旦情緒激動的片刻，他就會不

㊱ 參同註❶，頁638。

由自主的採用母語。

本文前項所言有關共同語的制定、方言與共同語的兼融，乃至多元的語言教育政策，其成功的基礎，便須建立在對本地不同語言系統的情感重視上。臺灣過去百年來的語言政策，基本上是壓抑了許多族群的方言母語才取得了成果，不論是日語也好，國語也好皆是如此。時至今日，類似的高壓語言政策已不再適用，因爲過去以爲次文化的方言，在本土政治、文化意識抬頭下受到了重視，甚至在一般交際中成了主流，不再受到鄙視。

以閩南語爲例，其實在過去百年的高壓語言政策下，不但沒有消失，更在百年的潛伏期中漸次壯大，顯然使用閩南語的閩南族群，其語言感情是濃厚而不可忽視的。另外在臺灣擁有四百萬人口的客家族群，其所使用的客語方言，近年來也在族群競爭、政治爭勝、保衛鄉土文化的觀念中愈發受到重視。在在顯示了新世紀的語言政策，必須重視且小心的照應臺灣島內的各種語言感情成份，除了不再高壓之外，均衡的疏導、不同語言情感間的交流，及其與共同語間的良好關係等，相對於政治而言，更是刻不容緩的議題。

族群、方言的多元，本身就是一個敏感的差異，尤其臺灣地狹人稠，有一九四九年隨國民政府撤守臺灣的大陸各省新移民，也有來台較早的閩南、客家族群，更有九大族的原住民族群。在擺脫過去百年的高壓語言政策後，各族群基於方言母語的感情，各種方言早已躲上台面，甚至多有較勁之意。如何疏導類似的紛爭，便賴正確「語言觀」的培養。「語言觀」即「語言觀念」指人們對某種語言的看法，包括對其功能、社會地位及發展前途等的價值判斷[37]。

---

[37] 同前註。

臺灣目前各種方言與主流共同語間的爭勝，其實便是各族群方言價值判斷提升所導致的語言觀分歧現象。

形成語言觀的因素頗爲複雜，其中交際功能是基本因素，此外還有政治、經濟狀況、宗教信仰、族群心理等社會因素；以及文化程度的高低、職業性質差異等個人因素。臺灣目前的社會情勢，正好是這些因素都產生世代交替現象的一個多元文化體，因此主流語言價值的不同角度思考，遂也應運而生，長此以往對族群間之融合並非好事。

當務之急應是培養正確的語言觀，及正確的語言價值判斷。綜合本文前諸項所論，未來的語言觀應是以「維持國語，扶助方言。」的平衡理念爲目標。透過自由的、平等的和開放的語言教育政策，使各族群、各方言間的協調性增加，不再是對立與競爭；而是社會交際與生活交際兼顧，才是各族群應有的正確語言觀。

㈤、結論：結合全民利益交集的語言政策

討論語言政策，必須涵蓋語言計畫、語言教育。語言政策是語言計畫的指導原則、語言計畫是語言政策的具體步驟，而語言教育則是語言計畫最具體的表現。三者的關係若以「畫圓圈」來表示，則圓心代表語言政策、語言計畫是把語言政策畫出來的圓規，而語言教育就是所畫出來的圓，三者相輔相成㊳。

其中的教育層面，則是觀察政策的最直接管道。臺灣的國語教育，近半世紀以來已算是成功的，不論那一族群的人，以國語爲主

㊳ 同註❿。

要的交際工具，在多數場合中是可以行得通的。但這並不代表臺灣各族群便願意主動或被動的放棄母語方言，相反的，民間在政治、經濟、鄉土文化等社會因素改變下，方言使用的機會與權力大增。在一九九三年教育部更宣佈要實施雙語教育，且從一九九六年起，國小三至六年級增設「鄉土教學活動」，其中便包括鄉土語言教學。這其實相當程度反映了臺灣目前社會文化環境的變遷與訴求，在未來語言政策的制定上是不可不慎的。

臺灣面對一個已然成型的多元文化社會，新世紀的語言政策、方針，必須揚棄過去百年來的單一思考，在共同語與各方言間求取平衡，而以「尊重語言權」為基本立場。因為語言權的尊重，可以確保每一個語族對國家資源有平等獲取的機會；也因對鄉土語言文化的彼此尊重，形成族群之相融而非對立。如此一來，語言的差異就不是困擾，而是多元社會的資產。透過平衡的語言政策，可以培養容納異己的民主精神，更促進了族群間的共存共榮。而如此的政策目標，又必須由語言教育的現代化、大眾化、實用化、本土化做起，相信這個完美的「圓形」語言工程，是新世紀的臺灣語言政策必須建立起的一條新路線。

Cultural Traditions and the Quest for Modernity in China : A Multi-Dimensional Problematique

羅多弼（Torbjörn Lodén）*

I

The concept of "China studies" can hardly be defined as an academic discipline with a specific set of theories and methods designed to resolve certain problems which have evolved over time. This concept refers rather to research efforts grounded in different academic disciplines which aim at illuminating and explaining aspects of Chinese culture and society. Thus China studies constitute an example of so-called area studies rather than an academic discipline in a conventional sense.

* 瑞典斯德哥爾摩大學亞太研究中心主任

Sometimes the concept of "Chine studies" is used synonymously with the older notion of "sinology ". But more often than not these respective notions are given somewhat different meanings. Whereas sinology for many users refers primarily to studies of premodern Chinese culture, the concept of China studies often refers to studies of 20th century Chinese society and culture.

In this context I use "China studies" in the broadest possible sense to refer to studies of Chinese culture or society in modern or premodern times.

Now the distinction between "area studies" and a theoretical "discipline" no longer appears as clear-cut as it once may have appeared. Traditional discipline in the natural sciences as well as the human sciences may no longer be viewed as based on specific sets of theories and methods designed to resolve specific problems. The tendency in recent times has rather been that one and the same discipline dissolves into sub-disciplines and that the boundaries between disciplines - be it physics and chemistry or sociology and anthropology – become blurred. We may even raise the question to what extent the ideal type of a theoretical discipline was ever realized.

Still there is reason to emphasize the distinction between "China studies" and "sinology" on the one hand and theoretical disciplines on the other in that the subject matter of the former is defined in terms of one culture or civilization, whereas the subject matter of the latter is defined in terms of theoretical approaches, even though these may not be based on well integrated and logically consistent premises, theories and methods.

No matter how they are defined "China studies" and "sinology" are Western notions defined primarily to refer to branches of scholarship which have developed in Europe and America.

But the greatest amount of research that can be classified in terms of these notions is carried out in China. "China studies" is generally translated into Chinese as *Zhongguo xue*, but as far as I know *Zhongguo xue* is used only to refer to research carried out about China in other countries and not to research efforts in China. "Sinology" has long been rendered into Chinese as *Hanxue*, which evokes in the minds of Chinese intellectuals the image of studies of premodern Chinese culture carried out in the spirit of the methods of textual criticism developed in China the 17th and 18th centuries, which paid homage to the scholarship of the ancient Han dynasty.

In China scholarship which could be classified as China studies or sinology actually takes place in a variety of disciplines such as history, literature, philosophy, art, sociology, political science, economics etc.

In recent years the notion of *guoxue* （national studies） - once coined by the great Zhang Taiyan in the early 20th century – has gained prominence to refer to studies of premodern Chinese culture, and Professor Zhang Dainian at Peking University says that guoxue refers to the same subject matter as the Western notion of *Hanxue*, i.e. sinology.

II

If China studies in the West are concerned with understanding "the other", in China these studies rather serve to deepen the understanding of "the self". While in China studies of Chinese culture and society are immediately related to defining one's own identity and to solving problems that are one's own problems, China scholars in the West are engaged in studies of the identities and problems of others.

But even of Western scholars China studies may ultimately have to do with the understanding of the self. The study of a foreign culture may be an endeavour to construct a mirror in which one may discover oneself. The history of Western China studies bears witness to innumerable examples of projections of concerns and anxieties of one's own culture on to Chinese culture.

In studying aspects of Chinese culture the Western scholar may create better conditions for communicating with China. Building bridges to Chinese culture, or engaging in intercultural communication, stands out as major task facing the practitioners of China studies in the West. In this regard, the equivalent in China of China studies in the West is studies of Western cultures and societies.

III

Although studies of Chinese society and culture may serve different purposes in China and the West, in approaching their research topics scholars in both regions still face some of the same basic questions of orientation and values. I would like here to draw attention to one such basic question which has to do with the attitude to the specificities of Chinese culture as opposed to the similarities which Chinese culture shares with other cultures.

We may assume that Chinese history and culture exhibit certain features that are specific and which have no exact equivalent in other cultures. But we may also assume that there are many ways in which Chinese culture resembles other cultures. The scholar must relate to the differences as well as to the similarities, and in the history of scholarship on Chinese culture and society in China and the West we may discern different orientations in this regard. We may, to simplify a complicated question to the point of oversimplification, distinguish between the particularists and the universalists.

The particularists – be they Chinese or Westerners – emphasize the specificity of Chinese culture and argue that the basic orientations of Chinese culture are different from European and Western culture and that, therefore, Chinese culture cannot be explained in terms of Western concepts, no can China's social problems be understood and analysed in terms of non-Chinese concepts. They argue that values considered valid in the Western world are not valid in China. The notion of a set of specific Asian values therefore seems appealing to many of them.

The universalists, on the other hand, tend to see similarities where the particularists see differences. To the extent that thee are basic differences, they assume that the specifically Chinese phenomena may still be explained in Western terms. They argue for the possibility of cultural translation.

This controversy involves two different issues which must be kept apart. One issue is to what extent there are basic cultural differences, the other whether the specific features of one culture may be understood and explained in terms of the other.

As for the first issue the difference of opinion should probably be seen as a difference of degree. For example, I know of no one who would deny that the history of Chinese thought as compared to the history of European thought does exhibit some distinguishing features; that, for example, much less attention is paid to logic and epistemology in traditional Chinese thought than in European thought.

The question to what extent there exist basic cultural specificities must be kept separate from the question of the translatability of these differences which is, as I see it, the core of this problematique.

Translations can never be perfect. A translation must be based on an interpretation of a certain text or phenomenon, and such interpretations are inevitably fraught with uncertainty. Some interpretations are more accurate than others, but there is hardly such a thing as a perfect interpretation. Once the interpretation is made the translator must find those terms and formulations in the target language best suited to convey the original content as interpreted. Even within the same culture and the same language interpretations are always provisional.

However, the fact that there is no such thing as a perfect interpretation and perfect translation does not mean that interpretations and translations are impossible or useless. On the contrary, it seems to me that interpretations are very close to the core of the human sciences and that there is hardly any qualitative difference between intracultural and intercultural interpretations. For me as a student of Chinese culture, trying to explain Chinese phenomena in Swedish or English words is indeed the essential part of my work.

In this controversy between particularists and universalists, which I have outlined in a somewhat simplified form, I side with the universalists. In the West it seems to me that particularism has too often been used to erect walls around Chinese culture rather than tearing them down, making Chinese culture much less accessible than it actually is. In China particularism seems to be used to oppose the opening up of China to the outside world and China's integration into the world, which I consider desirable – for the world and for China.

Recognizing that there are indeed many differences between the cultural traditions of China and the West, and viewing the specific features of one culture as valuable contributions to the cultural reservoir at the disposal of mankind, I believe that these specific features of one culture may preferably be considered variations of a number of basic unifying themes of human culture.

Furthermore, I think it is a most important task for China scholars to interpret and explain Chinese culture to people of different cultures over the world. Since there is no such thing a perfect interpretation, it is indeed valuable that Chinese phenomena are interpreted and explained from different points of view.

As far as cultural understanding is concerned one may seldom speak about one truth only. While we must be on our guard against the extreme relativism which postmodernism and other currents of contemporary thought have promoted during the past couple of decades, I think it is important to realize that different perspectives of a culture or a society may often reveal different complementary truths about that cultural or society.

IV

In studying Chinese culture scholars in China and in other countries often engage in joint projects, and I believe this is a very promising tendency. Based in Stockholm, I would like to see more cooperation in China studies between scholars in China and Sweden. In particular when it comes to studying the history of Sino-Swedish contacts in different fields I think we shoulder a heavy responsibility to cooperate much more than we have done so far. Also when it comes to some topics of basic research I think many topics are awaiting joint research efforts.

From a Swedish perspective much remains to be done, for example, in studying the development of trade between China and Sweden from the 18th century onwards and the activities of Swedish Christian missionaries in China during the hundred years from the middle of the 19th century and until the establishment of the People's Republic of

China.

V

I would like to some up some of the rather loose ends of this paper in six points:

1st, cultural interpretation and translation are essential aspects of China studies;

2nd, cultural interpretation and translation facilitate intercultural communication which is vitally important;

3rd, the cultural heritage of China should be seem as an important integral part of the cultural reservoir at the disposal of mankind;

4th, different perspectives of Chinese culture may be mutually complementary rather than exclusive and contribute to enriching the understanding of Chinese culture;

5th, in our studies of Chinese culture and society there is room for cooperation as well as division of labour between Chinese and Western scholars;

6th, free and unfettered flow of knowledge and information across the boundaries of states and nations is essential for scholarship on Chinese culture and society.

The 'Native' Researcher Revisited Some reflections on personal and structural components of Otherness

熊彪（Björn Kjellgren）*

摘　要

全球化過程使世界日趨密集。各種网絡與實踐向許多長期存在且被視爲永恆的文化邊境及國家邊境的觀念發起挑戰。這時也出現了不少往往被誤爲「傳統」或「保守」的文化逆流運動。

本文所涉及的近幾年在中國大陸出現的本土學者概念，在某種程度上可理解爲一種文化逆流運動。從一個國際性角度來看，這概念可以說是與後殖民主義以及東方主

* 瑞典斯德哥爾摩大學中文系博士生暨兼任講師

義相關聯的。具體而言，我將它置於美國人類學家的本土學者爭論、臺灣香港社會科學的本土化（或中國化）及中國大陸社會科學規範化的上下文中來理解。儘管如此，本文的目的不僅僅將本土學者概念置於一個上下文中，解構和批駁它，而主要是進一步理解它所指示的認識論及方法論的問題。

希望本文在提出異議的同時也促進學者之間的認識與交流。

每隻螞蟻都有眼睛、鼻子。它美不美麗；偏差有沒有一毫厘，有何關係？

——林　夕

Abstract

One of the revelations of our late modern era is that as the world grows increasingly dense in the process we usually refer to as globalisation, and numerous networks and practices of different characters challenge long-standing boundaries and level many cultural distinctions, the very same process simultaneously generates cultural counter-currents, often mistakenly interpreted as 'traditional' or 'conservative'. (Giddens 1990, 1991).

In this paper I will address the topic of the Chinese 'native researcher', which to some degree is such a phenomenon, generally linked to the broader issues of post-colonialism and orientalism. I have chosen this topic not merely to deconstruct and contextualise the notion of 'native researcher', which I will do, or debunk it, which I will also do, but foremost to enquire into the epistemological and methodological nexus which it refers to.

I hope with this enquiry both to mirror some of this ongoing debate, and to contribute, in a minute fashion, to the continuous dialogue between scholars from different camps, both of these being endeavors I believe to be the scholar's obligations.

The 'Native researcher' in Chinese ethnography

Exactly. how widespread or influential the idea of the native researcher is in contemporary mainland China is hard to determine. Incontrovertibly, the question of a researcher's ethnic identity becomes interesting only in mixed company and since that is not the case in the majority of research carried out in China, one may well guess that it is a small issue, but one bound to grow in time, however, with increased academic cooperation and cross-cultural exchange and influences.

In this paper I will refer to the concept as mirrored in the works of one of the contemporary rising stars in Chinese anthropology, Wang Mingming 王銘銘 (1997a, 1997b), whose writings on the topic, I believe, are good examples of the somewhat confused understanding of the concept among a younger generation of progressive mainland scholars.❶

❶ The term used by Wang is *bentu shehui yanjiuzhe* 本土社會研究者, 'native social researcher'. As for his own background, not without interest in this context, he was born in Fujian, received his higher education in Ecglangd and is now working in Beijing. Even though I will seem like his 'antagonist' in this

Wang Mingming (1997b, p. 20) evokes the doyen of Chinese anthropology, Fei Xiaotong 費孝通 (1993, pp. 163-65), and suggests that Chinese are much better suited for anthropological research in China than (western) foreigners.❷He advances mainly two reasons for this: Chinese researchers can identify interesting things faster than foreigners in China and can avoid what Wang calls 'epistemological problems' (renshilun wenti 認識論問題) often related to studies of 'the cultures of Others' (yiwenhua 異文化), e.g., when westerners study China. In this context, Wang sees advantages with the native researcher. He writes (p. 125):

> Research of ones own society is superior to the study of the culture of the Other in two major respects. Firstly, the native social researcher can more easily grasp the interrelatedness of the rules of society and culture with the life of man. Secondly, only from the perspective of his own society is it possible for the social scientist to understand his own role in society and, at the same time, find the appropriate social position for himself.

---

paper I am not at all concerned with the personal motives or politics behind Wang's writings and would like to point out that I deal with his works only as examples of a certain kind of resoning.

My own major experiences with field research, constituting the foundation for my understanding of the topic, come chiefly from research in Shenzhen and among the Chinese in Stockholm. I received my academic training in sociology and ethnology.

❷ Fei Xiaotong himself in his early days having received his letter of mastership from Malinowski(1923), who in a foreword to Fei's study and only justifies Fei as a native ethnographer (which, as we shall return to, was a matter of controversy within the discipline), but also writes that Fei possesses local knowledge that would be almost impossible for a Westerner to acquire. However misquotes Fei Xiaotong, who actually has a much more open-minded view on the topic - judging from the very same book Wang refers to.

(Bentu shehui yanjiu zai liang da fangmian jiao zhi yu yiwenhua yanjiu zhanyou youshi. Shouxian, bentu shehui yanjiuzhe geng yi yu bawo shehui yu wenhua guize yu ren benshen de shenghuo de xiangguanxing. Qici, zhi you zai bentu shehui de toushi zhong, shehui kexue gongzuozhe cai neng liaojie zishen zai shehui zhong de juese, bing geiyu zishen yi ge tieqie de shehui dingwei 本土社會研究在兩大方面較之於"異文化"研究占有優勢。首先，本土社會研究者更易於把握社會與文化規則與人本身生活相關性。其次，只有在本土社會的透視中，社會科學工作者才能瞭解自身在社會中的角色，並給予自身一個貼切的社會定位).❸

Before getting back to the Chinese native researcher, I believe we should contextualise the notion and seek some of its intellectual roots. The context I suggest is twofold and, although pointing in different directions, basically parts of the same process: on the mainly western arena it is the question of the native researcher as debated especially in American anthropology; closer to China, it is the sinicization of the social sciences as crystallised in Taiwan and Hong Kong, and, to a lesser degree, in mainland China.

"We" and "the natives" in western anthropology

In the anthropological profession as taught in the West, the

---

❸ It should be pointed out that although this thesis is presented in a generalistic voice, there is no doubt that Wang is here specifically referring to China as the 'native society', to western scholars (*xifang xuezhe* 西方學者) in China as those studying the 'culture of Others' and to Chinese researchers as 'native social reserachers'.

distinctions between the 'regular' cholars, i.e., those who studied alien cultures, and the 'native' scholars, who were seen as studying their respective cultures from within, were, and are still in some institutions, part of the disciplines received wisdom. The position of the native scholar was unique since his status as 'native' was independent of academic training and rested solely on his 'ties of blood' with the soil on which he worked. This was then sometimes seen as something exclusively positive, given the basic drive in anthropology to get the 'native's point of view', but it could also be interpreted as a hindrance to the scholar's much valued objectivity. The peril of 'going native' and the advice to new field-workers to 'stay off the women' both reflect this side of the anthropological stance (see Evans-Pritchard 1973). Thus, a distinction was made between 'native' and 'real' scholars.

Both academic and non-academic developments during the 1980s and early 1990s have in many ways made these distinctions obsolete. Rapid changes and increased social mobility in many of the countries previously seen as 'primitive' as well as in the so-called first world were the basic non-academic reasons. With more students and scholars working in the West having their roots in non-western countries, and with an increasing number of 'native scholars' in the countries once studied with the 'western gaze', many of whom are also influential participants in international scholarly debates, the notion of any scholar having a fixed and unchanging cultural identity has been increasingly untenable (cf. Narayan 1993). Western researchers on their side, having no longer any 'undiscovered natives' to map out, and responding to a self-reflective critique of their own discipline's colonial origin, have also increasingly turned to their 'own turf' for material. On top of this, of course, post-modernism caused the death of many well-established concepts. The notion of 'native scholar' has hardly any substantial value today in most western institutions. The post-positivistic turn of the social sciences, largely building on older continental theories, has also seriously undermined the simplistic notion of the 'native view' as still often given in the *emic-etic* dichotomy.

In its place, an understanding of the researcher's active participation in the creative process of any ethnography has appeared.

Unfortunately, insufficient attention may have been given to the ethnic or cultural identity of 'regular' scholars, and as the Daoists would say 'When you have western scholars - then you will also have non-western'. Although they exist, little has been written about 'africanised scholars' or 'asianised scholars' etc. Thus we still have the tacit notion of the native scholars; 'native' still being foremost a concept tied to crude notions of authenticity and cultural essentialism.

The Sinicization of the Social Sciences

A geographically closer older relative to the 'native scholar' in contemporary mainland China is the movement for indigenous or sinicized (bentuhua 本土化, zhongguohua 中國化) social sciences, the battle cries of which were first heard among Chinese scholars in America, Taiwan and Hong Kong in the early 1980s, and which became more topical in mainland China only during the 1990s.

The most vivid academic discipline engaged in this movement was social psychology, with leading names in Taiwan like Yang Guoshu 楊國樞 and Huang Guangguo 黃光國. Most of the social sciences were represented, however, and the movement had spiritual connections both to the field of literature and to philosophy, where new Confucians like Du Weiming 杜維明 can be said to have been brothers-in-arms.

This was a movement with two basic rationales. On the scholarly side it was an attempt to construct descriptions and theories based on non-western precepts and assumptions (such as the tacit understanding of the 'universal nature' of American research findings), which would make them more relevant to the local arena and less dependent on alien constructs which could obstruct the understanding of Chinese society. Observed sociologically, the movement was a social science version of the 'obsession with China'. Traditional Chinese ideas and values were to be examined and utilised in order not only to get a better understanding of local societies, but foremost to bring about a *Chinese* understanding of society and local culture among a general public, seen to be on the edge of totally abandoning their 'original' identity in the process of modernisation. What was worse, some even seemed to take pleasure in this shedding of skin, 'mistakenly' believing that all things modern were better than the traditional ones (e.g., Yang Guoshu 1987/1988). In trying to do this they frequently turned to the classics of the Chinese 'big tradition' for concepts and definitions (e.g., Huang Guangguo 1988a, 1988b, 1994; Cai & Xiao 1986). As with the 'native researchers' in anthropology, scholars engaged in this development were as a rule educated in the West i.e., - the United States - and their scholarship often had an air of 'Zhongti - Xiyong' 中體西用 with Chinese concepts originating from the Warring States juxtaposed with positivistic calculations from America.❹

In mainland China, with soft sciences such as sociology,

---

❹ Possibly, it was the rapid development in Taiwan during the very years these scholars stayed in America which made them aware of a 'loss of Chineseness' and prompted their reaction; a recovery of familiarity.

Among a younger generation of Taiwanese scholars *bentuhua* is quite differently understood. Being a scholarly wing of the movement for the 'taiwanisation of Taiwan' these interpret *bentuhua* as *taiwanhua* (taiwanisation) as opposed to older generations's still more influential *zhongguohua* with its extremely tight bonds to Chinese 'big tradition'.

anthropology and social psychology all being (re)born thanks to Deng Xiaopings reform program, the movement for *bentuhua* was not only associated with early ethnographic works by Fei Xiaotong and others, but also with Chinas contemporary political quest. Thus, some voices argued for *you Zhongguo tese de shehui kexue* 有中國特色的社會科學 'social sciences with Chinese characteristics' (Shi Xiuyin 1998) as an academic brother-in-arms to the official ideology of post-Mao China.

In as much as the concept of *bentuhua* was discussed in mainland China, however, it was usually raised together with the question of 'regularisation' (*guifanhua*規範化) of the social sciences. Was regularisation, much needed if China's research in social sciences was to be taken seriously in an international context, the same as Westernisation landing the Chinese researcher into the trap of Eurocentrism - which 'at least would be very embarrassing for any Chinese scholar', according to the mainland sociologist Huang Ping 黃平 (1995/1997, p. 219). What was the alternative, if any? How can one successfully sail between a Scylla of questionable research and a Charybdis of Western paradigms and definitions?

To this day, given the mainland's quest to become an international actor, most energy has naturally been spent on becoming familiar with already accepted (western) concepts and methods and the movement for *bentuhua* has not been left uncontradicted (e.g., Su 1994) nor has it gained support from any substantial quarter of the academic field (Shi Xiuyin 1998). As an example, nothing *at all* was mentioned about 'sinicized psychology' in a recapitulation of mainland developments of psychology by Zhao Liru in 1996.❺

❺ This does not mean that 'native' concepts are not at all used or taught, but it justly indicates the minor roles allotted to them.

This could of course be construed as the final capitulation to the western right to continue to define the standards of the field. Huang Ping (1995/1997, p. 218-219), although highly aware of both the personal and professional heterogeneous reality glossed over by the terms 'west' and 'western', thus states that the problem of *bentuhua* is hardly a global concern: Except for some non-western scholars working in the west, American and European scholars are not concerned with the problem of *bentuhua* the way Chinese scholars have to be when applying western paradigms to their own societies.

The basic problem, from my point of view, is the conspicuous unawareness in all of this of the fact that new academic trends and 'paradigms' today appear just as 'foreign' to the vast majority of western students and scholars as to our Chinese colleagues. Any new 'western' theory of class formation, of ethnicity, or of any other social phenomenon may be historically tied to an older debate within some western sphere, but this certainly does not mean that 'we in the west' would have any automatic understanding or unequivocal view on it. I do not mean to suggest here that we live in a world of cultural equilibrium, but maybe I could be so bold as to suggest that between two equally educated individuals from Europe and China, generally the Chinese would have the relative advantage of being more familiar with cultural concepts and trains of thoughts from Europe than the other way around, and that this not only is a sign of the much loathed western cultural hegemony forcing 'our' tradition on everyone else, but also a tremendous resource available to few Europeans.

As to the more specific strength and weakness of this theoretical approach they are clearly seen in, for example, a conceptual framework for studying interpersonal relationships proposed by Wang, Dong & Liu (1987), in which filial piety *xiao* 孝, loyalty *zhong* 忠, understanding *shu* 恕, faith *xin* 信, brotherly respect *ti* 悌 and righteousness *yi* 義 are taken as the fundamental modes of behaviour for different relations. These relations, based on professional fellowship *yeyuan* 業緣, ties of blood *xueqin* 血親 and/or local communality *diyuan* 地緣, can then be measured in intensity, direction, geographic and social distance, contradictions, speed of development and complexity. In this theoretical framework the given concepts are objectified, not questioned or challenged, but at the same time they fit smoothly into an analysis were the social categories that are studied are already well defined through, and with, these very same cultural concepts. This problem is far from uniquely Chinese or non-western; the very same problem, of course, exists in most social science research although most scholars tend to use a technical language and avoid everyday terms in order to get around the problem, or at least make the reader aware of the specific meaning attached to a certain term in the context of an investigation.

Undoubtedly, the sinicization of the social sciences is one of the single-handedly most important scholarly movements during the last twenty years, and I totally agree with Huang Guangguo❻s (1998) view on the importance of a 'multi-model research approach'(*duoyuan dianfan de yanjiu quxiang* 多元典範的研究趨向). It has opened the door to systematic and sensitive understanding and explanations of social phenomena previously marginalized either due to their 'poor fit' with established (American) concepts or because they were seen as totally unique and best treated on their own as 'things Chinese'. Nevertheless,

---

❻ (1998) Zhishi yu xingdong: Zhonghua wenhua chuantong de shchui xinli quanshi 知識與行動：中華文化傳統的社會心理詮釋 [Knowledge and Action: Explanatory Notes on the Social Psychology of the Chinese Cultural Tradition] Taibei: Xinli chubanshe 心理出版社。

the purpose of this scholarly trend. For my present purpose it is enough to point out that, as all scientific approaches, this movement too has its sunspots, and that some of these are related to our main concern, the 'native researcher' in Chinese ethnography.

The frequent merging of classical concepts from the 'big tradition' with everyday Chinese life, as well as the often almost ridiculous effects of the comparison of contemporary American practices with Chinese ideals, often void of any temporal aspects, more often than not only serve to confirm and defend old generalised notions of the anthropological Other (cf. Gabrenya & Hwang 1996, pp. 319-320).❼ Geoffrey Blowers (1996) further notes a tendency to exclusion when it comes to the study of typically Chinese phenomena (e.g., calligraphy, *fengshui*) using Chinese concepts. Many studies are primarily meant for a Chinese public only and often also use different theories of uniqueness (*teshulun* 特殊論), claiming that things Chinese can only be understood within an already existing framework of Chinese culture.❽ From this position, of course, there is but a small step to take to the advocacy not only of 'native theory' but also of 'native researchers'. Thus, we can now return to Wang Mingming and the Chinese native researcher.

Basic problems with the argument of the Native researcher

Let me point to some rather obvious problems with Wang's arguments: His initial standpoint is expressed thus: 'the native social

❼ This is, I would think, most effortlessly felt by those outside this dichotomy.

❽ Werker versions, no doubt, of the more rabid Japanese *Nihon-ron* 日本論 which often claims that not only can Japanese culture (and everything else Japanese) only be understood in its own right, but also only by the Japanese themselves.

researcher can more easily grasp the interrelatedness of the rules of society and culture with the life of man'. Since this hardly relates to a theoretical understanding of the interrelatedness between society, culture and man, in more practical terms it must suggest that Chinese researchers would be 'more efficient' given their language skills, their sensitivity and preexisting local knowledge, a thought which perhaps seems appealing at first, but is impaired in important ways.

First of all, the argument implies that there is but one Truth out there in the field, for the fittest researcher to find - something Wang elsewhere seems to contradict (1997b, pp. 317-318). Even though he in a post-colonial mode suggests that the Chinese researcher would probably come up with a more authentic description (*youshi* 優勢 is the term he uses, 1997a, p. 124) void of cultural prejudices, this echoes an older understanding of the ethnographer as a clinical explorer of already existing ideas, a map-maker of never-changing cultures, and ignores the fundamental post-positivist understanding of the social scientist as an active and innovative interpreter of a social reality in which he interacts, and as a generator of a certain presentation.❾

What phenomenon or question is interesting in a specific research situation is, to my mind, hardly self-evident or objectively determinable, but something for the researcher - and the reader - to determine subjectively, usually based upon an array of considerations, some of which we will return to later. As to the 'technical' aspect of the argument, I readily acknowledge that most researchers from outside a given country have to work for years to somewhat acquire the language skill and the accumulated knowledge of those who have grown up in that country.❿

❾ An understanding on the methodological level more than on the level of research techniques.

❿ This is of course equally true in respect to a researcher who is studying, for

Nonetheless, I strongly feel that one should not here confuse the two levels of sufficiency and mastery. As any trained researcher appreciates, being a 'native' is far from enough to become a good researcher, and personal differences between researchers influencing the success of the research, such as academic training and the abilities to listen and respect the people with whom one is dealing, although these are seldom discussed in sufficient detail, far outweigh any quality coming from national affiliation (cf. Hsu 1973; Fine 1993; McCrae, Costa & Yik 1996).

Now, one could argue that this is exactly what is hinted at; no doubt a person familiar with the relevant cultural codes of behaviour is more likely to make a favourable, or at least non-objectionable, appearance on the scene of investigation, thus more easily getting access to relevant data.

The implication, or recommendation if one so wishes, of this line of argument - that one should not study cultures other than ones own - raises difficulties related to the terms 'native' and 'own society' which constitutes the second major problem with the argument. It is surprising that Wang does not give this issue more attention, since Fei Xiaotong himself, also in the work quoted by Wang (Fei 1993), presents himself as basically a student of the cultures of Others (in his case the minorities of Southwest China) even though his teacher Malinowski may have seen it differently from his European perspective. As with the 'native scholar' in American anthropology, the designation 'native' only works through contrast, and although Wang's use of the term still constitutes the construction of the Chinese self as the Other, certainly the problem of ethnicity is somewhat easier in the China vs. the West scenario than in

---

example, a minority group in his own country whose language or customs he has to learn.

the American case, not least given the ethnical registration system in China which for all everyday purposes prevents the hyphen- or double hyphen-American situation to emerge.

Wang's argument would of course be feasible if one believed in clearly demarcated cultures in which all members were wholly socialized. But then the first problem would be where to draw the line between these islands: Can someone from Fujian claim to be a native in Sichuan? Can anyone from the city do meaningful research in the countryside? Can any man understand the lives of women? Can someone with a middle-class background write about the marginal man? Can a middle-aged researcher really understand youth culture? Can anyone today write with insight about the late Qing period? Etc., etc., *ad infinitum*. Secondly, how can a 'true native' possibly convey his findings to those of other cultures? And if not - what would be the goal of the whole enterprise? But, if one does *not* believe in this, as I would assume Wang does not, then there can only be relative, highly individual advantages and disadvantages connected to the matching of researcher and their fields of research. Furthermore, if one believes in the interpretive function of the researcher, it seems highly desirable to get as many different scholars as possible to do research, in order to get more versions, this polyphony also helping to diminish the potentially negative side-effects of studying other people.

The second argument, related to the 'epistemological problem of studying the Other', and summed up in the lines: 'only from the perspective of his own society is it possible for the social scientist to understand his own role in society and, at the same time, find the appropriate social position for himself', is perhaps less readily understood. It could be understood as 'one avoids putting oneself in the colonial or orientalist position if one keeps to one's own culture'. Understood this way, the argument is indeed forceful, for who in his right mind would voluntarily put himself in such a position?! However, the colonial or orientalist notion is then presented in a suspiciously simple way. When it comes to more qualitatively inclined studies carried out by a single, or a few, researchers - from whatever cultural or social background in whatever cultural or social setting - I strongly believe one should be careful not to commit the 'ecological fallacy'. Few would argue today, I imagine, that such a position is automatically connected to the colour or nationality of the researcher and one would have to read the specific works in order to pass judgement. Unless one argues - and this could well be done - that *all* knowledge work in 'colonial ways' if in the hands of the powerful. Then, unfortunately, the problem is that in the overwhelming majority of social studies this *is* the case. One could further argue that Chinese researchers in general hold more power, and are more determined to use their power, in relation to their objects of study than foreign researchers in China do. Social scientists working in their own country, with the possibility or even commission to influence decision makers, are often involved in social engineering in ways not readily open to ethnographers working in foreign countries.

If the epistemological problem on the other hand is that of 'being in the know', then the same arguments as above of course would apply, but with a focus more exclusively on the research situation, the interaction with informants etc.

The line about the 'role of the researcher' seems to be a hint in that direction, as is Wang's conception (1997a, p. 236) of western researchers as having lost their roles in the colonial romanticism of the culture of the Other (*zai 'yiwenhua' de zhiminshi langman zhong migan zishen juese* 在“異文化”的殖民式浪漫中迷感自身角色). Furthermore, Wang (1997b p. 124) explicitly writes that his arguments in favour of native researchers are not to be construed as excuses for 'expelling' western scholars from

Chinese territory, nor for asking them to stop doing their research.⓫ Again, I would argue that Wang's argument is badly underpinned here. Seldom is the researcher really seriously caught up in the local social structure of the field in which he is doing his research, be this in his own country or not. Agreeing a little more with some other, more open, lines of his (Wang 1997a, pp. 317-18), that the problem for foreigner researchers is that of becoming familiar with the Chinese scene while that of the Chinese is to be able to detached themselves from too familiar things so as to be able to see them at all, I would still say that the generalisation of researchers into the two categories of 'foreign' and 'domestic' conceals more than it reveals, especially when talking about such a highly complex society as China.⓬ Were Wang to do research in Shenzhen or Stockholm, where I have worked, the specific situations facing him would naturally be different from mine in many aspects, but his role as *researcher* would most probably be basically the same as mine in the eyes of my informants, and still I believe we would both understand our own roles in these settings and also find appropriate social positions for ourselves. Any ethnographer will keep, or will be kept at, a certain distance in the field, be it situated in his own culture or a foreign one, as also Fei Xiaotong (1993, p. 165) writes. On the other hand, besides being 'researchers', we would probably in our informants' eyes be performing other, very different roles connected to 'our position

---

⓫ According to him, the latter would be hard anyway since sinology has already become many western scholar's means of livelihood (*mousheng shouduan* 謀生手段) - as if he himself lived on air!

⓬ Similes of this kind are also somethimes heard from Chinese scholars in respict to such remote research as that on ancient poetry, which of course appear more ludicrous.

in society' and to power, though not personal power.⓭

That which remains

Having critically examined the concept of Chinese native researcher, a real, and widely felt difference between researchers (and their works) from different spheres *does* exist. This difference needs to be confronted.

The first hint about the real issues comes from feelings known, I believe, to many scholars: Huang Ping (1997, p. 206) remembers British sinologists at SOAS as being preoccupied with what he at the time (late 1980s) saw as a lot of never-ending common sense non-problems (*wufei shi changshi de wenti zhenglun bu xiu* 無非是常識的問題爭論不休), a conception that in character is fairly typical of many Chinese readers of western writing on China and one which is analogues to an often equally disparaging uninterest felt by many non-Chinese readers of Chinese scholarly literature, as well as scholars from different academic fields toward collegues in the same country. This, however, is not, as Wang's argument would have it, a question of the national or even ethnic belonging of the researcher. The 'native' researcher can also fall into this pit. A case in point is coincidently provided by Wang's own research into genealogies in Fujian (1997c), his home province. In a critical review of this study in the journal *Zhongguo shehui kexue* 中國社會科學 (Social Sciences in China), Cao Shuji 曹樹基 (1999, p. 132) does not mince words about the (lack of) qualities of this particular native researcher:

> Furthermore, the author really should not have committed this enormous amount of common knowledge errors regarding the

---

⓭ Lack of power is most likely one of the major reasons for an ethnographer ending up far from a colonial superior, as someone Laura Adams (1999) calls the 'mascot researcher'.

last 50 years' history of the Peoples Republic of China. His unfamiliarity *vis-a-vis* the Chinese society has reached a truly shocking level - is mistakes can serve as a sounding alarm clock to those followers of impetuous research.（另外，對於中華人民共和國近 50 年來的歷史，作者本不應該犯下如此天量的常識性錯誤，他對中國社會陌生已到了令人吃驚的地步，他的失誤可以爲浮躁學風的追隨者敲響警鐘。*Lingwai, duiyu Zhonghua renmin gongheguo jin 50 nian lai de lishi, zuozhe ben bu yinggai* fanxia ruci tianliang de changshixing cuowu, ta dui Zhongguo shehui mosheng yi dao le ling ren chijing de dibu, ta de shiwu keyi wei fuzao xuefeng de zhuisuizhe qiaoxiang jingzhong.）

These harsh words are not reproduced here as an evaluation of Wang's work, but as an example of the obvious fact that even the seemingly most local scientist is highly vulnerable to the critique that his blood is supposed to protect him from according to his thesis about the native researcher. However, it is of value to note that Cao's critique also focused on another problem with Wang's text: the dull presentation, which Cao sees as a result of Wang's conscious effort to have a dialogue with western scholars and their theories. This effort, Cao writes, has little value as it turns out that Wang cannot deliver what he promises but ends up only with tiresome repetitions of long well-known facts among western scholars and nothing new at all on his side of the Sino-Western dialogue. The reason behind this and many other feelings of tediousness of course lies in the above mentioned fact that every research and every text is aimed at a certain public with certain tastes and preferences. Here, it gets interesting to talk again of the importance of the 'native researcher', not as a possessor of a certain passport or certain looks, but foremost as a native of a certain structure.

I would argue that differences in research, the basic topic of this paper, stem from two sources: The first, already touched on above, is personal. Who you are and what education, training and experience you have must naturally influence your research, and more so if you work alone or in a small group, as most ethnographers do. Since the ethnography in the end is a written thing, the way you write, how you account for your views is not only a matter of taste but also very much part of the product. Do you use a detached 'we-voice' as a veil against personal disclosure and act the objective mirror, or are you the scientist-cum-artist whose monograph reads like - and maybe pretends to be - novel. These are to a certain extent personal choices, but only to an extent, limited as they are by the other source, the structural one.

The structural influences are to a large degree tied to the organisation in which one works. As the Swedish sociologist Goran Ahrne (1994) notes, we give up large parts of our individuality and personal freedom everyday when we go to work, doing the deeds of an organisation, being part of an organisation. ⓮ Every academic organisation, or position, is haunted by longings and fears tied to explicit and implied rules or guidelines postulating, among other things, goals for the research and codes of conduct, and giving hints about what deviations from the 'ideal activity' can be tolerated, what discussions are permissible. In our role as researcher with an institutional affiliation our ethnicity and nationality are secondary to political questions of priority, informing us about what is academically interesting and how this can be presented. A researchers institutional belonging can also substantially influence his work in terms of access and entrance to the field, and

---

⓮ This is something which of course can be felt as more or less restricting. When entering into an organisation we lose some and gain some power and other benefits, making it possible to realise things not achievable outside the organisation.

influence the role and power invested in him for the specific research, which of course must influence also the persons with whom he is working.

Structural influences, however, do not only stem from the researchers own organisation. In China as in Sweden and most countries where funding and grants for research are distributed by special institutions designated for this purpose, *their* demands and expectations are also very much a part of the researchers considerations.⑮To the extent that the organisation does not have its own organ of publication, or if the researcher aspires to be published elsewhere, the media also as a rule have formats to which the researcher must to some degree adjust.⑯

Conclusion

We live in a world where we should, I believe, generally strive less to emphasise the boundaries between people and try more to see both the commonality and complexity beyond the Us-and-Them dichotomy. However, we cannot for that reason overlook real differences and inequalities. What we can do, is to do away with the simple idea of 'nativeness' when this is connected to crude notions of authenticity and cultural essentialism and instead pay more attention to the substantial factors influencing research, writings and readings; i.e., those labeled personal and structural in this article. No doubt, more international

---

⑮ Ethnicity can of course also be utilised as a resource in the academic game. Any ethnographer would naturally stress his unique abilities or skills in situations where this would enhance his credibility or get him advantages in some other form.

⑯ This is of course one of the reasons behind the quest among researchers, institutions and even disciplines for their own media, as expounded on by Bourdieu and many others.

cooperation is one very important way to address the problem, another is to make structural influences more visible. Since the world is a truly multiplex place, scholars will - as this article is an example of - continue to disagree on each other's points of views even when we are basically in the same boat. This is something I consider good. But in order for this critique to lead somewhere, an expanded and broadened dialogue between scholars from different institutional backgrounds is necessary (personality being harder to account for although mixed research team would be a way to address also this issue). I sincerely hope this paper, in its modest way, contributes to that dialogue.

References

Adams, Laura L

(1999) 'The Mascot Researcher: Identity, Power and Knowledge in Fieldwork' *Journal of Contemporary Ethnography*, No 4

Ahrne, Goran

(1994) *Social Organizations: Interaction Inside, Outside and Between Organization. London: Sage*

Blowers, Geoffrey H

(1996) 'The Prospects for a Chinese Psychology' in: Bond (ed.) *The Handbook of Chinese Psychology*. Hong Kong: Oxford University Press

Cai Yongmei 蔡勇美 and Xiao Xinhuang 蕭新煌 (eds.)

(1986) *Shehuixue Zhogguohua* 社會學中國化 [The Sinicization of Social Science] Taibei: Juliu 巨流

Cao Shuji 曹樹基

(1999) 'Zhongguo cunluo yanjiu de dong-xifang duihua - ping Wang Mingming "Shequ de licheng" ' 中國村落研究的東西方對話 - 評王銘銘《社區的歷程》 (Sino-Western Dialogue on the Study of Chinese Villages - on *Development of Communities*) *Zhongguo shehui kexue* 中國社會科學 (Social Sciences in China), No 1

Evans-Pritchard, Edmund Evan

(1973) 'Some Reminiscences and Reflections on Fieldwork' *Journal of the Anthropological Society of Oxford*, Vol 4

Fei Xiaotong 費孝通

(1939) *Peasant Life in China: a Field Study of Country Life in the Yangtze Valley. London: Routledge & Paul Kegan*

(1993a) 'Zai shuo ren de yanjiu zai Zhongguo' 再說人的研究在中國 [More Remarks on the Study of Man in China] in: Beijing daxue shehuixue renleixue yanjiusuo 北京大學社會學人類學研究所 [Peking University Research Centre for Sociology and Anthropology] (red): *Dongya shehui yanjiu* 亞東社會研究 [Studies of East Asian Societies] Beijing: Beijing daxue chubanshe 北京大學出版社

(1993b) 'Ren de yanjiu zai Zhongguo - geren de jingyan' 人的研究在中國一個人的經驗 [The Study of Man in China - ersonal Experiences] in: Beijing daxue shehuixue renleixue yanjiusuo 北京大學社會學人類學研究所 [The Institute of Sociology and Anthropology Peking University] (red): *Dongya shehui yanjiu* 亞東社會研究 [Studies of East Asian Societies] Beijing: Beijing daxue chubanshe 北京大學出

版社

Fine, Gary Alan

(1993) 'Ten Lies of Ethnography: Moral Dilemmas of Field Research' *Journal of Contemporary Ethnography*, No 3

Gabrenya, Jr, William K and Hwang Kwang-kuo 黃光國

(1996) 'Chinese Social Interaction: Harmony and Hierarchy on the Good Earth' in: Bond (ed.) *The Handbook of Chinese Psychology*. Hong Kong: Oxford University Press

Giddens, Anthony

(1990) *Consequences of Modernity*. Cambridge: Polity Press/Blackwell

(1991) *Modernity and Self-identity: Self and Society in the Late Modern Age. Stanford: Stanford University Press*

Hsu, Francis L K

(1973) 'Role, Affect and Anthropology' *American Anthropologist*, No 79

Huang Guangguo 黃光國 (Hwang Kwang-Kuo)

(1988a) 'Renqing yu mianzi: Zhongguoren de quanli youxi' 人情與面子：中國人的權力遊戲 [*Renqing* and *mianzi*: The Chinese Power Game] in: Yang Guoshu 楊國樞 (ed.) *Zhongguoren de xinli* 中國人的心理 [The Psychology of the Chinese People] Taibei 臺北: Guiguan tushu gongsi 桂冠圖書公司

(1988b) *Rujia sixiang yu Dongya xiandaihua* 儒家思想與東亞現代化 [Confucianism and the Modernisation of East Asian] Taibei: Juliu 巨流

(1994) Hudonglun yu shehui jiaoyi: shehui xinlixue bentuhua de fangfalun wenti梛互動論與社會交易：社會心理學本土化的方法論問題 [Interdependence and Social Exchange: Methodological Problems of the Indigenousation of Social Psycholgy] *Bentu xinlixue yanjiu* 本土心理學研究 No 3

Huang Ping 黃平

(1995/1997) Cong bentuhua dao guifanhua: Zhangli yu pingheng□從本土化到規範化：張力與平衡 [From Indigenousation to Standardisation: Tension and Equilibrium] in *Wei wancheng de xushuo* 未完成的敘說 (Unfinished Relating). Chengdu: Sichuan renmin chubanshe 四川人民出版社 (originally in *Zhongguo Shuping* 中國書評, No 5)

(1997) 'Duanxiang "Haiwai Zhongguo yanjiu congshu" ' 斷想《海外中國研究叢書》 [Reflections on 'Collection of Overseas Chinese Studies'] in *Wei wancheng de xushuo* 未完成的敘說 (Unfinished Relating). Chengdu: Sichuan renmin chubanshe 四川人民出版社 (1998 published in *Hanxue shijie* 漢學世界, No 1)

McCrae, Robert R; Paul T Costa jr and Michelle S M Yik

(1996) Universal Aspects of Chinese Personality Structure in: Bond (ed.) *The Handbook of Chinese Psychology*. Hong Kong: Oxford University Press

Narayan, Kirin

(1993) 'How "Native" Is a native Anthropologist?' *American Anthropologist*, No 95

Shi Xiuyin 石秀印

(1998) 'Shehui xinlixue de bentuhua' 社會心理學的本土化 [Indigenous Social Psychlogy] in: Zhang Zhuo 張琢 (ed.) *Dangdai Zhongguo shehuixue* 當代中國社會學 (Chinese Sociology Today) Beijing: Zhongguo shehuikexue chubanshe 中國社會科學出版社

Su Guoxun 孫國勛

(1994) 'Lun shehuixue zhongguohua de liang nan wenti: cong "Kexue yanjiu wangling" kan "renqing yu mianzi" lilun moshi' 論社會學中國化的兩難問題從'科學研究綱領'看'人情與面子'理論模式 (The Dilemma of Sociological Sinicization: Criticism of 'Face and Favor' Model in the light of 'Scientific Research Programmes') *Xianggang shehui kexue xuebao* 香港社會科學學報 (Hong Kong Journal of Social Science), No 3

Wang Lei王雷, Dong Zhikai董志凱 and Liu Gongfu劉工力

(1987) *Renji guanxi jichu* 人際關係基礎 [The Basis for Interpersonal Relations] Shenyang: Liaoning daxue chubanshe 遼寧大學出版社

Wang Mingming 王銘銘

(1997a) *Shehui renleixue yu Zhongguo yanjiu* 社會人類學與中國

研究 (Social Anthropology and Its Studies of China) Beijing: Sanlian shudian 三聯書店

(1997b) 'Shehui renleixue de Zhongguo yanjiu - renshilun fanshi de gaiguan yu pingjie' 社會人類學的中國研究—認識論范式的概觀與評介 (Research on China from the Perspective of Social Anthropology and Appraisal of Epistomological Paradigms) *Zhongguo shehui kexue* (Social Sciences in China) 中國社會科學 1997, No 5

(1997c) *Shequ de licheng: Xicun hanren jiazu de gean yanjiu* 社區的歷程：溪村漢人家族的個案研究 (Development of Communities: Case Studies of Han Families in Xi Village) Tianjin: Tianjin renmin chubanshe 天津人民出版社

Yang Guoshu 楊國樞 (Yang Kuo-Shu)

(1987/1988)'Zhongguoren congshu xu' 中國傳統價值的穩定與變遷 [Preface to the Chinese book serie] in: Yang Guoshu 楊國樞 (ed.) *Zhongguoren de xinli* 中國人的心理 [The Psychology of the Chinese People] Taibei: Guiguan tushu gongsi 桂冠圖書公司

Zhao Liru 趙莉如

(1996) 'Xinlixue zai Zhongguo de fazhan ji qi xianzhuang, xia' 心理學在中國的發展及其現狀，下 (The History and Current Development of Psychology in China, part 2) *Xinlixue dongtai* 心理學動態 (Journal of Developments in Psychology), No 4

由《聊齋誌異》觀「唯情意識」

黃麗卿*

一

《聊齋誌異》（以下簡稱《聊齋》）係蒲松齡所著，爲清代文言小說的代表作。蒲氏生於明崇禎十三年（西元一六四〇年），卒於清康熙五十四年（西元一七一五年），正處在晚明清初變動不居的時代。蒲氏才能甚高，一生志在科舉，卻屢試不第，加上生活困頓，對社會百態、人情冷暖有深切感受，故將滿腹才學及心中不平寄託於《聊齋》，蒲松齡自稱《聊齋》爲「孤憤之書」，其「孤憤」可謂對現實而發❶。

《聊齋》一書的內容主題，依張春樹、駱雪倫的分類，可分爲四類。一是愛情故事，二是揭發官僚腐敗的故事，三是諷刺當時科

* 淡江大學中文系講師

❶ 《聊齋誌異·自序》云：「……集腋爲裘，妄續幽冥之錄；浮白載筆，僅成孤憤之書，寄託如此，亦足悲矣！」蒲松齡《聊齋誌異》會校會注會評本(一)。張有鶴輯校，臺北：里仁書局，1991年3 月。

舉制度及學風的故事，四是反映漢人反清情緒的故事❷。此書共四百餘篇，其中愛情故事近百篇，依陸又新對《聊齋》愛情篇章分類統計共分六種類型：一、人與人戀愛，二、人與狐戀愛，三、人與鬼戀愛，四、人與仙戀愛，五、人與妖戀愛，六、鬼與鬼戀愛。陸又新並就《聊齋》愛情故事的內涵及其藝術性加以探討❸，由此認爲：

> 基於小說家對人性及社會的關切，蒲松齡深切關懷青年男女最切身的問題——愛情與婚姻。《聊齋》中的愛情故事真實的反映了當時青年男女追求戀愛及幸福婚姻的各種心態❹。

此一看法正說明《聊齋》一書反映出社會各種問題，其中發憤而作之處甚多，因此如果論其人與異類相戀是與現實無涉，似乎有待商榷❺。本文就在此一研究基礎上對論題進行思考，從蒲松齡許多描寫人與異類之戀情的篇章中，大都表現不同情愛類型，由此可以觀其「唯情意識」，故在此將就其重情之論特別觀察，並藉由蒲氏之評論加以省察，由此且展開「唯情意識」時代精神之討論。

---

❷ 見張春樹、駱雪倫著〈蒲松齡聊齋誌異中的思想境界〉，幼獅月刊第四十四期。

❸ 見陸又新《聊齋誌異中的愛情》第二章。臺北：臺灣學生書局，1992年5月。

❹ 同❸，第五章，頁305。

❺ 見吳禮權《中國筆記小說史》第六章指出：「清前期的著名文言小說《聊齋》中的許多言情作品，在內容上全述人鬼、人妖、人狐等婚戀故事，純然與現實無涉」，頁266。臺北：臺灣商務印書館，1993年8月。

二

《聊齋》中所呈現之「唯情意識」爲何，本文首先將從其抒發情志的篇章中，就其強調「情」的部分作一探討，在論點中可觀《聊齋》對秉情以超越生死特別看重，由此提出「情之至者，鬼神可通」之論點，此一論點可否構成或足以說明其所要呈現的「唯情意識」？將從以下文本中加以觀察：在卷十一〈香玉〉文本中主角黃生視白牡丹精香玉爲愛妻，視冬樹精絳雪爲良友。因三人情深義重，故而有死而後生、生而求死的情節。當黃生初見香玉時便「愛而忘死」，香玉死後他兩次哭穴，作哭花詩五十首，日夜臨穴涕洟，其至情終於感動花神而使香玉復生；而黃生死，香玉也隨之憔悴而亡。

同時文本還描寫黃生與絳雪的友情，以誠相待，當絳雪有刀斧之難時，黃生全力相救，因此當黃生、香玉相繼死後，絳雪亦義不容辭以死殉友。更令人感動的是，黃生不以死爲悲而以爲樂，道出：「此我生期，非死期也，何哀爲！」黃生何以能坦然面對死亡，而體悟形軀之消亡只是短暫的，又能感知「他日牡丹下有赤牙怒生，一放五葉者，即我也。」主要是黃生已能呈現至情至性。因三人有著堅貞不渝、至情不悔之精神，故能有超越生死之表現，因此，蒲松齡稱：「情之至者，鬼神可通，花以鬼從，而人之魂寄，非其結於情者深耶？一去而兩殉之，即非堅貞，亦爲情死矣。」

對於超然於生死之外的情感，在卷二〈連城〉也有描寫。主角喬生爲一貧士，因受千金女連城資助而視其爲知己，不惜割胸肉以治其病，卻因貧寒未能獲其父擇婿允諾，得知連城死訊，持著「士爲知己者死，不以色也」一慟而絕，死後在陰間尋覓連城，他便「樂死不願生」，然其用情至深之精神，終得亡友之助，雙雙復活成親。喬生何以能有「樂死不願生」之精神，此從其所言：「僕不膺肉者，聊以報知己耳」。因有「報知己」之心，當連城一死，亦不願獨活，認爲到陰間反而有再見的希望，有此癡情不悔之心，故能有「樂死不願生」的想法。

又在卷二〈阿寶〉一篇道出主角孫子楚更是痴心忘我之典型，其魂魄依附鸚鵡身上，對阿寶表示其愛意，其言：「得近芳澤，於願已足」，經多次努力追尋，終能與阿寶結爲連理。其後孫子楚因病而亡，阿寶則以「君死，妾何能獨活」而殉情，其精神令冥王感動，而讓已死的孫子楚再生，和阿寶長相廝守。蒲松齡以「性痴則其志凝」，嘉許此段人間的至情至愛，因情既可重生，更能說明「能以至誠之心處之，天下不復有難處之事矣」❻。

另在卷二〈嬌娜〉中，狐女嬌娜對孔生有治病之恩，孔生對她則有「曾經滄海難爲水」之情，但等嬌娜婚嫁之後，孔生對其愛就昇華爲可爲她獻出生命，當嬌娜一家面臨滅頂之災時，孔生不以異類相欺，而是以「至情可酬知己」之心捨身相救，嬌娜見孔生死於旁，大哭道：「孔郎爲我而死，我何生矣！」當孔生被救醒後，嬌娜之夫雖已死，但他們仍持知己之情相惜相待。此一知己之情是孔生與嬌娜經歷生死交關而來，甚爲難得。但明倫稱其：「嬌娜能用情，能守禮，天眞爛漫，舉止大方，可愛可敬」❼。在此篇文本最

---

❻ 同註❶所引書，《聊齋》三會本卷二〈阿寶評〉，頁二三九。

❼ 同前註〈嬌娜評〉頁六五。

後蒲松齡稱許：「余於孔生，不羨其得豔妻，而羨其得膩友也，觀其容可以忘飢……」。

在各種男女之愛、知己之情中，因有至情相待而能超越生死，甚至打破人與異類相隔之界。此在人鬼之戀中有許多類似之例，如〈聶小倩〉，小倩雖爲女鬼，卻有感釆臣不爲財、色所惑，終能改過向善，並助釆臣以避禍，釆臣則救小倩於苦海之中，並讓小倩住在家中，小倩美麗、善良、親切、誠懇、樂於助人的形象，讓人忘其爲鬼，其美好的表現打破人鬼殊途之隔，終能與釆臣結婚生子。此份患難與共、眞誠相待之情，也可使人鬼心靈相通。卷五〈章阿端〉中戚生之妻死後，本應投胎轉世，但她堅決表示：「情之所鍾，本願長死，不樂生也」，此一愛情已置於生死之上。在卷三〈連鎖〉中，人鬼也可共成詩文良友，經由患難之交後，亦能結合相守。

至於秉情而生之力量甚大，可以在遭受百折千磨亦終不悔者，如卷五〈鴉頭〉，描寫狐精鴉頭爲情願與秀才王文逃離青樓，終因妖術抵不過鴇母而被拘禁十八年之久。由她在「幽室之中，暗無天日，鞭創裂膚，飢火煎心，易一晨昏，如歷年歲。」但爲求幸福婚姻生活，矢志不二、從一而終之愛情，付出了常人難以忍受之代價，最後願望終能實現。蒲松齡嘉許她說：「至百折千磨，之死靡它，此人類所難，而乃於狐得之乎，唐君謂魏徵更饒嫵媚，吾於鴉頭亦云。」狐女鴉頭不屈從於鴇母的淫威，大膽與王文私奔，可謂用情至深之表現。

其他能經由知己之情而不以妍媸易念者，可見〈瑞雲〉一篇，主角瑞雲係杭州名妓，色藝無雙，身價甚高，與賀生經由詩文相知，二人所重者爲「知己」，故瑞雲不因賀生無財相輕，賀生則以癡情獻知己，因此當瑞雲由美變醜，甚至醜狀類鬼，賀生則言出：「人生所重者知己，卿盛時猶能知我，我豈以衰故忘卿哉？」贖她回家，不顧別人訕笑，用情更深。其眞情終於感動仙人還其美貌，特別嘉許賀生：「天下惟眞才人爲能多情，不以妍媸易念也。」此一精神極爲可貴，此與傳統以「男才女貌」爲衡量情愛之觀念有極大不同。另在〈喬女〉篇也寫男女間「知己之感，許之以身」。男方能不嫌女方醜陋、已婚，誠意敬愛；而女方則認爲「妾以奇醜，爲世不齒，獨孟生能知我」，故「自省有以報知己」、能相識於患難之中，相濡以沫而生之情，相較於一見傾心之情，實有更深刻的見解。

從上述文本之觀察中，各篇皆表現出重情之傾向。首先，從標舉「情之至者，鬼神通之」，而能超越生死之外，樂死不願生者，如〈香玉〉、〈連城〉、〈阿寶〉、〈聶小倩〉等篇。其次，重情而能遭受百折千磨終不悔者如〈鴉頭〉。另外，能有知己之情而不以妍媸易念者如〈瑞雲〉、〈喬女〉等篇。皆足以說明蒲氏特別標舉重情之論。然而從「情之至者，鬼神通之」等論點中，是否可以觀其「唯情意識」，本文將再就其時代衍生之問題加以探索。

三

蒲氏在本文中所呈顯的「唯情意識」，是從「情之至者，鬼神通之」，而達到超然生死之外，因情而生，因情而亡等境界，由此開展其重情的思想。其論至情能超越生死之精神，呈顯出何種時代的意義？其論點在晚明已有相近之論，如湯顯祖所持「情至」之說，其《牡丹亭·題詞》論情之起時，「一往而深，生而可以死，死而可以生」並塑造杜麗娘爲「有情人」的典型，作爲「情至」的表現。又如馮夢龍更提倡「情教說」，特別指出「人而無情，雖曰生人，吾直謂之死矣」、「無情而人，寧有情而鬼・・・情鬼賢於情人」。

湯顯祖所言之「情至」之精神，主要是強調能超越生死而論，而馮夢龍其論情，亦持著「無情而人，寧有情而鬼」，二家何以如此深刻以論情之重要？此論在其時代開展出何種意義？

在樓宇烈〈湯顯祖哲學思想初探〉一文中對於宋明理學家將此處藉由宋明理學家中對「情」與「理」之論述加以省察：「情」與「理」的關係，大概可以歸納爲以下三個要點：「一、把『理』與『情』截然對立起來；二、把『理』說成是『純善』的，而把『情』看成是惡，是人欲；三、要求以『理』制『情』，直至滅『情』，因而提出了『革盡人欲，復盡天理』，或『存天理，滅人欲』。這也就是說，『理』中所無的，就不允許存在。」❽

因爲一般論者將「理」與「情」截然二分，並將「情」視爲惡的，是人欲，導致情欲在此一文化觀念往往呈現負面評價，而受到傳統禮教之壓抑、貶斥，故而「存天理，滅人欲」亦或爲理所當然之論，也因此，明代社會上長期以來，在「以禮節情」的傳統禮教觀念之下，一直給予女子甚多束縛，此從《明史》所收的節婦、烈女傳比《元史》以上的任何一代正史至少要多出四倍以上，可見當時婦女生活的悲慘。加上明代的皇帝和后妃又積極提倡「女德」，編刊多種婦女道德教科書，以毒害她們的精神生活。

清初此一傳統禮教觀念仍充斥於人民心中，此處或許正是《聊

---

❽ 見《湯顯祖研究論文集》，中國戲劇出版社，頁一五四。

齋》之所以強調「情」之重要，期能以情制禮，尊重「情」的合理性，故作品試圖從人與異類之戀中，一方面有意肯定自然情欲的重要，一方面則讚揚知己之愛或忠貞癡情之表現，在當時禮教社會中，情欲是被排斥的，然而蒲氏則特別強調，其中，尤其對於超然生死之外，「樂死不願生」、「因情而生」等精神推崇。從其對「情」體悟如此深刻，且多處表現於其作品中，隱然可見其自覺對社會衍生種種問題有所批判。此份自覺從何而來，在此將從晚明湯顯祖、馮夢龍等人之看法中加以觀察。

情之至者可以突破生死的界限，此可從湯顯祖在《牡丹亭》塑造杜麗娘之情愛典型以觀，此處亦正是《聊齋》「情之至者，鬼神可通」所強調之精神。另外，在〈牡丹亭·題詞〉中提出以「情」和「禮」相對，更對青年男女突破社會道德的禁制有所鼓舞，勇以追求愛情的自由。特別強調：

> 嗟夫！人世之事，非人世所可盡。自非通人，恆以理相格耳。第云理之所必無，要知情之所必有邪！❾

袁中郎也強調要順應人情的自然，並道出：

> 孔子所言絜矩，正是因，正是自然。後儒將矩字看作理字，便不因，不自然。夫民之所好好之，民之所惡惡之，是以民之情為矩，安得不平；今人只從理上絜去，必至內欺己心，外拂人情，如何得乎？夫非理之為害也，不知理在情內，而

---

❾ 《牡丹亭·題詞》，人民文學出版社。

> 欲拂情以為理，故去治彌遠。[10]

因人情可受尊重與地位之提高，由此馮夢龍敢於大膽提出「情」教，以取代「名」教的依據。於〈山歌序〉中已言：「借男女之眞情，發名教之僞藥。」

「情教說」所根據的情論，馮夢龍認爲「草木之生意，動而爲芽；情亦人之生意也。」情和草木之芽一樣，是人的生機的根本來源，「生在而情在焉。故人而無情，雖曰生人，吾直謂之死矣！」[11]

特別強調出：「無情而人，寧有情而鬼，但恐死而知耳；如有知而生人所不得遂之情，遂之於鬼，吾猶謂之情鬼賢於情人也。且人生而情死，非人；人死而情生，非鬼。」他對情的肯定，乃至於要在三不朽之外，另立一不朽。

從湯顯祖塑造杜麗娘爲天下有情人之形象，此一因情而亡，因情而生之精神，使天下人在感動之餘，也引發大家對情、理對立問題之反省。馮夢龍在《山歌》中是借男女自然情愛的歌詠，以發名教之僞藥。此外，在《情史》的〈情奔〉一篇的論述中，對情理問題有所斟酌，以眞情相許背棄既定之理。他說：

> 古者聘爲妻，奔爲妾。夫奔者，以情奔也。奔爲情，則貞爲非情也，又況道旁桃柳，乃望以歲寒之骨乎！春秋之法，使夏變夷，不使夷變夏，妾而抱婦之志焉，婦之可也？娼而行妾之事焉，妾之可也。彼以情許人，吾因以情許之；彼以眞

[10] 《袁宏道集箋校》，卷四十四，頁一一九三。

[11] 《情史》卷二十三，情通類總評，廣文書局。

情殉人，吾不得復以雜情疑之，此君子樂與人爲善之意⑫。

此大段之論與傳統之觀念大相逕庭，對於當時禮教有強烈的批判意味，由此更能對「情」予以合理的尊重。

面對「滅人欲」問題，蒲松齡主要是以人與異類之戀，從各種不同角度予以稱許，由此特別強調重情之論，並從靈魂基本上不受形體、物種的限制，且能相互溝通，此所謂「乃知天地間，有情皆可相契」，也可說一切動植物，只要有情，皆能與人接觸，以建立各種情愛。因此在〈素秋〉中，蒲松齡藉由書生俞愼明確指出：「禮緣情制，情之所在，異族何殊焉」，俞愼能不因素秋兄妹爲異類，而能建立起知己之情。

情之所在，則能制禮，此一以情制禮的觀點，實有其特殊意義，因爲相較於「以禮節情」的傳統禮教觀念，及宋明理學中「滅人欲」等論點而言，其批判意味已明顯可見。

因爲清初統治者在實行武力，籠絡兩種政策的同時，又於思想文化方面加強了統治，其中是大力提倡程朱理學，鞏固思想統治。此從康熙時代《性理精義》的編寫，《性理大全》的刊行頒佈，程朱派理學家李光地、湯斌、陸隴等人的受寵幸等，即可看出其倡理學，企圖以此束縛人們的思想。但明末清初之思想家對宋明以來極爲虛僞的理學、道學也有所反駁，對人欲問題更有重新討論，如王夫之所言：「人欲之大公，即天理之至正。」（〈讀四書大全記〉），已能將飲食男女之欲，視爲人們生活的正當要求。

面對「滅人欲」所衍生的種種問題，因此蒲氏透過文本中的困

---

⑫ 《情史》，情貞類總評，廣文書局。

境，對晚明以來重情之論有所省察，特別標舉「情之至者，鬼神通之」，並塑造情癡之典型加以表現。誠如但明倫所評：「此一情鍾於人則是情人，此一情鍾於妖則是情妖，此一情鍾於鬼則是情鬼，此一情鍾於花則是情種、情根、情苞、情蕊」⑬。其中對知己之情不僅有特別稱許，甚至擴及在無情物上寫痴情，如郎玉柱癡情於書，張幼量癡情於鴿，烏子才癡情於花，邢雲飛癡情於石。情痴、石痴等都意味著缺乏圓滑、見解偏頗的心態，在當時的禮教觀念中，大抵視之耽迷不悟的愚蠢，或是玩物喪志的惡習。然而蒲氏對此都賦予肯定的評價，認爲：

> 性痴則志凝，故書痴者文必工，藝痴者技必良；世之落拓而無成者，皆自謂不痴者也。且如粉花蕩產，盧雉傾家，顧痴人事哉！以是知慧黠而過，乃是真痴，彼孫子何痴乎⑭。

由此可見蒲氏所言之「情」，與世人所認知之情實有極大差異，世人對癡是從負面之意論斷，而蒲氏則從有慧黠予以肯定，其中即是「情之至者」的表現。尤其更可貴的是，蒲氏對男女之愛而能昇華爲知己之情特別稱許，此可從〈香玉〉、〈嬌娜〉等篇以觀之。

蒲松齡除著重感天動地之眞情、男女相知相感之情等之外，對於當時男女之間的情慾關係，甚至夫婦間的情慾生活，亦視之爲人之常情。如〈青娥〉中霍桓約妻同床，遭岳父斥罵，他理直氣壯地反駁言：「兒女之情，人所不免，長者何當伺我？」卷二〈嬰寧〉

---

⑬ 同註❶所引書《聊齋》三會本卷十一〈香玉〉評。

⑭ 同註❶所引書《聊齋》三會本卷二〈阿寶〉評。

中，她也把「大哥欲我共寢」這樣的話告訴母親，王生制止，她說：「背他人，豈得背老母。且寢處亦常事，何諱之？」卷十一〈書癡〉中郎玉柱嘗受到夫婦居室之樂，興奮以道：「我不意夫婦之樂，有不可言傳者。」且「逢人輒道」，還公然宣稱：「天倫之樂，人所皆有，何諱焉。」由上述直抒情慾之事，在禮教甚嚴的時代，實可謂驚世駭俗之言，而蒲松齡何以特別標舉情慾乃自然之事，此處似對道學家矯情虛僞的「滅人欲，存天理」之論有所駁斥。

結　論

蒲松齡透過《聊齋》所要呈現的「唯情意識」，實與晚明以來重情的思想相近，由此藉以對治「滅人欲」及種種衍生之問題，並可看出其論情呈現豐富意涵，舉凡直抒自然情欲、男女之愛、知己之情、人與宇宙萬物之情等。另外，從「情之至者，鬼神通之」以標舉「情癡」之典型，而論出「性癡則其志凝」中所涵有之眞智慧，正能藉此以凸顯傳統禮教之下不合理之制度，特別是其所論只要有眞情，則萬物皆可相契相知，由此實可看出一名知識份子對宇宙萬物的深刻關懷。而其展現之精神，誠如馮鎮巒於〈聊齋雜記〉稱許此書：「……多言鬼狐，款款多情；間及孝悌，俱見血性，較之水滸、西廂，體大思經，文奇義正，爲當世不易見之筆墨，深足寶貴。」

東坡「以詩爲詞」在文學史上的意涵

馬銘浩*

Abstract

Shwu Si's invention of "blending poems into lyrics" creates the heroic type of lyrics. And literature history in the past has given such new founding a high esteem in different aspects. The article is aimed at discussing the issues concerning the correlation between poems and lyrics, and the status of the literature and music in Chinese culture.

The first chapter deals with the aesthetic principles of lyrics. The second deals with Dwueng Pwuo's mastering of lyrics. The third focus upon the disintegration of songs and lyrics. The fourth gives an account of the changing of styles in

* 淡江大學中文系副教授

lyrics. The last chapter concludes that Dwueng Pwuo though deepens the lyrics' expressions in words, yet narrows its musical richness.

歷來論詞總以蘇軾爲豪放文人詞之代表，尤其在詞史上因蘇軾的詞作及其影響，改變詞的原始美學條件，所造成文類的異化現象，不僅影響到後代的詞作本質，更使得詩、詞兩種文類交互感通，引起文學史上常見所謂本色與變異的爭論。當然東坡詞在中國文學史上自有其特殊的價值，不管詩、詞、文、書畫均有其不可取代的地位。然而其地位的重要性，並不只限於發揮原始藝術的美學成就，而是博採縱取不同藝術的特色之後，以其個人的生命觀照所形成的新的美學觀點，詩的開展是如此；總結古文八大家的成就是如此；開創文人畫派是如此；文人詞的形成更是如此。是以，論述東坡詞在文學史上的價值時，其對詞的美學認知、創作手法及觀念變革等，所引起所謂「以詩爲詞」的命題，就顯得特別有意義了。文學史家對東坡詞的論述多從其詞作與音樂的分離、詞境擴大及詞的詩化等方面來論其作品❶，其實這些論述也都是在「以詩爲詞」的創作理念下所引發出來現象。是以本文即以東坡「以詩爲詞」在文學史上的問題爲主，討論此一文類感通所造成的涵化現象及其衍生而來的相關問題。

❶ 如劉大杰《中國文學發達史》將東坡詞的特點分成：「一、詞與音樂的初步分離。二、詞的詩化。三、詞境的擴大。四、個性分明。」葉慶炳的《中國文學史》則將蘇軾對宋詞的貢獻歸納爲：「一、詞始與音樂分離。二、以詩爲詞，詞境始大。」

一、詞的審美原則

胡夷新聲與里巷俗曲的結合產生了民間詞曲，加以文人詞的興起，二者揉合遂使得「詞」體正式走人中國文學史的殿堂。不管詞的來源是因著音樂關係而來的「倚聲說」；或是以文字意涵爲審美對象的「詩餘說」，其填詞形式上的音樂特性，和不同於詩歌風化效果，和以宴享娛樂爲主的內容寫作，形成了詞體的特殊審美原則，也可以說是詞體的原始本色。「倚聲說」主要是以其音樂性爲主要思考，如宋代王灼《碧雞漫志》所說：「蓋隋以來，今之所謂曲子者漸興，至唐稍盛，今則繁聲淫奏，殆不可數，古歌變爲古樂府，古樂府變爲今曲子，其本一也。」同時代胡仔的《苕溪漁隱叢話後集》則說：「唐初歌詞，多是五言詩，或七言詩，初無長短句。自中葉以後，至五代，漸變成長短句，及本朝則盡爲此體。」南宋朱熹的《朱子語類》更明確的提出：「古樂府只是詩，中間卻添許多泛聲。後來人怕失了那泛聲，逐一添個實字，遂成長短句，今曲子便是。」甚至沈括在《夢溪筆談》裡就指出了倚聲填詞的過程，其謂：「詩之外又有和聲，則所謂曲也。古樂府皆有聲有詞，連屬書之。如曰賀賀賀、何何何之類，皆和聲也。今管弦之中纏聲，亦其遺法也。唐人乃以詞填入曲中，不復和聲。」至於「詩餘說」則是在詩歌的範疇內，以文字爲審美對象，思考其本質。如宋代胡寅《題酒邊詞》認爲：「詞曲者，古樂府之末道也；古樂府者，詩之旁行也。……名之曰曲，以其曲盡人情耳。」張鎡《題梅溪詞》說：「自變體以來，司花傍輦之嘲，沈香亭北之詠，至於人主相友善，則世之文人才士，遊戲筆墨於長短句間。」明代錢允治的《國朝詩餘序》則寫道：詞者詩之餘，曲又詞之餘也。李太白有《草堂集》載〈憶秦娥〉、〈菩薩蠻〉二詞，爲千古詞家鼻祖，故宋人有《草堂詩餘》云。」最具有代表性的則屬清代紀昀等人在《四庫全書提要·御定歷代詩餘》裡所說的：「詩降而爲詞始於唐，若〈菩薩蠻〉、〈憶秦娥〉、〈憶江南〉、〈長相思〉之屬，本是唐人之詩，而句有長短，遂爲詞家權輿，故謂之詩餘。爲其上承於詩，下沿爲曲。」至於如清代汪森《詞綜·序》所說的：「自有詩而長短句即寓焉。〈南風〉之操、五子之歌是已。周之頌三十一篇，長短句屬十八；漢〈郊祀歌〉十九篇，長短句居其五；至〈短簫鐃歌〉十八篇，篇皆長短句，謂非詞之源乎！」很明顯地已經將詞的來源放入經學的思考脈絡中。

「倚聲說」重視詞和音樂發展變化的關係，「詩餘說」則力主詞在文字甚至經學審美範疇中的傳承地位。一重視式形變化；一重視內容風格。至清代常州詞派的張惠言論詞的起源時，提出另一種觀點，其謂：

> 詞者，蓋出於唐之詩人，采樂府之音，以制新律，因繫其詞，故曰「詞」。……其緣情造端，興於微言，以相感動，極風命謠。里巷男女，哀樂以道。賢人君子幽約怨悱不能自言之情，低徊要眇，以喻其致。❷

❷ 清·張惠言：〈詞選·序〉。

常州詞派對詞的立論主張雖然一向是強調其比興寄託的微言大義，但是在此所謂的「采樂府之音，以制新律」在一定程度上，也道出了詞的音律雖然雜源於曲子詞、教坊、大曲等不同來源，但定型爲詞體之後，其音律是不同於古音的事實。而所謂「里巷男女，哀樂以道」則是說出了詞以言情爲主的本質。

綜上之述，詞體的本色可從音律和內容風格二者來判斷。在音律上倚聲填詞，遵從以樂聲爲主的詞律，不可隨意以文字內容而改變因音律考量而形成的詞律；在內容風格上，因爲詞本起於里巷教坊，又在歌樓舞榭之中成長，所以言情，尤其是言男女之情就成爲了詞作內容的主流，以此而形成的風格自是以所謂的婉約、豔靡爲主，如明・王世貞所說：

> 詞須婉轉綿麗，淺至儇俏，挾春月煙花於閨幨內奏之。一語之豔，令人魂絕，一字之工，令人色飛，乃爲貴耳。至於慷慨磊落，縱橫豪爽，抑亦其次，不作可耳。❸

又

> 《花間》以小語致巧，世說靡也。《草堂》以麗字則妍，六朝隃也。即詞號稱詩餘，然而詩人不爲也。何者？其婉孌而近情也，足以移情而奪嗜，其柔靡而近俗也，詩嘽緩而就之，而不知其下也。❹

---

❸ 明・王世貞：〈弇州山人詞評〉。見於《詞話叢編》第二冊。

❹ 同註❸。

當然文類本質的轉化是隨著文化環境的變遷所做的調適，然而塡詞之制與婉約之風從詞體正式走入中國文學史的殿堂開始，至少到北宋蘇東坡爲止，仍是一般所共同承認的詞作方向。

二、東坡對詞體本色的掌握

東坡的詞作一改前人創作法則，改變詞體原始審美原則，使得產生本質上的變異，首先提出此一看法的是蘇門中的陳師道，其謂：

> 退之以文爲詩，子瞻以詩爲文，如教坊雷大使之舞，雖極天下之工，要非本色。❺

從此以後「以詩爲詞」似乎就成爲後人評論東坡詞的重要依歸，甚至因此而有所謂詞中的豪放派產生，以相對抗於婉約派。事實上，將東坡詞與韓愈文並舉而論，似乎標識著東坡係有意識的要突破詞體的創作模式❻。然而，當我們在討論這一問題，也應該要先認識東坡對詞體本色的了解程度，方能進一步探討「以詩爲詞」的意義。

東坡詞創作的時間甚晚，在其詞集中要到宋·熙寧五年（1072）東坡三十七歲任杭州判時的〈浪淘沙〉（昨日出東城）才見到正式的作品❼，在此之前東坡不管在詩或文方面都已有相當的成就。而詞

---

❺ 宋·陳師道：《後山詩話》。見於《歷代詩話》。

❻ 韓愈爲文時即不斷標榜著「破體爲文」的重要性，並有意識地以實際作品來實踐其理論。

❼ 以下東坡詞的編年係根據石淮聲、唐玲玲合編之《東坡樂府編年箋註》華正書局，民八十二年八月初版爲主。然而該書所編東坡的第一首詞作爲宋·

在歷經花間、南唐到北宋晏、歐、柳永諸人的實創之後，也已成爲當代社會流行的文體，只是其審美對象是以民間娛樂爲大宗，並非文人主要的創作對象。是以諸如柳永此等流行詞作之大家，儘管「凡有井水飲處即能歌柳詞」❽，在傳統文人的眼中也只能換來「淺近卑俗」❾、「好爲俳體、詞多媟黷」❿等評價，尚無法完全進入以文字爲審美主流的文人文學範疇中。所以當東坡剛開始寫作詞的時候，對於詞的特性掌握，其實和當時人的看法是很相近的，東坡在面對當時詞作相當有名的張先時，曾有以下的看法：

> （張先）清詩絕俗，甚典而麗，搜研物情，刮發幽翳，微詞婉轉，蓋詩之裔。⓫

又

> 子野詩筆老妙，歌詞乃其餘波耳。⓬

從東坡對張先詞的評價中，我們可以有以下兩種心得：第一、東坡仍然將詞定位爲「詩餘」的角色，是寫詩之外的娛樂休閒之作，若是詞作內容得到文人的肯定，也是因爲寫作模式符合詩歌所建立下

治平元年（1064）東坡二十九歲時的〈華清引〉，其間相隔八年後才又有〈浪淘沙〉。只是〈華清引〉的爭議性過大，龍榆生的《東坡樂府箋》等諸多編年也未編入此首作品，加以其風格迥異於東坡早期詞作，是以本文遂〈浪淘沙〉爲東坡的第一首詞作。

❽ 葉夢得：《避暑錄話》，卷下。

❾ 王灼：《碧雞漫志》。

❿ 劉熙載：《藝概·詞概》。

⓫ 蘇軾：〈祭張子野文〉，引於《蘇東坡全集》前集卷三十五。

⓬ 蘇軾〈張子野詞跋〉，引於吳訥《唐宋名賢百家詞》。

來的審美原則，也可說是「以詩爲詞」的思考基礎；第二、既然在東坡的創作意識中很明顯的將詩、詞分開，也了解在文學史上各有其不同的創作法則和審美對象，則又對於詞體的本色也應當有所了解才是。如果證諸於東坡早期詞作，我們更可以發現杭州時期東坡的詞多是以傳統流行且易入手的詞牌爲多⓭，在此時期東坡共作詞共約二十一題五十首，其中重複創作的依序有〔菩薩蠻〕五首、〔南鄉子〕五首、〔江城子〕三首、〔南歌子〕三首、〔減字木蘭花〕三首、〔行香子〕兩首，加上五代以來所流行的〔采桑子〕、〔訴衷情〕、〔清平樂、〔浪淘沙〕、〔臨江仙〕、〔蝶戀花〕、〔如夢令〕、〔定風波〕、〔阮郎歸〕等共三十首，就佔了該期詞作的一半以上。詞律上除了〔行香子〕結片的地方以一字領起三句對仗的方式，有所創變之外，其餘也大多都合於詞律的要求。內容上以送別、寄贈作品爲主，雖說偶然雜有個人對人生的部份感懷，然而此種創作模式，係自柳永以來即有，只可說是又承襲於柳永之處，卻不是自創的題材。在風格上仍語多細膩婉約，如「娟娟缺月西南落，相思撥斷琵琶索。枕淚夢魂中，覺來眉暈重」〈菩薩蠻〉、「舊恨前歡，心事兩無據。要知欲見無由，痴心猶自，倩人情，一聲傳語」〈祝英臺近〉、「玉人家在鳳凰山，水雲間，掩門閒，門外行人，立馬看弓彎。十里春風誰指似，斜日映，繡簾斑」〈江城子〉

⓭ 對東坡詞作的分期歷來多認爲任杭州通判時爲其與詞初期接觸的早期；密州、徐州時期爲成長期；黃州時期爲成熟高峰期；晚年則爲圓融期。當然這樣的分期法是以其所謂的「豪放文人詞」爲思考對象，然而縱觀其詞作將杭州任通判時期定位爲與詞接觸的初期，是可以理解並接受的，是以從此說。

等。

縱使東坡的初期詞作已有部份線索可以看出「文人詞」的痕跡，但是對於傳統詞體美學風格的掌握，卻不能因此視而不見。當然討論東坡早期的詞作，不能不重視其受到張先的影響。東坡任職杭州通判時曾與之交遊，並受其詞作影響，《苕溪漁隱叢話》卷三十九曾經引東坡之語說：

> 吾昔自杭移高密，與楊元素舟。而陳令舉、張子野皆從余過公擇於湖。遂與劉孝俱至松江。夜半月出，置酒垂虹亭上。子野年八十五，以歌詞聞於天下，作〈定風波令〉……坐客懽甚，有醉倒者，此樂未嘗忘也。

按張先大蘇軾四十六歲，和兩人可說是忘年之交，曾有兩首〈定風波令〉相互次韻唱和。而張先在當時是以詞作聞名的作家，其作品總是在風流韻事之中，夾雜有嚴肅的感懷，然而吟風弄月的內容卻是當時人對張先作品的觀感。《韻語陽秋》卷十九曾記載：

> 張子野八十五猶聘妾，東作詩謂「詩人老去鶯鶯在，公子歸來燕燕忙」是也。荊公文有詩云「篝火尚能書細字，郵筩還肯寄新詩」，其精力如此，宜其未能息心於粉白黛綠之間也。

也正風流多情，所以張先詞作多有贈妓的內容，用字遣詞多細膩婉約，所作詞調多有唐、五代以來的詞牌為多，如〔木蘭花〕十首、〔菩薩蠻〕九首、〔蝶戀花〕五首、〔定風波〕五首、〔清平樂〕三首、〔南鄉子〕三首等，張先使用二十六種舊調卻填了七十三首之多，共佔其一百四十五首小令中的一半，可見其音樂上的饒富古制。雖然後世柳永的慢詞帶來新機，是文人詞成立的重要機制，但我們卻更有理由相信張先詞作中對詞體本色的掌握，是眞接影響東坡早期詞作的要素，也更可以證明東坡對詞體本色的嫻熟。

三、樂律與文字的分離

改變以音樂爲主的塡詞機制，成爲以文字思考爲創作的主要對象，是「以詩爲詞」的文人詞之所以能夠成立的充要條件。而東坡在詞體文字與音樂分離的實作上，在歷代詞論中若是以文人詞爲思考脈絡，則多歌頌其對詞體開創之功，若是以音樂性著眼，則多非難東坡的不解音律。非難者之中以宋代周邦彥和李清照最具代表性，尤其李清照著〈詞論〉強調「詞別是一家」，要求詩、詞應有所分別，以相應於東坡以來詩詞相混所興起的文人詞，就批評蘇詞「皆句讀不葺之詩爾，又往往不協音律」⓮。其實這的看法在北宋是相當普遍的，范正敏就曾認爲：「子瞻之詞雖工，然而多不入腔，正以不能唱曲也」⓯。甚至蘇門中的晁補之也提到：「東坡詞，人謂多不諧音律，然居士詞橫放傑出，自是曲子中縛不住者」⓰。雖然在南宋以後有人爲其緩頰，如胡仔提出：「子瞻自言生平不善唱曲，故間有不入腔處，非盡如此」⓱、陸游則說：「世言東坡不能

⓮ 《詞話叢編》。

⓯ 《苕溪漁隱叢話》前集卷四十二引《遁齋閒覽》。

⓰ 《能改齋漫錄》卷十六。

⓱ 同註⓯，前集卷二十六。

歌，故所作樂府詞多不協。晁以道云：『紹聖初，與東坡別於汴上，東坡酒酣，自歌〈古陽關〉。』則公非不能歌，但豪放不喜裁翦以就聲律耳」⑱。其實不管東坡是不是故意不願遷就音律，還是不懂音律，其詞作比當時人不合於音律是可以確定的。

只是由於樂律的佚失，東坡詞如何的不入腔，如何的不諧律，現今幾乎已無從了解。或許有人依明代以來所編的的各種詞譜，依序排列對照來了解東坡詞的如何出格，然而這些詞譜所記的只是詞在文人化之後，改變審美態度，依詩的平仄法則所歸納出來的格律而非原始音律。龍榆生先生在《詞律質疑》中曾提出這樣的看法：

> 詞本依聲而作，聲必協律而後可歌，此必然之理，今無異議者也，然此所謂律者，乃律呂之律，依所屬宮調不同而異其作用，必準之管絃而俱合，付之歌喉而無所戾，初未嘗專以四聲清濁當之。……後世所謂依譜填詞，但按句讀長短之數，聲韻平上之差，便以爲能盡協律之能事。……則填詞必應月律方能諧美，此所謂律，即律呂之律，而關乎宮調方面者。自音譜失傳，吾人已無從懸其妙用矣。⑲

既然東坡詞的出律不可依現存的詞譜而論，則其「不入腔」、「不協律」的問題就無法就平仄格律上來討論。

若換個角度來思考這一個問題時，我們發現若以創作論的觀點來看，在東坡之前詞本來就是音律爲主，文字爲副。聲音之美是主

---

⑱ 陸游：《老學庵筆記》卷五。

⑲ 《詞學季刊》第一卷第三號。

要的審美標的，欣賞對象也擴及中下階層的民眾。主動的創造力是操之於樂工之手，縱使有少數文人能自度新曲，也是先思考曲調的曼妙，再求詞句的優美。而詞既是大眾娛樂所用，作詞者當須考慮其市場的接受度，與個人的藝術涵養，所以依舊詞牌填製社會大眾喜好的詞句內容，是最保守也最容易被欣賞者接受的方法。東坡詞與其說其不守音律，倒不如說是改變詞的審美結構。將創作主導權由樂工手中轉移至文人的意識，成爲文字爲主，音樂爲輔。將由耳聽的爲主的接受模式，轉成以眼視爲主的接受模式。若從音樂的角度來看東坡詞縮小了音樂成長的空間，若從抒情言志來看東坡詞則開拓了創作的道路。宋·沈義父的《樂府指迷》即指出：

> 如秦樓楚館所歌之詞，多是教坊樂工及鬧井做賺人所作，只緣音律不差，故多唱。之求其下語用字，全不可讀。

這是音樂的角度來看詞的成長。至如王灼《碧雞漫志》說：

> 東坡先生非醉心於音律者，偶爾作歌，指出向上一路，新天下耳目，弄筆者始知自振。

所謂「弄筆者始知自振」，可說將詞以欣賞者爲創作依歸，以討好欣賞者的模式，轉換成提升欣賞者以就創作者抒情言志的傳統。而所謂的「向上一路」更是就文字內容而言，對音樂環境來說可能就反其道而行了。

東坡詞共三百五十一首，共用了七十六種詞調，而且還集中在少數幾種常見的詞調中，如小令部份〔浣溪沙〕四十七首、〔減字木蘭花〕二十八首、〔菩薩蠻〕二十二首、〔南歌子〕十八首、〔南鄉子〕十七首、〔西江月〕十五首、〔蝶戀花〕十五首、〔臨江仙〕十四首、〔江神子〕十二首、〔定風波〕九首、〔點降脣〕七首、〔虞美人〕七首、〔行香子〕七首、〔漁家傲〕六首、〔木蘭花〕六首、〔如夢令〕五首；長調則有〔滿庭芳〕六首、〔水龍吟〕六首、〔滿江紅〕五首。共十九調只佔東坡詞所用詞調的四分之一，數量卻有二百四十九首，佔東坡所有詞作的十分之七。和東坡前後期的柳永、秦觀、周邦彥相比，柳詞共二百十二首，一百三十五調；秦詞八十七首，四十六調；周詞一百八十五首，一百十二調。可見得愈重視音律的詞家，其所運用的詞調愈多種，喜歡用各種不同的詞調來嘗試創作，反之愈不重視音律的詞家，所運用的詞調愈少，因爲東坡已分離出詞的音樂性，當成另一種詩體在創作⑳。詞調的存在除了部份合樂的理由外，最大的價值就在於保持著詞體形式上的特點，其長短句的形式有別於詩歌的整齊五、七言句式，是由形式稍微牽制著內容的發展，使不與詩歌完全相同。所以在其觀念中詞儘管是詩之裔，但詩、詞在形式上仍是有所分別的。也由於東坡始將詞的音律與內容分離，是以後世雖有周邦彥、李清照，甚至南宋張炎等人極力主張詞的音樂性，並有談論音律的作品，然而對傳統文人而言，學習音律終究是件難事，宋代就有多人以此爲畏途㉑，則遑論明代以後寫詞文人。是在自明代之後以仿詩歌平仄譜而得的詞譜遂應運而生，考之明代以後所產之的各詞譜，事實上是以吟頌

⑳ 黃文吉先生所著《北宋十大詞家研究》，文史哲出版社。亦持完相相同之觀點。本文之統計數字亦參酌該書。

㉑ 宋·張炎〈詞論〉：「詞之作必須合律，然律非易學，得之指授方可。……今詞人才說音律，便以爲難，正合前説，所以望望然而去之。」

爲主的平仄格律，而非合於音樂性的曲律，當然依平仄譜填詞，傳統文人亦樂而相配。清代萬樹的《詞律發凡》曾提道：

> 自沈吳分四聲以來，凡用韻樂府，無不調平仄者，至唐律以後，浸淫爲詞尤以諧聲爲主，倘平仄失調則不可入調。周、柳等制腔造譜，皆按宮調，故協於歌喉，播諸弦管，以迄白石、夢窗輩，各有所創，未有不悉音理而造格律者。

這樣的說法已是從詩化的觀念中脫胎而來，將音律與平仄格律強加湊和，所謂的「音理」事實上也是諧聲而已。但同時代的毛奇齡卻有以下的反省：

> 古者以宮、商、角、徵、羽、變宮、變徵之七聲，乘十二律，得八十四調。後人以宮、商、角、徵之四聲，乘十二律，得四十八調。蓋去徵聲與二變不用焉。四十八調至宋人詩餘猶分隸之。其調不拘長短，有屬黃鍾宮者，屬黃鍾商者，皆不相出入，非今之譜詩餘者，僅以小令、中調、長調分班部也。……近人不解聲律，動造新曲曰自度曲，試問其所自度曲隸何律？律隸何聲？聲隸何宮何調？而乃搁然妄作有如是耶！㉒

詞律從音律轉化成爲文人所習用的平仄譜，恐怕也是東坡「以詩爲詞」影響所及的一項副產品了。

㉒ 清·毛奇齡《西河詞話》卷二。

四、詞體風格的更替

即如前所言，詞本起於秦楚樓館，係供大眾聲色娛樂之產物，所以取悅欣賞對象是重要的美學任務，這其中除了聲音上的變化之外，演唱者仍具有關鍵性的地位，北宋中詞人李薦曾寫過一首〈品令〉來戲嘲善歌的老翁，其詞曰：

> 唱歌須是，玉人檀口，皓齒冰膚。意傳心事，語嬌聲顫，字如貫珠。老翁雖是解歌，無奈雪鬢雲霜。大家且道，是伊模樣，怎如念奴。

可知詞在當時已是一種表演藝術，所以觀賞者除了耳聽其音，還要目視其人，謳歌者的姿色也就成爲欣賞者要求條件之一，歌壇也因此而成爲年輕貌美歌妓的天下。唱詞既以女聲爲主流，其先天上的音色遂使得詞的風格自然就往婉約一路走去。文人做詞係提供給歌妓所唱，自五代以來詞家亦多以女子之口吻創作，鮮少作家個性的表現，是以內容亦多陰柔秀麗、風月情懷。王灼《碧雞漫志》卷一曾對此現象提出批評道：

> 古人善歌得名不擇男女。……唐時男有陳不謙、謙子意奴，高玲瓏、長孫元忠、候貴昌……。如有穆氏、方等、念奴、張紅紅、張好好……。今人獨重女音，不復問能否。而士大夫所作歌詞亦尚婉媚，古意盡失。

東坡詞一改社會風尚，不專爲女子歌妓做詞，也間接的改變了詞的審美情調，內容自然不拘於柔媚婉約一途。即如宋俞文豹《吹劍錄》所載：

> 東坡在玉堂日，有幕士善歌。因問：「我詞如何柳七？」對曰：「柳郎中詞只合十七、八女郎，執紅牙板，歌『楊柳岸曉風殘月』。學士詞，須關西大漢，銅琵琶。鐵綽板，唱『大江東去』。坡爲之絕倒。

一般對此記載的理解多爲詞中柳永婉約與東坡豪放的分別，然而妙齡少女與關西大漢的不同演唱型態，應該也是決定詞作內容風格的重要條件。

東坡以詩人之姿介入詞體創作，強調自我個性的呈現，改變爲歌妓做詞的創作型態。無疑是重內容輕形式，以文學作品服務於作者情志的寫作模式。就東坡而言：只是多一種形式供其揮灑。就詞體而言：卻擴大並改變了發展方向。如果細分東坡詞，可以分成供歌席娛樂所用的詞作，和抒發個人生命情志的詞作。前者多爲早期的作品，部份屬婉約風格；後者則大量集中在徐、密之後，今人所說的東坡詞豪放多是就此而論。所以談婉約與豪放的正、變說，是就詞體文類而論，談東坡「以詩爲詞」則是就作家創作主體而論。

當然「以詩爲詞」是緊扣著文學史的發展脈絡而來，即如葉嘉瑩先生所說：

> 自晚唐之溫庭均、韋莊，經過五代之馮延巳、李璟、李煜，以迄北宋之晏殊與歐陽修，其以精美之物象及深婉的情意以喚起讀的聯想與感動，並且將一己之人生際遇與學養胸襟都

> 逐漸融入小詞之中，這種演變之過程，可以說是明白可見的。於是當時在歌筵酒席間隨意寫付歌兒酒女去吟唱的本無個性的豔歌，及終於有了可以抒情寫志的作用，所以我們曾經將此一演化之過程，稱之爲「詩化」的過程。㉓

準此論，則東坡將詞詩化繼前人之功，是文學發展史上承繼傳統，開創新路的一環節。事實上，詩在中國文學史上自有其無法取代的崇高地位，尤其自漢代經學獨尊時，詩亦納入經學的思考體系之中。其中雖經六朝唯美文體的盛行，「詩言志」的經學思考卻早已深植文人心中。是以，當無限擴大詩學領域的同時，民間謠可以是詩，古樂府可以是詩，曲子可以是詩，當然詞也可以用詩的觀念進行創作，以滿足文人「詩言志」的理念。詞進入文人的創作領域時，雖然娛樂效果未減，但是在傳統文人心目中，其地位卻是遠在詩歌之下甚遠，東坡說張先詞是「詩之裔」、是寫詩後之餘波；〈與蔡景繁書〉說：「……頒示新詞，此古人之長短句也，得之驚喜。」〈答李季常書〉也提到：「又惠新詞，句句警拔，詩人之雄，非小詞也。但豪放太過，恐造物者不容人如此快活。」東坡也知道太過豪放的詞作並非詞之本色，易引來本色當行者的批評，但「詩言志」的最高指導原則，可以擺落詞體形式上的束縛，是以在內容與形式的抉擇上，東坡所選擇的是「曲子縛不住」的創作理念。

而詩歌理論在歷經代的發揚已到達相當成熟的階段，所以東坡由詩歌理念中獲得了完整的養份，其後期詞作的不限題材內容、表達作者個性等，也都是「以詩爲詞」理念的發揮。至如宋代所流行

㉓ 葉嘉瑩著《靈谿詞說·論秦觀詞》。

奪胎、換骨的詩法，其實在東坡詞中隱括、集句的創作方式中就已見端倪。其〈哨遍〉一詞在序中即明言：「陶淵明賦〈歸去來〉，有其詞而無其聲，余既治東坡，築雪堂於上，人俱笑其陋；獨鄱陽董毅夫過而悅之，有門鄰之意。乃取〈歸去來辭〉，稍加隱括，使就聲律，以遺毅夫，使家僮歌之，相從於東坡，釋耒而和之，古牛角而爲之節，不亦樂乎。」作〈浣溪沙〉隱括張志和之〈漁父〉，其序謂：「玄眞子〈漁父〉詞極清麗，恨其曲度不傳，故加數語，令以〈浣溪沙〉歌之。」並作詞如下：

> 西塞山邊白鷺飛，散花洲外片帆微，桃花流水鱖魚肥。
> 自庇一身青蒻笠，相隨到處綠蓑衣，斜風細雨不須歸。

諸如此類是稍微改變前人文意，重新改製之新曲。而集句之類如其〈南鄉子〉：

> 寒玉細凝膚（吳融句），清歌一曲倒金壺（鄭谷句）。冶葉倡條遍相識（李商隱句），爭如，豆蔻花梢二月初（杜牧句）。年少即須臾（白居易句），芳時偷得醉工夫（白居易句）。羅帳細垂銀燭背（韓偓句），歡娛，豁得平生俊氣無（杜牧句）。

這些作品或許只是遊戲之作，不可據以說明和「以詩爲詞」的直接關係，但環視宋代詩壇，此種創作方式多見於詩歌中，而少見於詞作。所以我們不能不承認東坡寫詞時受到詩歌創作意識影響之深。

五、結　語

歷來文學史在論及文體的質變時，有時太過度強調文類自身的演化，而忽略了文體係操縱於作家之手，作家、作品與讀者的三角依存關係，才能決定文體演化的方向。作家可能被社會需求帶著走，其作品也只在滿足社會大眾的快感；天才作家的誕生，則可能創作新的審美味口，讓社會大眾遵從，進而提升其審美層次。在作家創作慾望與讀者的滿足快感的牽引下，文體就可能漸進式的產生質變。詞在中國文學史上的演化，即是從滿足大眾審美味口的聲色之娛，經由文人的參與逐漸改變其本質，最終成爲以文人爲審美對象的小眾文學。這其中蘇軾就扮演了天才作家的角色，其出現無疑爲詞的新走向催生，而「以詩爲詞」的過程，也是將詞由全民共享的娛樂，轉化成爲只有少數文人能夠審美的新體。若從音樂的角度來說，東坡「以詩爲詞」使詞加快喪失其音樂性，成爲以文字爲唯一審美對象的文類；若從文學的角度來說，「以詩爲詞」，擴大了詞的格局和境界，使文人面對詞時「指出向上一路」，符合「詩言志」的文人傳統。然而我們今天所說的文學史，事實上也是以文人創作爲主體的菁英式文學，所以在建構文學史料時，自然就以文字審美爲主流，相對地，也容易在不自覺中排擠其他依附而生的藝術。所以就藝術史的發展來說：「以詩爲詞」對藝術發展的多樣性，具有嚴重的殺傷力。就文學史來說：「以詩爲詞」是文人有意識的將社會審美味口積極帶向精緻化的道路。而「詩言志」無疑地是中國文學史中一股強大的巨流，任何文類只要進入其思考領域，就很有可能爲其淹沒，被文人調整其本質，使其符合傳統詩歌理念中的價值。

Treasures of Another Kind: The Celebration and Condemnation of Metaphor, Lie and Illusion in Classical Chinese Poetics

Martin Svensson*

In what follows I will approach the closely interrelated topics of classical Chinese poetics and theories of language from a slightly unconventional perspective. In short, what is to be investigated is the relationship between some early texts dealing, with aural and optical illusions and what may tentatively be called the "reading of poetic imagery" in the Confucian scholar Mao Heng's exegesis of the *Book of Poems* (*Shijing,* China's oldest collection of poetry).❶Against the grain of customary Sinological thought, I will suggest that early Han Dynasty poetics(second century B.C.)originated in and advanced what contemporary critical parlance would call a philosophy of metaphoricity. And not only

---

* 馬丁，瑞典斯德哥爾摩大學中文系博士生暨兼任講師

❶ I am referring to Pauline Yu's already classic *The Reading of Imagery in the Chinese Poetic Tradition* (Princeton: Princeton University Press, 1987).

does this tradition speculate most suggestively on the linkage between lying, metaphoric poetry and illusion; it also contains precicely what Sinology has dogmatically denied: musings on the the Chinese written character as a medium for poetry (albeit from an angle diametrically opposed to Pound's).

Now, if I am aiming, at a "new" understanding, what constituted the old, conventional comprehension of Han Dynasty poetics? With remarkable synergy, sinologists of this expiring century have used the concept of *cosmology* in their attempts to define the essential difference between the Chinese and Western systems of thought. Against the Occidental, Platonic division of the world into phenomena and ideas one has posed cosmology's scheme, whereby all things constantly and simultaneously interact and exert influence on one another. Informed by this model (which no doubt did flourish in the latter Han), the sinologist has intimated that the Occidental notion of metaphor - divided into sensuous vehicle and abstract tenor-is inapplicable to the Chinese figure of speech which may, initially and falsely, be mistaken for a Western metaphor. By way of example, when the first piece of the *Book of Poems,* on Mao Heng's interpretation, describes a "virtuous" bird as an image of the equally "virtuous" young lady whom the poem celebrates, it is not a case of metaphoricity.❷Why? Simply because the bond between bird and woman must be understood as having existed *prior to* and *independently of* the poet's poetic description of it.❸Consequently we must not understand the Chinese poet as a clever maker of metaphors - he merely

---

❷ See Wang 1988: 8. I follow the sequential order given in Karlgren 1950.

❸ Yu 1988: 33: "...the connections between subject and object ... are viewed in the Chinese tradition as already pre-established."

describes, in literal language, a world already full of correspondences, a *metaphorical world.* From another point of view, we may also say that the Chinese "(non-)metaphor" does not, and cannot, *lie*. When the Anglophonic brute says that he "fancies that bird," he is literally lying, since he is not referring to a fowl but to a woman (albeit in foul language). By contrast, when the Chinese poet depicts a certain bird known for its virtuous behaviour in order to indicate the virtue of his female protagonist, he is merely presenting one of two halves of a cosmological unity.

The ingenious and seductive poetics of cosmology has frequently been substantiated by strategical misreadings of pivotal Han Dynasty texts, most notably the *Great* and the *Minor Prefaces.* These documents have been interpreted as describing, a spontaneous bard who, swayed by cosmological forces, passively reflects the external world, rather than an active calculating poet who can manipulate language and fabricate metaphors. I have put forward my objections to these misreadings in another context.[4] What I wish to do here is to dispute and complicate the reduction of two complex and diverse traditions to a few slogans; to counteract the blurring of the boundary between philosophy and rhetoric; to question the importance of the much later cosmological paradigm for early Han Dynasty poetics; and, most importantly, to reveal the debate on illusion, lies and metaphoric deviation that constituted the context in which Mao Heng's exegesis of the *Poems* was performed.

I will begin by discussing two well-known tales from the essay "Mistrusting Similitude" in *Mr. Lü's Annals* (third century B.C.) and,

---

[4] The Great *Preface* is a short essay on the origin and function of poetry (*shi*); the Minor *Prefaces* consist of short exegetical comments on each poem in the *Book of Poems.* See Svensson: Forthcoming.

then, go on to contrast the suspicion with which the phenomena of illusion, doubleness and ambiguity are treated there with the idea that illusion is, indeed, a prerequisite for ritual activity - an assumption implicit in the Confucian thinker Xun Qing's contemporary "Discourse on Ritualism." And from Xun's exposure and espousal of illusionary rhetoric I shall return to Mr. Lü and demonstrate how, paradoxically, the very same principle also applies to his theory of metaphor, tacitly developed in an essay named "Treasures of Another Kind." Finally, having thus traced the demarcation line that separates the damnable illusion that occurs in, and disturbs, everyday life from the illusion actually favoured by rites and witty language, I will proceed to Mao Heng's discussion of poetry *qua* ritualized discourse and try to unravel the poetics underlying his *Commentary on the Book of Poems,* starting from what seems like a mere cursory remark on the fourth stanza of poem 192, "Zheng yue." A close, not to say obsessive, reading of poem and commentary will reveal that Mao's conception of clever poetic discourse - rhetoric - was indeed founded on this paradoxical, simultaneous embrace and rejection of illusion and metaphor.

In the Western philosophical tradition, "illusion" is a time-honoured theme and a close relative to other noble topics such as mimesis, imagery, metaphor, trompe l'oeil etc. My usage of this concept as a reference to a thought pattern that underlies and shapes certain aspects of early Confucianism is, of course, itself a metaphor and, as such, always an approximation. Although I would argue that "illusion," in the common sense of the word, corresponds fairly well to what the authors of the above-mentioned texts had in mind when they were discussing the problem of *si* 似, "similarity," I urge the reader simultaneously to recall and resist the works of "illusionists" such as Ernst Gombrich, W.J.T. Mitchell, or Jean Baudrillard. Also the writings of Maurice Blanchot and

Gilles Deleuze, which sometimes come astonishingly close to the texts that are our main concern here, should be approached with extreme caution.

As an indication of my rather less sophisticated usage of the concept, I shall give two examples of the illusion. First, consider the scene in Arthur C. Clarke's 2001 when the protagonist has succeeded in breaking through to what we, acknowledging the limits of human language, may call a "parallel universe"; and how he finds himself in what he will soon discover is only a *replica* of an ordinary American hotel room, containing furniture, magazines, a bowl of flowers - an illusion procured by the friendly creatures of this other dimension to make him "feel at home" (Clark 1968: 240-49). As I conceive the term, this eerie doubleness, where there are two instances of the same outward shape but where only one of them reflects the *real thing,* is the very essence of the illusion. From a psychological point of view, consider also how the discovery (the "disillusion") of the objects' true status entails a sense of vertigo and nausea at the intense similarity between original and copy, and at the gulch that separates the snugness of one's tellurian home from this otherworldly, "unheimlich" apparition.

If this exemplifies an illusion that may be temporarily joyful but, in the long run, unpleasant and puzzling, the other version I have in mind lacks this negative side. The illusion of the *continuum* makes us expect that the next moment will to a very high degree resemble, or at least be a safe and logical progression from, the preceding one. We expect the sun to rise again tomorrow morning as it has always done, even though it is possible that some hitherto unknown cosmological force will extinguish the solar ball during the night. Under the same law of habit, we presume that the tennis ball we have just hit will follow its trajectory without, let us say, stopping in mid-air and dropping vertically to the ground as if it had hit an invisible wall. What these two differently structured and, seemingly, banal cases of illusion have in common is the dependence on the ordinary, patterned course of events and the disturbing and/or seductive possibility of the extraordinary. The illusion, as construed by these two examples, is thus always a dialectic play (lat. *lusus*) of convention and the breaking of convention, of expectation and astonishment. And, as we shall see, the illusion is the rhetorical tool par excellence in early Chinese poetics.

One
Metaphor and illusion in early Chinese thought

Mr. Lü's ghostly signifier

Like most Confucian literature of the time, the collection of philosophical essays from the first centuries B.C. that goes under the name of *Mr. Lü's Annals* (*Lüshi chunqiu* 呂氏春秋) deals mostly with ethical and "political" problems: What are the duties of a ruler and of his ministers? Is rebellion against a dissolute royal house permissible? How does one, at one and the same time, maximize the happiness of the populace and keep them from growing too strong? Not surprisingly - since a peaceful and prosperous society was thought to depend on, and establish, orderliness and preciseness - a prevalent topic is the necessity of unity, of oneness, and, correspondingly, the exigency to eliminate ambiguity, deviation and excess. And this theme is not limited to political discourse, but relates directly to central questions in contemporary theories of poetry and language - hence its relevance to us.

As an example of the book's political theory we may consult an essay suitably called "Sticking to One [Principle]" ("Zhi yi" 執一), where the text says:

> An army must be unified by a general, a state by a ruler, and the whole World by an emperor. The emperor must stick to one [principle] to keep the world together [*turn zhi* 摶之]. Order follows oneness; chaos follows twoness [*Yi ze zhi, er ze luan* 一則治二則亂] (*lüshi:* 1132)

For reasons that will appear later, we should note that a variant of the last, slogan-like sentence of this piece appears in a chapter with a similar message called "No Twotiming" ("Bu er" 不二) as "Order follows oneness; chaos follows deviation [or 'otherness' *yi* 異]" 一則治異則亂 (Ibid.: 1134).

These rather trite fragments well exemplify the so-called Legalist strain of early Confucianism. Fortunately, things become more stimulating as we proceed to the real object of our interest, the discussion of the *impediments* to this much desired unity, clarity and perceptiveness in the chapter named "Mistrusting Similitude" ("Yi si" 疑似).❺"The similarity in appearance between different objects is the cause of great confusion," the opening line states, and what follows is the author's somewhat flimsy musings on the fact that our faculties of perception are sometimes unable to distinguish between outside appearance and the inner, true nature of an object or, indeed, of a human being. The

---

❺ Ironically, the character *yi*疑, here translated as"to mistrust,"is itself ambiguous, being also synonymous with *si* 似, "similitude." Cf. Chen Qiyou's discussion, *Lüshi*: 1498-99.

deceptive play between surface and essence (in my non-metaphysical adaption from lat. *esse* , "to be") may appear at all times and at all levels, thus the text says:

> The [deceptive] similarity between ordinary stones and jade is what worries the trader in jade... That people with shallow understanding but with sophistical discourse may *seem* to possess thorough knowledge is what worries the virtuous ruler. The ruler of a declining state only *seems* wise and its ministers only *seem* loyal. The similarity between disparate things puzzles the ignoramus and spurs the sage to intense brainracking. Thus, Mozi wept when he came upon a fork in the road [*dao* 道] (Ibid.: 1497).❻

The image of the great thinker Mozi 墨子 (fl. 5th century B.C.) at the forked road sums up the whole discussion: Mozi weeps because the wrong road is, according to the surface appearance presented to his senses, identical to the correct one but leads to an unwanted, Incorrect destination. In a nutshell, the formula of Mozi's conundrum and, of course, of similitude in general, is that there is only one form (shared by the identical roads) corresponding to *two* different contents (the two destinations). And in the two folksy tales that follow this passage, the same formula is elaborated on and turned into an embryonic semiotic theory.

> In Claremont... lived a ghost fond of assuming the shape of a passerby's son, grand son or brother. One day, a fellow from the village travelled to the market and, upon his drunken return, the

---

❻ The expression "forked road" evokes a pun on *dao* 道, "road," "way," "The Way."

> ghost assumed his son's shape, led him by the arm and abused him. At home, and no longer drunk, the man approached his son: *I'm your father! How could you be so cruel! Why did you make fun of me when I was drunk!* His son wept and kowtowed: *No! I did nothing of the kind! Yesterday I went to collect debts in Eastville, just ask anyone!* Persuaded, the father commented: *Damn! It must be that ghost I've been hearing about.* He decided to return to the market the following day for another drinking bout, hoping to meet the ghost again and, if given the chance, stab him to death. And so, the next morning he went and got drunk again. The son, meanwhile, fearing that his father would be unable to return home, went out to meet him. *But as the father saw his real son he drew out his sword and stabbed him.*
>
> The old man killed his own son because his wits had been confused by the duplicating ghost (Ibid.: 1498).

"*Das* ist des Pudels Kern!" Let us make a few remarks regarding this ghastly chain of events, whose pattern we are slowly beginning to recognize. The son's facade has been usurped, doubled, and when the father sees his son's countenance the first time he returns from the market he is the victim of an uncanny illusion, just as the hero of Clark's novel who finds in the parallel universe a replica (with the accurate cover but with papers lacking print) of the *Washington Telephone Directory* (Clark 1968: 243). Once the father has realized that an alien entity has assumed his son's shape, the stage is set for a tragedy. Now the story, as hitherto told, will repeat itself, but with a stand-in for the leading man. The comical twist that the plot banks on is that the second time the "disillusioned" father returns to the village and sees his son's countenance, he is *once more* illusion's victim, and this because two things have happened. First, he has come to the bizarre conclusion that his son's outer appearance can be perfectly and spectrally duplicated in an act of evil mimesis and that the link between form and content is thus arbitrary. Second, he is seduced by the repetition of events, the continuum: in the morning he goes to the market again, gets drunk again, returns home again and-again-meets someone or something resembling his son. Our tragic anti-hero is so confident that he has learnt the new rules of the game (*"son" equals ghost*) that, at this time and in this situation, he forgets that his son's shape is now radically ambiguous and can contain the ghost *as well as* his true son. This second time, the ghost's trick is *not* to assume the son's shape.

Before leaving this exemplary tale of the illusion that may follow in the wake of extreme similitude I will make a point that, at this stage, may seem conceited. We are using excerpts from *Mr. Lü's Annals* and Xun Qing to facilitate an eccentric look at Han Dynasty theories of poetic language. Allow me, therefore, to attempt a translation of the formula of illusion into semiotic terms. What we have called, variously, "form," "appearance," "outer shape," or "surface" corresponds to what pre-Saussurian semiotics called *signans,* the concrete and material form of a sign, the actual sound or written mark that represents a word. Similarly, the "content," the "thing," the "essence" that is presented to one's perception by way of the surface may be understood as the semiotic *signatum,* the "meaning" of the sign/word that is attached to its *signans.*

Theoretically and ideally, a sign consists of a signans and a signatum in absolute harmony. But if I were to use the word "dog" to refer to a feline animal, the conventionally established link between signans and signatum, between the three letters combined into d-o-g and the concept of the canine beast considered Man's Best Friend, would be broken. Moreover, people whom I would tell I had a "dog" at home would be under the illusion that my pet barked instead of mewed. As for the ghost story, we may say that it relates a tale about a signans (the son's shape) that, suddenly and with frightful consequences, acquires a *second* signatum (the ghost) adjuncted to its conventional one (the "essence" of the real son). Now, I should like to suggest that, at an allegorical level, the text could be understood as a warning about a ghostly (or, indeed, *spiritual*) meaning that may enter a word from the outside and disturb our conventional perception of things, a meaning injected into language perhaps by "people with a shallow understanding but with sophistical discourse." A warning, that is, issued by dogmatic Confucian scholars against metaphorical, ambiguous and illusory language in the quest for Confucius' celebrated "rectification of names" (*zheng ming*).

Let us ruminate on this interpretation as we proceed.

The drum signal

The incompetent last king of the Zhou Dynasty (1099-771 B.C.), You 幽 and his notably depraved queen Bao Si 褒姒 are, seemingly, the main characters of the chapter's second tale about the illusory change of identities. The story implies that what ended the Zhou was the changed meaning of an alarm signal brought about by Bao Si's sexual desire.

> The two capitals of the Zhou Dynasty, Feng and Hao, were both close to the territory held by the barbarous Rong people and, therefore, [the royal house] and the various vassals agreed on [*yue* 約] building a fort by the Royal Road, and putting on its roof powerful drums that could be heard for miles. In the event of an attack from the Rong, the drums would spread the news and the vassals' troops would hasten to assist their emperor. When the Rong finally attacked, King You beat on the drums,

> and the vassal's troops duly arrived. Bao Si was exuberant and took great pleasure in the spectacle. king You desired his queen's laughter, so he pounded the drums a great many times and the troops kept coming to the capital, only to find that there was no attack. It went so far that, when the Rong finally did attack again, no vassal responded to the king's drum. The king expired at the foot of Black Horse Mountain, and the whole world laughed at his death. With the "No Attack" he lost the "Real At tack" 以無寇失眞寇 (*Lüshi:* 1497-98).

Now, quite obviously, this is a story not about King, You and Bao Si, but about the moving fate of a sign, the drum signal. The tale's plot, furthermore, is so perfectly analysable in semiotic terms that the sinologist, in constant fear of accusations of hermeneutic colonialism, need not be ashamed of applying this "Western" method to an ancient Chinese text. If the sound of the drum is the signal's signans, its two signata are the two antagonistic meanings alluded to in the cryptic last sentence: "Real Attack" and "No Attack." The shift of the meaning attributed to the signal and the story's progression may be regarded from the perspective of the interplay between addresser and addressee. At the first stage, the signal signifies "attack" for both king and vassals. When the king attempts to amuse Bao Si with the sight of bloodthirsty soldiers, thus breaking the original agreement, the signal has the signatum "attack" for the vassals and the signatum "no attack" for the king and queen. Finally, the tables are turned and the signal signifies "attack" for the king and "no attack" for the vassals.

From this I allow myself to draw three conclusions. The semiotic system implicit in this text holds that a sign consists of two parts, identifiable with the signans/signatum dichotomy described above, and, secondly, that the relation between the two units - form and content, word and meaning - is arbitrary and explicitly the outcome of a mutual "agreement" (*yue* 約) between two or more parties, hence the deleterious possibility of a multitude of signata.❼Finally, and as a corollary to the above, this tripartite formula stands in salient opposition to cosmological language theories claiming that the relationship between *ming* and *shi*, word and object, is *not* arbitrary but that they are bound together by a cosmic link that prohibits and condemns any gliding of meaning. (I am not suggesting, however, that the ideal of a perfect relationship between word and world is incompatible with the message of the tale, which is ostentatiously negative.)

My audacious attempt a minute ago to transpose into semiotic terminology the deceitful play with outward appearance and identity that constituted the plot of the ghost story has now become, I hope, fully understandable and, indeed, unavoidable. In this tale, the movement between convention and deviation takes place, if not yet at the level of language proper, then at least at the similarly abstract level of one of man's representational systems. The "similarity" (si) of which the chapter's title speaks, refers here to the *alarm signal's outward similarity to itself,* while its meaning is ever volatile. Through human manipulation the percussional sign deviates from its customary meaning while it retains its habitual appearance (the drum *sounds* the same), very much like the ghost's manipulative replication of the drunken merchant's son (the ghost-"son" looks like the original). From another aspect, and expressed in sexual terms, the signans copulates with two signata simultaneously, a promiscuity with disastrous results. Moreover, and not without interest for us, what Mr. Lü, in panic and in warning, has described is the

---

❼ Yue refers, of course, precicely to the arbitrariness of the relation between *Ming* and *shi* in Xun Qing's "Zheng ming," *Xunzi jijie*: 420.

formula of the metaphor.

Xunzi's funeral scene: Illusion become mimesis

We are about to turn into a gloomier neighbourhood. Until now, the Confucian voice has spoken anxiously and Warningly about the image or signal whose customary usage is abruptly altered so that “war” suddenly means “peace” and a father suddenly slaughters his beloved son. Any everyday visual or aural impression, this voice tells us, may be an illusion deviating from the order of things as we have come to know them. *Death*, likewise, breaks the everyday pattern and puzzles us. And perhaps, to some extent, our confusion stems from the perplexity we feel towards death's own illusion, its cruel little joke, the corpse. The “remains” of a person are precisely that exterior form, that image, which remains after its content is gone. In semiotic parlance, the cadaver is a signans without a signatum, or, with new and more abstract signatum. The body on the slab *looks like* the person who walked among us but is, in fact, not.

Xun Qing's “Discourse on Ritualism” (“Li lun” 禮論) contains a most captivating description of the funeral objects with which Zhou Dynasty graves were furnished. Unlike most contemporary treatises on the same subject, this passage goes on to explain the strange nature of the interred goods and interpret their significance as ritual objects. Xun Qing probably did so because the meaning of the already ancient and ossified burial rituals was not wholly clear to the people of the third century B.C., at the same time as it was assumed that every step, gesture and movement of these rites somehow embodied the wisdom of antiquity.[8]

---

[8] Cf. Xun Qing's description of the rituals as a mysterious mode of action inherited from the sagely “Hundred Kings” of ancient times in *Xunzi jijie*: 369

Here, we should reiterate the well-known fact that the concept of "ritualism" (li 禮) occupied a preeminent position in Confucian thought, and that ritualized behaviour involved not only a fastidious adherence to age-old ceremonies but, more specifically, a fondness for, let us say, an "indirect" mode of expression. For instance, ancient documents record many instances of diplomats discoursing by way of poetry quoted out of context, a custom called *fushi*. In order not to appear too forward. (and thus boorishly uncultivated), these dignitaries would quote (fu) a stanza of a well-known poem which, metaphorically and ideally, corresponded to the situation at hand.❾I propose that a similar logic is at work Xun Qing's hermeneutics of entombment.

The immediate reason for Xun's long treatise seems to have been Mozi's radical demand for a halt to the absurdly expensive arid excessive funeral rites advocated by the conservative Confucian camp.❿Xun responds that even birds and beasts go through the process of mourning their dead by returning to their old dwellings(*gu xiang* 故鄉), howling and moaning at the place they used to share with the dead one, before they can leave the sorrow behind（*qu zhi* 去之）.⓫And if this is so, Xun Qing asks, how could man, with his greater intelligence, refrain from treating the dead as well as he did when they were alive? On a casual first reading, this seems to be the very message of the passage, yet its real argument is quite different and much more refined.

("Li lun,"): "[As for the rites], there is still no knowledge of their origin."

❾ See also the "Appreciating Straightforwardness" (*Gui zhi* 貴直) chapter of Mr. *Lü's* Annals and its illuminating tale of the forthright Neng Yi.

❿ *See Xunzi jijie*: 371.

⓫ Note Xun's anthropomorphic usage of the word *guxiang*, a word invested with nostalgia denoting man's birth place.

"The funeral rite," Xun Qing begins,

> embellishes death with life. One should accompany the dead [to their final resting place] in much the same manner as one did when they were alive, following the same principles in death as in life, in their absence as in their presence: one princip!e for the beginning and the end (Ibid.: 372).

Were it not for the crucial notion of "embellishing" the mortal realm with objects and principles drawn from the realm of life, one could misconstrue this opening passage as describing the *denial* of the death of the loved one, a grave misunderstanding.

> Immediately after death has occurred, bathe the head and body, tie the hands, and put food in the mouth, just as in life （*xiaing sheng zhi* 象生執）. If you do not wash the hair, then wet it and comb it three times only. If you do not bathe the body, then wet a towel and wipe the body three times only.⑫

But, to our bewilderment, in the next passage the predominant principle of "as in life, so in death" is Suddenly challenged:

⑫ Transl. modif. Dubs 1928: 235. I have chosen not to discuss the question of the difference between the articles "for the living" (*sheng qi*) and those "for the dead" (*ming qi*). It is clear from the rhymed, penultimate sentence ("the 'objects used in life' have a certain polish...") that, for Xun, the two categories of things are alike in their illusory imitation of usable objects. *Ming* (*shen ming zhi; ming bu yong*) may mean "illuminate, indicate; *sheng may*, of course, mean "raw, unrefined."

> Fill the ears and put in the ear plugs. Provide raw rice for food, put withered bones in the mouth, *going against the way of doing things in life* （*fan sheng shu* 反生術） (Ibid., emphasis added).

From now on, Xun is concerned with the significance of the rites for the *mourner,* not the dead. As he later says (*Xunzi jijie*: 366), they serve to "emphasize [or 'reduplicate'] the grief [*zhonglchong ai* 重哀]," referring perhaps to the painful repetition of the recognition of death's advent that will eventually turn into an acceptance of the new situation and a reorientation for the mourner - the process which Freud called a work-of-mourning.

> Arrange the three suits of underclothing; wrap the girdle around without fastening it...tie up the hair, but do not put on the hat or the hairpin. When displaying the funeral goods, the hat is helmet-shaped but the hair lacks clips. The clay water and wine jars are empty and not filled [*xu er bu shi* 虛而不實]. There is a fine bamboo mat but no bed. The wooden articles have not been finished, the pottery articles have not been shaped into complete objects, and the articles made of bamboo and reeds have no core. The wind-instruments are all there, but not attuned to each other; the zither's strings are there but have not been tuned in concert. The chariots are interred but with the horses facing the wrong direction. This announces that [these objects] are not used [*gao bu yong ye* 告不用也].The "objects used in life" [*sheng qi* 生器] go into the grave, symbolizing the shift from one road to another [x*iang xi dao* 象徙道]." [These objects] are full of omissions and never brought to their perfection [*lüe er bu jin* 略而不盡]. They have appearance, but no utility. The chariots are led to the tomb and bu ried, [but] the metal rein-ends, the reins and the horse collars

> do not follow, in order to show [*ming* 明] that [these objects] are not used. The announcement of the shift of road and the display of uselessness all serve to emphasize/double one's grief. Hence, the "objects used in life" have a certain polish but no utility, and the "luminous objects" [*ming qi* 明器] have outward appearance, but no usefulness...Thus the inter ment is the respectful concealment of [the person's] form [*xing* 形] (*Xunzi jijie:* 368-71)

What is, admittedly, a prosaic translation at least hints at the highly rhetorical and succinct style of the passage: the repetitions, the puns, the subtle analogies. And with our senses sharpened by Mr. Lü's instances of illusion, we immediately recognize the opposition of form to content as the dominant theme here. Yet, Xun's contemplation of the illusion differs conspicuously from Lü's. The objects marked by death's presence have the outward appearance of their mundane counterparts in the warm sun, but a human, premeditated act has deprived them of their essence, i.e. their *function,* a destructive act which makes possible their conversion into *signs.* ⓭ And this *deliberate* destruction (or negation) of a minute but vital part is what indicates the deviation from Mr. Lü's unwanted and negative illusion to what Xun conceives of as a rhetorical manipulation of signs.

At this juncture, Xun's analysis urges us to focus on both the illusion in its very illusion-ness, and to ask ourselves what the rhetorical movement from functionable object to uselessness actually says. An answer to the latter question comes from the last sentence quoted above which speaks of the corpse as the form (*xing*) of the dead person: the form

---

⓭ Cf. Maurice Blanchot's astounding discussion of the image, corpse and broken utensil in "Les deux versions de l'imaginaire" in *L'espace* litteraire (rpt. Paris: Gallimard, 1996), 346-49.

of the once living individual is interred along with the forms (*mao*) of the once usable objects. The funeral goods with their eerie ambience are thus not only illusory images of functional utensils but, moreover, *imitations of the corpse* declaring that the dead body is now useless and without function. But why this doubling, this second illustration that the death objects perform, this time of the corpse? We find the answer in Xun Qing's remark about the "doubling of grief" (*chong ai*): the unperfected funeral goods serve as a guarantee that the mourner will not reverse his journey into the underworld by mistaking the objects in the crypt for *usable* objects and, thereby, be induced to elude the work-of-mourning and again direct his attention to everyday life⓮(The original, crass reason

⓮ Which, as we remember, is exactly what animals do automatically when they return to their old dwelling to moum.

Content-wise, there is a slight but substantial difference between Xun Qing's speculations on the significance and mode of signification of the funeral rites, and those expressed in the three canonical books on rites and ritualism that originate from roughly his time, the *Zhou li*, the *Yi li* and the *Li ji* (all three included in Ruan 1979). On two occasions in the *Li ji,* Confucius makes passing comments on the usage of the *ming qi.* In the first place ("Dan gong," Ruan 1979: 1289) he alleges that these strange, unperfected objects are the results of a necessary compromise between treating the deceased as forever extinct by burying them without any funeral goods ("inhumane, not permissible"), and treating them as though they were still alive through the interment of fully usable objects ("dim-witted, not permissible"). Although terse and somewhat obscure, this paragraph suggests that the ultimate motif behind the burial of the quasi-perfected goods was, not primarily to please the manes, but to allow the living to keep within the limits of "humaneness" (*ren* 仁) and, thereby, the ritual system. Likewise, in. the second passage ("Dan gong," Ruan 1979: 1303), Confucius says that makers of the *ming qi* show a true insight into the principles of mourning (*sang zhi dao* 喪之道) when they do not render the funeral goods into usable objects, and when they make effigies of chariots and horses out of clay and hay, respectively, instead of putting real horses and chariots in the

that the objects were left half-done may, of course, have been that they were simply not intended for any practical purpose.)

At a more general level, the lugubrious Xun conceptualizes the phenomenon of death, not by anthropomorphizing death into a Grim Reaper but, negatively, by describing, death as the *lack* of an unspecifiable entity which renders the dead person useless, just like a chariot which cannot be properly used without horses. Thus, death is lack and uselessness, as illustrated by the funeral objects (directly fashioned after the corpse) that "have appearance, but no utility" and of which the jars - empty and hollow in want of wine and water - vividly represent the deceased person's absence from the pleasures and necessities of daily life.

But the *third* act of imitation, derived from the illusion's illusionness, remains unaccounted for. On the one hand, the crucial and meaningful flaw in the objects that illustrates the corpse's uselessness can be detected only at close range. Conversely, and requiring a distant point of view, the elaborate display of faulty goods, i.e. the creation of an

---

grave. In a similar fashion, he condemns the usage of wooden replicas (*yong* 俑) as "inhumane" *(bu ren* 不仁), since they bear too strong a resemblance to people of flesh and blood and, therefore, to the archaic, barbaric and "inhumane" custom of human sacrifice. It is apparent that what concerns Confucius in this context, and what stirs his sympathies and antipathies, is man's adherence to ritual conduct and the practice of "humanness," and not a concern for the spirits. Now, if both Xun Qing and Confucius are concerned with the importance of the burial rites for the living, they differ markedly in their interpretation of the *ming qi* and, in particular, of the reasons for which they must differ from objects intended for use by the living. For Confucius, as we have seen, the unhewn objects have the double purpose of enabling man to treat the deceased "humanely" without appearing foolish while, at the same time, signifying the distance from life and, therefore and more importantly, from human sacrifices.

illusory scene, illustrates the *corpse's* illusion-ness. Just as we, from a distance, may mistake the burial goods put on display for everyday objects intended to be used and consumed, a reclining corpse may be taken for a sleeping - but living - body. Thus, the funeral objects mimic *both* the corpse's emptiness, uselessness and its uncanny, illusion-inducing resemblance to its former owner. The jar, for example, illustrates both the body's mortal lack (the jar is empty), *and* the possibility of the illusion that the body's external form, which so resembles the deceased, may contain a living person (you know that the jar is empty only after a thorough examination; from afar an empty jar looks like a full jar) Moreover, the flickering between illusion and illustration means that the two modes must be infinitely close in time but *never simultaneous*. This crucial, rhetorical moment is located at the very borderline where both interpretations are possible: *now here/now gone; now living/now dead.* And at the utmost extreme of Xun Qing's interpretation of the burial scene, this vertiginous vacillation between delusion and truth gives rise to a truly sublime mimesis of the mourner's despair: *it can't be true/it is true; she can't be dead/she is dead.*

We learnt from Mr. Lü that an illusion is the traumatic disturbance of the conventional meaning routinely attached to an external appearance. Here, Xun celebrates the change of the meaning and function of the funeral goods. Why? Two things make this change acceptable. The first is the ritual setting which admits, and possibly demands, deviations from the normal laws of literalness (as in the *fushi* practice). A playful answer to the second question is provided by the text itself: the funeral objects, it says, "go into the grave, symbolizing the *shift from one road to another.*" In order to explain the process of signification involved in the ritual perversion of everyday objects Xun plays with the ambiguity of the word *dao:* "road," "way," "method," "the Way (*Tao*)," "order," "speech." Thus, the phrase *xiang xi dao* 象徙道 means something like "representing the chance of *dao.*" In other words, the funeral objects not only signify a shift from the material road with which we associate the horse and chariot or, metaphorically, from the old order made obsolete with the arrival of death; they also indicate a change in the conventional mode of *speech.* Inside the death ritual, the straightforward language of the living is no longer applicable, simply because such language *cannot adequately describe death* or the lack it produces in the human body. Instead, we must resort to the ritualized and metaphorical language that emerges from the illusion of the corpse (which, of course, is precisely what Xun proves: the very moment he makes the pun on *dao*).

The possibility of a crossing over from illusion to illustration is, in more ways than one, a pivotal point, for it can serve as a basis of an experimental theory of early Chinese rhetoric. Here, unconventional ("metaphoric" or "symbolic") meaning is presumed to be achieved through an act of *deprivation or depreciation* that brings about an illusion which, in its turn, produces the aberrant meaning sought after by the skilled poet. Accordingly, the Chinese rhetorician-cum-language abuser starts off with the full presence of a sign (a signal, a body, an object, a word), its form and its conventional, comfortable meaning only to rid the sign of its established meaning in a violent act that conserves the sign's form but produces a new meaning. "Violence" correctly connotes illicitness and intrusion, and the shift of signification alone with the maintenance of form in the texts from *Mr. Lü's Annals,* and the body's similar transformation into a corpse are all described in negative terms. However, Xun Qing's analysis of the entombment rites and their ,production of meaning must be considered in a wholly different light, for in the dominion of rites and death, illusion and illustration, illustration and illusion are praised. Poetry, too, finds itself in this dominion, but does that mean that poetic language too is a ghost language, a death language?

TWO

"That which seems to be, but is not" - Illusion as a trope and the advent of Chinese metaphoricity in the Mao Commentary

Treasures of another kind

Before we proceed to poetry proper, in this case the *Book of Poems,* let me retrace my argument thus far by recalling the image of Mozi crying at the "forking road" (*qi dao* 歧道). Although the author did not intend a pun on the various meanings of *dao* ("road," "principle," "speech"), I will allow myself to comment briefly on a metaphorical reading of the phrase *qi dao.* Why cry over forking speech or, with Xun Qing, a "shift" in speech? If, as I have argued, the forking road presents the wanderer anxious to reach his goal with the vexing choice between two identically looking roads of which only one leads to the correct destination, then bipartite speech (delivered by Sophists and feared by rulers) provides the listener with ambiguous words, such as metaphors. Thus read, the phrase *qi dao* expresses the horror for unstable language, just as the "Yi si" chapter as a whole warns about the terrors which may follow our confrontation with unstable identities.

Speculative as it may be, this reading is able to locate the weak, inconsistent and utterly ironical moment in the text's argument, the moment when it condemns metaphoricity precisely by way of a metaphor. Allow me now to exemplify, without the speculative gesture, this paradox in the essay "Treasures of Another Kind" ("Yi bao" 異寶) from *Mr. Lü's Annals* (*Lüshi:* 666). We have encountered this specific "otherness" (*yi* 異) already in the motto "Order follows oneness; chaos follows otherness" 一則治異則亂. And in the Confucian dialectic of convention and deviation, *yi* ("to differ," "deviate," "other") assumes the same role as *xi* ("to move") and *qi* ("forking"), in that they all represent the digression from a hitherto followed road, principle (*dao*) or meaning. As for the character pronounced *bao in* modem Mandarin, and meaning "treasures," it is ideographic to the extent that it represents various valuables - jade, a cowrie-shell and earthen goods - together under a roof. I use the word "ideographic" (tabooed by contemporary sinology) not to suggest that the "image" of valuable objects stacked under a roof could *only* mean "treasures" (it could just as well signify "storehouse," for example, or even represent another word as a phonetic loan), but to indicate that the linkage between 寶 and "treasures" is not completely arbitrary. I would also claim that once the link between the character and its meaning has been established, the components that the character *bao* consists of cannot but exert a certain influence over the definition of what a "treasure" is.

"Yi bao" starts with a statement that warrants minute attention: "It was not the case," it is said, that "the [sagely] men of yore lacked treasures [*bao*]." "What they treasured was 'something else' 古之人非無寶也其所寶者異也. Later, in the well-known story of the righteous Wu Yuan, who had fled from the state of Chu because of its corrupt government, there appears a certain old fisherman who helps Wu despite the fact that he would have been amply rewarded by the Chu ruler had he captured the fugitive. The author asks, what did this humble but sagely fisherman consider a treasure? Obviously not the piece of material wealth that reader and author conventionally associate with the word "treasure" and the character *bao*寶, but rather the nobler and more abstract "treasure" of assisting an upright man and, thus, a moral society. Now, we may choose to describe the linguistic operation somewhat differently. Let us assume that the relater of this chain of events was puzzled by the old man's indifference to worldly riches and tried to find a way of describing the logic behind his refusal. The fisherman's behaviour remains nameless until the author comes up with the assumption that the man *did,* in fact, receive treasures, but the treasures *of another kind* which are the satisfaction that comes from performing a virtuous act. On this interpretation, it is the presence in the narrative of the treasures - the valuables promised by the state of Chu - that generates the new, metaphoric meaning of *bao* as a "treasure" which is not a treasure of jade and cowrie-shells, but a "treasure" in a sublimated, nobler sense, a "treasure" within quotation marks.

What they treasured was 'something else' 其所寶者異也 The text literally says that what the ancient sages valued was *yi*, "otherness," "deviation." And this is, in fact, a crucial moment in our inquiry into Confucian theories on language and rhetoric, for what this phrase articulates is Mr. Lü's paradoxical damnation of illusion's intrusion into everyday matters and his embrace of its appearance in literary language. The very concept of *yi,* under attack elsewhere in the *Annals be*cause it refers to the whole vexed sphere of ambiguity, illusion and deviation, is here "treasured" for its power to enrich language by the linguistic illusion called metaphor. We find in "Yi bao" exactly the same mechanism as in, most obviously, King You's manipulation of the drum-signal from its conventional signification into an "other" meaning but also in Xun Qing's analysis of the funeral rituals. The rhetoric of "otherness" begins by presenting us with an anomaly: objects for practical use in a tomb or material riches in the hands of an empty-handed fisherman. And so this rhetorical strategy leads to an instant of conceptual chaos and illusion which is transformed into clear, logical meaning as soon as we discover that the entombed goods have been deprived of their usefulness and the "treasure" of the precious objects formerly piled up together under a roof. The *illusion* of the fisherman's material wealth turns into a perfect *illustration* of his spiritual wealth once we have reevaluated *bao* and grasped its other meaning.

Hence, what underpins this chapter of *Mr. Lü's Annals* is a celebration of metaphoricity, the epitome of a treasure "of another kind." Let us return to this example, as Claude Levi-Strauss would say, as a "tool to think with."

The object of my attention in the following, crowning part of the article is a "tropological movement" - a subtle, rhetorical play on and with images of nature - that Mao Heng detects in a *Shijing* poem, and which is directly linked to the themes of illusion and lying and to the pattern of norm and deviation that we have explored above. Furthermore, this "movement" (or poetic technique) is intimately related to the trope that Mao Heng categorizes as a *xing* 興, but which differs significantly (in the literal sense of the word) from the canonical definition he gives of that rhetorical figure in his bombastic comment on "Guan ju," the very first of the *Poems.* In the last section, I will thus first demonstrate how the "canonical" xing explains (or produces) metaphorical meaning and, second, how the "ironical" subspecies of the xing pertains to Mao's remarkable speculations on the illusion as a poetic trope. Finally, I will reveal how these two editions of the same trope *themselves* come to constitute a dialectic pair of rule and variation, and how the so-called ironic xing thereby establishes itself as a mocking illusion of the already elusive, illusion-inducing standard version - that is, as an illusion of the illusion.

To forestall unnecessary misunderstanding, it is vital to grasp that I am first and foremost concerned with Mao's *Confucian* reading of the *Shijing, not* with what the poems "themselves" may be construed as saying outside the system of Confucian doctrine. Also, I will treat Mao's second century B.C. *Commentary in* perfect isolation from all other contemporary hermeneutical works on the *Poems.*

What, then, is a "xing"? Let us tentatively (and not quite accurately) call it a "metaphor," but only on the condition that we immediately forget all about this Occidentalist gesture. I have, in another context (Svensson 1996), described the xing as a tool used - and quite possibly invented - by Mao Heng to explain the rhetorical modus of the ancient *Poems* and, in particular, how the poems' descriptions of natural sceneries may function as metaphors of the human action that they take as their main subject. (This is the hermeneutic mechanism behind Mao's interpretation of the description of a virtuous bird as an image of a virtuous lady, as discussed above.) I have also suggested how the xing, as an indicator of metaphorical meaning in the poetic text, although employed by Mao to make *everything* into metaphors of Confucian virtue, had the unwanted but fascinating side-effect of opening up these poetic texts for *other,* illicit and counter-Confucian metaphorical interpretations. Finally, and also in the same context, I have implied that the success of the xing to a large extent depended on *the force* that Mao could exert as an authority on the *Poems.* In other words, although Mao would triumphantly discourse on the metaphoricity of the poetic text, and stimulate the. growth of a Chinese rhetoric, he could never appeal to his readers' rationality when he, for instance, insisted on a moralizing reading of what, on the surface, is a straightforward love poem. He could only claim to *know* that the *Poems* were, in the words of another Confucian classic, a "storehouse of righteousness," and attempt to find the means and power to demonstrate it. [15]But to those who doubted the a priori dictum about the exonerated *Poems,* e.g. the anti-Confucian movement of the 1920s, Mao would always appear as a charlatan using the xing as a magic wand, pointing it to this or that image, phrase or line, and claiming it to be a metaphor.

It is my position that, although many of Mao's moralizing interpretations can find no support in the texts themselves, he had the genius of perceiving the rhetorical mechanisms of the poetic text and, not least, of being able to sum up the fragments of a long-standing tradition of allegorico-metaphorical interpretation, systematize it and present it as a hermeneutical method. Even to those who abhor Confucian exegesis and consider it a thick, nauseating film smeared on the "fresh" and vigorous *Poems,* Mao Heng's achievement should stand out as remarkable.

The *Shijing* poem "Zheng yue" 正月, is a Iong lamentation about governmental chaos. As far as we know, during the early Han Dynasty it was understood as a critique articulated by high ranking noblemen (*daifu*) against the same King You that brought about the end of the Zhou Dynasty by beating the war drum one time too many. It is a reading not unwarranted by the poem itself, for the eighth stanza does mention the wicked Bao Si by whom, in Mao's words, "King You was led astray" (Wang 1988: 670). For us, however, the question is not the exact temporal or geographical situation referred to but the literary technique employed by the narrator. For although the *Commentary* does not define it as a xing, the "Zheng yue" persistently employs a rhetorical figure of speech that, at one point, will prompt Mao to provide us with a clue to his conception of poetic creation.

---

[15] *Zuozhuan,* Xi 27, Ruan 1979: 1822.

The poem starts by describing a disturbing anomaly:

正月繁霜　It is the *zheng* month, ample is the frost
我心憂傷　our hearts - grieved and hurt
民之訛言　The false words of the populace
亦孔之將　are heavily execrated (Wang 1988: 665)

The *zheng*-month, Mao points out, refers to the fourth month of the *Xia* calendar and, thus, to a time of year that normally does not see any frost (ibid.). For the sake of argument, we should here distinguish between two alternative readings. On the one hand, we could interpret these lines literally and decide that the speaker is shocked and distressed at nature's untimeliness, a deviation that, according to the ancient Chinese mantic tradition, could be interpreted as a disastrous omen. But we could also understand the image of frost in the fourth month as a rhetorical trope used by the skilful poet to set the tone for a poem that will describe a *saeculum* out of joint and deviating from the path of true virtue. Naturally (and fortunately), we don't have to make this choice, but can be content with letting the letter and the spirit exist side by side. As for our understanding of *Mao's* reading of "Zheng yue," what speaks against the rhetorical, more sophisticated interpretation is, of course, the plain fact that Mao does not label the image given in the first two lines a "xing," as he would normally do to indicate a phrase that should not be taken literally. Yet, considering Mao's comments on the later, similarly structured stanzas we must let our attention linger here for a few more moments.

Now, if a poet depicts the ground as covered by hoar-frost, not as an actual description of a late spring, but purely as an *image* of deviation and unnaturalness, would he not be engaging in rhetoric? And what is rhetoric's master trope, the metaphor, if not *literally a lie* (a definition that should be read twice)? And what theme do the last two lines introduce if not *lying*? And can it be a mere coincidence that the character *e* 訛 - meaning both "lie" and "rhetorical persuasion" - consists of the two components "word" (*yan* 言) and "change" (*hua* 化), thus indicating a mutated word or a transformation brought about by speech? At this stage, let us merely remark that it would be amusingly ironic if the first two lines should literally be a lie, while the following two lines accuse *other* people of lying - a paradoxical stance toward the Janus-faced phenomenon of the metaphor/illusion that we recognize from Mr. Lü.

As suggested by my polemical account of the poetics of cosmology, the distinction drawn between rhetoric and literalness is not mere scribble in the margins of the grand tradition of *Shijing* interpretation, but the actual bone of contention between two factions of Sinology. Although I am inclined to describe both the *Poems* and the Han Dynasty exegesis thereof as refined, rhetorical and metaphorical, the general tendency is to present them (and Chinese literature in general) as literal, concrete and the result of a spontaneous outburst from the poet. A Chinese poem, on this latter interpretation, is simply the literal/literary representation of an actual event as experienced by an actual person.

In any case, the poem's description of springtime hoar-frost presents a nature that behaves unnaturally and breaks the narrator's expectations of the stable and cyclic path of the seasons - the continuum of cosmos. When the theme of lying reappears in the fifth stanza, it is impossible to avoid the nagging suspicion that the author is, in fact, using a rhetorical lie in his vehement denouncement of linguistic trickery.

謂山蓋卑　They say "a mountain is low"
爲岡爲陵　["But"? "That"?] there are ridges and cliffs
民之訛言　The mutated words of the populace
寧莫之懲　Why has no one put a stop to them? (ibid.: 667)

Mao's interpretation of this stanza demands elaborate detective work, but let us first consider the stanza in its own right. Rhetorically, this is effective stuff: only a regime led by a corrupt ruler such as King You can claim that "up" is "down" and that a mountain - that which by definition is high - is low. As with Mr. Lü's "treasure," there is an instance of linguistic abuse, the mountain with its high ridges and cliffs is "low," and thus not a mountain. (In the next stanza [ibid.], the "populace" is reported as saying that heaven is "high" and that the earth is "thick" - unmistakable truths - but at that stage even the most obvious statement by these perverters of language can no longer be trusted.) But are we to take this alleged quotation at face value? Should we really believe that the "populace" (a derogative term for immoral nobles) is literally trying to convince the narrator that this blatantly false statement is true? And why, of all things, talk about *mountains* in the first place? I submit the hypothesis that the poet purposely chose "mountain," as a token of something high, paired it with the adjective "low" and put the whole contradictory phrase in the mouth of his enemies to illustrate their perverse and absurd behaviour. Moreover, the "a-mountain-is-low" concept is perfectly consistent with the ironic vacillation between norm and deviation, expectation and disappointment that "Zheng yue" takes as its theme. As I hinted above, however, the drawback of this admittedly potent trope is the absurd paradox that the poet must be untruthful in his description of the perverters of truth.

However, Mao's inconspicuous but mind-boggling comment on the first line (or, perhaps, on the first two lines) demands that the "mountain-is-low" statement be taken metaphorically: "On the throne is not a Superior Man, but a Petty Man." The metaphor itself is quite commonplace in the *Commentary,* where the *Poems'* descriptions of high mountains are frequently interpreted as metaphors of high social position and those who possess it. Instead, the cause of our predicament is Mao's failure to tell us if it is the populace or the poet himself who is asserting that the "mountain is low," and if the "cliffs and ridges" are to be understood as parts of a *high* mountain (and, thus, as a refutation of the claim that the "mountain is low") or as an "inferior version" of a mountain (thus saying that "it is no mountain - only cliffs and ridges"). Post-maoist annotators of the *Poems* have explored these possibilities ad nauseam and we may sum them up thus: if the lying populace is the speaker, then either the second line must be taken as their claim that the "mountain" consists only of cliffs and ridges (the king is a Petty Man), or it should be understood as the poet's refutation of their "lies": it *is* a mountain look at the high cliffs and ridges (the king *is* indeed a Superior Man). In this latter case, we must construe the whole narrative as uttered by the poet as a remonstration with, and defence of, his king, warning the ruler about the lying, populace about to rebel. If, on the other hand, it is the poet himself who articulates the oxymoronic words about the low mountain, then he is literally lying in order to verbalize a metaphorical truth, namely that what is supposed to be elevated (a "mountain," a ruler) is, in fact, not so. And what would be gained by such a perverse use of language ("high is low") is the sense, indeed, that a Petty Man holding the position destined for the Superior Man is as twisted, illogical and utterly counter-intuitive as calling "up" "down." In this latter case, there would, again, be a conspicuous and slightly comical tension between the literal-lie-as-metaphorical-truth constituted by the first lines and the accusation hurled against the populace that they are liars. In the former case, we would more or less have the same situation - rhetorically speaking - but with the difference that the first two lines could be understood as an example of the populace's lies. However, this would not make a great difference for our purposes, since what the poet (according to Mao) would then be calling a lie would not be the metaphorical mode of expression per se - the literal lie - but what the metaphor contends, namely that the king is a Petty Man.

This exposition, somewhat baroque in its details, of Mao's reading of a single line is warranted because of the information it brings us about the relations-hip between lying and rhetoric (i.e. metaphoricity), and we may illustrate that liaison by comparing what I alleged above was an interpretation closer to the text itself with the readings inspired by Mao's metaphorical rendition. If the poem itself exemplifies the "lies of the populace" by the blatant lie that "a mountain is low," then Mao, on our former reading, overpasses the literal lie ("the mountain is low") to find a *metaphorical lie* ("the king is a Petty Man"). Or, again, if the voice belongs to the narrator, the literal lie simply becomes a metaphorical truth ("the king *is* a Petty Man").

My argument, by way of this relentless contemplation of one and the same phrase from different angles, is that *Mao nowhere condemns metaphoricity* itself as a perverted use of language. And this insight makes possible a new set of questions. We may now begin to ask ourselves what kind of lie is tolerable and even lauded, and which lies are despised, and if the schizophrenic word *e* ("mutated speech, lie, persuasion") may help us understand the rhetorical principles obeyed by the *Shijing* poet.

Also the eleventh stanza - exceptional in its illustration of threat and terror - is based on the pattern of convention and deviation:

魚在于沼　The fish is in the pond
亦匪克樂　yet he cannot rejoice
潛雖伏矣　although by diving down it can hide on the bottom
亦孔之炤　Yet the [light] greatly illuminates him
憂心慘慘　the grieved heart is in pain,
念國之爲虐　thinking of the cruelty carried out by the state (ibid.: 672)

The first line, as we have come to expect, is deceptive. Everything seems to be in perfect order with the fish being in its proper and natural environment. The second line follows the rhetorical pattern by deviating from the expectation of joy and harmony promised by the first line, while the third and fourth lines lead us down to the depths of the lake, and also to a submeaning hidden below the textual surface. When "He ming" 鶴鳴, *Shijing* poem 184, says that "fish are swimming in deep waters/or [in the shallow water] at the islets" Mao interprets it as a metaphor of the superior man (*junzi*) who should be "hidden yet obvious" (a notion probably derived from a citation of "He ming" by Xun Qing).⑯Mao's argument is that the actions of a sage should influence the world without an obvious manifestation of power. The Confucian *junzi* should *be* but not be seen and, therefore, Mao comments that "fine fish hide in the depths; small, inferior fish swim around the islets" (Wang 1988: 672) Here, in "Zheng Yue's" description of a state in turmoil, the "fine" fish, as an image of the virtuous man, attempts to hide at the bottom but is, even here, threatened and terrorized by a malevolent and all-penetrating sunlight - King You's *Lichtzwang* - that illuminates the creature driven by righteous instincts. *Our* dry and self-evident observation, dazzled perhaps by the intrusive vision of the ferocious sun, is that this stanza is not a literal account of the behaviour of fish but, quite obviously, a metaphor of how an evil and corrupt government disturbs the natural behaviour of the virtuous man and invades his most intimate space.

At this point, I will for a brief moment consider the position of the cosmological sinologist who remains unconvinced that the poet of

---

⑯ See *Xunzi jijie*, ("Ru xiao"): 128. The "fine" fish is clearly another variation of the same "hidden but obvious" trope. For the connection between Xun and Mao, see Chen Huan's *Shi Maoshi zhuanshu* (Taipei: Xuesheng, 1967).

"Zheng yue" cold- heartedly used the vernal hoar-frost and frightened fish as mere fictitious *images of* political corruption. Rather, on his or her view, the first and fourth stanzas literally describe the omens sent down by Heaven as indications of the impending fall of the grand Zhou Dynasty.[17] Differently put, the cosmological world view makes the poet assume that such anomalies are commonplace when a ruling dynasty is about to fall. Consequently, the disturbed fish does not *resemble* Mao's and Xun's Superior Man in his distress at the corrupt regime; rather, both fish and man are simultaneous but different *symptoms* of the disturbance of nature that coincides with the declining dynasty. We should also formulate the same idea from another aspect, and make it clear that a cosmological poet or hermeneut would not make an *ontological* distinction between fish and man in this text. The fish would remain a fish without ever being reduced to a mere image of anything else. Now, should we like to express these beliefs in modem terminology we could say that, according to the Cosmologist view, natural phenomena and human actions coexist in the text on identical premises, and that the poet (or Mao) links fish and man metonymically - not metaphorically, since they are parts of the same string of occurences but do not bear any external resemblance to each other. The sinologist, it is implied, must not succumb to the seduction of the Occidental tradition, with its penchant for abstraction and symbolism, and be led to falsify the wholly other Chinese tradition by finding therein the cunning metaphors of the

---

[17] For an exemplary early interpretation of natural anomalies as portents of a coming dynastical change, cf. Baiyang Fu's comments on the earthquakes that (allegedly) took place during the second year of King You's reign in the "Bian wu" chapter of the *Shuo yuan,* compiled by Liu Xiang (79-8 B.C.). *Shuo yuan duben* 説苑讀本 (Taipei: Sanmin, 1996), 637-8.

Western poet.⑱

I will challenge the premises of this paradigm in a moment, for the time has now come to hasten to the heart of the matter. It is in his comment on the fourth stanza that Mao is moved to pinpoint and name the frustrating pattern of naturalness and deviation, this ironic pattern of promise and disappointment. The first lines of the stanza go:

瞻彼中林　look at the middle of that forest,

侯薪侯蒸　[there is] only firewood and brushwood (ibid.: 667)

Mao comments that " 'Firewood and brushwood' says that it has the appearance [of a forest] but is [in fact] not 薪蒸，言似而非" (ibid.). In the world gone awry that the poem describes, this is yet another sign of disappointment and deviation. On a first, naive reading, the forest/firewood illusion seems to have two functions. On the one hand, it pertains to the poem's general pattern of thing turning out to be different from one's expectations. On the other hand, the image opposes genuineness and solidity (trees, forest) to lightness and inferiority (firewood as an inferior "version" of trees). With reference to the situation of the state, the poem says that what may look imposing from the outside is, on a closer look, mere rubbish: an illusion that vanishes with the *reevaluation of the second glance* and the advent of truth that follows in its wake. But as we shall see, Mao's words about that which "seems to be but is not" (*si er fei* 似而非) also apply to the whole rhetorical apparatus involved here.

The first line describes how the eye of the narrator catches the sight

---

⑱ See Svensson Forthcoming. The Chinese tradition is anything but a monolith, and we should make a sharp distinction between the poetics of Kong Yingda's Tang Dynasty *Preface* to the *Poems* and that expressed in the Han Dynasty *Great Preface*.

-the appearance - of a forest. That image is then contradicted by the statement that the "forest" consists merely of fire- and brushwood. But notice that, like Mr. Lü in his tales about the ghost and the drum signal, what Mao focuses on is explicitly the dialectic between appearance and essence, between *being* and *seeming to be.* In the terms of the rhetorician, it is precisely by describing a situation (that which *is*) by an incorrect word that the poet can reach an illusion and, thereafter, a metaphorical meaning. In this context, then, the word "forest" (*lin* 林) is a misnomer. A forest is, by definition, an assembly of trees and a "forest" lacking trees can, strictly speaking, not be a forest, just as a "treasure" (*bao*) without valuables cannot be a treasure in the ordinary sense of the word, or as a low "mountain" is not really a mountain. But here, in the fourth stanza of the "Zheng yue," it is not *nature* or Heaven that lets us down by deviating from its own, presumed naturalness, as may have been the case when nature sent down frost in the fourth month. Here, the deviation is calculated and takes place at the level of language, in other words: at the rhetorical level.

In the example of Mr. Lü's "treasures of another kind," the author used the word *bao*, denoting material riches, to refer to a non-material "treasure." What this metaphorical (mis-) use of *bao* aimed at, then, was the concept of an *anti-treasure.* Instead of a treasure of money and jade, the old angler preferred the "treasure" of virtue. Let us describe the metaphoric process that shapes Mr. Lü's tale like this: *formerly* people wanted anti-treasures (virtue); now people only want treasures (material riches); *therefore* the world of today is a greedy, inferior version of former times. Similarly, but in inverted order, Mao's forest/firewood trope says that *at first* I saw a forest; *then* I discovered that what *looked like* a forest was an anti-forest, merely firewood; *therefore* nowadays things are not what they seem to be on the surface, they are illusory.

Both tropes foreground a word ("treasurer", "forest") whose conventional denotation they abuse in order to produce a meaning that reaches beyond the literal sense of the words.

The shift from conventional to rhetorical meaning is so much more striking in the original because of the ideographic nature of the two characters *bao* and *lin. Bao,* as we already know, depicts certain valuable items under a roof. Likewise, the character that we have translated as "forest" - *lin* 林 - is a recognisable depiction of two trees. The concretion of the latter character contrasts noticeably and comically with the factual misapprehension: just as the poet wished, we actual*ly see* the trees of the forest and can hardly believe our eyes when, in the next line, we come upon only firewood and brushwood. This is the *rhetorical moment put fully into practice*, when the reader faces a perfect ambiguity: is it a forest or just fire- and brushwood? But, again, the narrator is himself "at fault" for misnaming the firewood a forest. Unless we believe that this stanza is actually and ultimately about a man mistaking firewood for a forest, and that he wrote down his experience second-by-second, we cannot be in doubt that the first two lines are part of the well-known rhetorical pattern of convention and deviation. Now we can, with full confidence, point our finger at the poet and accuse *him* of the very crimes that he spends thirteen carefully embroidered stanzas denouncing: lies and usurpation. On Mao's reading, to be able to say (*yan* 言) that things today are not what they seem to be, the poet purposely calls the fire- and brushwood a "forest." The *si er fei*, that linguistic illusion, has become a sought-after, man-made trope.

Now we understand the true colours of a poet who indulges in irony: he is a "misnamer," i.e. a disturber of the holy alliance between signans and signatum, and the character for misnaming is precisely *e* 訛, "mutated speech," "lie" or "persuasion by words." The character *e*, in its

Janus-faced ambiguity, can thus be raised as an emblem for the rhetorical vacillation between lie and truth, illusion and illustration used by the Chinese man of letters. When the poet, in the fifth stanza, alleged that the "populace" says "the mountain is low," he was describing a despicable act of lying, namable by the word *e* 訛, *by means of* a sophisticated trope of persuasion, that could also be referred to as *e* 訛.

We can now answer the question that we tentatively posed above: what separates the negative from the positive, the pure and damnable illusion or lie from the acceptable and praised rhetorical trope? The answer is disappointingly simple-hearted and, in all fairness, I have been begging it from the very beginning: the difference is not one of structure but of approach. The illusion that rhetoric generates is actually appreciated and useful as metaphorical meaning. Rhetorical tropes are lies with a purpose, in contradistinction to the destructive "mutated speech" of ghosts, evil kings or the "populace," the meaning of which cannot be elevated into a higher significance. And the best illustration of this is in the first and last stanzas of "Jie nan shan" 節南山 (poem 191), where it finally becomes perfectly clear that *e,* in its benevolent form as persuasion, includes the accepted form of lying that we call metaphoricity (Ibid.: 657-64).

In the final stanza of that poem the narrator himself suddenly appears and presents his aim: "I, Jia Fu, made this recitation...to change your heart by words/to make you protect and cultivate the ten thousand city-states" 家父作誦…式訛爾心以蓄萬邦. "To change by words" is my translation of e 訛, as it appears in this context.⑲According to Mao's Commentary, and to what this lengthy poem itself reveals about the situation in which it was vocalized, its narrator is a noble of the

---

⑲ "Change" 化 is Zheng Xuan's rendition. See Wang 1988: 664.

declining Zhou Dynasty addressing the Grand Master Yin 師尹 of Zhou, exhorting him to lead a virtuous life that the populace may emulate.[20] What concerns us, of course, is how this admonition is carried out, and we will do no more than consult the two lines that open the poem: High and steep is South Mount/with its stones piled amass. Now, a remonstration in ten stanzas directed to one of the most powerful men of the ruling dynasty would not begin with a literal - and therefore, in this context, nonsensical - description of a pile of stones. Instead, and most probably as an accurate reconstruction of the author's intention, Mao interprets the majestic mountain as a "xingish" metaphor of the grand Master Yin (ibid.: 657). Thus, just as the fushi, the rhetorical e involves metaphoricity and analogy.

Furthermore, if Mao has instinctively described the rhetorical modus of "Zheng yue" with the formula of "si er fei" he has, in the same stroke, described the formula for Mr. Lü's two tales of the signal that "seemed to be" what it was not (i.e. an alarm signal) and the external shape of a person that was not what it seemed to be" (the beholder's son or a ghost). Apart from these negative examples, the formula also accurately describes Xun Qing's funeral scene of objects, which were seemingly intended for the corpse but which possessed a hardly discernable flaw that destroyed the discrepancy and transformed them (with the "appearance

---

[20] *Min* ("populace") often denotes, not only the demographic group of the lower classes, but also the plebeian instinct to *copy,* mindlessly, the external world or, in other words, to be *overwhelnied* by the tendencies of the contemporary world. The Confucian contempt for the inherently shapeless and perfectly mouldable populace is expressed in the Qi-school comment on "jie nan shan": "if you love righteousness the *min* will [turn toward=] cherish humaneness (*ren*) and their customs will be fine; if you love profit the min will love what is perverted and their customs will degenerate." See Wang 1988: 657.

but not utility") into an illustration of the corpse and thus of death itself. And, interestingly enough, it also describes the illusory usage of *bao,* a word *that seems* to refer to material riches but that is, in fact, not doing so.

To return to the fictitous dialogue with my cosmologist opponent above, it is the case that in both classical Chinese and English, the phrase "si er fei" expresses, superfluously, what the notion of *si*, or "similarity," must refer to on its own, namely an external resemblance without common identity between two (or more) objects. But by adding ... *~er fei*, "...but not being," Mao emphasizes the ontological inferiority of the thing "that resembles": it can only beguile the hasty, first glance but never the scrutinizing second look, for it *is not* the object it resembles. A true cosmologist would never, like Mao Heng, take such an obsessive interest in the illusion (often man-made, as in the drum-signal, funeral objects, *bao,* and forest), and the possibility of representational systems to produce illusions and, thus, metaphors.

Let us formulate and discuss the central problem by way of an extended analysis of the *bao* example. What the whole story demonstrates is the birth of a metaphor through the catachretic act of misnaming. A *bao* is a treasure of material valuables - this is the fundamental point implied by the author. The act which at first is un-namable is the fisherman's refusal to accept the treasure he is promised by Chu for Wu Yuan, and the reason it cannot be named is that the story is written from the perspective of a much later, degenerated society where greed is the rule and lack of lust for treasures is incomprehensible. We could also put it like this: what is so utterly puzzling is the fisherman's refusal to treat the treasure as the treasure *it is*. In Chinese (as with "treasure" in English), the verbal form of *bao* means exactly "to treat as a treasure," so when the fisherman refuses to *bao* (verb) the *bao* (noun) he refuses to acknowledge the treasure's existence as a treasure. The treasure of material valuables is therefore no longer a "treasure" (since it does not qualify as a "treasure" under the new rules), but the *verb remains. And* apparently, the fisherman "treasures" Wu Yuan (and, metonymically, virtue) higher than material riches, because he chooses to help Wu Yuan rather than receive the treasure, an act that generates the catachresis: the fisherman treasures *another,* metaphorical "treasure" (the *yi bao* of the chapter's title). And, as I said above, the "treasure" of virtue and righteousness should always be imagined as enclosed in quotation marks so that we won't mistake the Superior Man's love of virtue for the vulgar man's love of riches, its very antithesis. What remains identical to itself in the story is the external appearance of the character *bao* - its signans - just as the drum-signal itself remains unaltered despite King You's breach of semantic convention.

To solve the crux of the unspeakable act, the author could simply have begun the story by saying that formerly men "loved" virtue more than riches, but by measuring everything in terms of material riches, and by describing the love of virtue in terms of an anti-treasure, the author describes a former righteousness that is now so utterly lost that it can only be described as *negative greed.* The literal lie - the assertion that one could treasure an anti-treasure - has been transformed into a metaphorical truth.

Let us, for the last time, consider Xun Qing's burial rites. There, the new rhetorical meaning emerged only with the destruction or deprivation of the objects' functionality (which I, in stark contrast to Heidegger and Blanchot, have called their "being"), which is made abundantly clear through Xun's insistence on the difference between appearance and uselessness. *Before* the illusion was exposed the objects signified "life"; *afterwards* they illustrated *death* through an imitation of the corpse. Similarly, the metaphorical meaning of *bao* can occur only when the signans "bao" 寶 has been deprived of its conventional signatum, "material riches," through the fisherman's rejection of the treasure. Both tropes move from concretion to abstraction; from jade, money and earthenware to virtue; from the concrete and vital acts of drinking wine or riding a chariot to the abstraction of all abstractions, death.

In a moment I will go on to Mao's canonical definition of the xing, and demonstrate that the ironical xing is itself a deviation from a set norm. But I will anticipate my final conclusion and suggest that, in general, for a xing to qualify as a xing, it must present the reader with an image whose ultimate meaning cannot be deduced from its face value. It must present an image that "resembles (something else) but is not."

Mao's canonical xing: "Guan ju."

My attempt to provide a general introduction to Mao's poetics requires a few more details about its historical and intellectual background. The 305 poems of which the *Book of Poems* consists date from approximately 1000 - 600 B.C. During the Han Dynasty, and with the emergence of Confucianism as a state doctrine, *the Poems* were used to disseminate and exemplify Confucian philosophy by way of allegoresis and metaphorical interpretations. Three rivalling "schools" of *Shijing* interpretation now appeared: Lu, Qi and Han. As we already know, during the second century B.C. the Confucian scholar Mao Heng wrote yet another commentary on the *Poems,* simply called the *Mao Commentary.* Mao gained in popularity (not least due to invention of the xing as a tool for literary analysis) and his *Commentary* was, subsequently, recognized as the orthodox version of *Shijing*-exegesis whereas the other three schools fell into oblivion.

Here, I intend to do little more than present an analysis of Mao's momentous comment on the first *Shijing* poem, "Guan ju," that will elucidate and put in perspective what has been said above and what will be said below. It follows, then, that I will only be able to scratch the surface of what is Mao's most generous exposition of his hermeneutic method. Now, what reason do I have for appending the pompous adjective "canonical" to the exegetic procedure that Mao performs here? There are, in fact, several interrelated reasons for what is a rather loose usage of the word. First, Mao's comment on "Guan ju" is so studious and detailed that one gets the impression that he is here taking great pains to persuasively explain the principles of the xing-method. Since the *Commentary* otherwise often consists of very terse comments on the meaning of the xing-images or explanations of obscure characters, the sheer abundance of the comment suggests that it occupies a privileged place in Mao's work. Second, and on the same note, the position of "Guan ju" as the first poem of what, indeed, had already become a book of monumental importance also indicates that Mao must have felt a need to take immediate control of these peculiar texts that he claimed speak allegorically of virtue through love poems, which, as such, could easily be misinterpreted. Third, the metaphorical construction of what Mao here names a xing is by far the most cornmon subspecies of the xing in general. Finally - and this is a speculation that would require a more extensive presentation of evidence than I have space for - I would suggest that, despite the allegorical minutiae, Mao's exploration of the metaphorical organisation of "Guan ju" is more convincing than many of his shorter, sometimes incomprehensively terse, comments on later poems. Therefore, I have considered it justifiable, as well as practical, to assume the model presented in Mao's notes on "Guan ju" as the prototype from which the variations of the xing (of which we shall discuss only the ironic xing) deviate.

The critical reader may also wish to know by what right I will split into subspecies what seems to have been one coherent concept to Mao Heng. The answer lies precisely in that question's emphasis on the modem notion of "concept." Mao's xing is, more than anything else, a pragmatic and not particularly lawbound *method* that emerged from the Confucian scholar's need to explain why and how a passionate love poem could speak of virtue, and it is best described as the crucial component of Mao's exegetical machinery for the transformation of poetry into Confucian doctrine. Conversely, the xing should be regarded neither as the *poet's* technique for the organization of imagery nor as his method, like the Western metaphor, of expanding language and expressing the hitherto inexpressible.㉑This change of perspective makes it easier to understand how "xing" came to be the generic name of several, slightly different interpretational methods.

What distinguishes the canonical xing (as opposed to the ironical digression presented below) is that the metaphorical message of the natural image which Mao in his analysis calls "xing" mirros *positively* the human situation that the poem speaks of.

The poem begins thus:

關關雎鳩　Guan guan [cries] the osprey
在河之洲　On the islet of the river (Ibid.: 8)

Mao comments:

> This is a xing. "Guan guan" are harmonious calls. Although the jujiu [...] is a passionate bird the males and females live in

㉑ I have discussed the pragmatic nature of the xing in "What happened when Mao Heng read the *Odes*? A study of the exercise of hermeneutic authority in Han China," *Journal of the Oriental Society of Australia*, (forthcoming).

> separation from each other. The queen - consort takes joy in the virtue of her lord, nothing is not harmonious or not in concord and their sexuality does not degenerate into wantonness. It is sincere and firm, profound and deep, like the *jujiu's* living in separation. If things are like this, they can be used to influence and change that which is under heaven. If man and woman live in separation then father and son will love each other; if father and son love each other then ruler and subject will respect each other; if ruler and subject respect each other then the proceedings of the royal court will be well-regulated; if the proceedings of the royal court are well-regulated then the kingly way will be perfected. 興也關關和聲也雎鳩…鳥摯而有別……后妃說樂君子之德，無不和諧又不淫其色，愼固幽深若雎鳩之有別，然後可以風化天下，夫婦有別則父子親，父子親則君臣敬，君臣敬則朝廷正，朝廷正則王化成 (ibid.).

Here, in Mao's comment on the first two lines of the *Poems,* we find the thematic key-words that keep appearing in different combinations all through the *Commentary*: regulation, hierarchic rigour and harmony are the concepts that underlie Mao's interpretation. The negativity of Mao's idiom ("nothing is not harmonious," no wantonness") presents disharmony, fornication and chaos as the *prima materia* that must be fought and negated. By describing harmony in terms of negated disharmony and "correct" sexuality in terms of negated sexual misconduct, Mao underlines the fragility of a state in which "the kingly way" has been perfected and discloses the Confucian scholar's fear of sexuality, excess, licentiousness, hierarchic derangement. Sex, we observe, is the very pivot of human society: if man and woman only regulate their sexual behaviour the primary condition for a paradisiacal society is fulfilled.

Conversely, if sexuality is allowed to Go on the rampage the world will go awry, the two parallel hierarchies - that of the family and that of the government - will break down and chaos will take over. The language of negation is paradoxical in that it simultaneously confirms the existence of that which it wishes to condemn, just as the xing, as I suggested above, paves the way for the deviant readings it sets out to abolish.

Turning our attention to the poem's rhetorical arrangement, we find that the *jujiu* - bird - conventionally rendered as "osprey" - does not merely refer to a bird that Mao describes as passionate yet chaste. "Osprey" has a secondary and more important signatum: the queen celebrated for her chasteness. The bird and the woman are linked on a textual level by means of similitude since that avian animal and this human animal share the characteristic of having a well-ordered sex life. This linkage is manifested most clearly in the *Commentary* by Mao's use of the metaphorical copula *ruo* 若, "like" or "as." The osprey is thus present in the text as a description of queen-consort, and this description is made possible through the presence of a *tertium comparationis* - the shared characteristic that allows *this to* refer to *that* - in this case, a well-regulated sex life.

The cosmological sinologist can now be heard grumbling disapprovingly that the *poem itself* simply juxtaposes nature and human action into a parataxis without discriminating between what is ontologically superior and inferior. But what concerns us is *Mao's* distinction between image (the xing) and that image's referent (the woman/queen), and this act of distinguishing is undoubtedly metaphorical. Furthermore, from our knowledge of the *si er fei*-trope we know both of Mao's interest in the opposition of appearance to essence and the crucial notion of the rhetorical lie - the *e* - through which a metaphorical truth may appear. And thus we have the conceptual tools that will allow us to understand fully how the xing operates with regard to "Guan ju." Retaining, Mao's perspective, we should, firstly, understand the word "osprey" as disrupted by the same radical ambiguity that characterized Mr. Lü's "treasure." With Mao, "osprey" abandons its conventional meaning (or "signatum") and now refers to the queen through a *tertium comparationis,* just as *bao* could metaphorically refer to the sense of satisfaction achieved through a lofty deed because benevolence is as *valuable* to the Superior Man as a treasure is to a lesser person. Secondly, we may also describe the xing as *a si er fei,* a rhetorical lie where the signans "osprey" (i.e. the characters 雎鳩) *resembles itself* but is deprived of its conventional signatum, its essence and function. As with Xun's funeral objects, the deliberate act of destruction or deprivation creates an illusion and, subsequently, a metaphorical meaning. Thirdly, it is thus apparent that the "xingish" poem involves and banks on the rhetorical moment of suspense that leaves the reader hanging between illusion and illustration, appearance and essence. The first time the xing is read it is construed as a description of an osprey. But the intelligent (pure and virtuous) reader's *second glance* grasps the purely rhetorical connection between the depiction of nature and the human action described immediately thereafter and, understanding the xing as an image of the latter, is able to decode the metaphorical meaning,. Yet, in the infinitely short moment - the rhetorical moment - that separates the two modes of reading the reader is captivated by the illusion, like Xun's desperate mourner who for a second is gripped by the idea that the body may still contain the departed, or like the poet in front of the forest-like non-forest.

And indeed, from Mao's "xingish" perspective, the birds *qua* birds are non-ssential; their only function is to brine, out the "virtue" that he claims is the queen's. If the birds did not have a feature pertinent to the context, their precence in the poem would in Mao's eyes simply be incomprehensible and absurd - their crying cacophonous - since he knows a priori that the *Poems* are a "storehouse of righteousness." This means that, even though Mao may have fancied invisible, cosmological threads combining the birds and the human animal, such a conception of the world is virtually irrelevant on the textual, i.e. rhetorical, level where Mao uses the xing to distinguish between picture and depicted and reads the lines about the quacking osprey as a metaphor of the queen.

A final observation before we proceed to the next lines of the poem: hitherto we have only read Mao's comment on the very first two lines of "Guanju." A "direct," "naïve" and non-Confucian reading would probably understand the first poem as a charming song about passionate love, as in later stanzas where the "lord" is described as "seeking" his girl while tossing and turning in his sleep. The enormous tension between the poem per se and the Confucian message that Mao must find therein explains the copiousness of Mao's comments as well as his "negative" idiom. Since the poem itself speaks of passionate love Mao must make a direct and violent counter-attack to make the poem speak of non-passion and of sexual regulation; hence the allegory, the metaphors and the mass of words whose function it is to add force to his comments (sometimes, one suspects, by confusing the reader). Hence, also, the structure of negativity. Mao realizes that the poem is explicitly speaking of passion and that this fact cannot easily be swept under the rug. But by making the ospreys (and thus the two people) creatures of sexual moderation Mao is able to negate, on the meta-textual level, the theme of passion. Consequently, the "lord's" (*junzi* 君子) feverish longing for the girl now becomes the Superior Man's (*junzi*) longing for a chaste mate and for a relationship characterized by non-closeness (i.e. distance), non-fomication and non-disharmony:

窈窕淑女　The chaste and goood girl -

君子好逑　A fine mate for the lord (ibid.: 9)

Mao comments:

> *Yaotiao* means "dark and secluded" [... This says=] means that the queen-consort has the virtue of the *jujiu*-bird. This dark and secluded, chaste and loyal girl is fit to be the lord's good mate 窈窕幽閒也…言后妃有關雎之德，是幽閒貞專善之女宜爲君子好匹 (ibid.: 10).

"Dark and secluded" refers, in all probability, to the seclusion of the palace to which the chaste queen-consort is confined. We are beginning to grasp the rhetorical structure of the poem: the image of the bird, screaming on an isolated islet in the river, is here taken as a metaphor of the queen in her seclusion, a chaste "girl" determined to keep her (sexual) integrity intact. More importantly, we can now distinguish between the two kinds of figurality at work in the poem: allegory and metaphoricity. On the one hand we have Mao's allegorical identification of the poem's personae as the king and the queen. Such an act of identification is not warranted by the text itself but builds on extratextual information supplied by Mao, the hermeneutic authority, in an act of interpretational violence corrupting the text's integrity. On the other hand Mao establishes a metaphorical linkage w*ithin* the text: the ospreys function as a metaphor of the girl. We have already concluded that the characteristic shared by the bird and the young couple is sexual moderation. Now, Mao identifies the tertium comparationis as virtue (*de* 德): virtuous is the osprey and virtuous is the girl/queen. The linkage itself between the osprey and the girl is not completely arbitrary since both tenor (girl) and vehicle (osprey) are mentioned by the text. The xing, therefore, is a hermeneutical tool that enables Mao to establish a metaphorical linkage between the initial description of a natural scene and the human action that follows.

As proposed above, the parallelistic structure of "Guanju" itself suggests a metaphorical relation between the osprey and the personage of the poem. Therefore, we could say that Mao's xing actually reveals the imagistic structure of this piece in a non-violent act of interpretation. To reveal the imagistic structure and to interpret it are, however, two widely different acts. The irony of the xing is that the very concept that Mao invented as a means of transforming a non-ideological text into Confucian dogma can very easily end up as a lethal weapon directed against Mao himself. Once we have grasped the parallelistic and metaphorical structure revealed by Mao's xing we cannot but identify the islet-confined and screaming osprey with the "girl," thereby opening up the text for a "deviant" and forbidden reading that understands the girl as the unreachable object of the young man's feverish dreams or, equally probable, as a young girl alienated, in a most physical manner on her islet, by her lust.

This schizophrenia between what the poem explicitly says and what Mao wants it to say, between the perverse, sexual and excessive reading that the xing inevitably suggests and the approved, Confucian reading that Mao's xing aims at is always inherent in Mao's hemeneutics. At this level, the xing is characterized by a painful tension between Mao's pragmatism (the xing is used to transform the text) and the purely rhetorical scheme that the xing reveals (the *jujiu* is a metaphor of the amorous couple, but what it actually *tells* us about them, we can only guess).

The ironic xing

As I have already hinted, my so-called canonical model accurately describes how Mao's concept xing functions and how it is structured in most - but not all - cases. Now, what characterizes the sub-species of the xing that I call "ironic" is precicely a discrepancy between the opening natural scene and the human action spoken of immediately thereafter, which the poem in the final analysis "is about." In Mao's hermeneutics the "xing" tag means that the image in question should not be taken literally but, in the majority of cases, metaphorically. But in the ironic poem, the representation of nature (whose metaphorical interpretation and relation to the human setting are overdetermined by the canonical xing-practice) describes a situation which stands in total opposition to what is taking place in the human realm.

As an example we shall consider Mao's reading of the first two lines of "Shan you fusu" 山有扶蘇 (poem 84):

山有扶蘇　On the mountain there are *fusu*-trees
隰有荷華　In the swamps there are lotus flowers (ibid.: 354-55)

Mao comments that these lines are "a xing..., saying that high and low, big and small all obtain what is appropriate [for them]" 興有…言高下大小各得其宜 (ibid.). As we already know, Mao's semiotic system frequently interprets the high mountain as a metaphor of high position and, in particular, of the ruler, while the lowlying swamps refer to the lowly minister. What the xing is describing, then, is the fortunate and appropriate situation where a Superior Man rules and the petty man occupies a lowly position, just as the *fusu*-tree and the lotus flower are found in their natural and proper habitats.

But to this blessed order is contrasted the disorder of the following lines:

不見子都　I do not see Zi Du
乃見狂且　I only see a mad man!

We are familiar with the playful vacilliation between norm and deviation, and the rhetorical purposes it can be put to. When all four lines have been read, the xing and the ideal it describes turn into an illusion. But if Mr. Lü showed us that it is actually possible to call a non-treasure a treasure and to make an alarm-signal into a pleasure-signal, then another contemporary annotation on the *Poems,* the *Minor Preface,* acknowledges the instance of linguistic abuse but repudiates the irony by saying that this poem "criticizes befuddlement. What is called 'beautiful' is not beautiful" 刺忽所美非美然 (ibid.). In other words, the xing metaphorically praises a situation in which the Superior Man is on the throne when, in fact, a mad man is in power. The xing - and thus the clever poet himself - *lies,* but with a purpose, since the whole piece should be understood as a critique of confusion, or, from the perspective of "Mistrusting Similitude," of the inability of detecting the rotten core underneath the polished exterior. The comparison with Mr. Lü's metaphorical usage of *bao* is felicitous since the *Preface,* in its comment on this poem, banks on a similar abuse of language, whereby the conventional meaning of a word *(mei,* "beautiful") is used to refer to an object to which it is not applicable (the "non-beautiful" *–fei mei* - mad man). The difference, of course, lies in the *Preface's* refusal of the oxymoron: you cannot praise as "beautiful" what, conventionally speaking, is not so.

Mao assumes the same ironic relation between the xing and the world but gives the poem a different spin by commenting that "Zi Du was someone praised and loved by his [generation=] contemporaries" 子都世之美好者也 (ibid.). According to Mao, the poem's narrator expects to see the throne occupied by the honourable Zi Du (whose historical identity has never been disclosed), but finds it usurped by a maniac. The first lines promise order, the following ones deliver only disorder; the human world disappoints us by negating the ideal that the xing has set up.

The event of the ironic xing, when the illusion of the "xingish" metaphor itself becomes an illusion, is indeed a suitable and comical end to our brief investigation into the Chinese rhetoric of illusion. The reader, happy to have grasped the code of metaphorical interpretation from the canonical xing, comes to the ironic poem only to find that he is *again* illusion's victim, like the unfortunate merchant first fooled by the impersonating ghost and, then once again, by the illusion of the illusion. And perhaps, at least at this point, Mr. Lü's ghost story could be understood as a parable of the dancers of reading thoroughly allegorical and metaphorical texts: one may end up slaying them in an act of combined annoyance and love.

An Endnote on Essence, Appearance and The Poetics of Deviation

Against the backdrop of the prevalent poetics of cosmology I have attempted to demonstrate how warmly ritual, poetic and hermeneutic literature during the third and second centuries B.C. embraced the rhetorical play with literal and metaphorical meaning.

In the texts chosen for our investigation we found descriptions of what, at first sight, appeared to be two diametrically opposed phenomena but which, after closer scrutiny, were revealed to be identically structured. Both occurrences involved the confusing doubling of a familiar object's external appearance that resulted in the beholder's inability to distinguish between the original (and its essence or meaning) and the copy (having appearance but no substance). We defined this phenomenon by the Western concept of illusion and realized that what had momentarily beguiled us was the drastic disparity between the authors' assessment of the illusion. However, Xun Qing's brilliant and poetic analysis of the funeral rites indicated that the peculiar frenzy of the illusion - so feared by Mr. Lü - could be manipulated and used to express the previously inexpressible, and we claimed this manipulation of signs to be a *rhetorical* act. Xun's fervent insistence on the difference between essence (or function) and form confirmed our earlier hypothesis and his interpretation of the useless funeral objects as an illustration of the similarly useless corpse emphasized the critical *rhetorical moment*, when the very illusion-ness of the illusion is revealed and turned into a metaphorical truth. Returning to Mr. Lü's "Treasures of another kind" we were surprised to find therein a fullfledged theory of the metaphor *qua* linguistic illusion and literal lie. We were now able to demarcate a vast space within the Confucian world of thought where rhetorical and linguistic illusions were not dreaded but actually welcome, yet often indicated by words and concepts denoting deviation and even falsehood: *yi, xi dao, qi dao, e*. We could now revise our understanding of *Mr. Lü's Annals* and conclude that what makes some illusions so loathsome is their interference in and disturbance of everyday life, whereas in language, rituals and poetry the illusion is expected and accepted.

What characterizes and provides the illusion with its rhetorical potency is the deviation from its beholder's expectations. In our analysis of Mao's reading of "Zheng yue" we made the important discovery that the principle of deviation unites and links the three concepts *e, si er fei* and *xing*. The radical ambiguity of *e,* meaning both "lie" and "rhetorical persuasion," illustrated with utmost clarity the Confucian weakness for the linguistic illusion, the mutated and/or transforming word. And, in what perhaps constituted the apex of our investigation, Mao's *si er fei* confirmed and expressed the Confucian obsession with the dialectics of essence and appearance, divulging how the clever poet turns a literal lie into a metaphorical truth.

We had now reached the stage where we could approach what I called Mao's "canonical" xing. In other words, we had obtained enough knowledge about the Confucian speculations on rhetoric to avoid the cosmologist's pitfalls and to grasp that the xing is Mao's exegetic tool for distinguishing vehicle (the xing, the natural description) from tenor (the human situation described in the poem). As demonstrated in the reading of "Guan ju," Mao's "xingish" act establishes a rhetorical hierarchy by indicating which image is to be read purely as a description of another. The xing is, consequently, a thoroughly rhetorical concept (or tool), and does *not* philosophize on the order of cosmos. Expressed in terms with which we are familiar, the phrase designated "xing" is itself a *si er fei,* a linguistic sign that resembles itself but *is* another. Furthermore, Mao's poet is a clever metaphorizer, a creator of similitude, and not a spontaneous medium unable to do anything but passively reflect the outside world.

Finally, the ironic sub-species of the xing, in its turn, should be regarded as a deviation from the positive correspondence between tenor and vehicle in Mao's canonical Ur-version. When the reader encounters a harmonious nature described in the first lines, s/he expects a happy human situation and is surprised by the next lines' *negation* of the harmony "promised" by the xing. The ironical poem, on Mao's reading, must therefore be understood as the brilliant gem of Confucian rhetoric: a deviation in two stages.

It is in *this* historical and intellectual context - the Confucian discourse on illusion, rhetoric, metaphors and lies - that we should understand Mao's xing and his hermeneutic project.

國家圖書館出版品預行編目資料

世紀之交：觀念動向與文化變遷
第二屆中瑞漢學國際學術會議論文集

淡江大學中國文學系主編. – 初版. –
臺北市：臺灣學生，2003[民 92]
面；公分

ISBN 957-15-1146-3 (精裝)
ISBN 957-15-1147-1 (平裝)

1. 漢學 – 論文，講詞等

030.7　　91016569

世紀之交：觀念動向與文化變遷

第二屆中瑞漢學國際學術會議論文集

編者：淡江大學中國文學系
出版者：臺灣學生書局
發行人：孫善治
發行所：臺灣學生書局
臺北市和平東路一段一九八號
郵政劃撥帳號：00024668
電話：(02)23634156
傳真：(02)23636334
E-mail：student.book@msa.hinet.net
http：//studentbook.web66.com.tw
本書局登記證字號：行政院新聞局局版北市業字第玖捌壹號
印刷所：宏輝彩色印刷公司
中和市永和路三六三巷四二號
電話：(02)22268853

定價：精裝新臺幣四八〇元
平裝新臺幣四一〇元

西元二〇〇三年二月初版

03009

ISBN 957-15-1146-3 (精裝)
ISBN 957-15-1147-1 (平裝)